2/96

Chile
a country study

Federal Research Division
Library of Congress
Edited by
Rex A. Hudson
Research Completed
March 1994

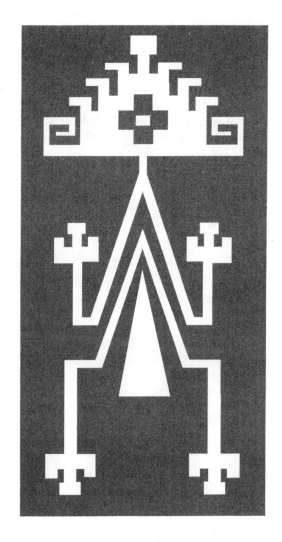

On the cover: A figure *(lukutuel)* from a seventeenth-century
Mapuche woman's belt called *ñimintrarüwe*

Third Edition, First Printing, 1994.

Library of Congress Cataloging-in-Publication Data

Chile : a country study / Federal Research Division, Library of
Congress ; edited by Rex A. Hudson. — 3rd ed.
    p.   cm. — (Area handbook series, ISSN 1057-5294)
(DA pam ; 550-77)
    "Supersedes the 1982 edition of Chile : a country study, edited
by Andrea T. Merrill."—T.p. verso.
    "Research completed March 1994."
    Includes bibliographical references (pp. 381-417) and index.
    ISBN 0-8444-0828-X
    1. Chile. I. Hudson, Rex A., 1947- . II. Library of Con-
gress. Federal Research Division. III. Series. IV. Series:
DA pam ; 550-77.
F3058.C5223   1994   94-21663
983—dc20   CIP

Headquarters, Department of the Army
DA Pam 550-77

For sale by the Superintendent of Documents, U.S. Government Printing Office
Washington, D.C. 20402

Foreword

This volume is one in a continuing series of books prepared by the Federal Research Division of the Library of Congress under the Country Studies/Area Handbook Program sponsored by the Department of the Army. The last two pages of this book list the other published studies.

Most books in the series deal with a particular foreign country, describing and analyzing its political, economic, social, and national security systems and institutions, and examining the interrelationships of those systems and the ways they are shaped by cultural factors. Each study is written by a multidisciplinary team of social scientists. The authors seek to provide a basic understanding of the observed society, striving for a dynamic rather than a static portrayal. Particular attention is devoted to the people who make up the society, their origins, dominant beliefs and values, their common interests and the issues on which they are divided, the nature and extent of their involvement with national institutions, and their attitudes toward each other and toward their social system and political order.

The books represent the analysis of the authors and should not be construed as an expression of an official United States government position, policy, or decision. The authors have sought to adhere to accepted standards of scholarly objectivity. Corrections, additions, and suggestions for changes from readers will be welcomed for use in future editions.

Louis R. Mortimer
Chief
Federal Research Division
Library of Congress
Washington, DC 20540-5220

Acknowledgments

The book editor would like to thank the chapter authors for reviewing and commenting on various chapters. Their expertise contributed greatly to the overall quality of the book.

The authors are grateful to individuals in various agencies of the United States government, international organizations, private institutions, and Chilean diplomatic offices who offered their time, special knowledge, or research facilities and materials to provide information and perspective. None of these individuals, however, is in any way responsible for the work of the authors.

Thanks also go to Ralph K. Benesch, who oversees the Country Studies/Area Handbook Program for the Department of the Army. In addition, the book editor would like to thank members of the Federal Research Division who contributed directly to the preparation of the manuscript. These include Sandra W. Meditz, who reviewed all textual and graphic materials, served as liaison with the sponsoring agency, and provided numerous substantive and technical contributions; Marilyn L. Majeska, who managed editing; Andrea T. Merrill, who edited the tables, figures, and Bibliography and managed production; and Barbara Edgerton and Izella Watson, who did the word processing. Thanks also go to Vincent Ercolano, who performed the copyediting of the chapters; Cissie Coy, who performed the final prepublication editorial review; and Joan C. Cook, who compiled the index. Linda Peterson and Malinda B. Neale of the Library of Congress Printing and Processing Section performed the phototypesetting, under the supervision of Peggy Pixley.

David P. Cabitto provided invaluable graphics support, including preparation of several maps and the cover and chapter illustrations. He was assisted by Harriett R. Blood, who prepared the topography and drainage map, and by the firm of Greenhorne and O'Mara.

Finally, the book editor acknowledges the generosity of the individuals and the public, private, diplomatic, and international agencies who allowed their photographs to be used in this study.

Contents

Chapter 4. Government and Politics 197

Arturo Valenzuela

List of Figures

Preface

Like its predecessor, this study is an attempt to examine objectively and concisely the dominant historical, social, environmental, economic, governmental, political, and national security aspects of contemporary Chile. Sources of information included books, journals, other periodicals and monographs, official reports of governments and international organizations, and numerous interviews by the authors with Chilean government officials. Chapter bibliographies appear at the end of the book; brief comments on sources recommended for further reading appear at the end of each chapter. To the extent possible, place-names follow the system adopted by the United States Board on Geographic Names. Measurements are given in the metric system; a conversion table is provided to assist readers unfamiliar with metric measurements (see table 1, Appendix). A glossary is also included.

Spanish surnames generally are composed of both the father's and the mother's family names, in that order, although there are numerous variations. In the instance of Eduardo Frei Ruiz-Tagle, for example, Frei is his patronymic and Ruiz-Tagle is his mother's maiden name. In informal use, the matronymic is often dropped, a practice that usually has been followed in this book, except in cases where the individual could easily be confused with a relative or someone with the same patronymic. For example, Frei Ruiz-Tagle, the current president, is the son of former president Eduardo Frei Montalva.

The body of the text reflects information available as of March 31, 1994. Certain other portions of the text, however, have been updated. The Introduction discusses significant events that have occurred since the completion of research, the Country Profile includes updated information as available, and the Bibliography lists recently published sources thought to be particularly helpful to the reader.

Table A. Chronology of Important Events

Period	Description
SIXTEENTH CENTURY	
October 21, 1520	Ferdinand Magellan first European to sight (but not identify) Chilean shores.
1535–37	Diego de Almagro leads first Spanish expedition to explore Chile.
1540	Pedro de Valdivia conquers Chile.
February 12, 1541	Valdivia founds Santiago.
1553–58	Indigenous Araucanian uprising.
1557	Mapuche rebel chief Lautaro defeated.
1560s	Alonso de Ercilla y Zúñiga composes epic poem "La Araucana."
SEVENTEENTH CENTURY	
1603	First army-like force, or militia, established in Chile.
1609	Pope Paul V authorizes war against Araucanians.
1643	Although warfare against Araucanians continues, Indians help Spaniards repel invasion of southern Chile by Brouwer expedition.
1647	Earthquake destroys Santiago.
EIGHTEENTH CENTURY	
1730	Earthquake causes great destruction in Santiago and most of central Chile.
1759–96	Bourbon reforms give Chile greater independence from Viceroyalty of Peru.
1791	Governor Ambrosio O'Higgins y Ballenary outlaws *encomiendas* and forced labor.
NINETEENTH CENTURY	
September 18, 1810	Criollo leaders of Santiago declare independence from Spain.
1814–17	The Reconquest (La Reconquista).
October 2, 1814	Spanish troops from Peru reconquer Chile at Battle of Rancagua.
February 12, 1817	Troops led by Bernardo O'Higgins Riquelme, father of Chile, and General José de San Martín defeat Spanish in Battle of Chacabuco.

Table A.—Continued

Period	Description
1817	O'Higgins (1817–23) becomes supreme director of Chile.
April 5, 1818	Chile wins formal independence after San Martín defeats last large Spanish force in Battle of Maipú.
August 1818	First provisional constitution approved in plebiscite.
1818–30	Period of civil wars.
April 17, 1830	Liberals defeated by Conservatives at Battle of Lircay.
1830–61	Period of Conservative rule.
1830–37	"Portalian State" initiated by businessman Diego Portales Palazuelos, who dominates politics.
1833	New Portalian constitution implemented.
1836–39	Chile wages war against Peru-Bolivia Confederation.
January 1839	Chile wins war by defeating Peruvian fleet at Casma on January 12 and Bolivian Army at Yungay on January 20.
1861–91	Period of Liberal rule.
1879–83	Chile wages war against Bolivia and Peru in War of the Pacific.
1883	Chile seals victory with Treaty of Ancón.
1891	Civil war pits supporters of President José Manuel Balmaceda Fernández against Congress, which wins.
TWENTIETH CENTURY 1891–1925	Period of Parliamentary Republic.
1925	Chile's second major constitution approved.
1945	Gabriela Mistral wins Nobel Prize for Literature.
September 4, 1970	Popular Unity's Salvador Allende Gossens wins presidential election.
1971	Pablo Neruda wins Nobel Prize for Literature.

Table A.—Continued

Period	Description
September 11, 1973	Military led by General Augusto Pinochet Ugarte overthrows Allende government.
September 1973–90	Period of military rule under General Pinochet.
1980	New military-designed constitution is approved in a plebiscite.
1988	Plebiscite held on Pinochet rule.
1990	Transition to democracy begins with presidency of Patricio Aylwin Azócar.
March 11, 1994	Aylwin is succeeded by Eduardo Frei Ruiz-Tagle.

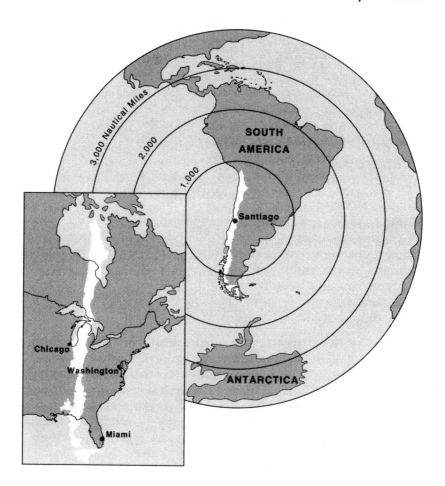

Country

Official Name: Republic of Chile (República de Chile).

Short Name: Chile.

Term for Citizen(s): Chilean(s).

Capital: Santiago.

NOTE—The Country Profile contains updated information as available.

Geography

Size: Totals 756,950 square kilometers (nearly twice the size of California); land area: 748,800 square kilometers, including Easter Island (Isla de Pascua; 118 square kilometers), Islas Juan Fernández (179 square kilometers), and Isla Sala y Gómez but excluding claimed Chilean Antarctic Territory (Territorio Chileno Antártico), which covers 1,249,675 square kilometers (not recognized by the United States).

Coastline: 6,435 kilometers (continental Chile).

Maritime Claims: Contiguous zone: twenty-four nautical miles; continental shelf: 200 nautical miles; exclusive economic zone: 200 nautical miles; territorial sea: twelve nautical miles.

Disputes: Bolivia has sought a sovereign corridor to Pacific Ocean since ceding Antofagasta to Chile in 1883; Río Lauca water rights in dispute between Bolivia and Chile; short section of southern boundary with Argentina indefinite; Lago del Desierto (Desert Lake) region under international arbitration as a result of a border conflict between Argentina and Chile; Chile's territorial claim in Antarctica partially overlaps Argentina's claim.

Topography and Climate: One of narrowest countries in world, averaging 177 kilometers wide (ninety kilometers wide at thinnest point in south and 380 kilometers across at widest point in north). Rugged Andes Mountains run down eastern side of country. Cordillera Domeyko (Domeyko mountain chain) in northern part of country runs along coast parallel to Andes. Five north-to-south natural regions: far north (Norte Grande), consisting of dry brown hills and sparse vegetation and containing extremely arid Atacama Desert and Andean plateau; near north (Norte Chico), a semi-arid region between Río Copiapó and Santiago; central Chile (Chile Central), most densely populated natural region, including three largest metropolitan areas—Santiago, Valparaíso, and Concepción—and fertile Central Valley (Valle Central), with temperate, Mediterranean climate; heavily forested south (Sur de Chile), south of Río Bío-Bío, containing cool and very rainy (especially during winter) lake district and crisscrossed by hundreds of rivers; and far south (Chile Austral), sparsely populated, forested, constantly cold and stormy, with many fjords, inlets, twisting peninsulas, and islands. Land use: 7 percent arable (of which 29 percent irrigated), 16 percent meadows and pasture, 21 percent forest and woodland, and 56 percent other, including 1 percent irrigated. Temperate rain forest totals 14,164,045 hectares. Annual rate of deforestation (1981–85): 0.7 percent. Nearly 607,030 hectares clear-cut (stripped of all trees) since 1978. Seasons: spring—September 21 to December 20; summer—December 21 to March 20; autumn—March 21 to June 20; and winter—June 21 to September 20.

Principal Rivers: Aconcagua, Baker, Bío-Bío, Imperial, Loa (Chile's longest at about 483 kilometers), Maipo, Maule, Palena, Toltén, and Valdivia.

Principal Lakes: Del Toro, General Carrera, Llanquihue, Puyehue, Ranco, Rupanco, Sarmiento, and Villarrica.

Society

Population: 13.7 million (July 1993 estimate), with 1.6 percent average annual population growth rate between 1982 and 1992. Projected annual population growth rate 1.5 percent for 1991–2000. Density in 1993 eighteen persons per square kilometer, with great regional variations. Valparaíso Region, Bío-Bío Region, and Metropolitan Region of Santiago contained 63 percent of population, with about 39 percent of total population, or 5.3 million people, in Metropolitan Region of Santiago (1992). Population about 86 percent urban, 14 percent rural. Urban population annual growth rate in 1960–91, 2.6 percent; projected 1991–2000, 1.8 percent. Of some 335 communities nationally in 1993, poorest twenty-one located in regions of La Araucanía (eleven), Bío-Bío (five), and Coquimbo (five), together containing 2.6 percent of national population.

Ethnic Groups: Mestizo (mixed native American and European ancestry), 66 percent; European, 25 percent; native American, 7 percent; and other, 2 percent. Under law of September 28, 1993, state recognizes Mapuche (also called Araucanian), Aymara, Rapa Nui, Quechua, Colla, Alacalufe, and Yagán as main indigenous communities. Native Americans totaled 1.3 million in 1992, including 928,069 Mapuche, 48,477 Aymara, and 21,848 Rapa Nui. Quechua and Aymara located in north; Alacalufe and Ona in south; Mapuche, who speak Mapudungu, in south and central Chile, mostly around Temuco; Pascuene and Huilliche on Easter Island. Only Mapuche and former Huilliche islanders managing to survive culturally on mainland.

Official Language: Spanish (called Castellano in Chile).

Education and Literacy: As of 1966, primary education eight years and secondary education four years. School year runs from March through December. In mid-1980s primary school attendance varied between 93 percent and 96 percent; by 1989 secondary school enrollment had risen to 75 percent. Students in universities and professional institutes numbered about 153,100 in 1989. Adult literacy rate 94.6 percent, with average of 7.5 years of schooling (1992).

Health: Heavy investments in programs for very poor and in water and sanitation systems helped lower infant mortality rates and raise life expectancy, giving country a relatively high human development index (HDI) world ranking of thirty-sixth in 1992. Proportion of Chileans living in poverty decreased from 45 percent in 1985 to 33 percent in 1992. Birthrate 22.4 per 1,000 population; fertility rate 2.4 children born per woman (1993); mortality rate 5.6 deaths per 1,000 population (1992). In 1993 life expectancy estimated at seventy-one years for males and seventy-seven years for females (total). Estimated 1993 infant mortality rate below 1991 rate of 14.6 per 1,000 live births. Population with access to health services in 1988–90, 95 percent; to safe water, 86 percent rural/urban average, 100 percent urban; to sanitation, 83 percent. Twenty-eight recorded cholera cases in first nine months of 1993, with no deaths. In 1984–89 population per physician averaged 1,230. Social security benefits expenditures as a percentage of GDP: 9.9 percent (1980–89).

Religion: In 1992 census, of population aged fourteen years and older (totaling 9,775,222), 76 percent declared themselves Roman Catholic, 13 percent Evangelical or Protestant, 7 percent indifferent or atheist, and 4 percent other, including small Jewish, Muslim, and Christian Orthodox communities. Roman Catholic Church source of significant opposition to military regime of General Augusto Pinochet Ugarte (1973–90), playing key role in protection of human rights. Roman Catholic Church's influence in society has diminished since 1970s because of substantial growth of Pentecostal (Evangelical) churches.

Economy

Salient Features of the Economy: International trade liberalized since 1979. Has had fundamentally sound market economy. Since 1990 democratically elected government has maintained export-led growth, fiscal discipline, and relatively low inflation. Exchange-rate policy, based on daily adjustments of nominal exchange rate and aimed at encouraging exports, has been at center of country's economic success. Gross domestic public investment in 1991: 2.9 percent of GDP; gross domestic private investment in 1991: 15.9 percent of GDP. Gross national savings in 1992: 18.4 percent of GDP. Average annual rate of inflation 20 percent in 1980–90 period. Inflation 18.7 percent in 1991, 12.7 percent in 1992, and 12.2 percent in 1993; projected to be 10.0 percent in 1994 and 9.0 percent in 1995. Unemployment in 1992 about 4.5 percent, according to National Statistics Institute. Estimated 1994 budget US$11.4 billion.

Gross Domestic Product (GDP): One of Latin America's most economically developed countries, with a diversified, free-market economy. In 1992 GDP US$33.7 billion. In 1992 GDP per capita between US$2,515 and US$2,800, rising to US$3,160 in 1993. During 1990–93 period, poorest 20 percent of population experienced increase in income of 30 percent. GDP growth rate in 1992: 10.4 percent. Slowed to 6 percent in 1993. GDP growth projected by Central Bank to be 4.5 percent in 1994, and by Economist Intelligence Unit (EIU) to be 8 percent in 1995.

Gross National Product (GNP): In 1990 GNP about US$25.5 billion; 2.8 percent annual growth rate in 1980–90 period. In 1992 GNP per capita US$2,550; 1.1 percent annual per capita growth rate in 1980–90 period.

Agriculture: Agriculture, forestry, and fishing accounted for 8.2 percent of GDP in 1992, according to EIU, or 6.2 percent according to Inter-American Development Bank (IDB). Exports totaled US$1.2 billion (1991). Major crops: apples, corn, grapes, plums, potatoes, rice, sugar beets, and wheat, as well as forest products. Leading agricultural export: fruit. Leading agricultural imports: bananas, coffee, corn, cotton, dry milk, rice, soybean, sugar, tea, and wheat. Although free-market oriented, agricultural sector protected by "price bands." Agriculture accounted for 18 percent of labor force (1989–91).

Industry: One of most highly industrialized countries in Latin America. Manufacturing accounted for 20.8 percent of GDP (1992), according to EIU, or 35.9 percent, according to IDB. Industrial exports totaled US$4 billion (1992), surpassing copper exports (US$3.9 billion) for first time, but slowed in 1993. Industry accounted for 20.8 percent of labor force (1992). Mining accounted for 6.7 percent of GDP (1992), with copper still most important product in 1993, despite plunging prices (accounting for 30 percent of total value of exports in 1991). World's leading copper producer since 1982. Estimated 2 million tons of copper produced in 1993, up from 1.9 million tons in 1992. Opening of new copper mines and increasing output at existing mines expected to boost country's share of world copper production from 17.5 percent in 1990 to about 33 percent in 2000, or 3.3 million tons by 2000. Chile produces about twenty-four nonmetallic minerals, with exports amounting to US$191 million (1993).

Energy: National energy reliance on petroleum and natural gas, 60 percent; hydroelectric power, 25 percent; and coal, 15 percent. In 1992 kilowatt capacity 5,769,000; kilowatt-hours produced, 22,010 million. Annual rate of change in commercial energy consumption (1980–90), 2.9 percent. However, electricity demand rose by 8 percent in 1993, and growth of more than 6 percent was expected for 1994. Domestic oil consumption estimated at 138,527 barrels per day (1991). Oil reserves declining at 10 percent per year; stood at 300 million barrels in 1992. Estimated 17.9 billion barrels per day produced in 1991, equivalent to only 13 percent of domestic oil consumption. In 1992 Argentina and Chile agreed to build a trans-Andean oil pipeline. Gas production amounted to about 4 billion cubic meters in 1991. Work began on gas pipeline from Argentina in 1992.

Services: Accounted for 29.1 percent of GDP (1992), according to EIU, or 57.9 percent, according to IDB. Employed 26.4 percent of labor force (1991). Tourism one of key service industries. Total visitors—half of them from Argentina—grew from 1.35 million in 1991 to estimated 1.5 million in 1992; visitors spent estimated US$900 million in 1992 and 1993.

Balance of Payments: Continued trade surpluses since 1982 led to accumulation of unprecedented US$9.9 billion in international reserves by end of 1993. Country's foreign investment inflow in first eleven months of 1993 rose to US$2.3 billion, a 92 percent increase over same period of 1992. Current account deficit in 1993 estimated at about 4.5 percent of GDP, or US$1.9 billion. Expected to broaden to US$2.4 billion, or 5.3 percent of GDP, in 1994. However, capital account surplus in 1993 created US$800 million overall balance of payments surplus (US$50 million more than in 1992). Balance of payments surplus in 1994 estimated at only US$100 million, with current account deficit of US$2.4 billion.

Imports: Principally petroleum, wheat, capital goods, spare parts, motor vehicles, and raw materials, mainly from European Union (EU), United States, Japan, and Brazil. Imports expenditures in 1993 estimated at US$10.1 billion, with 20 percent growth of imports of capital goods. Liberal import policy. Import duty a flat 11 percent for most products, except for expensive luxury goods or commodities governed by price band, which often carry additional surtaxes; regional accords aiming to cut tariffs to zero. Imports also subjected to 18 percent value-added tax (VAT) on c.i.f. (cost, insurance, and freight) value. Duty-free imports of materials used in products for export within 180 days, with prior authorization. Free-zone imports, if reexported, exempt from duties and VAT. Central Bank approval needed for all imports.

Exports: Principally copper (accounting for about 35 percent of exports), industrial products, molybdenum, iron ore, wood pulp, seafood, fruits, and nuts, mainly to EU, United States, Japan, and Brazil. Constituted 34 percent of GDP in 1990; 7 percent annual growth rate 1980–90. International recession and lower commodity prices caused value of exports to fall 7 percent in 1993, but exports constituted about 36 percent of GNP that year. Estimated 1993 total export earnings of US$9.3 billion down by US$800 million, creating country's first trade deficit in more than a decade. In 1991–93 Japan was Chile's largest export market, surpassing Chile's exports to United States. In 1993 Chile was third-largest supplier of wine to United States, after Italy and France.

Foreign Debt: Despite substantial improvement in country's exports, foreign debt rose from US$17.4 billion in 1991 to US$18.9 billion in 1992 (or US$19.1 billion according to International Monetary Fund) to an estimated US$20.2 billion in 1993. However, net foreign debt (total debt minus net international reserves) declined from 47 percent of GDP in 1989 to 21 percent of GDP in 1993. By early 1991, Chile was upgraded to status of nonrestructuring country, meaning that its debt was now considered recoverable, thus facilitating access to voluntary capital markets. In June 1991, Chile became first Latin American country to benefit from reduction in debt with United States within framework of President George Bush's Initiative for the Americas agreement. In December 1993, Standard and Poor Corporation, a United States credit rating agency, raised Chile's credit rating from investment-grade (BBB) to BBB + for long-term debt in foreign currency.

Fiscal Year (FY): Calendar year.

Exchange Rate: On September 13, 1994, Ch$405.9 = US$1.

Transportation and Telecommunications

Roads: Totaled 79,025 kilometers, including 9,913 kilometers of paved roads, 33,140 kilometers of gravel roads, and 35,972 kilometers of improved and unimproved earth roads. Pan American Highway (Longitudinal Highway), running length of country, forms 3,600-kilometer backbone of road system, with transversal roads leading from it east and west. Southern extension of about

1,100 kilometers, Southern Highway, from Puerto Montt to Puerto Yungay, opened in 1988. International highways also include Arica-Santos Highway to Bolivia and Trans-Andean Highway between Valparaíso and Mendoza, Argentina.

Motor Vehicles: 1.7 million (1994), including 1,034,370 automobiles, 403,842 vans, 49,006 buses, 126,698 trucks, 80,558 motorcycles, and 46,014 other commercial vehicles. An additional 202,000 motor vehicles expected to be registered in 1994.

Railroads: Mostly state owned, operated by State Railroad Company (Empresa de Ferrocarriles del Estado—EFE). Totaled 7,766 kilometers. Privately owned lines, totaling 2,130 kilometers, mostly in desert north, where northern terminal is Iquique. No passenger trains to northern Chile from Santiago. Four international railroads: two to Bolivia, one to northwest Argentina, and one to Peru. In 1992 Congress approved privatization of EFE, with only infrastructure remaining state owned. After period of neglect, government investment in EFE infrastructure was expected in 1993 to total US$98 million. In July 1993, Chile and Brazil invited Bolivia and Argentina to participate in joint effort to build interoceanic railroad line between Chilean and Brazilian coasts. Santiago has underground railroad system (metro).

Ports: Nine main ports: Antofagasta, Arica, Coquimbo, Iquique, Puerto Montt, Punta Arenas, San Antonio, Talcahuano (country's best harbor and its main naval station), and Valparaíso; also nine others. Only four or five have adequate facilities; about ten are used primarily for coastal shipping, restricted to Chilean flag vessels. Northern mining ports include Caldera, Chañaral, Coquimbo, and Huasco. Petroleum and gas ports include Cabo Negro, Clarencia, Puerto Percy, and San Gregorio. Main forest product ports San Vicente and Lirquén on Concepción Bay. Transnational transport of goods by road between Chilean ports of Antofagasta, Arica, Iquique, and Valparaíso and Brazilian ports of Santos and Porto Alegre. Government building US$10 million commercial port in Punta Arenas to service growing number of foreign vessels, cruise liners, and scientific ships en route to Antarctica. Puerto Ventanas—first private port in country, located on Quinteros Bay, in Valparaíso Region—opened in 1993.

Waterways: 725 kilometers of navigable inland waterways, mainly in southern lake district; Río Calle Calle provides waterway to Valdivia.

Airports and Air Transport: 390 total, of which 351 are usable airports, forty-eight of them paved. Two international airports: Comodoro Arturo Merino Benítez International Airport at Pudahuel outside Santiago; Chacalluta International Airport, Arica. Three main Chilean carriers: National Airlines (Línea Aérea Nacional de Chile—LAN-Chile), Fast Air, and Chilean Airlines (Línea Aérea del Cobre—Ladeco). By 1993 air transportation market had grown by 56 percent since 1990. United States share of United States-Chile market increased from 34 percent in 1990 to 62 percent in late 1993.

Telecommunications: 342 radios, 205 televisions, and sixty-eight telephones per 1,000 people in 1990. Broadcast stations included 167 AM, no FM, 131 TV, and twelve shortwave stations. Modern telephone system based on extensive microwave relay facilities. Total telephones in 1991 about 768,000. In October 1993, Chilesat, a Telex Chile subsidiary, joined the Americas-1, Columbus-2, and Unisur cable networks, a fiber-optics telecommunications system through submarine cables linking South America with North America and Europe.

Government and Politics

Government: Multiparty republic with presidential system based on 1980 constitution, amended and approved by referendum in July 1989, with fifty-four reforms. Executive, legislative, and judicial branches. Executive power with president directly elected; successive reelection not allowed. Presidential candidates must win majority or face runoff. Under constitutional reform approved by Congress in February 1994, presidential term reduced from eight to six years, the traditional term. Eduardo Frei Ruiz-Tagle, elected president of Christian Democratic Party (Partido Demócrata Cristiano—PDC) on November 23, 1991, won presidential election held on December 11, 1993, and assumed presidency on March 11, 1994. National Security Council (Consejo de Seguridad Nacional—Cosena) includes president of republic, presidents of Supreme Court and Senate, and heads of armed forces and police. Bicameral National Congress (hereafter, Congress; located in Valparaíso): Senate, with forty-six members, including eight designated senators, serving eight-year terms; and Chamber of Deputies with 120 members serving four-year terms. Courts include Supreme Court (seventeen judges), sixteen appellate courts, and a number of military courts.

Administrative Subdivisions: Twelve regions (*regiones*), and Metropolitan Region of Santiago. Regions each headed by an intendant (*intendente*). Regions subdivided into total of fifty-one provinces (*provincias*), each headed by a governor (*gobernador*) and 300 municipalities (*municipalidades*), each headed by a mayor (*alcalde*) appointed by municipal council (in towns with fewer than 10,000 inhabitants) or by president of the republic (in towns with more than 10,000 inhabitants). Lowest subdivision, communes (*comunas*). Santiago, like other cities, headed by mayor.

Politics: Governing coalition, Coalition of Parties for Democracy (Concertación de Partidos por la Democracia—CPD), dominated by PDC and socialists, expected to retain control in Congress, but without increase in legislative strength it may be unable to introduce important constitutional reform, such as composition of Constitutional Tribunal, membership and functions of Cosena, and promotion of military officers.

Political Parties: Left—Communist Party of Chile (Partido Comunista de Chile—PCCh) discredited since October 1988 plebiscite (which PCCh claimed regime would not allow Pinochet to lose), revolution in Eastern Europe, and disintegration of Soviet Union. Party for Democracy (Partido por la Democracia—PPD), which is an independent-minded creation of the Socialist Party (Partido Socialista) and a member of Aylwin government's CPD coalition, became second most popular party in 1993, after PDC. United Popular Action Movement (Movimiento de Acción Popular Unitario—MAPU), a Mapuche leftist party, quit CPD in June 1993. Christian Left (Izquierda Cristiana), a minor leftist party and CPD member. Humanist-Green Alliance (Alianza Humanista-Verde—AHV) also left CPD in 1993. Center—PDC had most followers in 1993, with 36.2 percent of overall votes. Radical Party (Partido Radical) supporting Frei Ruiz-Tagle in 1993. Right—National Renewal (Renovación Nacional). Independent Democratic Union (Unión Demócrata Independiente—UDI), political voice of former military regime's economic and political elite. Although National Renewal dominant rightist party, it and UDI main rivals for leadership of right. Union of the Centrist Center (Unión de Centro Centro—UCC) also a rightist party. On July 3, 1993, center-right parties—National Renewal, UDI, UCC, National Party (Partido Nacional), and Liberal Party (Partido Liberal)—agreed to form coalition called Union for the Progress of Chile (Unión por el Progreso de Chile). However, center-right remained in disarray prior to December 1993 elections.

Foreign Relations: Pro-West, pro-democracy. Maintains relations with more than seventy countries. Since restoration of democratic government in 1990, has reestablished political and economic ties with other Latin American countries, North America, Europe, and Asia. United States-Chilean relations have improved considerably since return to democracy and progress on issue of 1976 assassination in Washington of former Chilean ambassador to United States Orlando Letelier and United States citizen Ronnie Moffitt. Although shunning multilateral regional integration schemes, entered into bilateral tariff-cutting accords with individual Latin American countries—including Argentina, Bolivia, Colombia, and Mexico—in early 1990s, as well as negotiated framework trade agreement with United States in October 1990. Since joining Rio Group in 1990, has played active role in promoting democracy within inter-American system.

International Agreements and Membership: Member of Agency for the Prohibition of Nuclear Weapons in Latin America and the Caribbean; Economic Commission for Latin America and the Caribbean; General Agreement on Tariffs and Trade; Group of Eleven; Group of Seventy-Seven; Inter-American Development Bank; International Atomic Energy Commission; International Bank for Reconstruction and Development; International Civil Aviation Organization; International Criminal Police Organization; International Labor Organization; International Maritime Satellite Organization; International Monetary Fund; International Office for Migration; International Telecommunications Satellite Organization; International Telecommunications Union; Latin American Integration Association; League of Red Cross and Red Crescent Societies; Organization of American States; Organization of Copper Exporting Countries; Rio Group; United Nations and its main affiliated organizations; World Federation of Trade Unions; World Health Organization; World Intellectual Property Organization; and World Tourism Organization.

National Security

Armed Forces: Despite seventeen years of military rule (1973–90), still exceptionally professional and generally free of factionalism or partisan politics. In 1993 combined strength at least 91,800 (including 54,000 army, 25,000 navy, and 12,800 air force). Army reserves additional 50,000.

Defense Budget: Defense budget averaged US$1 billion annually in 1990–93. Annual average imports of major conventional arms US$212 million in 1987–91; as a percentage of national imports in 1990, 3.0 percent.

Military Units: Army organized into seven military areas (*áreas militares*—AMs)—headquartered in Antofagasta, Santiago, Concepción, Valdivia, Punta Arenas, Iquique, and Coihaique—and seven divisions, one for each AM. Navy organized into four naval zones, headquartered in Iquique, Punta Arenas, Talcahuano, and Valparaíso. Operational command includes Fleet, Submarine Command, and Transport Force. Navy includes Navy Infantry Corps (3,000 marines), Naval Aviation (750 members), and Coast Guard (1,500 members). Air force organized into three commands—Combat Command, Personnel Command, and Logistical Command—four air brigades, and twelve groups or squadrons. Air brigades headquartered in Iquique, Santiago, Puerto Montt, and Punta Arenas. Also operated an air base on King George Island, in Chilean Antarctic Territory.

Military Equipment: Ground forces equipped with forty-seven AMX–13 light tanks and twenty-one AMX–30 medium battle tanks from France; fifty M–41, sixty M–24, and 150 M4A3/M51 Super-Sherman tanks from United States/Israel; and 500 armored personnel carriers (APCs) from Brazil and 60–100 from United States. Navy ships include six missile destroyers, four missile frigates, and four submarines. Marines equipped with forty French APCs. Air force equipment includes sixteen F–5 fighters from United States, fifteen Dassault Mirage fighters from France, and thirty-three Hawker Hunters from Britain, as well as twenty Chilean-made strike aircraft and sixty-eight trainers (made partially or wholly by Chile).

Police: Official name: Forces of Order and Public Security. Consist of two separate law enforcement forces: Carabineros (national, 31,000-member paramilitary police force) and Investigations Police (national, 4,000-member plainclothes organization). Carabineros organized into three main zones—Northern Zone, Central Zone, and Southern Zone—with marine and air sections. Investigations Police operate in support of Carabineros and intelligence services of armed forces. For example, Investigations Police operate an antinarcotics force. In addition to law enforcement and traffic management, Carabineros engage in narcotics suppression, border control, and counterterrorism. Italy and Spain pledged to help Aylwin government finance and train civilian-based security force capable of combating terrorist threat.

Insurgents: Various terrorist groups still sporadically active in 1993: pro-Cuban Movement of the Revolutionary Left (Movimiento de la Izquierda Revolucionaria), United Popular Action Movement-Lautaro (Movimiento de Acción Popular Unitario-Lautaro), Lautaro

Youth Movement (Movimiento de Juventud Lautaro), Manuel Rodríguez Patriotic Front (Frente Patriótica Manuel Rodríguez), and Maoist-oriented Manuel Rodríguez Patriotic Front-Autonomous (Frente Patriótica Manuel Rodríguez-Autónomo). None a serious threat to national security, but each capable of occasional acts of terrorism.

Introduction

THE SOUTHERNMOST NATION of Latin America and one of the longest and narrowest nations in the world, Chile may derive its name from the indigenous Mapuche word "Chilli," which may mean "where the land ends." The Spanish conquistadors had heard about Chilli from the Incas of Peru, who had tried but had failed to conquer the land. In any case, the few survivors of Diego de Almagro's first Spanish expedition south from Peru in 1535–37 called themselves the "men of Chilli."

Despite its geographical isolation by formidable barriers—the Andes Mountains on its eastern flank, the Atacama Desert in its northernmost area, and the Pacific Ocean on its western side—Chile traditionally has been one of South America's best educated and most stable and politically sophisticated nations. Chile enjoyed constitutional and democratic government for most of its history as a republic, dating from 1818, particularly after adoption of its 1833 constitution. After a period of quasi-dictatorial rule in the 1920s and early 1930s, Chile developed a reputation for stable democratic government. Chileans have also benefited from state-run universities, welfare institutions, and, beginning in 1952, a national health system.

Throughout the 1970–90 period, Chilean national identity was tested as the country was subjected to profound political, economic, and social changes. Although the country began the 1970s by embarking on what soon proved to be a disastrous experiment in socialism, it ended the 1980s with a widely acclaimed free-market economy and a military government that had committed itself, albeit inadvertently through a plebiscite, to allowing a transition to democracy in 1990. Since the restoration of democracy, Chile has served as a model for other developing nations and the East European countries that are attempting to make a similar transition to democratic government and an antistatist, free-market economy. Yet the Chileans endured rough times before finding an economic prescription that worked for them.

During the ill-fated Popular Unity (Unidad Popular) government of its Marxist president, Salvador Allende Gossens (1970–73), Chile experienced uncharacteristic economic and political turbulence. As economic and political conditions deteriorated rapidly in August 1973, the Chilean Armed Forces and even the moderate Christian Democratic Party (Partido Demócrata Cristiano—PDC), Chile's largest single party, began to view the Allende government's socialist economic policies as a threat. On September 11, 1973, the armed forces shocked the world by attacking the lightly defended presidential palace, La Moneda, with army troops and aerial bombardment. Led by newly appointed army commander General Augusto Pinochet Ugarte, the bloody coup seemed incongruously violent for a country of Chile's democratic and civil traditions, especially considering that Allende had been elected democratically and had won a substantial 43 percent of the vote in the March 1973 congressional elections. Not having fought a real war since the War of the Pacific (1879–83) against Peru and Bolivia, the army seemed to welcome a pretext for reminding Allende's supporters of the military option contained in their own national motto, "By reason or by force."

In the "Historical Setting" chapter, historian Paul W. Drake summarizes various explanations for Allende's downfall and the coup as posited by analysts of the different political tendencies. Drake takes a similarly egalitarian approach to assessing blame, noting that "there was ample blame to go around" and that "groups at all points on the political spectrum helped destroy the democratic order by being too ideological and too intransigent." Prior to the coup, Chilean society had become polarized between Allende's supporters and the growing opposition, particularly during the culmination of the constitutional crisis in August 1973. In political terms, society was divided into three hostile camps—the Marxist left, the Christian Democratic center, and the conservative right. In "The Economy" chapter, economists Sebastian Edwards and Alejandra Cox Edwards blame the downfall of the Allende government to a large extent on its disregard of "many of the key principles of traditional economic theory." In their analysis, Allende's Popular Unity government was at fault, not only because of its monetary policies but also because of its lack of attention to the role that the real exchange rate plays in a country's international competition and balance of payments.

The Allende episode has remained politically charged during the past two decades, as evidenced by the march by Socialists and Communists on La Moneda and their skirmishes with police on the occasion of the twentieth anniversary of Allende's overthrow. A peculiar aspect of the historiography of the military coup, one that is illustrative of the political sensitivities surrounding it, is how Allende's death has been described. Some scholars have mentioned both versions of his death—the official military account that he committed suicide and the left-wing version that he was assassinated by the military. Others, including historian Mark Falcoff, have used the more noncommittal phrase that Allende "died in the coup." Thanks in large part to the assassination myth that Cuban president Fidel Castro Ruz and Colombian novelist Gabriel García Márquez helped to create, the left-wing version is still widely believed. Available evidence, however, is adequate to reasonably conclude that Allende committed suicide with the AK–47 assault rifle given him by Castro. Scholars such as Paul E. Sigmund and James Dunkerley believe Allende's death was a suicide, and reference sources and mainstream news media tend to use this version.

It is fairly well known that Allende was a long-time admirer of Chilean president José Manuel Balmaceda Fernández (1886–91), who shot himself to death while inside the Argentine legation on September 19, 1891, the day after his term ended. Balmaceda committed suicide as a result of his defeat in the Civil War of 1891 between his supporters and those of the National Congress (hereafter, Congress). In the weeks before the 1973 military coup, Allende, who like Balmaceda had overstepped his constitutional authority, had made his obsession with suicide as a last resort known to various individuals, including French president François Mitterrand. The coup and Allende's death were a tragic denouement to a chapter in Chilean history that most Chileans probably would like to forget, just as they would like to forget the repression that followed.

After the overthrow of the Allende government, Chile was plunged into a long period of repressive military rule. According to the National Commission on Truth and Reconciliation (the Rettig Commission), an eight-member investigatory body created by the government of Patricio Aylwin Azócar (1990–94), the armed forces and security forces were responsible for the deaths of 2,115 Chileans in the years following the 1973 coup, as well as the systematic torture or imprisonment of thousands of other opponents of the Pinochet regime.

Beginning with the Allende government and continuing with the military regime of General Pinochet (1973–90), Chile underwent two decades of social, economic, and political restructuring. As political scientist Arturo Valenzuela points out in the ''Government and Politics'' chapter, the Pinochet regime, ironically, proved to be ''the longest and most revolutionary government in the nation's history.'' Although the Pinochet regime adopted a system of local government administration based on corporatism (see Glossary), it avoided the corporatist economic policies often associated with authoritarian military rulers and favored by Chile's industrial bourgeoisie and landowning class. Instead, Pinochet was guided by the so-called ''Chicago boys'' (see Glossary), economists trained at the University of Chicago by Milton Friedman, a spokesman for monetarism (see Glossary). Determined to transform Chile's statist economy, Pinochet embraced the free-market, export-oriented economic model recommended by these advisers. The policies called for integrating the Chilean economy into the world economy, privatizing nationalized industries as well as the social security and health sectors, sharply reducing the number of public employees, adopting monetarist policies, deregulating the labor market, and carrying out a sweeping tax reform, among other measures.

By the late 1980s, the Chilean economy was again booming, and other developing countries were looking to it as an economic model. The regime's drive to privatize was an important indicator of the transition to a market economy. Of about 550 firms under state control in the 1970s, fewer than fifty remained so by the end of 1991. Whether Chile's structural transformations could have been carried out by a democratic government is unclear. By the early 1990s, Argentina's democratically elected president, Carlos Saul Menem, had achieved comparable reforms without sacrificing democracy or human rights. However, the success of the Pinochet model in Chile probably had less to do with authoritarianism per se than it did with the authoritarian implementation of antistatist, free-market policies.

Fortunately for the future of Chilean democracy, Pinochet was unable to carry out his plan to permanently abolish traditional political parties and institutions and continue ruling as Chile's president for most of the 1990s. His mistake (and Chile's gain) was to hold a plebiscite on a key provision of the Pinochet constitution, which voters had approved on September 11, 1980. The 1980 constitution provided for the gradual restoration of democracy by 1989, but it would have extended Pinochet's presidency through most of the 1990s. An overconfident Pinochet proceeded with the constitutionally mandated plebiscite on October 5, 1988, and was shocked when nearly 55 percent of registered voters indicated their preference for open elections in late 1989, while only 43 percent voted for allowing Pinochet to remain president through 1997. According to Arturo Valenzuela in the "Government and Politics" chapter, the opposition basically outfoxed Pinochet and won the plebiscite "following Pinochet's rules."

Aylwin, a Christian Democrat, easily won the long-awaited presidential election on December 14, 1989, as the candidate of the Coalition of Parties for Democracy (Concertación de Partidos por la Democracia—CPD), winning 55.2 percent of the vote. In concurrent congressional elections, the CPD also won a majority of elected seats in both houses of Congress. However, the coalition was unable to offset the nine Pinochet-designated senators, making the CPD's plans for further reform of the military-designed constitution unattainable for the foreseeable future.

When Aylwin (1990–94) took office as president on March 11, 1990, he inherited one of the strongest economies in Latin America, although the gross domestic product (GDP—see Glossary) growth rate in 1990 was only 2.1 percent. In addition to continuing Pinochet's free-market policies, Aylwin enhanced the former regime's foreign trade policy by further reducing import tariffs from 15 percent to 11 percent. Whereas the free-market policies adopted by Uruguay in 1990 met with strong resistance from a population accustomed to a generous cradle-to-grave welfare system, in Chile similar policies met with support from all sectors of society. Chile emerged not only as a showcase of a successful transition to moderate democratic government but also as a widely admired economic model for the developing world, achieving a GDP growth rate of 5.5 percent in 1991, with an unemployment rate of only 6.5 percent, and an unprecedented 9 percent GDP growth rate in 1992. The GDP growth rate reportedly slowed to about 5.5 percent in 1993, but the economy remained strong. In 1993 unemployment was only 5 percent, and inflation was down to 12 percent. Moreover, thanks to the economic policy of President Aylwin's minister of finance, Alejandro Foxley Riesco, total investment in Chile in 1993 was an impressive 27 percent of GDP, while Chile invested a comparable percentage of its GDP in other countries, including Argentina.

Chile's economic reforms had their downside. As Samuel Valenzuela points out, the Pinochet regime's social and economic policies led to increased socioeconomic inequalities, and urban and rural poverty remained extensive. The severe structural transformations, combined with the two harsh recessions and high debt-service obligations, aggravated the already high inequality of income distribution. According to Chilean sociologists Cristóbal Kay and Patricio Silva, who was health undersecretary in the early 1990s, extreme poverty (see Glossary) still affected nearly 55 percent of the rural population in 1990. The standard of living of many Chileans was further reduced by the declining quality of schooling and health care and inadequate land reform. Although the regime made heavy investments in programs for the very poor, thus helping to lower the infant mortality rate and raise life expectancy, its land reform measures were not particularly effective. Chile in 1987 remained in the category of countries with high inequality in the distribution of landholdings, with a Gini coefficient (see Glossary) of 0.64, according to the United Nations Development Programme.

The Aylwin government funneled at least 20 percent more resources into social programs, such as education, housing, and health, by raising taxes and seeking foreign assistance. Under the Aylwin government, the income of the lowest quintile of the population increased by 30 percent in 1990–93. By 1992 the proportion of Chileans living in poverty had decreased to 33 percent, from 45 percent in 1985. This amounted to 4.2 million Chileans living in poverty in 1993, with 1.2 million living in extreme poverty.

The Aylwin government also continued the privatization of social security, begun by the military regime in 1981. By the end of Aylwin's term, Chile's pension reform was the envy of the world. Officials from developing as well as developed nations were visiting Chile to see how it was done. By 1994 the system was managing assets of US$19.2 billion, giving Chile a savings rate similar to some Asian nations. Thanks in large part to its pension fund, Chile now has a strong capital market consisting of stocks, bonds, and other financial instruments.

As a democratic political model, the Aylwin government had a major handicap, namely the military, which, according to Arturo Valenzuela, has served as a virtually autonomous power within the government. With the help of its rightist allies in Congress, the military demonstrated its influence by derailing the Aylwin government's cautious but determined attempts to prosecute military officers for past human rights abuses. Aylwin refused to support the enactment of a blanket amnesty law, such as the one approved by Uruguay's General Assembly for military officers accused of human rights abuses committed between 1973 and 1978.

The military's rightist allies in Congress also thwarted the Aylwin government's attempts to enact reforms, such as one that would have eliminated the designated senators and another that would have replaced the military-designed binomial electoral system (see Glossary) with a system of proportional representation. Despite his setbacks in enacting reforms, Aylwin made good use of the strong presidential powers provided by the Pinochet-designed constitution. For example, he succeeded in enacting a constitutional reform law restoring the country's tradition of elected local governments and another limiting the power of the military courts to trying only those military personnel on active duty.

Aylwin's generally very successful presidency, particularly his handling of the economy, assured a continuation of democratic government under another politically moderate president, Eduardo Frei Ruiz-Tagle, the well-regarded son of Eduardo Frei Montalva (1964–70), one of Chile's most respected presidents. Frei Ruiz-Tagle entered politics only in 1989, when he ran successfully for a Senate seat from Santiago. He was elected PDC president in 1991, winning 70 percent of the vote. Although a consensus candidate for the PDC presidency, Frei was particularly favored by the PDC's right-wing faction, popularly known as the *guatones* (fat men). The party's other factions—the left-wing's *chascones* (bushy-haired men) and the center's *renovadores* (renewalists)—favored other candidates.

On May 23, 1993, Frei defeated his Socialist Party (Partido Socialista) rival, Ricardo Lagos Escobar, to obtain the CPD's presidential nomination, with a lopsided vote of 60 percent to 38 percent. Thanks in part to Aylwin's strong performance in the social, economic, and political areas, in part to Frei's political inheritance, and in part to continued divisiveness among the rightist parties, there was never any doubt that Frei would win. As chairman of the Senate's key Finance and Budget Committee, Frei had earned a reputation as a fiscal moderate. His positive public rating, according to a Center for Public Studies (Centro de Estudios Públicos—CEP)-Adimark poll of July 1993, was a remarkable 75 percent, even higher than Aylwin's 73 percent positive rating.

Indeed, Frei's coalition easily won the presidential election on December 11, 1993, with 57.4 percent of the vote, compared with 24.7 percent for Arturo Alessandri Besa, Frei's closest challenger and candidate of the newly formed center-right coalition called the Union for the Progress of Chile (Unión por el Progreso de Chile). Frei received the largest popular mandate of any Chilean leader since 1931. In sharp contrast to the presidential elections of September 4, 1970, the unexciting elections of December 11, 1993, lacked left-wing and right-wing rhetoric. The vast majority of Chileans, enjoying Latin America's strongest economy, were apparently content to let the government remain in the hands of the political center, namely Frei Montalva's son. Although Frei Ruiz-Tagle, unlike his late father, is not known for his public oratory, Chileans regarded his low-key, nonconfrontational, and statesmanlike campaigning style, as well as his penchant for consensus-building, as positive traits.

Frei Ruiz-Tagle appears to have a better chance than Aylwin had to make the executive stronger vis-à-vis the military, not only because of his powerful mandate but also because the political right is becoming less protective of the military's prerogatives within the military-designed political system. In addition, Frei Ruiz-Tagle, unlike his father's rightist alliance, allied himself with the Socialist Party, thus strengthening social and political harmony. Nevertheless, daunting challenges in the form of military resistance face Frei in his plans to seek to amend the Pinochet-era constitution. These plans include abolishing the designated Senate seats, reforming the electoral system, and making the army commander, General Pinochet, and the other military commanders accountable to elected officials. Frei's political agenda also includes less politically sensitive goals, such as improving secondary and higher education, consolidating Chile's political democracy, modernizing public services, and giving priority to rural development and eradication of poverty.

On the foreign front, Frei appears to be inclined to reverse Chile's uninterest in regional trade pacts. In particular, his government is reassessing the potential benefits of joining the Southern Cone Common Market (Mercado Común del Cono Sur—Mercosur; see Glossary) and expects that Chile will become an associate member by January 1995. After the United States Congress ratified the North American Free Trade Agreement (NAFTA—see Glossary) in November 1993, Chile began lobbying to join a similar agreement with the United States (one that would drop the "North" from NAFTA), citing President William Jefferson Clinton's position that Chile is "next in line" to join NAFTA. Total bilateral trade between Chile and the United States amounted to US$4.1 billion in 1993.

Frei's coalition maintained a majority (seventy) of the 120 seats in the lower house of Congress, the Chamber of Deputies, but fell short of the eighty it needed for a two-thirds voting bloc. Its lack of majority support in the forty-six-member Senate also seemed to preclude passage of constitutional amendments, which require a three-fifths majority in both houses. Like its predecessor, the Frei government's efforts are likely to be hampered by the nonelected senators appointed by the Pinochet regime (of whom only eight are still serving) and by the binomial electoral system, which the military adopted for the 1989 elections in order to strengthen the hand of the rightists.

Furthermore, unlike its pre-coup democracy, Chile's democracy of the 1990s is expected to remain fettered by a military with a strong institutional role in government, a military that will not likely tolerate a departure from the economic policies that constitute the principal accomplishment of its seventeen years in power. Even Frei's stated intention to push legislation to relieve the Copper Corporation (Corporación del Cobre—Codelco) of its constitutional obligation to give the armed forces 10 percent of its annual earnings entails a risk of antagonizing the military. In 1993 this contribution amounted to US$197 million, almost one-fifth of the total defense budget. However, one casualty of a financial scandal at Codelco that broke in January 1994 could be the army. The copper unions asked the army to give up its 10 percent share of

Codelco's annual sales as a patriotic gesture. Although the army ignored this request, Congress was planning to discuss military spending later in the year, leaving open the possibility that the army could be compelled to make the sacrifice to head off additional budget cuts.

Frei's relations with the military may determine how successful he is in achieving his stated objectives, but confrontation with the military does not appear to be his style. Indeed, in his address to Congress on May 21, 1994, Frei avoided the most controversial issue, his lack of power to appoint or dismiss the military commanders. The only feasible resolution of the dilemma of Pinochet's continuing influence in government and what Frei's government refers to as "authoritarian enclaves" may need to await the general's scheduled retirement in 1997. Even then, Chile's transition to democracy will not be fully consolidated until reform of constitutional anachronisms, such as the immunity of military commanders from presidential dismissal, the binomial electoral system, and the designated senators. However, there is no guarantee that Pinochet's departure will allow for the rapid implementation of these needed reforms.

September 15, 1994   Rex A. Hudson

Chapter 1. Historical Setting

A textile figure depicting a tree (temu, *meaning the tree* Temu divaricatum), *from a seventeenth-century Mapuche woman's belt called* ñimintrarüwe

FROM ONE OF THE MOST neglected outposts of the Spanish Empire, Chile developed into one of the most prosperous and democratic nations in Latin America. Throughout its history, however, Chile has depended on great external powers for economic exchange and political influence: Spain in the colonial period, Britain in the nineteenth century, and the United States in the twentieth century.

Chile's dependence is made most evident by the country's heavy reliance on exports. These have included silver and gold in the colonial period, wheat in the mid-nineteenth century, nitrates up to World War I, copper after the 1930s, and a variety of commodities sold overseas in more recent years. The national economy's orientation toward the extraction of primary products has gone hand in hand with severe exploitation of workers. Beginning with the coerced labor of native Americans during the Spanish conquest, the exploitation continued with mestizo (see Glossary) peonage on huge farms in the eighteenth and nineteenth centuries and brutal treatment of miners in the north in the first decade of the twentieth century. The most recent victimization of workers occurred during the military dictatorship of Augusto Pinochet Ugarte (1973–90), when unions were suppressed and wages were depressed, unemployment increased, and political parties were banned.

Another persistent feature of Chile's economic history has been the conflict over land in the countryside, beginning when the Spaniards displaced the indigenous people during their sixteenth-century conquest. Later chapters of this struggle have included the expansion of the great estates during the ensuing four centuries and the agrarian reform efforts of the 1960s and 1970s.

Politically, Chile has also conformed to several patterns. Since winning independence in 1818, the nation has had a history of civilian rule surpassed by that of few countries in the world. In the nineteenth century, Chile became the first country in Latin America to install a durable constitutional system of government, which encouraged the development of an array of political parties. Military intervention in politics has been rare in Chile, occurring only at times of extraordinary social crisis, as in 1891, 1924, 1925, 1932, and 1973. These interventions often brought about massive transformations; all the fundamental changes in the Chilean political system and its constitutions have occurred with the intervention of the armed forces, acting in concert with civilian politicians.

From 1932 to 1973, Chile built on its republican tradition by sustaining one of the most stable, reformist, and representative democracies in the world. Although elitist and conservative in some respects, the political system provided for the peaceful transfer of power and the gradual incorporation of new contenders. Undergirding that system were Chile's strong political parties, which were often attracted to foreign ideologies and formulas. Having thoroughly permeated society, these parties were able to withstand crushing blows from the Pinochet regime of 1973–90.

Republican political institutions were able to take root in Chile in the nineteenth century before new social groups demanded participation. Contenders from the middle and lower classes gradually were assimilated into an accommodating political system in which most disputes were settled peacefully, although disruptions related to the demands of workers often met a harsh, violent response. The system expanded to incorporate more and more competing regional, anticlerical, and economic elites in the nineteenth century. The middle classes gained political offices and welfare benefits in the opening decades of the twentieth century. From the 1920s to the 1940s, urban laborers obtained unionization rights and participated in reformist governments. In the 1950s, women finally exercised full suffrage and became a decisive electoral force. And by the 1960s, rural workers achieved influence with reformist parties, widespread unionization, and land reform.

As the political system evolved, groups divided on either side of six main issues. The first and most important in the nineteenth century was the role of the Roman Catholic Church in political, social, and economic affairs. Neither of the two major parties, the Conservative Party and the Liberal Party, opposed the practice of Catholicism. However, the Conservatives defended the church's secular prerogatives; the Liberals (and later the Nationals, Radicals, Democrats, and Marxists) took anticlerical positions.

The second source of friction was regionalism, although less virulent than in some larger Latin American countries. In the north and south, reform groups became powerful, especially the Conservatives holding sway in Chile's Central Valley (Valle Central), who advocated opposition to the establishment. Regional groups made a significant impact on political life in Chile: they mobilized repeated rebellions against the central government from the 1830s through the 1850s; helped replace a centralizing president with a political system dominated by the National Congress (hereafter, Congress) and local bosses in the 1890s; elected Arturo Alessandri Palma (1920–24, 1925, 1932–38) as the chief executive representing the north against the central oligarchy in 1920; and cast exceptional percentages of their ballots for reformist and leftist candidates (especially Radicals, Communists, and Socialists) from the 1920s to the 1970s. Throughout the twentieth century, leaders outside Santiago also pleaded for administrative decentralization until the Pinochet government devolved greater authority on provincial and municipal governments and even moved Congress from Santiago to Valparaíso.

The third issue dividing Chileans—social class—grew in importance from the nineteenth century to the twentieth century. Although both the Conservatives and the Liberals represented the upper stratum, in the nineteenth century the Radicals began to speak on behalf of many in the middle class, and the Democrats built a base among urban artisans and workers. In the twentieth century, the Socialists and Communists became the leaders of organized labor. Along with the Christian Democratic Party, these parties attracted adherents among impoverished people in the countryside and the urban slums.

In the twentieth century, three other issues became salient, although not as significant as divisions over social class, regionalism, or the role of the church. One was the cleavage between city and country, which was manifested politically by the leftist parties' relative success in the urban areas and by the rightist groups in the countryside. Another source of strife was ideology; most Chilean parties after World War I sharply defined themselves in terms of programmatic and philosophical differences, often imported from abroad, including liberalism, Marxism, corporatism (see Glossary), and communitarianism (see Glossary). Gender also became a political issue and divider. After women began voting for president in 1952, they were more likely than men to cast ballots for rightist or centrist candidates.

As Chile's political parties grew, they attracted followers not only on the basis of ideology but also on the basis of patron-client relationships between candidates and voters. These ties were particularly important at the local level, where mediation with government agencies, provision of public employment, and delivery of public services were more crucial than ideological battles waged on the national stage. Over generations, these bonds became tightly woven, producing within the parties fervent and exclusive subcultures nurtured in the family, the community, and the workplace. As a result, by the mid-twentieth century the parties had politicized schools, unions, professional associations, the media, and virtually all other components of national life. The intense politicization of modern Chile has its roots in events of the nineteenth century.

During the colonial period and most of the twentieth century, the central state played an active role in the economy until many of its functions were curtailed by the military government of General Pinochet. State power was highly centralized from the 1830s to the 1970s, to the ire of the outlying provinces.

Although normally governed by civilians, Chile has been militaristic in its dealings with native peoples, workers, and neighboring states. In the twentieth century, it has been a supporter of arbitration in international disputes. In foreign policy, Chile has long sought to be the strongest power on the Pacific Coast of South America, and it has always shied away from diplomatic entanglements outside the Americas.

Pre-Columbian Civilizations

At the time the Spanish arrived, a variety of Amerindian societies inhabited what is now Chile. No elaborate, centralized, sedentary civilization reigned supreme, even though the Inca Empire had penetrated the northern land of the future state. As the Spaniards would after them, the Incas encountered fierce resistance from the indigenous Araucanians, particularly the Mapuche tribe, and so did not exert control in the south. During their attempts at conquest in 1460 and 1491, the Incas established forts in the Central Valley of Chile, but they could not colonize the region. In the north, the Incas were able to collect tribute from small groups of fishermen and oasis farmers but were not able to establish a strong cultural presence.

The Araucanians, a fragmented society of hunters, gatherers, and farmers, constituted the largest native American group in Chile. A mobile people who engaged in trade and warfare with other indigenous groups, they lived in scattered family clusters and small villages. Although the Araucanians had no written language, they did use a common language. Those in what became central Chile were more settled and more likely to use irrigation. Those in the south combined slash-and-burn agriculture with hunting.

The Araucanians, especially those in the south, became famous for their staunch resistance to the seizure of their territory. Scholars speculate that their total population may have numbered 1 million at most when the Spaniards arrived in the 1530s; a century of European conquest and disease reduced that number by at least half. During the conquest, the Araucanians quickly added horses and European weaponry to their arsenal of clubs and bows and arrows. They became adept at raiding Spanish settlements and, albeit in declining numbers, managed to hold off the Spaniards and their descendants until the late nineteenth century.

The Araucanians' valor inspired the Chileans to mythologize them as the nation's first national heroes, a status that did nothing, however, to elevate the wretched living standard of their descendants. Of the three Araucanian groups, the one that mounted the most resistance to the Spanish was the Mapuche, meaning "people of the land."

Conquest and Colonization, 1535–1810

Politics and War in a Frontier Society

Chile's first known European discoverer, Ferdinand Magellan, stopped there during his voyage on October 21, 1520. A concerted attempt at colonization began when Diego de Almagro, a companion of conqueror Francisco Pizarro, headed south from Peru in 1535. Disappointed at the dearth of mineral wealth and deterred by the pugnacity of the native population in Chile, Almagro returned to Peru in 1537, where he died in the civil wars that took place among the conquistadors.

The second Spanish expedition from Peru to Chile was begun by Pedro de Valdivia in 1540. Proving more persistent than Almagro, he founded the capital city of Santiago on February 12, 1541. Valdivia managed to subdue many northern Amerindians, forcing them to work in mines and fields. He had far less success with the Araucanians of the south, however.

Valdivia (1541–53) became the first governor of the Captaincy General of Chile, which was the colonial name until 1609. In that post, he obeyed the viceroy of Peru and, through him, the king of Spain and his bureaucracy. Responsible to the governor, town councils known as *cabildos* administered local municipalities, the most important of which was Santiago, which was the seat of a royal *audiencia* (see Glossary) from 1609 until the end of colonial rule.

Seeking more precious metals and slave labor, Valdivia established fortresses farther south. Being so scattered and small, however, they proved difficult to defend against Araucanian attack. Although Valdivia found small amounts of gold in the south, he realized that Chile would have to be primarily an agricultural colony.

In December 1553, an Araucanian army of warriors, organized by the legendary Mapuche chief Lautaro (Valdivia's former servant), assaulted and destroyed the fort of Tucapel. Accompanied by only fifty soldiers, Valdivia rushed to the aid of the fort, but all his men perished at the hands of the Mapuche in the Battle of Tucapel. Valdivia himself fled but was later tracked down, tortured, and killed by Lautaro. Although Lautaro was killed by Spaniards in the Battle of Mataquito in 1557, his chief, Caupolicán, continued the fight until his capture by treachery and his subsequent execution by the Spaniards in 1558. The uprising of 1553–58 became the most famous instance of Araucanian resistance; Lautaro in later centuries became a revered figure among Chilean nationalists. It took several more years to suppress the rebellion. Thereafter, the Araucanians no longer threatened to drive the Spanish out, but they did destroy small settlements from time to time. Most important, the Mapuche held on to their remaining territory for another three centuries.

Despite inefficiency and corruption in the political system, Chileans, like most Spanish Americans, exhibited remarkable loyalty to crown authority throughout nearly three centuries of colonial rule. Chileans complained about certain policies or officials but never challenged the regime. It was only when the king of Spain was overthrown at the beginning of the nineteenth century that Chileans began to consider self-government.

Chileans resented their reliance on Peru for governance, trade, and subsidies, but not enough to defy crown authority. Many Chilean criollos (creoles, or Spaniards born in the New World) also resented domination by the *peninsulares* (Spaniards, usually officials, born in the Old World and residing in an overseas colony), especially in the sinecures of royal administration. However, local Chilean elites, especially landowners, asserted themselves in politics well before any movement for independence. Over time, these elites captured numerous positions in the local governing apparatus, bought favors from the bureaucracy, co-opted administrators from Spain, and came to exercise informal authority in the countryside.

Society in Chile was sharply divided along ethnic, racial, and class lines. *Peninsulares* and criollos dominated the tiny upper class. Miscegenation between Europeans and the indigenous people produced a mestizo population that quickly outnumbered the Spaniards. Farther down the social ladder were a few African slaves and large numbers of native Americans.

The Roman Catholic Church served as the main buttress of the government and the primary instrument of social control. Compared with its counterparts in Peru and Mexico, the church in Chile was not very rich or powerful. On the frontier, missionaries were more important than the Catholic hierarchy. Although usually it supported the status quo, the church produced the most important defenders of the indigenous population against Spanish atrocities. The most famous advocate of human rights for the native Americans was a Jesuit, Luis de Valdivia (no relation to Pedro

Pedro de Valdivia,
founder of Santiago
and Chile's first governor
Courtesy Embassy of
Chile, Washington

de Valdivia), who struggled, mostly in vain, to improve their lot in the period 1593–1619.

Cut off to the north by desert, to the south by the Araucanians, to the east by the Andes Mountains, and to the west by the ocean, Chile became one of the most centralized, homogeneous colonies in Spanish America. Serving as a sort of frontier garrison, the colony found itself with the mission of forestalling encroachment by Araucanians and by Spain's European enemies, especially the British and the Dutch. In addition to the Araucanians, buccaneers and English adventurers menaced the colony, as was shown by Sir Francis Drake's 1578 raid on Valparaíso, the principal port. Because Chile hosted one of the largest standing armies in the Americas, it was one of the most militarized of the Spanish possessions, as well as a drain on the treasury of Peru.

Throughout the colonial period, the Spaniards engaged in frontier combat with the Araucanians, who controlled the territory south of the Río Bío-Bío (about 500 kilometers south of Santiago) and waged guerrilla warfare against the invaders. During many of those years, the entire southern region was impenetrable by Europeans. In the skirmishes, the Spaniards took many of their defeated foes as slaves. Missionary expeditions to Christianize the Araucanians proved risky and often fruitless.

Most European relations with the native Americans were hostile, resembling those later existing with nomadic tribes in the United

States. The Spaniards generally treated the Mapuche as an enemy nation to be subjugated and even exterminated, in contrast to the way the Aztecs and the Incas treated the Mapuche, as a pool of subservient laborers. Nevertheless, the Spaniards did have some positive interaction with the Mapuche. Along with warfare, there also occurred some miscegenation, intermarriage, and acculturation between the colonists and the indigenous people.

The Colonial Economy

The government played a significant role in the colonial economy. It regulated and allocated labor, distributed land, granted monopolies, set prices, licensed industries, conceded mining rights, created public enterprises, authorized guilds, channeled exports, collected taxes, and provided subsidies. Outside the capital city, however, colonists often ignored or circumvented royal laws. In the countryside and on the frontier, local landowners and military officers frequently established and enforced their own rules.

The economy expanded under Spanish rule, but some criollos complained about royal taxes and limitations on trade and production. Although the crown required that most Chilean commerce be with Peru, smugglers managed to sustain some illegal trade with other American colonies and with Spain itself. Chile exported to Lima small amounts of gold, silver, copper, wheat, tallow, hides, flour, wine, clothing, tools, ships, and furniture. Merchants, manufacturers, and artisans became increasingly important to the Chilean economy.

Mining was significant, although the volume of gold and silver extracted in Chile was far less than the output of Peru or Mexico. The conquerors appropriated mines and washings from the native people and coerced them into extracting the precious metal for the new owners. The crown claimed one-fifth of all the gold produced, but the miners frequently cheated the treasury. By the seventeenth century, depleted supplies and the conflict with the Araucanians reduced the quantity of gold mined in Chile.

Because precious metals were scarce, most Chileans worked in agriculture. Large landowners became the local elite, often maintaining a second residence in the capital city. Traditionally, most historians have considered these great estates (called haciendas or *fundos*) inefficient and exploitive, but some scholars have claimed that they were more productive and less cruel than is conventionally depicted.

The haciendas initially depended for their existence on the land and labor of the indigenous people. As in the rest of Spanish America, crown officials rewarded many conquerors according to the *encomienda* (see Glossary) system, by which a group of native Americans would be commended or consigned temporarily to their care. The grantees, called *encomenderos,* were supposed to Christianize their wards in return for small tribute payments and service, but they usually took advantage of their charges as laborers and servants. Many *encomenderos* also appropriated native lands. Throughout the sixteenth and seventeenth centuries, the *encomenderos* fended off attempts by the crown and the church to interfere with their exploitation of the indigenous people.

The Chilean colony depended heavily on coerced labor, whether it was legally slave labor or, like the wards of the *encomenderos,* nominally free. Wage labor initially was rare in the colonial period; it became much more common in the eighteenth and nineteenth centuries. Because few native Americans or Africans were available, the mestizo population became the main source of workers for the growing number of latifundios (see Glossary), which were basically synonymous with haciendas.

Those workers attached to the estates as tenant farmers became known as *inquilinos.* Many of them worked outside the cash economy, dealing in land, labor, and barter. The countryside was also populated by small landholders (*minifundistas*), migrant workers (*afuerinos*), and a few Mapuche holding communal lands (usually under legal title).

Bourbon Reforms, 1759–96

The Habsburg dynasty's rule over Spain ended in 1700. The Habsburgs' successors, the French Bourbon monarchs, reigned for the rest of the colonial period. In the second half of the eighteenth century, they tried to restructure the empire to improve its productivity and defense. The main period of Bourbon reforms in Chile lasted from the coronation of Charles III (1759–88) in Spain to the end of Governor Ambrosio O'Higgins y Ballenary's tenure in Chile (1788–96).

The Bourbon rulers gave the *audiencia* of Chile (Santiago) greater independence from the Viceroyalty of Peru (see fig. 2). One of the most successful governors of the Bourbon era was the Irish-born O'Higgins, whose son Bernardo would lead the Chilean independence movement. Ambrosio O'Higgins promoted greater self-sufficiency of both economic production and public administration, and he enlarged and strengthened the military. In 1791 he also outlawed *encomiendas* and forced labor.

The Bourbons allowed Chile to trade more freely with other colonies, as well as with independent states. Exchange increased with Argentina after it became the Viceroyalty of the Río de la Plata

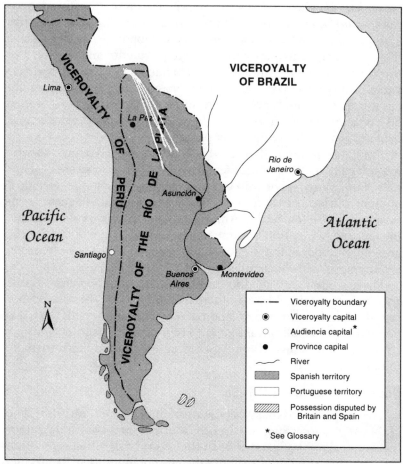

Source: Based on information from A. Curtis Wilgus, *Historical Atlas of Latin America*, New
York, 1967, 112.

Figure 2. Three South American Viceroyalties, ca. 1800

in 1776. Ships from the United States and Europe were engaging
in direct commerce with Chile by the end of the eighteenth century. However, the total volume of Chilean trade remained small
because the colony produced few items of high unit value to out-
siders.

Freer trade brought with it greater knowledge of politics abroad,
especially the spread of liberalism in Europe and the creation of
the United States. Although a few members of the Chilean elite
flirted with ideals of the Enlightenment, most of them held fast to
the traditional ideology of the Spanish crown and its partner, the
Roman Catholic Church. Notions of democracy and independence,

let alone Protestantism, never reached the vast majority of mestizos and native Americans, who remained illiterate and subordinate.

Wars of Independence, 1810–18

Aristocratic Chileans began considering independence only when the authority and legitimacy of the crown were cast in doubt by Napoleon Bonaparte's invasion of Spain in 1807. Napoleon replaced the Spanish king with his brother, Joseph Bonaparte. On the peninsula, Spanish loyalists formed juntas that claimed they would govern both the motherland and the colonies until the rightful king was restored. Thus, Chileans, like other Spanish Americans, had to confront the dilemma of who was in charge in the absence of the divine monarch: the French pretender to the throne, the Spanish rebels, or local leaders. The latter option was tried on September 18, 1810, a date whose anniversary is celebrated as Chile's independence day. On that day, the criollo leaders of Santiago, employing the town council as a junta, announced their intention to govern the colony until the king was reinstated. They swore loyalty to the ousted monarch, Ferdinand VII, but insisted that they had as much right to rule in the meantime as did subjects of the crown in Spain itself. They immediately opened the ports to all traders.

Chile's first experiment with self-government, the Old Fatherland (Patria Vieja, 1810–14), was led by José Miguel Carrera Verdugo (president, 1812–13), an aristocrat in his mid-twenties. The military-educated Carrera was a heavy-handed ruler who aroused widespread opposition. One of the earliest advocates of full independence, Bernardo O'Higgins Riquelme, captained a rival faction that plunged the criollos into civil war. For him and for certain other members of the Chilean elite, the initiative for temporary self-rule quickly escalated into a campaign for permanent independence, although other criollos remained loyal to Spain. Among those favoring independence, conservatives fought with liberals over the degree to which French revolutionary ideas would be incorporated into the movement. After several efforts, Spanish troops from Peru took advantage of the internecine strife to reconquer Chile in 1814, when they reasserted control by winning the Battle of Rancagua on October 2. O'Higgins and many of the Chilean rebels escaped to Argentina.

During the Reconquest (La Reconquista) of 1814–17, the harsh rule of the Spanish loyalists, who punished suspected rebels, drove more Chileans into the insurrectionary camp. More and more members of the Chilean elite were becoming convinced of the necessity of full independence, regardless of who sat on the throne of Spain. As the leader of guerrilla raids against the Spaniards, Manuel Rodríguez became a national symbol of resistance.

When criollos sang the praises of equality and freedom, however, they meant equal treatment for themselves in relation to the *peninsulares* and liberation from Spanish rule, not equality or freedom for the masses of Chileans. The criollos wanted to assume leadership positions previously controlled by *peninsulares* without upsetting the existing social and economic order. In that sense, the struggle for independence was a war within the upper class, although the majority of troops on both sides consisted of conscripted mestizos and native Americans.

In exile in Argentina, O'Higgins joined forces with José de San Martín, whose army freed Chile with a daring assault over the Andes in 1817, defeating the Spaniards at the Battle of Chacabuco on February 12. San Martín considered the liberation of Chile a strategic stepping-stone to the emancipation of Peru, which he saw as the key to hemispheric victory over the Spanish. Chile won its formal independence when San Martín defeated the last large Spanish force on Chilean soil at the Battle of Maipú on April 5, 1818. San Martín then led his Argentine and Chilean followers north to liberate Peru; fighting continued in Chile's southern provinces, the bastion of the royalists, until 1826 (see Genesis of the Armed Forces, 1814–36, ch. 5).

Civil Wars, 1818–30

From 1817 to 1823, Bernardo O'Higgins ruled Chile as supreme director (president). He won plaudits for defeating royalists and founding schools, but civil strife continued. O'Higgins alienated Liberals and provincials with his authoritarianism, Conservatives and the church with his anticlericalism, and landowners with his proposed reforms of the land tenure system. His attempt to devise a constitution in 1818 that would legitimize his government failed, as did his effort to generate stable funding for the new administration. O'Higgins's dictatorial behavior aroused resistance in the provinces. This growing discontent was reflected in the continuing opposition of partisans of Carrera, who was executed by the Argentine regime in Mendoza in 1821, as were his two brothers three years earlier.

Although opposed by many Liberals, O'Higgins angered the Roman Catholic Church with his liberal beliefs. He maintained Catholicism's status as the official state religion but tried to curb the church's political powers and to encourage religious tolerance as a means of attracting Protestant immigrants and traders. Like the church, the landed aristocracy felt threatened by O'Higgins, resenting his attempts to eliminate noble titles and, more important, to eliminate entailed estates.

Bernardo O'Higgins Riquelme,
father of Chile
Courtesy Embassy of
Chile, Washington

O'Higgins's opponents also disapproved of his diversion of Chilean resources to aid San Martín's liberation of Peru. O'Higgins insisted on supporting that campaign because he realized that Chilean independence would not be secure until the Spaniards were routed from the Andean core of the empire. However, amid mounting discontent, troops from the northern and southern provinces forced O'Higgins to resign. Embittered, O'Higgins departed for Peru, where he died in 1842.

After O'Higgins went into exile in 1823, civil conflict continued, focusing mainly on the issues of anticlericalism and regionalism. Presidents and constitutions rose and fell quickly in the 1820s. The civil struggle's harmful effects on the economy, and particularly on exports, prompted Conservatives to seize national control in 1830.

In the minds of most members of the Chilean elite, the bloodshed and chaos of the late 1820s were attributable to the shortcomings of liberalism and federalism, which had been dominant over conservatism for most of the period. The abolition of slavery in 1823— long before most other countries in the Americas—was considered one of the Liberals' few lasting achievements. One Liberal leader from the south, Ramón Freire Serrano, rode in and out of the presidency several times (1823–27, 1828, 1829, 1830) but could not sustain his authority. From May 1827 to September 1831, with the exception of brief interventions by Freire, the presidency was occupied by Francisco Antonio Pinto Díaz, Freire's former vice president. In August 1828, Pinto's first year in office, Chile abandoned its short-lived federalist system for a unitary form of government, with separate legislative, executive, and judicial branches. By adopting a moderately liberal constitution in 1828, Pinto alienated both the Federalists and the Liberal factions. He also angered the old aristocracy by abolishing estates inherited by primogeniture (*mayorazgo*—see Glossary) and caused a public uproar with his anticlericalism. After the defeat of his liberal army at the Battle of Lircay on April 17, 1830, Freire, like O'Higgins, went into exile in Peru.

Aristocratic Republicanism, 1830–91

Scholars have long pondered why Chile was the first country in Latin America to achieve stable civilian rule in a constitutional, electoral, representative republic. They have also asked why Chile was more successful at constitutional government thereafter than its neighbors. One part of the answer is that Chile had fewer obstacles to overcome because it was less disturbed by regional, church-state, and ethnic conflicts. The geographically compact and relatively homogeneous population was easier to manage than the far-flung groups residing in many of the other new states of the hemisphere. As the nineteenth century wore on, slow settlement of the frontiers to the north and south provided a safety valve without creating a challenge to the dominance of the Central Valley.

As with regionalism, the church issue that rent many of the new republics was also muted in Chile, where the Catholic Church had never been very wealthy or powerful. Some historians would also argue that Chilean criollos, because they lived on the fringe of the empire, had more experience at self-government during the colonial period. In addition, the Chilean elite was less fearful than many other Spanish Americans that limited democracy would open the door to uprisings by massive native or black subject classes. At the same time, the ruling class was cohesive and confident, its members connected by familial and business networks. The elite was powerful partly because it controlled the main exports, until foreigners took over trade late in the nineteenth century. The rapid recovery of the export economy from the devastation of the wars of independence also helped, as economic and political success and stability became mutually reinforcing. Capitalizing on these advantages, however, would require shrewd and ruthless political engineers, victory in a war against Chile's neighbors, continued economic growth, and some luck in the design, timing, and sequence of political change.

The Conservative Era, 1830–61

Members of the first political parties, the Conservatives (*pelucones,* or bigwigs) and the Liberals (*pipiolos,* or novices), began to coalesce around the church-state issue. Not only more favorably inclined toward the church, the Conservatives were also more sympathetic than the Liberals toward the colonial legacy, authoritarian government, the supremacy of executive powers, and a unitary state. After their victory at the Battle of Lircay, the Conservatives took charge, spearheaded by a Valparaíso merchant, Diego Portales Palazuelos.

The Portalian State, 1830–37

Although never president, Portales dominated Chilean politics from the cabinet and behind the scenes from 1830 to 1837. He installed the "autocratic republic," which centralized authority in the national government. His political program enjoyed support from merchants, large landowners, foreign capitalists, the church, and the military. Political and economic stability reinforced each other as Portales encouraged economic growth through free trade and put government finances in order.

Portales was an agnostic who said that he believed in the clergy but not in God. He realized the importance of the Roman Catholic Church as a bastion of loyalty, legitimacy, social control, and stability, as had been the case in the colonial period. He repealed Liberal reforms that had threatened church privileges and properties.

Portales brought the military under civilian control by rewarding loyal generals, cashiering troublemakers, and promoting a victorious war against the Peru-Bolivia Confederation (1836–39). After defeating Peru and Bolivia, Chile dominated the Pacific Coast of South America. The victory over its neighbors gave Chile and its new political system a psychological boost. Chileans experienced a surge of national enthusiasm and cohesion behind a regime accepted as legitimate and efficacious.

Portales also achieved his objectives by wielding dictatorial powers, censoring the press, and manipulating elections. For the next forty years, Chile's armed forces would be distracted from meddling in politics by skirmishes and defensive operations on the southern frontier, although some units got embroiled in domestic conflicts in 1851 and 1859. In later years, conservative Chileans canonized Portales as a symbol of order and progress, exaggerating the importance of one man in that achievement.

The "Portalian State" was institutionalized by the 1833 constitution. One of the most durable charters ever devised in Latin

America, the Portalian constitution lasted until 1925. The constitution concentrated authority in the national government—more precisely, in the hands of the president, who was elected by a tiny minority. The chief executive could serve two consecutive five-year terms and then pick a successor. Although Congress had significant budgetary powers, it was overshadowed by the president, who appointed provincial officials. The constitution also created an independent judiciary, guaranteed inheritance of estates by primogeniture, and installed Catholicism as the state religion. In short, it established an autocratic system under a republican veneer.

The first Portalian president was General Joaquín Prieto Vial, who served two terms (1831-36, 1836-41). President Prieto had four main accomplishments: implementation of the 1833 constitution, stabilization of government finances, defeat of provincial challenges to central authority, and victory over the Peru-Bolivia Confederation. During the presidencies of Prieto and his two successors, Chile modernized through the construction of ports, railroads, and telegraph lines, some built by United States entrepreneur William Wheelwright. These innovations facilitated the export-import trade as well as domestic commerce.

Prieto and his adviser, Portales, feared the efforts of Bolivian general Andrés de Santa Cruz y Calahumana to unite with Peru against Chile. These qualms exacerbated animosities toward Peru dating from the colonial period, now intensified by disputes over customs duties and loans. Chile also wanted to become the dominant South American military and commercial power along the Pacific. Portales got Congress to declare war on Peru in 1836. When a Chilean colonel who opposed the war killed Portales in 1837, this act and the suspicion that Peruvians were involved in the assassination plot inspired an even greater war effort by the government.

Two Conservative Presidencies, 1841-61

Chile defeated the Peruvian fleet at Casma, Peru, on January 12, 1839, and the Bolivian army at Yungay, Peru, on January 20. These Chilean victories destroyed the Peru-Bolivia Confederation, made Chile lord of the west coast, brought unity and patriotism to the Chilean elites, and gave Chile's armed forces pride and purpose as a military with an external mission. The successful war also helped convince the European powers and the United States to respect Chile's coastal sphere of influence. Subsequently, the country won additional respect from the European powers and the United States by giving them economic access and concessions, by treating their citizens well, and by generally playing them off against each other.

*A church in
Chíuchíu in
northern Chile
Courtesy Embassy of
Chile, Washington*

Since its inception, the Portalian State has been criticized for its authoritarianism. But it has also been praised for the stability, prosperity, and international victories it brought to Chile, as well as the gradual opening to increased democracy that it provided. At least in comparison with most other regimes of the era, the Portalian State was noteworthy for being dominated by constitutional civilian authorities. Although Portales deserves some credit for launching the system, his successors were the ones who truly implemented, institutionalized, legitimized, and consolidated it. From 1831 to 1861, no other country in Spanish America had such a regular and constitutional succession of chief executives.

Manuel Bulnes Prieto (president, 1841–51), hero of the victories over the Chilean Liberals at the Battle of Lircay in 1830 and over the Bolivian army at Yungay in 1839, became president in 1841. As a decorated general, he was the ideal choice to consolidate the Portalian State and establish presidential control over the armed forces. He reduced the size of the military and solidified its loyalty to the central government in the face of provincial uprisings. As a southerner, he was able to defuse regional resentment of the dominant Santiago area. Although Bulnes staffed his two administrations mainly with Conservatives, he conciliated his opponents by including a few Liberals. He strengthened the new political institutions, especially Congress and the judiciary, and gave legitimacy to the constitution by stepping down at the end of his second term in office. Placing the national interest above regional or military loyalties, he also helped snuff out a southern rebellion against his successor.

Intellectual life blossomed under Bulnes, thanks in part to the many exiles who came to Chile from less stable Spanish American republics. They clustered around the University of Chile (founded in 1842), which developed into one of the most prestigious educational institutions in Latin America. Both foreigners and nationals formed the "Generation of 1842," led mainly by Liberal intellectuals and politicians such as Francisco Bilbao Barguin and José Victorino Lastarria Santander. Through the Society of Equality, members of the group called for expanded democracy and reduced church prerogatives. In particular, they defended civil liberties and freedom of the press, seeking to constrain the government's authoritarian powers.

Bulnes presided over continued prosperity, as production from the farms and mines increased, both for external and for internal consumption. In response to foreign demand, especially for wheat during the California and Australia gold rushes, agricultural exports increased. Instead of importing scarce and expensive modern capital and technology, landowners expanded production. They did this primarily by enlarging their estates and absorbing more peasants into their work forces, especially in the central provinces, where the vast majority of Chileans toiled in agriculture. This expansion fortified the hacienda system and increased the numbers of people attached to it. The growth of the great estates also increased the political power of the landed elites, who succeeded in exercising a veto over agrarian reform for a century.

In the mid-1800s, the rural labor force, mainly mestizos, was a cheap and expanding source of labor. More and more of these laborers became tenant farmers (*inquilinos*). For a century thereafter, many workers would remain bound to the haciendas through tradition, lack of alternatives, and landowner collusion and coercion. Itinerant rural workers and even small landowners became increasingly dependent on the great estates, whether through part-time or full-time work. The landed elites also inhibited industrialization by their preference for free trade and the low wages they paid their workers, which hindered rural consumers from accumulating disposable income. For a century, the lack of any significant challenge to this exploitive system was one of the pillars of the social and political hierarchy.

Liberals and regionalists unsuccessfully took up arms against Bulnes's Conservative successor, Manuel Montt Torres (president, 1851–61). Thousands died in one of the few large civil wars in nineteenth-century Chile. The rebels of 1851 denounced Montt's election as a fraud perpetrated by the centralist forces in and around Santiago. Some entrepreneurs in the outlying provinces also backed the rebellion out of anger at the government's neglect of economic interests outside the sphere of the central landowning elites. Montt put down the uprising with help from British commercial ships.

From 1851 to 1861, Montt completed the construction of the durable constitutional order begun by Portales and Bulnes. By reducing church prerogatives, Montt eased the transition from a sequence of Conservative chief executives to a series of Liberals. As a civilian head of state, he was less harsh with his Liberal adversaries. He also promoted conciliation by including many northerners as well as southerners in the government.

Benefiting from the sharp growth in exports and customs revenues in the 1850s, Montt demonstrated the efficacy of the central government by supporting the establishment of railroads, a telegraph system, and banks. He created the first government-run railroad company in South America, despite his belief in laissez-faire. He also initiated the extension of government credit to propertied groups. Under President Montt, school construction accelerated, laying the groundwork for Chile to become one of the most literate nations in the hemisphere. Expanding on the initiative started by Bulnes, Montt also pushed back the southern frontier, in part by encouraging German immigration.

As the next presidential succession approached, a second rebellion ensued in 1859. The rebels represented a diverse alliance, including Liberals who opposed the right-wing government and its encroachments on civil liberties, Conservatives who believed the president was insufficiently proclerical, politicians who feared the selection of a strongman as Montt's successor, and regionalists who chafed at the concentration of power in Santiago. Once again, Montt prevailed in a test of arms, but thereafter he conciliated his opponents by nominating a successor acceptable to all sides, José Joaquín Pérez Mascayano (president, 1861-71).

Under Bulnes and Montt, economic elites had resisted paying direct taxes, so the national government had become heavily dependent on customs duties, particularly on mineral exports. Imports were also taxed at a low level. The most important exports in the early years of independence had been silver and copper, mined mainly in the northern provinces, along with wheat, tallow, and other farm produce. The Chilean elites eagerly welcomed European and North American ships and merchants. Although these elites debated the issue of protectionism, they settled on low tariffs for revenue. Despite some dissent and deviations, the dominant policy in the nineteenth century was free trade—the exchange of raw materials for manufactured items—although a few local industries took root. Britain quickly became Chile's primary trading partner. The British also invested, both directly and indirectly, in the Chilean economy.

The Liberal Era, 1861–91

Following Pérez's peaceful ten-year administration, Chilean presidents were prohibited from running for election to a second consecutive term by an 1871 amendment to the constitution. Pérez was succeeded as president by Federico Errázuriz Zañartu (1871–76), Aníbal Pinto Garmendia (1876–81), and Domingo Santa María González (1881–86), the latter two serving during the War of the Pacific (1879–83). All formed coalition governments in which the president juggled a complicated array of party components.

The Liberal Party (Partido Liberal), the Conservative Party (Partido Conservador), and the National Party (Partido Nacional) were formed in 1857. Once the Liberal Party replaced the Conservative Party as the dominant party, the Liberal Party was in turn challenged from the left by the more fervent reformists of the Radical Party (Partido Radical). A spin-off from the Liberal Party, the Radical Party was founded in 1861. Reformists of the Democratic Party (Partido Democrático), which in turn splintered from the Radical Party in 1887, also challenged the Liberal Party. The National Party also vied with the Conservatives and Liberals to represent upper-class interests. Derived from the Montt presidency, the National Party, which represented the elite and the landed aristocracy, took a less proclerical, more centrist position than that of the Conservatives. Party competition escalated after the electoral reform of 1874 extended the franchise to all literate adult males, effectively removing property qualifications.

Like Montt, most Liberal chief executives were centrists who introduced change gradually. Their administrations continued to make incremental cuts in church privileges but tried not to inflame that issue. Secularization gradually gained ground in education, and Santa María transferred from the church to the state the management of birth, marriage, and death records.

Even during internal and external conflicts, Chile continued to prosper. When Spain attempted to reconquer Peru, Chile engaged in a coastal war (1864–66) with the Spaniards, whose warships shelled Valparaíso. Once again, Chile asserted its sway over the west coast of South America. Farming, mining, and commerce grew steadily until the world depression of the 1870s, when Chile again turned to a war against its Andean neighbors.

War of the Pacific, 1879–83

Chile's borders were a matter of contention throughout the nineteenth century. The War of the Pacific began on the heels of an international economic recession that focused attention on resources in outlying zones. Under an 1866 treaty, Chile and Bolivia divided the disputed area encompassing the Atacama Desert at 24° south latitude (located just south of the port of Antofagasta) in the understanding that the nationals of both nations could freely exploit mineral deposits in the region. Both nations, however, would share equally all the revenue generated by mining activities in the region. But Bolivia soon repudiated the treaty, and its subsequent levying of taxes on a Chilean company operating in the area led to an arms race between Chile and its northern neighbors of Bolivia and Peru.

Fighting broke out when Chilean entrepreneurs and mine-owners in present-day Tarapacá Region and Antofagasta Region, then belonging to Peru and Bolivia, respectively, resisted new taxes, the formation of monopoly companies, and other impositions. In those provinces, most of the deposits of nitrate—a valuable ingredient in fertilizers and explosives—were owned and mined by Chileans and Europeans, in particular the British. Chile wanted not only to acquire the nitrate fields but also to weaken Peru and Bolivia in order to strengthen its own strategic preeminence on the Pacific Coast. Hostilities were exacerbated because of disagreements over boundary lines, which in the desert had always been vague. Chile and Bolivia accused each other of violating the 1866 treaty. Although Chile expanded northward as a result of the War of the Pacific, its rights to the conquered territory continued to be questioned by Peru, and especially by Bolivia, throughout the twentieth century.

War began when Chilean troops crossed the northern frontier in 1879. Although a mutual defense pact had allied Peru and Bolivia since 1873, Chile's more professional, less politicized military overwhelmed the two weaker countries on land and sea. The turning point of the war was the occupation of Lima on January 17, 1881, a humiliation the Peruvians never forgave (see War of the Pacific, 1879–83, ch. 5). Chile sealed its victory with the 1883 Treaty of Ancón, which also ended the Chilean occupation of Lima.

As a result of the war and the Treaty of Ancón, Chile acquired two northern provinces—Tarapacá from Peru and Antofagasta from Bolivia. These territories encompassed most of the Atacama Desert and blocked off Bolivia's outlet to the Pacific Ocean (see fig. 3). The war gave Chile control over nitrate exports, which would

Source: Based on information from David P. Werlich, *Peru: A Short History*, Carbondale, Illinois, 1978, 110–11.

Figure 3. Territorial Adjustments among Bolivia, Chile, and Peru, 1874–1929

dominate the national economy until the 1920s, possession of copper deposits that would eclipse nitrate exports by the 1930s, greatpower status along the entire Pacific Coast of South America, and an enduring symbol of patriotic pride in the person of naval hero Arturo Prat Chacón. The War of the Pacific also bestowed on Chile's armed forces enhanced respect, the prospect of steadily increasing force levels, and a long-term external mission guarding the borders with Peru, Bolivia, and Argentina. In 1885 a German military officer, Emil Körner, was contracted to upgrade and professionalize the armed forces along Prussian lines. In subsequent years, better education produced not only a more modern officer corps but also a military leadership capable of questioning civilian management of national development (see Development of the Armed Forces, ch. 5).

After battling the Peruvians and Bolivians in the north, the military turned to engaging the Araucanians in the south. The final defeat of the Mapuche in 1882 opened up the southern third of the national territory to wealthy Chileans who quickly carved out immense estates. No homestead act or legion of family farmers stood in their way, although a few middle-class and immigrant agriculturalists moved in. Some Mapuche fled over the border to Argentina. The army herded those who remained onto tribal reservations in 1884, where they would remain mired in poverty for generations. Like the far north, these southern provinces would become stalwarts of national reform movements, critical of the excessive concentration of power and wealth in and around Santiago.

Soon controlled by British and then by United States investors, the nitrate fields became a classic monocultural boom and bust. The boom lasted four decades. Export taxes on nitrates often furnished over 50 percent of all state revenues, relieving the upper class of tax burdens. The income of the Chilean treasury nearly quadrupled in the decade after the war. The government used the funds to expand education and transportation. The mining bonanza generated demand for agricultural goods from the center and south and even for locally manufactured items, spawning a new plutocracy. Even more notable was the emergence of a class-conscious, nationalistic, ideological labor movement in the northern mining camps and elsewhere.

Prosperity also attracted settlers from abroad. Although small in number compared with those arriving in Argentina, European immigrants became an important element of the new middle class; their numbers included several future manufacturing tycoons. These arrivals came from both northern and southern Europe. People also emigrated from the Middle East, Peru, and Bolivia. Although most immigrants ended up in the cities of Chile, a minority succeeded at farming, especially in the south. In the early twentieth century, a few members of the Chilean elite tried to blame the rise of leftist unions and parties on foreign agitators, but the charge rang hollow in a country where less than 5 percent of the population had been born abroad.

Downfall of a President, 1886–91

The controversial downfall of President José Manuel Balmaceda Fernández (1886–91) represented the only occasion when power was transferred by force between 1830 and 1924. This event resulted in the most important alteration in the constitutional system between 1833 and 1925. In many respects, the Balmaceda episode was the culmination of two trends: the growing strength of Congress in relation to the president, and the expanding influence of foreign capital in the mining zone. In essence, the rebels opposed Balmaceda's plans to expand the role of the executive branch in the political and economic systems.

Although scholars have debated whether the uprising against Balmaceda was mainly a fight over political or economic privileges, the bulk of research has supported the primacy of political over economic issues. From the 1830s to the 1880s, Congress had gradually asserted more and more authority over the budget and over cabinet ministers. Balmaceda tried to circumvent that budgetary power and break the hold of congressmen and local bosses on congressional elections.

Complaining about the heavy-handed rule of the president, and in particular his interference in congressional elections, Congress led a revolt against Balmaceda in 1891. Conservatives generally supported the rebels; Liberals and Democrats backed the president. Along with some renegade Liberals, the newly emergent Radical Party aligned with the so-called congressionalists, not wishing to see legislative prerogatives curtailed just as the party was gaining clients and strength. Those provincials resentful of the growing centralization of political and economic power in and around Santiago also backed the rebellion, especially in the north. Initially, the navy, the armed service that included the highest percentage of aristocrats, sided with the rebels; the army sided with the president.

The rebellion also attracted British entrepreneurs worried by Balmaceda's threat to encroach on the independence and revenues of the foreign-owned nitrate mines. Although not opposed to foreign investment, Balmaceda had proposed a greater role for the state and higher taxes in the mining sector. Tension mounted because nitrate sales were in a slump, a recurring problem because of the volatility of that commodity's price on international markets. The most famous British mine owner was John North, the "nitrate king," who was angry that his nitrate railroad monopoly had been terminated by Balmaceda. Although not directly involved, the United States supported Balmaceda as the legal president.

The insurgents won the bloody but brief Civil War of 1891 when the army decided not to fight the navy. As a result of the rebel victory, Congress became dominant over the chief executive and the nitrate mines increasingly fell into British and North American hands. Having gained asylum in the Argentine embassy, Balmaceda waited until the end of his legal presidential term and then committed suicide. As Portales became a legendary hero to the right, so Balmaceda was later anointed by the left as an economic nationalist who sacrificed his life in the struggle for Chilean liberation.

Already tense as a result of the civil war over Balmaceda, United States-Chilean relations deteriorated further as a result of the *Baltimore* incident. In late 1891, sailors from the U.S.S. *Baltimore* brawled with Chileans during shore leave in Valparaíso. To avert a war with an angry United States, the Chilean government apologized and paid reparations.

Parliamentary Republic, 1891–1925

The so-called Parliamentary Republic was not a true parliamentary system, in which the chief executive is elected by the legislature. It was, however, an unusual regime in presidentialist Latin America, for Congress really did overshadow the rather ceremonial office of the president and exerted authority over the chief executive's cabinet appointees. In turn, Congress was dominated by the landed elites. This was the heyday of classic political and economic liberalism.

For many decades thereafter, historians derided the Parliamentary Republic as a quarrel-prone system that merely distributed spoils and clung to its laissez-faire policy while national problems mounted. The characterization is epitomized by an observation made by President Ramón Barros Luco (1910–15), reputedly made in reference to labor unrest: "There are only two kinds of problems: those that solve themselves and those that can't be solved." At the mercy of Congress, cabinets came and went frequently, although there was more stability and continuity in public administration than some historians have suggested.

Political authority ran from local electoral bosses in the provinces through the congressional and executive branches, which reciprocated with payoffs from taxes on nitrate sales. Congressmen often won election by bribing voters in this clientelistic and corrupt system. Many politicians relied on intimidated or loyal peasant voters in the countryside, even though the population was becoming increasingly urban.

The lackluster presidents and ineffectual administrations of the period did little to respond to the country's dependence on volatile nitrate exports, spiraling inflation, and massive urbanization. They also ignored what was called "the social question." This euphemism referred mainly to the rise of the labor movement and its demands for better treatment of the working class. Critics complained that the upper class, which had given Chile such dynamic leadership previously, had grown smug and lethargic, thanks to the windfall of nitrate wealth.

In recent years, however, particularly when the authoritarian regime of Augusto Pinochet is taken into consideration, some scholars have reevaluated the Parliamentary Republic of 1891–1925. Without denying its shortcomings, they have lauded its democratic stability. They have also hailed its control of the armed forces, its respect for civil liberties, its expansion of suffrage and participation, and its gradual admission of new contenders, especially reformers, to the political arena.

In particular, two young parties grew in importance—the Democratic Party, with roots among artisans and urban workers, and the Radical Party, representing urban middle sectors and provincial elites. By the early twentieth century, both parties were winning increasing numbers of seats in Congress. The more leftist members of the Democratic Party became involved in the leadership of labor unions and broke off to launch the Socialist Workers' Party (Partido Obrero Socialista—POS) in 1912. The founder of the POS and its best-known leader, Luis Emilio Recabarren Serrano, also founded the Communist Party of Chile (Partido Communista de Chile—PCCh), in 1922.

Urbanization

Beginning in the middle of the nineteenth century, Chile's cities grew rapidly. They absorbed a trickle of immigrants from abroad and then vast numbers of migrants from the Chilean countryside. Improved transportation and communications in the second half of the nineteenth century facilitated these population movements. Although Santiago led the way, smaller cities such as Valparaíso and Concepción also swelled in size.

The founding of the Industrial Development Association (Sociedad de Fomento Fabril—Sofofa) in 1883 was another indication

A weaver in Donihue in central Chile Courtesy Embassy of Chile, Washington

of urbanization. It promoted industrialization long before the intense efforts of the 1930s to the 1960s. Manufacturing grew in importance in the latter decades of the nineteenth century and the opening decades of the twentieth. Most industry remained small-scale, with most of the labor performed by artisans. Protected industrialization did not become the vanguard of economic development until the period between the world wars.

The urban middle class also grew in size and became more politically assertive by the turn of the century. Whereas the economy and the society became more urban and diversified, the political system lagged behind, remaining mainly in the hands of the upper class. Nevertheless, more members of the middle class began appearing in party leadership positions, especially among the Democrats and Radicals. They were also prominent in the Chilean Student Federation (Federación de Estudiantes de Chile—FECh), based at the University of Chile. Equally important was their presence among the top commanders in the armed forces, who increasingly identified primarily with middle-class interests.

In the closing years of the nineteenth century, labor organizations gathered force, first as mutual aid societies and then increasingly as trade unions. In the opening decades of the twentieth century, labor organizing, unrest, and strikes reached new levels of intensity. In the northern nitrate and copper mines, as well as in the ports and cities, workers came together to press demands for better wages and working conditions. Attracted strongly to anarchist, anarcho-syndicalist, and socialist ideologies, they were harshly repressed during the Parliamentary Republic. The government carried out several massacres of miners in the nitrate camps; the most notorious took place in Iquique in 1907. Thus, a pattern of violent clashes between soldiers and workers took shape.

Organizational efforts in the mines and cities culminated in the creation of the first national labor confederation, the Workers' Federation of Chile (Federación Obrera de Chile—FOCh), in 1909. The organization became more radical as it grew and affiliated with the PCCh in 1922, under the leadership of Recabarren. Its greatest strength was among miners, whereas urban workers were more attracted to independent socialism or to anarcho-syndicalism. The latter movement grew out of resistance societies and evolved into the Industrial Workers of the World (IWW). Unlike the FOCh, the IWW spurned ties with political parties.

The emergence of working-class demands and movements spawned the so-called social question. Intellectuals and writers began criticizing the ruling class and the Parliamentary Republic for their neglect of workers and of social ills. New census data and other studies at the beginning of the twentieth century shocked the proud Chilean elite with revelations about the extent of poverty, illiteracy, and poor health among the vast majority of the population. Especially alarming were infant mortality figures that far exceeded those of Western Europe. Realization of the squalor and anger of the working class inspired new reform efforts.

Arturo Alessandri's Reformist Presidency, 1920–25

President Arturo Alessandri Palma (1920–24, March–October 1925, 1932–38) appealed to those who believed the social question should be addressed, to those worried by the decline in nitrate exports during World War I, and to those weary of presidents dominated by Congress. Promising "evolution to avoid revolution," he pioneered a new campaign style of appealing directly to the masses with florid oratory and charisma. After winning a seat in the Senate representing the mining north in 1915, he earned the sobriquet "Lion of Tarapacá." As a dissident Liberal running for the presidency, Alessandri attracted support from the more reformist Radicals and Democrats and formed the so-called Liberal Alliance. He received strong backing from the middle and working classes as well as from the provincial elites. Students and intellectuals also rallied to his banner. At the same time, he reassured the landowners that social reforms would be limited to the cities.

Alessandri also spoke to discontent stemming from World War I. Although Chile had been neutral, the war had disrupted the international commerce that drove the economy. German development of artificial nitrates was especially damaging, and thereafter copper would gradually surpass nitrates as the leading export, taking over conclusively in the 1930s. Inflation and currency depreciation compounded the country's economic woes.

During and after the war, the United States displaced Britain as Chile's most important external economic partner, first in trade and then in investments. American companies, led by Kennecott and Braden, took control of the production of copper and nitrates. As corporate investors, bankers, salesmen, advisers, and even entertainers, such as actor and humorist Will Rogers, came to Chile, a few Chileans began to worry about the extent of United States penetration.

As the candidate of the Liberal Alliance coalition, Alessandri barely won the presidency in 1920 in what was dubbed "the revolt of the electorate." Chilean historians consider the 1920 vote a benchmark or watershed election, along with the contests of 1938, 1970, and 1988. Like other reformers elected president in the twentieth century—Pedro Aguirre Cerda (1938–41), Gabriel González Videla (1946–52), and Salvador Allende Gossens (1970–73)—Alessandri had to navigate skillfully through treacherous waters from the day he was elected until his inauguration, warding off attempts to deny him the fruits of victory. Mass street demonstrations by his middle- and working-class supporters convinced the conservative political elite in Congress to ratify his narrow win.

After donning the presidential sash, Alessandri discovered that his efforts to lead would be blocked by the conservative Congress. Like Balmaceda, he infuriated the legislators by going over their heads to appeal to the voters in the congressional elections of 1924. His reform legislation was finally rammed through Congress under pressure from younger military officers, who were sick of the neglect of the armed forces, political infighting, social unrest, and galloping inflation.

In a double coup, first military right-wingers opposing Alessandri seized power in September 1924, and then reformers in favor of the ousted president took charge in January 1925. The latter group was led by two colonels, Carlos Ibáñez del Campo and Marmaduke Grove Vallejo. They returned Alessandri to the presidency that March and enacted his promised reforms by decree. Many of these reforms were encapsulated in the new constitution of 1925, which was ratified in a plebiscite.

31

Military Interventions, 1925-32

As in 1891 and 1973, the military intervened in national politics in the 1920s partly because of economic distress, partly to break a stalemate between the legislative and executive branches, and, above all, to change the political system. Colonel Ibáñez (president, 1927–31, 1952–58), quickly promoted to general, became the dominant power. He ruled, either behind or on the seat of power, until the economic crisis caused by the Great Depression (see Glossary) in 1931 prompted his resignation.

The 1925 Constitution

The 1925 constitution was the second major charter in Chilean history, lasting until 1973. It codified significant changes, including the official separation of church and state, thus culminating a century of gradual erosion of the political and economic power of the Roman Catholic Church. The constitution also provided legal recognition of workers' right to organize, a promise to care for the social welfare of all citizens, an assertion of the right of the state to infringe on private property for the public good, and increased powers for the now directly elected president in relation to the bicameral Congress, in particular concerning the removal of cabinet ministers, who heretofore had often been removed at the whim of the legislature.

Presidential and congressional elections were staggered so that a chief executive could not bring a legislature in on his coattails. The new constitution extended presidential terms from five to six years, with immediate reelection prohibited. It established a system of proportional representation for parties putting candidates up for Congress. The government was divided into four branches, in descending order of power: the president, the legislature, the judiciary, and the comptroller general, the latter authorized to judge the constitutionality of all laws requiring fiscal expenditures.

The Office of the Comptroller General of the Republic (Oficina de la Contraloría General de la República) was designed by a United States economic adviser, Edwin Walter Kemmerer. In 1925 he also created the Central Bank of Chile (see Glossary) and the position of superintendent of banks, while putting the country on the gold standard. His reforms helped attract massive foreign investments from the United States, especially loans to the government.

Although a labor code was not finalized until 1931, several labor and social security laws enacted in 1924 would govern industrial relations from the 1930s to the 1970s. The legislation legalized unions and strikes but imposed government controls over unions.

Union finances and elections were subjected to government inspection. The laws also restricted union activities and disallowed national confederations, which therefore subsequently arose outside the legal framework. Only factories with at least twenty-five workers could have an industrial union, even though approximately two-thirds of the industrial enterprises employed four or fewer workers, in effect artisans. Workers in smaller shops could form professional unions with workers of the same skill employed nearby. Agricultural unions remained virtually outlawed or extremely difficult to organize until the 1960s. The code left unions disadvantaged in their bargaining with employers and therefore reliant on political parties as allies. Those allies were crucial because the new code made the state the mediator in labor-management disputes.

Carlos Ibáñez's First Presidency, 1927–31

After a weak successor served in the wake of Alessandri's resignation in 1925, Ibáñez made himself president in a rigged election in 1927. He based his reign on military support (especially from the army), on repression (especially of labor unions, leftists, and political parties), and on a flood of loans from private lenders (especially from New York). He also created the national police, known as the Carabineros. His expansion of the central government found favor with the middle class. While Ibáñez promoted industry and public works, the economy fared well until torpedoed by the Great Depression.

According to the League of Nations (see Glossary), no other nation's trade suffered more than Chile's from the economic collapse. Unemployment approached 300,000, almost 25 percent of the work force. As government revenues plummeted, deficits grew. Chile suspended payments on its foreign debt in 1931 and took its currency off the gold standard in 1932. Expansion of the money supply and increased government spending thereafter generated inflation and rapid recovery. Also helpful was an emphasis on import-substitution industrialization (see Glossary) and the revival of exports, especially copper.

Rather than run the risk of civil war, Ibáñez went into exile in Argentina in July 1931 to avert clashes with demonstrators protesting his orthodox economic response to the depression and generally oppressive rule. His regime was followed by a kaleidoscope of governments, made and unmade through elections and military coups. The most notable short-lived administration was the twelve-day Socialist Republic of 1932, led by an air force commander, Marmaduke Grove, who would establish the Socialist Party (Partido Socialista) in 1933. Exasperated by depression and instability,

Chileans finally restored civilian rule by reelecting Alessandri to the presidency in 1932. Although the depression capsized civilian governments in most of Latin America, it discredited military rule in Chile. Now the 1925 constitution took full effect; it would remain in force until the overthrow of Salvador Allende Gossens in 1973.

Mass Democracy, 1932–73

From 1932 to 1973, Chile was the only country in Latin America to sustain electoral democracy at a time when major Marxist parties led the workers. Its stable multiparty political system bore more resemblance to West European than to Latin American models. Chileans took great pride in their representative democracy, and many looked with contempt on their more tumultuous neighbors.

Out of the turmoil of the depression, new political forces arose that shifted the political spectrum to the left. The Conservatives and the Liberals grew closer together as the combined forces on the right, now more fearful of socialism than of their traditional enemies in the anticlerical camp. The Radicals replaced the Liberals as the swing party in the center, now that they were outflanked on the left by the growing PCCh and the Socialist Party. A small group of Catholics known as the Falange broke away from the Conservative Party in 1938 to form a new party, the National Falange (Falange Nacional). It offered a non-Marxist, centrist vision of dramatic reform, a vision that would take wing in the 1950s under the name of Christian Democracy.

Alessandri's Second Presidency, 1932–38

Under the steady hand of the veteran Alessandri, reelected in December 1932 with 55 percent of the vote, Chile rapidly reinstated its interrupted democracy and revived its shattered economy. Although still a centrist reformer at heart, Alessandri now became the paladin of the right because the new Socialist left had outflanked him. He put into practice both the 1925 constitution and the 1931 labor code; reshuffled military commands; supported a 50,000-member civilian paramilitary force, the Republican Militia (Milicia Republicana), during 1932–36 to keep the armed forces in the barracks and to threaten leftists; and cut unemployment by promoting industry and public works.

In accordance with long-standing Chilean foreign policy principles, Alessandri sought to avoid entanglement in European conflicts. He cultivated good relations with both Britain and Germany, while remaining friendly with the United States. He declared neutrality in the Spanish Civil War, as the Chilean government had done during World War I.

The Socialists, Communists, and Radicals denounced Alessandri for insufficient economic nationalism and inadequate attention to the needs of working people. Heeding the new policy of the Comintern (see Glossary), adopted in 1935, the Chilean Communists backed away from proletarian revolution, which they had advocated obediently from 1928 to 1934. Now they promoted broad, reformist electoral coalitions in the name of antifascism. With slight deviations and name changes, the PCCh sustained this accommodative approach from 1935 until 1980.

Prodded by the Communists, the Radicals and Socialists aligned in 1936 with the Confederation of Chilean Workers (Confederación de Trabajadores de Chile—CTCh), a by-product of union growth and solidarity, to forge the Popular Front (Frente Popular). The Popular Front was given impetus by Alessandri's crushing of a railroad strike that year. The coalition also included the old Democrat Party, which was gradually supplanted by the Socialist Party until the former disappeared in the early 1940s. Similar to multiparty alliances in Europe and to populist coalitions in Latin America, the Popular Front galvanized the middle and working classes on behalf of democracy, social welfare, and industrialization. Its redistributive, populist slogan was "Bread, Roof, and Overcoat," coined by the 1932 Socialist Republic.

The Popular Front barely beat Alessandri's would-be rightist successor in the presidential contest of 1938 with 50.3 percent of the vote. One key to the Popular Front's victory was its nomination of a mild-mannered Radical, Pedro Aguirre Cerda, rather than the inflammatory Socialist, Marmaduke Grove. The other key was a bizarre sequence of events in which a group of Chilean fascists (members of the National Socialist Movement), backing Ibáñez's independent bid for the presidency, staged an unsuccessful putsch on the eve of the election. The slaughter of the putschists by forces of the Alessandri government prompted the fascists to throw their votes to the Popular Front. Although not numerous, those ballots put the Popular Front over the top.

The incongruous alignment of Nazis behind the antifascist Popular Front showed how far Chilean politicians would go to subordinate ideology to electoral considerations. Thus, a coalition that included Socialists and Communists captured the presidency quite early in twentieth-century Chile. Future president Salvador Allende served briefly as minister of health in this period.

Running under the slogan "To Govern Is to Educate," Aguirre Cerda (president, 1938–41) won an electoral majority in 1938. However, less than 5 percent of the national population actually voted for him. Until the rapid expansion of the electorate in the

1950s, less than 10 percent of the national population voted for presidential candidates. Only literate males over the age of twenty-one could vote in most elections until the 1950s; of those eligible to vote, approximately 50 percent usually registered, and the vast majority of those registered cast ballots. Women were allowed to exercise the franchise in installments, first for municipal elections in 1935, then for congressional contests in 1951, and finally for presidential races in 1952.

As had been the case with other Chilean electoral victories by left-wing candidates, tense days passed between the counting of the ballots and the ratification of the results by Congress. Opponents of the left schemed to prevent the takeover by their nemeses or to extract concessions before accepting defeat. Aguirre Cerda assured rightists of his moderate intentions, and the Alessandri government presided over his peaceful inauguration. The military quashed a single coup attempt in 1939.

Popular Front Rule, 1938–41

Led by the centrist Radical Party, the administration of the Popular Front assimilated the Socialists and Communists into the established bargaining system, making potentially revolutionary forces into relatively moderate participants in legal institutions. Although the official Popular Front ended in 1941, that bargaining system, with Marxist parties usually backing reformist Radical presidents, lasted until 1952.

Aguirre Cerda, like all Chilean presidents in the 1930s and 1940s, essentially pursued a model of state capitalism in which government collaborated with private enterprise in the construction of a mixed economy. The Popular Front promoted simultaneous import-substitution industrialization and welfare measures for the urban middle and working classes. As in the rest of Latin America, the Great Depression and then the onset of World War II accelerated domestic production of manufactured consumer items, widened the role of the state, and augmented dependence on the United States. All these trends dissuaded Marxists from demanding bold redistributive measures at the expense of domestic and foreign capitalists.

Aiming to catch up with the more affluent West, Chile's Popular Front mobilized the labor movement behind national industrial development more than working-class social advances. Although workers received few material benefits from the Popular Front, the number of legal unions more than quadrupled from the early 1930s to the early 1940s. Still, unions represented only about 10 percent of the work force.

Prior to his illness and death in November 1941, President Aguirre Cerda labored to hold his coalition together, to overcome the implacable opposition of the right-wing parties, and to fulfill his promises of industrialization and urban social reform. The Socialists and Communists quarreled incessantly, especially over the PCCh's support of the 1939 German-Soviet Nonaggression Pact between Hitler and Stalin. Early in 1941, the Socialist Party withdrew from the Popular Front coalition because of its animosity toward the PCCh, its rival claimant to worker loyalty and Marxist inspiration. Because the Conservatives and Liberals blocked nearly all legislation in Congress, little social reform was accomplished, except for improvements in housing and education. To appease right-wingers, the president clamped down on rural unionization.

From the 1920s into the 1960s, this modus vivendi between urban reformers and rural conservatives held fast. Progressives carried out reforms in the cities for the middle and working classes, while denying peasants union rights. Thus were preserved the availability of low-cost foodstuffs for urban consumers, control of the countryside for *latifundistas* (large landowners), and domination of the rural vote by right-wing politicians. From time to time, Marxist organizers threatened to mobilize the rural work force, and time and again they were restrained by their centrist political allies, who needed to reassure the economic and political right-wingers. When peasants protested this exploitation, they were repressed by landowners or government troops.

The greatest achievement of the Popular Front was the creation in 1939 of the state Production Development Corporation (Corporación de Fomento de la Producción—Corfo) to supply credit to new enterprises, especially in manufacturing. Partly with loans from the United States Export-Import Bank, Corfo contributed greatly to import-substitution industrialization, mainly for consumer items. The economically active population working in industry grew from 15 percent in 1930 to 20 percent in 1952, where it hovered for two decades. From the end of the 1930s to the start of the 1950s, Corfo supplied almost one-fourth of total domestic investments.

Juan Antonio Ríos's Presidency, 1942–46

A Radical even more conservative than Aguirre Cerda, Juan Antonio Ríos Morales (president, 1942–46), won the 1942 presidential election with 56 percent of the vote. Although the formal Popular Front had been terminated, the Socialists and Communists still gave their votes to Ríos to avoid a return of Ibáñez as the candidate of the Conservatives and Liberals. Under the stringencies of wartime, the new president further soft-pedaled social reform and emphasized industrial growth, under the slogan, "To Govern Is to Produce." Although he made some improvements in housing and health care, Ríos concentrated on promoting urban enterprises.

Ríos continued his predecessor's policy of neutrality in World War II. Although sympathetic to the Allies, many Chileans worried about the vulnerability of their Pacific Coast. Because of a desire for closer economic and security ties with the United States, Ríos finally bowed to pressure from Socialists, Communists, and other staunch antifascists, severing relations with the Axis in January 1943.

Even after breaking relations, Chile was never satisfied with the amount of aid and Lend-Lease military equipment it received from the United States. The United States, in turn, was equally discontent with languid Chilean action against Axis agents and firms. Nevertheless, Chile subsidized the Allied cause by accepting an artificially low price for its copper exports to the United States while paying increasingly higher prices for its imports. The war boosted Chile's mineral exports and foreign-exchange accumulation. At the same time, United States trade, credits, and advisers facilitated state support for new enterprises, including steel, oil, and fishing.

Not unlike Ibáñez in the 1920s, Ríos hoped to develop the national economy through external alignment with the "Colossus of the North." After displacing Britain as Chile's most important economic partner in the 1920s, the United States faced a period of German competition in the 1930s and then reasserted its economic dominance in the 1940s. That economic domination would last until the 1980s.

As Ríos's health deteriorated in 1945, another Radical, Alfredo Duhalde Vásquez (president, June–August 1946), took over as interim chief executive. Reacting against Ríos's conservatism and Duhalde's antilabor policies, progressive factions of the Radical Party joined with the Communists to field a left-wing Radical, Gabriel González Videla, for president in the 1946 election. González Videla also received the backing of most Socialists.

Trying to revive the reformist spirit of 1938, González Videla eked out a plurality of 40 percent against a field of rightist contenders. Once again, the candidate of the left had to walk a tightrope from election to inauguration because Congress had the right to pick either of the two front-runners when no one polled an absolute majority. González Videla ensured his congressional approval by granting landowners new legal restrictions on peasant unionization, restrictions that lasted from 1947 until 1967. He also appeased the right by including Liberals in his cabinet along with Radicals and Communists, the most exotic ministerial concoction

Chileans had ever seen, again demonstrating the politician's ability to cut deals transcending ideology.

Gabriel González Videla's Presidency, 1946–52

Chile quickly became enmeshed in the Cold War, as Moscow and especially Washington meddled in its affairs. That friction resulted in the splitting of the CTCh in 1946 into Communist and Socialist branches and then the outlawing of the PCCh. The Socialists were now opposed to the Communists and aligned with the American Federation of Labor-Congress of Industrial Organizations (AFL–CIO), having grown closer to United States labor interests during World War II.

Once in office, González Videla (president, 1946–52) rapidly turned against his Communist allies. He expelled them from his cabinet and then banned them completely under the 1948 Law for the Defense of Democracy. The PCCh remained illegal until 1958. He also severed relations with the Soviet Union, Yugoslavia, and Czechoslovakia.

Controversy still swirls around the reasons for this about-face. According to González Videla and his sympathizers, the repression of the Communists was necessary to thwart their plots against his government, although no evidence has been found to substantiate that claim. According to the Communists and other critics of González Videla, he acted under pressure from the United States and out of a desire to forge closer economic and military bonds with the dominant superpower. Historians have established that the president wanted to appease the United States, that the United States encouraged a crackdown on Chilean Communists, and that the United States government appreciated González Videla's actions and thereafter expanded the scope of its loans, investments, and technical missions to Chile. The United States and Chile also agreed to a military assistance pact while González Videla was president. However, no conclusive evidence has come to light that the United States directly pushed him to act.

Although González Videla feared Communist intentions and respected the wishes of the United States government, he also turned against the PCCh for other reasons. He hoped to mollify right-wing critics of his government, especially landowners, to whom he guaranteed a continuing moratorium on peasant unionization. He sought to remove any ideological justification for a military coup. He also wanted to weaken the labor movement in a time of economic uncertainties, slow growth, and rising inflation, when the PCCh was promoting strikes. González Videla's banning of the

Communists coincided with his movement away from social reform in favor of the promotion of industrial growth.

As the Radical years (1938–52) drew to a close, Popular Front-style coalition politics reached a dead end. The Radicals had swerved to the right, the Socialists had splintered and lost votes, and the Communists had been forced underground. Although the middle and upper classes had registered some gains in those fourteen years, most workers had seen their real income stagnate or decline. Often a problem in the past, inflation had become a permanent feature of the Chilean economy, fueled by the deficit spending of a government that had grown enormously under the Radical presidents. Progress had been made in industrialization, but with little benefit to the majority of the population. Promoting urban industries did not generate the growth, efficiency, employment, or independence promised by the policy's advocates. World War II had left the country more dependent than ever on the United States, which by then had become the dominant economic power in Latin America.

Populist development strategies had proved viable during the 1930s and 1940s. The protection and credit that went along with import-substitution industrialization had kept manufacturers satisfied. Although penalized and forced to accept low prices for their foods, agriculturalists welcomed expanding urban markets, low taxes, and controls over rural workers. The middle class and the armed forces had applauded state growth and moderate nationalism. The more skilled and organized urban workers had received consumer, welfare, and union benefits superior to those offered to other lower-class groups.

These allocations postponed any showdown over limited resources, thus enabling right and left to compromise. Political institutionalization and accommodation prevailed, partly because the unorganized urban poor and especially the rural poor suffered, in effect, from marginality (see Glossary). Starting in the 1950s, however, social demands outpaced slow economic growth, and the political arena became increasingly crowded and heated. In addition, accelerated mobilization, polarization, and radicalization by ideologically competing parties placed more and more stress on the "compromise state" to reconcile incompatible demands and projects.

By 1952 Chileans were alienated by multiparty politics that produced reformist governments, which would veer to the right once in office. Chileans were tired of *politiquería* (petty politics, political chicanery, and pork-barrel politics). Citizens were also dismayed by slow growth and spiraling inflation. They showed their displeasure by turning to two symbols of the past, the 1920s dictator Ibáñez and the son of former president Alessandri.

In an effort to "sweep the rascals out," the voters elected the politically unaffiliated Ibáñez back to the presidency in 1952. Brandishing his broom as a symbol, the "General of Victory" ran against all the major parties and their clientelistic system of government. He made his strongest attacks on the Radicals, accusing them of mismanagement of the economy and subservience to the United States.

Along with the short-lived Agrarian Labor Party (1945–58), a few Communists backed Ibáñez in hopes of relegalizing the PCCh; a few Socialists also supported him in hopes of spawning a workers' movement similar to Peronism (see Glossary) in Argentina. Other leftists, however, endorsed the first token presidential campaign of Salvador Allende in order to stake out an independent Marxist strategy for future runs at the presidency. Allende received only 5 percent of the vote, while Ibáñez won with a plurality of 47 percent. As it always did when no candidate captured an absolute majority, Congress ratified the top vote-getter as president.

Ibáñez's Second Presidency, 1952–58

Like the Radicals before him, Ibáñez entered office as a reformer governing with a center-left coalition and ended his term as a conservative surrounded by rightists. Along the way, he discarded his promises of economic nationalism and social justice. Also like the Radicals, he left festering problems for subsequent administrations.

Early in his administration, Ibáñez tried to live up to his billing as a nationalistic reformer. He rewarded those who had voted for him in the countryside by setting a minimum wage for rural laborers, although real wages for farm workers continued to fall throughout the decade. He also postured as a Latin American spokesman, hailing Juan Domingo Perón when the Argentine leader visited Chile.

After two years of expansionary fiscal policies in league with reformers and a few leftists, Ibáñez converted to a conservative program to stem inflation and to improve relations with the United States copper companies. As the effort to move import-substitution industrialization beyond the stage of replacing foreign consumer goods bogged down, the economy became mired in stagflation. The rates of industrialization, investment, and growth all slowed. Monetarist policies proposed by a team of United States experts, known as the Klein-Saks Mission, failed to bring inflation under control. Price increases averaged 38 percent per year during the 1950s.

Persistent inflation stoked a debate among economists over causes and cures. Emphasizing deep-rooted causes and long-term solutions, advocates of structuralism (see Glossary) blamed chronic inflation primarily on foreign trade dependency, insufficient local production (especially in agriculture), and political struggles over government spoils among entrenched vested interests. Their opponents, advocates of monetarism (see Glossary), attributed rising prices principally to classic financial causes such as currency expansion and deficit spending. Like the Klein-Saks Mission, the monetarists recommended austerity measures to curb inflation. The structuralists denounced such belt-tightening as recessionary, inimical to growth, and socially regressive. The monetarists replied that economic development would be delayed and distorted until expansionary monetary and financial policies were corrected (see Evolution of the Economy, ch. 3).

Adopting a monetarist approach, in 1955 Ibáñez made concessions to the United States copper companies, chiefly Anaconda and Kennecott, in an effort to elicit more investment. These measures reduced the firms' taxes and raised their profits but failed to attract much capital. Discontent with this experience underlay subsequent campaigns to nationalize the mines.

Ibáñez also enacted reforms to increase the integrity of the electoral system. Under the new plan, the secret ballot system was improved in 1958, and stiff fines for fraud were established. These reforms reduced the sway of landowners and facilitated the growth of the Christian Democrat and Marxist political movements among peasants.

Ibáñez's middle- and working-class support flowed over to the Christian Democrats and the Marxists. The Christian Democratic Party (Partido Demócrata Cristiano—PDC) was founded in 1957 with the merger of three conservative elements: the National Falange, founded in 1938; the Social Christian Conservative Party; and the remnants of the Agrarian Labor Party that had backed Ibáñez. The Christian Democrats espoused reformist Catholic doctrines that promised a society based on communitarianism. The new party appealed strongly to the middle class, women, peasants, and rural-urban migrants. Its displacement of the Radicals as the preeminent centrist party meant that a pragmatic organization was replaced by an ideological group less amenable to coalition and compromise. At the same time that the center was hardening its position, the right and the left were also becoming more dogmatic and sectarian.

Relegalized by Ibáñez in 1958, the PCCh formed an enduring electoral alliance with the Socialists known as the Popular Action

Front (Frente de Acción Popular—FRAP). The Marxist parties embraced more militant projects for the construction of socialism and disdained alliances behind centrist parties. They replaced Popular Front politics with "workers front" politics. The PCCh and the Socialist Party became more exclusive and radical in their ideological commitments and in their dedication to the proletariat. Of the two parties, the Socialist Party posed as more revolutionary, especially after the 1959 Cuban Revolution.

As they had in the 1930s, the Marxist parties experienced success in the 1950s in tandem with a unified national trade union movement. Dismayed by runaway inflation, the major labor unions replaced the fractionalized CTCh with the United Federation of Chilean Workers (Central Única de Trabajadores de Chile— CUTCh) in 1953. The Communists and Socialists, with their enduring strength in older unions in mining, construction, and manufacturing, took command of the new confederation.

As the 1958 election approached, the electorate divided into three camps well-defined by their predominant class and ideology. The right represented mainly Conservatives and Liberals, the upper class, rural dwellers, the defenders of capitalism, and the status quo. In the center, the Christian Democrats and Radicals spoke largely for the middle class and the proponents of moderate social reforms to avoid socialism. On the left, the Socialists and Communists championed the working class, advocating a peaceful transition to socialism. Rural-urban migrants and women had gained social and political importance. The percentage of the population registered to vote in presidential contests had risen from about 11 percent in the 1940s to 17.5 percent in 1952 and then to 21 percent in 1958. In the 1958 election, the right—Conservatives and Liberals—hoped to return to power for the first time since 1938. Their standard-bearer was Jorge Alessandri Rodríguez, an engineering professor and the son of Chile's most recent rightist president. He posed as an independent who was above party politics, offering technocratic solutions to the nation's problems. In the center, the Radicals, with candidate Luis Bossay Leyva, and the Christian Democrats, who nominated Eduardo Frei Montalva, vied for moderate votes. On the left, the reunited Socialists and Communists backed Salvador Allende.

In a preview of the 1970 election, the 1958 vote split three ways: 31 percent for Alessandri, 29 percent for Allende, and 40 percent for the rest, including a strong third-place showing by Frei with 21 percent. If it had not been for the 3 percent of the votes snared by a populist defrocked priest, the 15 percent won by the Radicals, and the low percentage (22 percent) of women casting ballots for Allende, the Marxists could easily have captured the presidency in 1958, several months before the Cuban Revolution. As it was, they and the Christian Democrats were highly encouraged to build their electoral forces toward another face-off in 1964. An especially noteworthy shift was the transfer of many peasant votes from the right to the columns of Christian Democrat and Marxist politicians promising agrarian reform.

Jorge Alessandri's Rightist Term, 1958–64

Once again, Congress approved the front-runner as president. Alessandri promised to restrain government intervention in the economy and to promote the private sector, although he did not envision reliance on the market to the extent that later would occur under Pinochet. With a slender mandate, the opposition in control of the legislature, and a modest program, the president accomplished little of note.

Alessandri did, however, maintain political and economic stability. He temporarily dampened inflation, mainly by placing a ceiling on wages. This measure sparked mounting labor protests in the early 1960s. The economy grew and unemployment shrank. He also passed mild land reform legislation, which would be implemented mostly by his successors. His action was partly the result of prodding by the United States government, which backed agrarian reform under the auspices of the Alliance for Progress (see Glossary) in hopes of blunting the appeal of the Cuban Revolution. At the same time, Alessandri tried to attract foreign investment, although he had no intention of throwing open the economy, as would be done under Pinochet. By the end of Alessandri's term, the country was burdened with a rising foreign debt.

In the 1964 presidential contest, the right abandoned its standard-bearers and gave its support to Frei in order to avert an Allende victory in the face of rising electoral support for the leftists. The center-right alliance defeated the left, 56 percent to 39 percent. The reformist Frei enjoyed strong United States support, both during and after the campaign. He also had the backing of the Roman Catholic Church and European Christian Democrats. Frei ran particularly well among women, the middle class, peasants, and residents of the shantytowns (*poblaciones callampas*). Allende was most popular with men and blue-collar workers.

Although Frei and Allende were foes on the campaign trail, they agreed on major national issues that needed to be addressed: greater Chilean control over the United States-owned copper mines, agrarian reform, better housing for the residents of the sprawling shantytowns, more equitable income distribution, expanded educational opportunities, and a more independent foreign policy. They both criticized capitalism as a cause of underdevelopment and of the poverty that afflicted the majority of Chile's population. To distinguish his more moderate program from Allende's Marxism, Frei promised a "Revolution in Liberty."

Eduardo Frei's Christian Democracy, 1964–70

After the 1965 elections gave them a majority of deputies in Congress, the Christian Democrats enacted ambitious reforms on many fronts. However, as a single-party government, they were often loath to enter into bargains, compromises, or coalitions. Consequently, rightists and leftists often opposed their congressional initiatives, especially in the Senate.

One of the major achievements of Eduardo Frei Montalva (president, 1964–70) was the "Chileanization" of copper. The government took 51 percent ownership of the mines controlled by United States companies, principally those of Anaconda and Kennecott. Critics complained that the companies received overly generous terms, invested too little in Chile, and retained too much ownership. Nevertheless, copper production rose, and Chile received a higher return from the enterprises.

Frei believed that agrarian reform was necessary to raise the standard of living of rural workers, to boost agricultural production, to expand his party's electoral base, and to defuse revolutionary potential in the countryside. Consequently, in 1967 his government promoted the right of peasants to unionize and strike. The administration also expropriated land with the intention of dividing it between collective and family farms. However, actual redistribution of land fell far short of promises and expectations. Conflict arose in the countryside between peasants eager for land and landowners frightened of losing their rights and their property.

During the tenure of the Christian Democrats, economic growth remained sluggish and inflation stayed high. Nevertheless, Frei's government improved income distribution and access to education, as enrollments rose at all levels of schooling. Under the aegis of "Popular Promotion," the Frei government organized many squatter communities and helped them build houses. This aided the PDC in its competition with the Marxists for political support in the burgeoning *poblaciones*. At the same time, Frei enacted tax reforms that made tax collection more efficient than ever before. The Christian Democrats also pushed through constitutional changes to strengthen the presidency; these changes later would be used to advantage by Allende. The PDC also revised electoral regulations, lowering the voting age from twenty-one to eighteen and giving the franchise to people who could not read (about 10 percent of the population was illiterate).

Although friendly to United States investors and government officials, the Frei administration took an independent stance in foreign affairs—more collegial with the developing nations and less hostile to the Communist-bloc nations. For instance, Frei restored diplomatic relations with the Soviet Union and most of its allies. Chile also gave strong backing to multilateral organizations, including the Latin American Free Trade Association (LAFTA—see Glossary), the Andean Group (see Glossary), the Organization of American States (OAS—see Glossary), and the United Nations. Meanwhile, aid and investment from the United States multiplied. Under Frei, Chile received more aid per capita from the United States than did any other country in Latin America.

After the two governments that followed the Christian Democrats, Chileans would look back with nostalgia on the Frei administration and its accomplishments. At the time, however, it was hounded by the right for being too reformist and by the left for being too conservative. While some on the right began forming paramilitary units to defend their property, some on the left began encouraging illegal seizures of farms, housing plots, and factories. Among the masses, the Christian Democrats raised expectations higher than they intended.

As the next presidential election approached, Frei remained personally popular, but his party's strength ebbed. With no clear winner apparent, the 1970 campaign shaped up as a rerun of 1958, with the right, center, and left all fielding their own candidates. The right hoped to recapture power and brake the pace of reform with former president Jorge Alessandri as the candidate of the National Party (Partido Nacional), established in 1965 by Conservatives and Liberals. In the center, the Christian Democrats promised to accelerate reform with a progressive candidate, Radomiro Tomic Romero. The left vowed to head down the road toward socialism with Salvador Allende as its nominee for the fourth time.

Under the leadership of the Socialist Party and the PCCh, the leftist coalition of 1970 called itself Popular Unity (Unidad Popular). Joining the alliance were four minor parties, including the shrunken Radical Party and defectors from the Christian Democrats, most notably the United Popular Action Movement (Movimiento de Acción Popular Unitario—MAPU). The coalition was reminiscent of the Popular Front of 1936–41, except that it was led by the Marxist parties and a Marxist candidate. Farther to the left, the Movement of the Revolutionary Left (Movimiento de la

Izquierda Revolucionaria—MIR), a small organization headed by radicalized students, scoffed at the electoral route, called for armed struggle, and undertook direct assaults on the system, such as bank robberies (see Terrorism, ch. 5).

To the surprise of most pollsters and prognosticators, Allende nosed out Alessandri 36.2 percent to 35 percent in the September 4, 1973, elections; Tomic trailed with 27.8 percent of the vote. In the Cold War context of the times, the democratic election of a Marxist president sent a shock wave around the globe. The seven weeks between the counting of the ballots and the certification of the winner by Congress crackled with tension. Attempts by the United States and by right-wing groups in Chile to convince Congress to choose the runner-up Alessandri or to coax the military into staging a coup d'état failed. A botched kidnapping planned by right-wing military officers resulted in the assassination of the army commander in chief, General René Schneider Chereau, on October 22, 1970, the first major political killing in Chile since the death of Portales in 1837. That plot backfired by ensuring the armed forces' support of a constitutional assumption of power by Allende.

After extracting guarantees of adherence to democratic procedures from Allende, the Christian Democrats in Congress followed tradition and provided the votes to make the front-runner Chile's new president. Although a minority president was not unusual, one with such a drastic plan to revolutionize the nation was unique. Allende was inaugurated on November 3, 1970.

Salvador Allende's Leftist Regime, 1970–73

The Allende experiment enjoyed a triumphant first year, followed by two disastrous final years. According to Popular Unity, Chile was being exploited by parasitic foreign and domestic capitalists. The government therefore moved quickly to socialize the economy, taking over the copper mines and other foreign firms, oligopolistic industries, banks, and large estates. By a unanimous vote of Congress in 1971, the government totally nationalized the foreign copper firms, which were mainly owned by two United States companies, Kennecott and Anaconda. The nationalization measure was one of the few bills Allende ever got through the opposition-controlled legislature, where the Christian Democrats constituted the largest single party.

Socialization of the means of production spread rapidly and widely. The government took over virtually all the great estates. It turned the lands over to the resident workers, who benefited far more than the owners of tiny plots or the numerous migrant laborers. By 1972 food production had fallen and food imports had risen. Also during

1971–72, the government dusted off emergency legislation from the 1932 Socialist Republic to allow it to expropriate industries without congressional approval. It turned many factories over to management by the workers and the state.

In his first year, Allende also employed Keynesian measures to hike salaries and wages, thus pumping up the purchasing power of the middle and working classes. This "consumer revolution" benefited 95 percent of the population in the short run because prices were held down and employment went up. Producers responded to rising demand by employing previously underused capacity.

Politically, Allende faced problems holding his Popular Unity coalition together, pacifying the more leftist elements inside and outside Popular Unity and, above all, coping with the increasingly implacable opposition. Within Popular Unity, the largest party was the Socialist Party. Although composed of multiple factions, the Socialist Party mainly pressed Allende to accelerate the transition toward socialism. The second most important element was the PCCh, which favored a more gradual, legalistic approach. Outside Popular Unity, the most significant left-wing organization was the MIR, a tiny but provocative group that admired the Cuban Revolution and encouraged peasants and workers to take property and the revolutionary process into their own hands, much faster than Allende preferred.

The most important opposition party was the PDC. As it and the middle sectors gradually shifted to the right, they came to form an anti-Allende bloc in combination with the National Party and the propertied class. Even farther to the right were minuscule, paramilitary, quasi-fascist groups like Fatherland and Liberty (Patria y Libertad), determined to sabotage Popular Unity.

The Popular Unity government tried to maintain cordial relations with the United States, even while staking out an independent position as a champion of developing nations and socialist causes. It opened diplomatic relations with Cuba, China, the Democratic People's Republic of Korea (North Korea), the Democratic Republic of Vietnam (North Vietnam), and Albania. It befriended the Soviet Union, which sent aid to the Allende administration, although far less than Cuba received or than Popular Unity had hoped for.

Meanwhile, the United States pursued a two-track policy toward Allende's Chile. At the overt level, Washington was frosty, especially after the nationalization of the copper mines; official relations were unfriendly but not openly hostile. The government of President Richard M. Nixon squeezed the Chilean economy by terminating financial assistance and blocking loans from multilateral organizations, although it increased aid to the military, a sector unenthusiastic toward the Allende government. It was widely reported that at the covert level the United States worked to destabilize Allende's Chile by funding opposition political groups and media and by encouraging a military coup d'état. Most scholars have concluded that these United States actions contributed to the downfall of Allende, although no one has established direct United States participation in the coup d'état, and very few would assign the United States the primary role in the destruction of that government.

During the second and third years of Popular Unity, demand outstripped supply, the economy shrank, deficit spending snowballed, new investments and foreign exchange became scarce, the value of copper sales dropped, shortages appeared, and inflation skyrocketed, eroding the previous gains for the working class. A thriving black market sprang up. The government responded with direct distribution systems in working-class neighborhoods. Worker participation in the management of enterprises reached unprecedented proportions. The strapped government could not keep the economy from going into free fall because it could not impose austerity measures on its supporters in the working class, get new taxes approved by Congress, or borrow enough money abroad to cover the deficit.

Although the right was on the defensive in Allende's first year, it moved on the offensive and forged an alliance with the center in the next two years. In Congress this center-right coalition erected a blockade against all Popular Unity initiatives, harassed Popular Unity cabinet ministers, and denounced the administration as illegitimate and unconstitutional, thus setting the stage for a military takeover. The most acrimonious battle raged over the boundaries of Popular Unity's "social property area" (*área de propriedad social*), which would incorporate private holdings through government intervention, requisition, or expropriation. The Supreme Court and the comptroller general of the republic joined Congress in criticizing the executive branch for overstepping its constitutional bounds.

Allende tried to stabilize the situation by organizing a succession of cabinets, but none of them guaranteed order. His appointment of military officers to cabinet posts in 1972 and 1973 also failed to stifle the opposition. Instead, it helped politicize the armed services. Outside the government, Allende's supporters continued direct takeovers of land and businesses, further disrupting the economy and frightening the propertied class.

The two sides reached a showdown in the March 1973 congressional elections. The opposition expected the Allende coalition to suffer the typical losses of Chilean governments in midterm elections, especially with the economy in a tailspin. The National Party and PDC hoped to win two-thirds of the seats, enough to impeach Allende. They netted 55 percent of the votes, not enough of a majority to end the stalemate. Moreover, Popular Unity's 43 percent share represented an increase over the presidential tally of 36.2 percent and gave Allende's coalition six additional congressional seats; therefore, many of his adherents were encouraged to forge ahead.

In the aftermath of the indecisive 1973 congressional elections, both sides escalated the confrontation and hurled threats of insurgency. Street demonstrations became almost daily events and increasingly violent. Right-wing groups, such as Fatherland and Liberty, and left-wing groups, such as the MIR, brandished arms and called for a cataclysmic solution. The most militant workers formed committees in their neighborhoods and workplaces to press for accelerated social change and to defend their gains. The opposition began openly knocking on the doors of the barracks in hopes that the military would provide a solution.

The regular armed forces halted an attempted coup by tank commanders in June 1973, but that incident warned the nation that the military was getting restless. Thereafter, the armed forces prepared for a massive coup by stepping up raids to search for arms among Popular Unity's supporters. Conditions worsened in June, July, and August, as middle- and upper-class business proprietors and professionals launched another wave of workplace shutdowns and lockouts, as they had in late 1972. Their 1973 protests against the government coincided with strikes by the trucking industry and by the left's erstwhile allies among the copper workers. The Nationalists, the Christian Democrats, and conservative students backed the increasingly subversive strikers. They called for Allende's resignation or military intervention. Attempts by the Catholic Church to get the PDC and Popular Unity to negotiate a compromise came to naught. Meanwhile, inflation reached an annual rate of more than 500 percent. By mid-1973 the economy and the government were paralyzed.

In August 1973, the rightist and centrist representatives in the Chamber of Deputies undermined the president's legitimacy by accusing him of systematically violating the constitution and by urging the armed forces to intervene. In early September, Allende was preparing to call for a rare national plebiscite to resolve the impasse between Popular Unity and the opposition. The military obviated that strategy by launching its attack on civilian authority on the morning of September 11. Just prior to the assault, the commanders in chief, headed by the newly appointed army commander,

General Augusto Pinochet Ugarte, had purged officers sympathetic to the president.

Allende committed suicide while defending (with an assault rifle) his socialist government against the coup d'état. Although sporadic resistance to the coup erupted, the military consolidated control much more quickly than it had believed possible. Many Chileans had predicted that a coup would unleash a civil war, but instead it ushered in a long period of repression.

Debate continues over the reasons for Allende's downfall. Why did he fail to preserve democracy or achieve socialism? Critics of the left blamed Allende for going to extremes, destroying the economy, violating the constitution, and undermining the spirit if not the letter of democracy. Right-wing critics in particular accused the left of even plotting an armed takeover, a charge that was never proved. Critics also assailed Popular Unity for being unclear about the limits of its reforms and thus frightening the middle class into the arms of the opposition. Critics of the right accused Popular Unity, in conjunction with the United States, of ruining the economy and of calling out the armed forces to protect its property and privileges. Observers in general scolded the far left for its adventurous excesses. The far left retorted that Popular Unity failed because it was too timid to arm the masses. Critics of the Christian Democrats chastised them for refusing to compromise, locking arms with the rightist opposition, and failing to defend democracy.

Many analysts would concur that there was ample blame to go around. In the view of many Chileans, groups at all points on the political spectrum helped destroy the democratic order by being too ideological and too intransigent. Many observers agree that a minority president facing adamant domestic and foreign opposition was extremely unlikely to be able to uphold democracy and create socialism at the same time. In the late 1980s, polls also showed that most Chileans did not want to try the Popular Unity experiment again, especially in light of its aftermath.

Military Rule, 1973–90

The armed forces justified the coup as necessary to stamp out Marxism, avert class warfare, restore order, and salvage the economy. They enshrined the National Security Doctrine, which defined their primary task as the defeat of domestic enemies who had infiltrated national institutions, including schools, churches, political parties, unions, and the media. Although civilians filled prominent economic posts, military officers took most government positions at the national and local levels. Immediately on seizing power, the military junta—composed of the commanders in chief of the army, navy, air force, and Carabineros—issued a barrage of decrees to restore order on its own terms.

The first phase of the dictatorship (1973–75) was mainly destructive, aimed at rapid demobilization, depoliticization, and stabilization. The armed forces treated Popular Unity as an enemy to be obliterated, not just as an errant political movement to be booted from office. The military commanders closed Congress, censored the news media, purged the universities, burned books, declared political parties outlawed if Marxist or if in recess otherwise, and banned union activities.

The worst human rights abuses occurred in the first four years of the junta, when thousands of civilians were murdered, jailed, tortured, brutalized, or exiled, especially those linked with the Popular Unity parties. The secret police, reporting to Pinochet through the National Intelligence Directorate (Dirección Nacional de Inteligencia—DINA), replaced in 1977 by the National Information Center (Centro Nacional de Información—CNI), kept dissidents living in fear of arrest, torture, murder, or "disappearance."

Throughout the second half of the 1970s, the Roman Catholic Church and international organizations concerned with human rights denounced the widespread violations of decency in Chile. Although officially neutral, the Roman Catholic Church became the primary sanctuary for the persecuted in Chile from 1975 to 1985 and so came into increasing conflict with the junta.

The former members of Popular Unity went underground or into exile. In the early years of the dictatorship, their main goal was simply to survive. Although the Communists suffered brutal persecution, they managed to preserve their organization fairly intact. The Socialists splintered so badly that their party nearly disappeared by the end of the 1970s. Draconian repression left the Marxists with no capacity to resist or counterattack. They did, however, manage to rally world opinion against the regime and keep it isolated diplomatically. By the end of the 1970s, most Christian Democrats, after initially cooperating with the junta, had also joined the opposition, although not in any formal coalition with any coherent strategy for restoring democracy.

Pinochet soon emerged as the dominant figure and very shortly afterward as president. After a brief flirtation with corporatist ideas, the government evolved into a one-man dictatorship, with the rest of the junta acting as a sort of legislature. In 1977 Pinochet dashed the hopes of those Chileans still dreaming of an early return to democracy when he announced his intention to institutionalize an authoritarian regime to preside over a protracted return to civilian rule in a "protected" democracy.

Pinochet established iron control over the armed forces as well as the government, although insisting that they were separate entities. He made himself not only the chief executive of the state but also the commander in chief of the military. He shuffled commands to ensure that loyalists controlled all the key posts. He appointed many new generals and had others retire, so that by the 1980s all active-duty generals owed their rank to Pinochet. He also improved the pay and benefits of the services. The isolation of the armed forces from civilian society had been a virtue under the democracy, inhibiting their involvement in political disputes; now that erstwhile virtue became an impediment to redemocratization, as the military remained loyal to Pinochet and resisted politicization by civilians.

Although aid and loans from the United States increased spectacularly during the first three years of the regime, while presidents Nixon and Gerald R. Ford were in office, relations soured after Jimmy Carter was elected president in 1976 on a platform promising vigorous pursuit of human rights as a major component of his foreign policy. During the Carter administration, a significant source of contention was the 1976 assassination in Washington of the former Chilean ambassador to the United States by agents of Pinochet's secret police. The target, Orlando Letelier, had served under Allende. In response to United States criticism, General Pinochet held his first national plebiscite in 1978, calling for a yes or no vote on his defense of Chile's sovereignty and the institutionalization of his regime. The government claimed that more than 75 percent of the voters in the tightly controlled referendum endorsed Pinochet's rule.

Neoliberal Economics

By the mid-1970s, the dictatorship switched from destroying the old order to constructing its version of a new Chile. The junta not only overturned decades of democratic government but also decades of statist economic policies, which had mainly protected industrialists and organized workers. The new economic program was designed by civilian technocrats known as the "Chicago boys" (see Glossary) because many of them had been trained or influenced by University of Chicago professors. The government instituted a dramatic conversion to free-market economics in 1975.

After curbing inflation and returning a significant amount of property to its former owners, the administration embarked on a radical program of liberalization and privatization, slashing tariffs as well as government welfare programs and deficits. As a result, the economy grew rapidly from 1976 to 1981, a feat heralded as the "Chilean miracle." That growth was fueled by the influx of private foreign loans until the debt crisis of the early 1980s. Financial conglomerates became the major beneficiaries of the open economy and the flood of foreign bank loans. Exports of nontraditional commodities, especially fruit, timber, and fish products, also grew impressively; the value of new exportables came to equal that of copper sales. Despite high growth in the late 1970s, income distribution became more regressive, and unemployment stayed in double digits. The underemployed informal sector also mushroomed in size. The regime responded with a "minimum employment" public works program (see The Military Government's Free-Market Reforms, 1973–90, ch. 3).

In conjunction with the liberalization of the economy, the junta implemented a series of social reforms to reduce the role of the central government in social security, labor disputes, health care, and education. These reforms fit with the desire to shrink the central government, decentralize administration, and privatize previous state functions. Critics charged that the welfare state was being dismantled to leave citizens at the mercy of the marketplace. The regime retorted that it was focusing its social assistance on the poorest of the poor to meet basic needs, and it pointed with pride to improvement in such indicators as infant mortality (see Welfare Institutions and Social Programs, ch. 2; Economic Results of the Pensions Privatization, ch. 3).

The most important of the government's so-called modernizations in social policy was the 1979 Labor Plan. The regime had already outlawed the CUTCh, Marxist union leaders, several Marxist unions, union elections, strikes, and collective bargaining. Nevertheless, after bearing the brunt of repression in 1973–74, unions gradually revived in the late 1970s. Little by little, cooperation increased between Marxist and Christian Democrat union leaders, the latter making gains because the former were outlawed. Although a few unions supported the government, most firmly opposed the regime and its economic program. The Labor Plan sought to codify the dictatorship's antilabor policies. It placed stringent limits on collective bargaining, strikes, and other union activities, especially any participation in politics. Almost all labor unions rejected the Labor Plan and aligned with the opposition (see Unions and Labor Conflicts, ch. 3).

The 1980 Constitution

At the height of the economic boom, the regime moved to legitimize and regularize its reforms and its tenure. Its new "constitution of liberty" was approved in a controlled plebiscite in 1980, in which the government claimed to have received 67 percent of the vote. Both leftists and Christian Democrats had called for a no vote. Because there were no safeguards for the opposition or for the balloting, most analysts expressed doubts about the government's percentage and assumed that the constitution may have won by a lesser margin. According to the new constitution, Pinochet would remain president through 1989; a plebiscite in 1988 would determine if he would have an additional eight years in office. The document provided for military domination of the government both before and after the 1988 plebiscite.

The constitution's approval marked the institutionalization of Pinochet's political system. In the eyes of the military, a dictatorship had now been transformed into an authoritarian regime, rule by exception having been replaced by the rule of law. When the new charter took effect in 1981, the dictatorship was at the peak of its powers, politically untouchable and economically successful. At that moment, few would have predicted that the dispirited and fragmented opposition would take power by the end of the decade.

The imposition of the authoritarian constitution cast further gloom on the divided and dejected opposition. The PCCh now made a historic reversal, claiming that all forms of struggle, including armed insurrection, were justified against the dictatorship. Most political parties on the left or in the center, however, continued searching for a peaceful path to redemocratization.

The Crisis of 1982 and the Erosion of Military Rule

From 1982 to 1990, Chile underwent a prolonged journey back to democracy. During that process, the country experienced five crucial changes. First, the economic collapse in 1982 provoked some adjustments to the neoliberal model and sparked widespread protests against the regime. That recession was compounded by the international debt crisis.

Second, although most of the regime's supporters in the business community and the armed forces held fast, the 1980s witnessed a weakening of their attachment to authoritarianism and a few defections from their ranks. Third, civilian society became emboldened. A series of demonstrations against Pinochet during 1983–85 spread from organized labor to the middle class and finally ended up concentrated among the residents of the urban shantytowns. Fourth, the previously repressed and dormant political parties came back to life. They took charge during the 1988 plebiscite that effectively ended the Pinochet regime and the subsequent 1989 elections for president and Congress. Fifth, after being surrounded by like-minded dictators in South America, Pinochet became isolated as a tide of democratization swept the continent, and the United States and Europe began applying pressure for Chile to join the trend.

In sum, from its apogee in the 1980 plebiscite to its exit in 1990, the authoritarian regime lost support and saw its opponents gain momentum and eventually power. During its first decade, however, the dictatorship had brought about profound and seemingly durable changes. Politically, it had pulverized the revolutionary Marxist left. Economically, it had moved Chile's focus from the state to the market. Socially, it had fostered a new emphasis on individualism and consumerism, widening the gap between rich and poor, even while helping some of the most destitute. What it had failed to do was to extirpate the preference of most Chileans for democracy.

*   *   *

Among works in English, an outstanding general history is Brian Loveman's *Chile: The Legacy of Hispanic Capitalism*. For the colonial period, Eugene H. Korth provides a useful introduction in *Spanish Policy in Colonial Chile*. The subsequent Bourbon years are covered by Jacques A. Barbier in *Reform and Politics in Bourbon Chile, 1755-1796*.

For the nineteenth century, the work to begin with is Simon Collier's *Ideas and Politics of Chilean Independence*. The development of the system of land tenure is examined by Arnold J. Bauer in *Chilean Rural Society from the Spanish Conquest to 1930*. The country's external relations are analyzed by Robert N. Burr in *By Reason or Force*. Works covering the nitrate era and the Balmaceda controversy include Thomas F. O'Brien's *The Nitrate Industry and Chile's Crucial Transition, 1870-1891;* Michael Monteón's *Chile in the Nitrate Era;* Maurice Zeitlin's *The Civil Wars in Chile, 1851 and 1859;* and Harold Blakemore's *British Nitrates and Chilean Politics, 1886-1896*.

Chilean relations with the United States can be surveyed in Fredrick B. Pike's *Chile and the United States, 1880-1962* and in William F. Sater's *Chile and the United States*. General coverage of the economy is found in Markos J. Mamalakis's *The Growth and Structure of the Chilean Economy*. A classic work on the copper industry is Theodore H. Moran's *Multinational Corporations and the Politics of Dependence*. The development of organized labor is explained in Peter de Shazo's *Urban Workers and Labor Unions in Chile, 1902-1927* and in Alan Angell's *Politics and the Labour Movement in Chile*. On rural conflicts, valuable sources include Brian Loveman's *Struggle in the Countryside* and Thomas C. Wright's *Landowners and Reform in Chile*. Concerning the role of the Catholic Church, the key source is Brian H. Smith's *The Church and Politics in Chile.* The armed forces are covered in Frederick M. Nunn's *The Military in Chilean History.*

The evolution of the political system is discussed by Timothy R. Scully in *Rethinking the Center.* Political developments leading up to the tragedy under Allende are traced by Paul W. Drake in *Socialism and Populism in Chile, 1932–52,* by Federico G. Gil in *The Political System of Chile,* and by James F. Petras in *Politics and Social Forces in Chilean Development.*

The two most controversial governments in Chilean history have generated a voluminous literature. On the Allende experiment, the best books to start with are Stefan de Vylder's *Allende's Chile;* Edy Kaufman's *Crisis in Allende's Chile;* Ian Roxborough, Philip O'Brien, and Jackie Roddick's *Chile: The State and Revolution;* Paul E. Sigmund's *The Overthrow of Allende and the Politics of Chile, 1964–1976;* Barbara Stallings's *Class Conflict and Economic Development in Chile, 1958–1973;* Arturo Valenzuela's *The Breakdown of Democratic Regimes: Chile;* and Peter Winn's *Weavers of Revolution.*

The first half of the Pinochet period is dissected by J. Samuel Valenzuela and Arturo Valenzuela in *Military Rule in Chile,* the second half by Paul W. Drake and Iván Jaksić in *The Struggle for Democracy in Chile, 1982–1990,* and the entire seventeen years by Pamela Constable and Arturo Valenzuela in *A Nation of Enemies.* Analyses of the dictatorship's economic innovations are provided in Sebastian Edwards and Alejandra Cox Edwards's *Monetarism and Liberalization* and in Alejandro Foxley Riesco's *Latin American Experiments in Neoconservative Economics.* (For further information and complete citations, see Bibliography.)

Chapter 2. The Society and Its Environment

A Mapuche rug representing a chilko, *a plant reputed to cure cardiovascular illnesses*

THE DEVELOPMENT OF CHILEAN SOCIETY since the country broke away from Spain early in the nineteenth century reflects in many ways a significant incongruity. On the one hand, the nation's political institutions and many of its social institutions developed much like their counterparts in the United States and Western Europe. On the other hand, the economy had a history of insufficient and erratic growth that left Chile among the less developed nations of the world. Given the first of these characteristics, Chilean society, culture, and politics have struck generations of observers from more developed nations as having what can be described, for want of a better expression, as a familiar "modernity." Yet this impression always seemed at odds with the lack of resources at all levels, the highly visible and extensive urban and rural poverty, and the considerable social inequalities.

Chile's location on the far southern shores of the Americas' Pacific Coast made international contacts difficult until the great advance in global air travel and communications of the post-World War II period. This relative isolation of a people whose main cultural roots lay in the Iberian-Catholic variant of Western civilization probably had the paradoxical effect of making Chileans more receptive to outside influences than would otherwise have been the case. The small numbers of foreign travelers reaching the country in the nineteenth and early twentieth centuries usually found a warm welcome from people eager to hear of the latest trends in leading nations. The immigrants to the country were similarly accepted quite readily, and those who were successful rapidly gained entry into the highest social circles. One result was a disproportionate number of non-Iberian names among the Chilean upper classes. Moreover, many Chileans, the wealthy as well as artists, writers, scientists, and politicians, found it virtually obligatory to make the long voyage to experience firsthand the major cities of Europe and the United States, and they rapidly absorbed whatever new notions were emerging in more advanced nations.

At the same time, Chile's physical isolation probably buttressed the commitment of the nation's leaders in all walks of life to building strong national institutions, which then developed their peculiarly Chilean features. For example, the rich could not easily envision sending their children to universities in Europe or the United States, and this created a demand that would not otherwise have existed for strong domestic centers of higher learning. A feeling of pride in these various institutions soon developed that contributed to the Chileans' strong sense of national identity.

This combination of openness to outside influences and commitment to the nation is undoubtedly related to the relative "modernity" that has been a feature of Chilean life since independence from Spain. From the very first national administrations, there was a strong expression of commitment to expanding the availability of education to both boys and girls, principally at the primary level. The University of Chile was established by the national government in 1842 and soon had a large, centrally located building in Santiago. In a matter of decades, the university became one of the most respected institutions of higher learning in Latin America. Women were admitted to the University of Chile beginning in 1877, making it a world pioneer in coeducational instruction; by 1932 about a third of the university's enrollment was female.

In the Americas, Chile was second only to Uruguay in creating state-run welfare institutions, adopting a relatively comprehensive social security system in 1924, more than a decade before the United States. A national health system was created by pooling existing state-founded institutions into a comprehensive organization in 1952. Under this program, curative and emergency care were provided free of charge to workers and the poor; in the early 1960s, preventive care became available to all infants and mothers.

However, inadequate development of the economy undermined Chile's relatively modern institutional edifice. The lack of resources often led to sharp conflicts between different groups trying to obtain larger pieces of a meager pie. As better placed and politically more influential groups were able to draw disproportionate benefits for themselves, inequalities were generated, as was made apparent by the wide disparities in the pension benefits that were paid by the state-run system. Despite the government's early commitment to public education, budgetary limitations meant that illiteracy decreased very slowly. By 1930 about a quarter of the adult population still could not read or write, a low proportion by Latin American standards but a far cry from the universal literacy existing at the time in France, Germany, and Belgium, whose educational systems had served as models for Chilean public education. Primary school attendance only approached universal levels in the 1960s, and full adult literacy was not achieved until the 1980s. The lack of educational opportunities limited social mobility, and investments in new technologies often ran into the difficulty of not having properly trained workers. The nation's industries, mines, and farms had at their disposal a large pool of unskilled or semiskilled workers, and for most jobs the wages, benefits, and working conditions were generally deplorable. On numerous occasions, worker demands met with heavy-handed repression, and class divisions became deep fault lines in Chilean society.

The military government that took over after the bloody coup of 1973 embarked on a different course from that followed by the country's governments over the previous half-century. Based on economic neoliberalism, the military regime's primary objectives were to reduce the size of the state and limit its intervention in national institutions. Most state-owned industries and the state-run social security system were privatized, private education at all levels was encouraged, and labor laws limiting union rights were enacted. Although new programs enhancing prior efforts to deal with the poorest segments of the population were successfully put into place, the authoritarian regime's overall social and economic policies led to increased inequalities.

At the start of the 1990s, Chile began to recover its democratic institutions under the elected government of Patricio Aylwin Azócar (president, 1990–94). Committed to redressing the social inequalities that had developed under the military regime, the new government allocated more resources to programs and institutions in education and health in order to improve their quality and the population's access to them. Although the Aylwin administration made some changes in these institutions, there was no attempt to undo the privatization of the social security system, which was now based on individual capitalization schemes rather than on the old state-run, pay-as-you-go system.

In 1993 and early 1994, there was a sharp sense of optimism regarding the Chilean economy. High rates of economic growth were expected to last through the 1990s. With its newfound economic dynamism, Chile seemed poised in the early 1990s to begin resolving the long-standing incongruity of a relatively advanced social and political system coexisting with a scarcity of means.

Geography

A Long, Narrow Nation

In a classic book on the natural setting and people of Chile, Benjamín Subercaseaux Zañartu, a Chilean writer, describes the country's geography as *loca* (crazy). The book's English translator renders this term as "extravagant." Whether crazy or extravagant, there is little question that Chile's territorial shape is certainly among the world's most unusual. From north to south, Chile extends 4,270 kilometers, and yet it only averages 177 kilometers east to west.

On a map, Chile looks like a long ribbon reaching from the middle of South America's west coast straight down to the southern tip of the continent, where it curves slightly eastward. Cape Horn, the southernmost point in the Americas, where the Pacific and Atlantic oceans turbulently meet, is Chilean territory. Chile's northern neighbors are Peru and Bolivia, and its border with Argentina to the east, at 5,150 kilometers, is one of the world's longest (see fig. 4).

Chile's shape was determined by the fact that it began as a Spanish settlement on the western side of the mighty cordillera of the Andes, in the central part of the country. This range, which includes the two tallest peaks in the Americas—Aconcagua (6,959 meters) and Nevado Ojos del Salado (6,880 meters)—is a formidable barrier, whose passes to the Argentine side are covered by a heavy blanket of snow during the winter months. As a result, Chile could expand beyond its original colonial territory only to the south and north. The colony grew southward by occupying lands populated by indigenous groups, and it grew northward by occupying sections of both Peru and Bolivia that were eventually awarded to Chile in the aftermath of the War of the Pacific (1879–83).

The northern two-thirds of Chile lie on top of the telluric Nazca Plate, which, moving eastward about ten centimeters a year, is forcing its way under the continental plate of South America. This movement has resulted in the formation of the Peru-Chile Trench, which lies beyond a narrow band of coastal waters off the northern two-thirds of the country. The trench is about 150 kilometers wide and averages about 5,000 meters in depth. At its deepest point, just north of the port of Antofagasta, it plunges to 8,066 meters. Although the ocean's surface obscures this fact, most of Chile lies at the edge of a profound precipice.

The same telluric displacements that created the Peru-Chile Trench make the country highly prone to earthquakes. During the twentieth century, Chile has been struck by twenty-eight major earthquakes, all with a force greater than 6.9 on the Richter scale (see Glossary). The strongest of these occurred in 1906 (registering an estimated 8.4 on the Richter scale) and in 1960 (reaching 8.75). This latter earthquake occurred on May 22, the day after another major quake measuring 7.25 on the Richter scale, and covered an extensive section of south-central Chile. It caused a tidal wave that decimated several fishing villages in the south and raised or lowered sections of the coast as much as two meters. The clash between the earth's surface plates has also generated the Andes, a geologically young mountain range that, in Chilean territory alone, includes about 620 volcanoes, many of them active. Almost

sixty of these had erupted in the twentieth century by the early 1990s. More than half of Chile's land surface is volcanic in origin.

About 80 percent of the land in Chile is made up of mountains of some form or other. Most Chileans live near or on these mountains. The majestically snowcapped Andes and their precordillera elevations provide an ever-present backdrop to much of the scenery, but there are other, albeit less formidable, mountains as well. Although they seemingly can appear anywhere, the non-Andean mountains usually form part of transverse and coastal ranges. The former, located most characteristically in the near north and the far north natural regions, extend with various shapes from the Andes to the ocean, creating valleys with an east-west direction. The latter are evident mainly in the center of the country and create what is commonly called the Central Valley (Valle Central) between them and the Andes. In the far south, the Central Valley runs into the ocean's waters. At this location, the higher elevations of the coastal range facing the Andes become a multiplicity of islands, forming an intricate labyrinth of channels and fjords that have been an enduring challenge to maritime navigators.

Much of Chile's coastline is rugged, with surf that seems to explode against the rocks lying at the feet of high bluffs. This collision of land and sea gives way every so often to lovely beaches of various lengths, some of them encased by the bluffs. The Humboldt current, which originates northwest of the Antarctic Peninsula (which juts into the Bellingshausen Sea) and runs the full length of the Chilean coast, makes the water frigid. Swimming at Chile's popular beaches in the central part of the country, where the water gets no warmer than 15°C in the summer, requires more than a bit of fortitude.

Chilean territory extends as far west as Polynesia. The best known of Chile's Pacific islands is Easter Island (Isla de Pascua, also known by its Polynesian name of Rapa Nui), with a population of 2,800 people. Located 3,600 kilometers west of Chile's mainland port of Caldera, just below the Tropic of Capricorn, Easter Island provides Chile a gateway to the Pacific. It is noted for its 867 monoliths (Moais), which are huge (up to twenty meters high) and mysterious, expressionless faces sculpted of volcanic stone (see fig. 5). The Islas Juan Fernández, located 587 kilometers west of Valparaíso, are the locale of a small fishing settlement. They are famous for their lobster and the fact that one of the islands, Isla Robinson Crusoe, is where Alexander Selkirk, the inspiration for Daniel Defoe's novel, was marooned for about four years.

Natural Regions

Chile may have a "crazy" geography, but it is also a land of

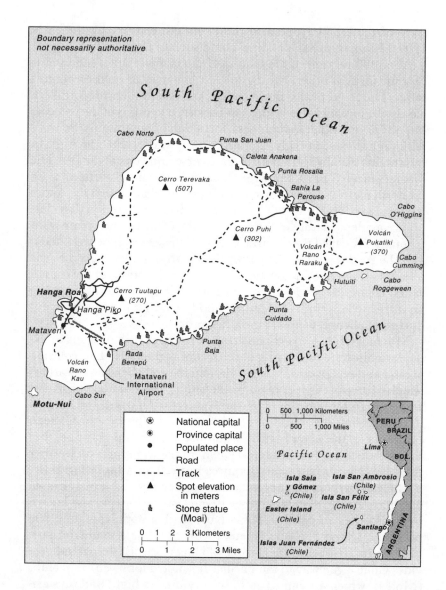

Figure 5. Easter Island (Isla de Pascua), 1986

unparalleled beauty, with an incredible variety that has fascinated visitors since the Spanish conquest. Because Chile extends from a point about 625 kilometers north of the Tropic of Capricorn to a point hardly more than 1,400 kilometers north of the Antarctic Circle, within its territory can be found a broad selection of the earth's climates. For this reason, geographically it is possible to

A monolith (Moai)
on Easter Island
Courtesy Embassy of
Chile, Washington

speak of several Chiles. The country usually is divided by geographers into five regions: the far north, the near north, central Chile, the south, and the far south. Each has its own characteristic vegetation, fauna, climate, and, despite the omnipresence of both the Andes and the Pacific, its own distinct topography.

The Far North

The far north (Norte Grande), which extends from the Peruvian border to about 27°south latitude, a line roughly paralleled by the Río Copiapó, is extremely arid. It contains the Atacama Desert, one of the driest areas in the world; in certain sections, this desert does not register any rainfall at all. Average monthly temperatures range at sea level between about 20.5°C during the summer and about 14°C during the winter. Most of the population lives in the coastal area, where the temperatures are more moderate and the humidity higher. Contrary to the image of monochrome barrenness that most people associate with deserts, the landscape is spectacular, with its crisscrossing hills and mountains of all shapes and sizes, each with a unique color and hue depending on its mineral composition, its distance from the observer, and the time of day.

In the far north, the land generally rises vertically from the ocean, sometimes to elevations well over 1,000 meters. The Cordillera Domeyko in the north runs along the coast parallel to the Andes. This topography generates coastal microclimates because the fog that frequently forms over the cold ocean waters, as well as any low clouds, is trapped by the high bluffs. This airborne moisture condenses in the spines and leaves of the vegetation, droplets that fall to the ground and irrigate the plants' roots. Beyond the coastal bluffs, there is an area of rolling hills that encompasses the driest desert land; this area ends to the east with the Andes towering over it. The edges of the desert in some sections have subterranean aquifers that have permitted the development of forests made up mainly of *tamarugos,* spiny trees native to the area that grow to a height of about twenty-five meters. Most of those forests were cut down to fuel the fires of the many foundries established since colonial times to exploit the abundant deposits of copper, silver, and nitrate found in the area. The result was the creation of even drier surface conditions.

The far north is the only part of the country in which there is a large section of the Andean plateau. The area receives considerable rainfall during the summer months in what is commonly known as the "Bolivian winter," forming shallow lakes of mostly saline waters that are home to a number of bird species, including the Chilean flamingo. Some of the water from the plateau trickles down the Andes in the form of narrow rivers, many of which form oases before being lost to evaporation or absorption into the desert sands, salt beds, and aquifers. However, some rivers do manage to reach the Pacific, including the Río Loa, whose U-shaped course across the desert makes it Chile's longest river. The water rights for one of the rivers, the Río Lauca, remain a source of dispute between Bolivia and Chile. These narrow rivers have carved fertile valleys in which an exuberant vegetation creates a stark contrast to the bone-dry hills. In such areas, roads usually are built halfway up the arid elevations in order to maximize the intensive agricultural use of the irrigated land. They offer spectacular panoramic vistas, along with the harrowing experience of driving along the edges of cliffs.

In the far north, the kinds of fruits that grow well in the arid tropics thrive, and all kinds of vegetables can be grown year-round. However, the region's main economic foundation is its great mineral wealth. For instance, Chuquicamata, the world's largest open-pit copper mine, is located in the far north. Since the early 1970s, the fishing industry has also developed enormously in the main ports of the area, most notably Iquique and Antofagasta (see The Current Structure of the Economy, ch. 3).

The Near North

The near north (Norte Chico) extends from the Río Copiapó

to about 32°south latitude, or just north of Santiago. It is a semiarid region whose central area receives an average of about twenty-five millimeters of rain during each of the four winter months, with trace amounts the rest of the year. The near north is also subject to droughts. The temperatures are moderate, with an average of 18.5°C during the summer and about 12°C during the winter at sea level. The winter rains and the melting of the snow that accumulates on the Andes produce rivers whose flow varies with the seasons, but which carry water year round. Their deep transverse valleys provide broad areas for cattle raising and, most important, fruit growing, an activity that has developed greatly since the mid-1970s.

As in the far north, the coastal areas of the near north have a distinct microclimate. In those sections where the airborne moisture of the sea is trapped by high bluffs overlooking the ocean, temperate rain forests develop as the vegetation precipitates the vapor in the form of a misty rain. Because the river valleys provide breaks in the coastal elevations, maritime moisture can penetrate inland and further decrease the generally arid climate in those valleys. The higher elevations in the interior sections are covered with shrubs and cacti of various kinds.

Central Chile

Central Chile (Chile Central), home to a majority of the population, includes the three largest metropolitan areas—Santiago, Valparaíso, and Concepción. It extends from about 32°south latitude to about 38°south latitude. The climate is of the temperate Mediterranean type, with the amount of rainfall increasing considerably and progressively from north to south. In the Santiago area, the average monthly temperatures are about 19.5°C in the summer months of January and February and 7.5°C in the winter months of June and July. The average monthly precipitation is no more than a trace in January and February and 69.7 millimeters in June and July. By contrast, in Concepción the average monthly temperatures are somewhat lower in the summer at 17.6°C but higher in the winter at 9.3°C, and the amount of rain is much greater. In the summer, Concepción receives an average of twenty millimeters of rain per month; in June and July, the city is pounded by an average of 253 millimeters per month. The numerous rivers greatly increase their flow as a result of the winter rains and the spring melting of the Andean snows, and they contract considerably in the summer. The combination of abundant snow in the Andes and relatively moderate winter temperatures creates excellent conditions for Alpine skiing.

The topography of central Chile includes a coastal range of mountains running parallel to the Andes. Lying between the two mountain ranges is the so-called Central Valley, which contains some of the richest agricultural land in the country, especially in its northern portion. The area just north and south of Santiago is a large producer of fruits, including the grapes from which the best Chilean wines are made. Exports of fresh fruit began to rise dramatically in the mid-1970s because Chilean growers had the advantage of being able to reach markets in the Northern Hemisphere during that part of the world's winter. Most of these exports, such as grapes, apples, and peaches, go by refrigerator ships, but some, such as berries, go by air freight.

The southern portion of central Chile contains a mixture of some excellent agricultural lands, many of which were covered originally with old-growth forests. They were cleared for agriculture but were soon exhausted of their organic matter and left to erode. Large tracts of this worn-out land, many of them on hilly terrain, have been reforested for the lumber, especially for the cellulose and paper industries. New investments during the 1980s in these industries transformed the rural economy of the region. The pre-Andean highlands and some of the taller and more massive mountains in the coastal range (principally the Cordillera de Nahuelbuta) still contain large tracts of old-growth forests of remarkable beauty, some of which have been set aside as national parks. Between the coastal mountains and the ocean, many areas of central Chile contain stretches of land that are lower than the Central Valley and are generally quite flat. The longest beaches can be found in such sections.

The South

Although many lovely lakes can be found in the Andean and coastal regions of central Chile, the south (Sur de Chile) is definitely the country's most lacustrine area. Southern Chile stretches from below the Río Bío-Bío at about 38° south latitude to below Isla de Chiloé at about 43.4° south latitude. In this lake district of Chile, the valley between the Andes and the coastal range is closer to sea level, and the hundreds of rivers that descend from the Andes form lakes, some quite large, as they reach the lower elevations. They drain into the ocean through other rivers, some of which (principally the Río Calle Calle, which flows by the city of Valdivia) are the only ones in the whole country that are navigable for any stretch. The Central Valley's southernmost portion is submerged in the ocean and forms the Golfo de Ancud. Isla de Chiloé, with its rolling hills, is the last important elevation of the coastal range of mountains.

The south is one of the rainiest areas in the world. One of the wettest spots in the region is Valdivia, with an annual rainfall of

Volcán Osorno, Chile's most perfectly shaped volcano, overlooking nearby
Lago Llanquihue, and a Lutheran church, representative of the
strong German influence in the region
Courtesy Ramón Miró
A lake near Coihaique in southern Chile
Courtesy Inter-American Development Bank

2,535.4 millimeters. The summer months of January and February are the driest, with a monthly average precipitation of sixty-seven millimeters. The winter months of June and July each produce on average a deluge of 410.6 millimeters. Temperatures in the area are moderate. In Valdivia the two summer months average 16.7°C, whereas the winter months average 7.9°C.

The lakes in this region are remarkably beautiful. The snow-covered Andes form a constant backdrop to vistas of clear blue or even turquoise waters, as at Lago Todos los Santos. The rivers that descend from the Andes rush over volcanic rocks, forming numerous white-water sections and waterfalls. The vegetation, including many ferns in the shady areas, is a lush green. Some sections still consist of old-growth forests, and in all seasons, but especially in the spring and summer, there are plenty of wildflowers and flowering trees. The pastures in the northernmost section, around Osorno, are well suited for raising cattle; milk, cheese, and butter are important products of that area. All kinds of berries grow in the area, some of which are exported, and freshwater farming of various species of trout and salmon has developed, with cultivators taking advantage of the abundant supply of clear running water. The lumber industry is also important. A number of tourists, mainly Chileans and Argentines, visit the area during the summer.

Many of Chile's distinctive animal species have been decimated as they have been pushed farther and farther into the remaining wilderness areas by human occupation of the land. This is the case with the *huemul*, a large deer, and the Chilean condor, the largest bird of its kind; both animals are on the national coat of arms. The remaining Chilean pumas, which are bigger than their California cousins, have been driven to isolated national parks in the south by farmers who continue to hunt them because they occasionally kill sheep and goats.

The Far South

In the far south (Chile Austral), which extends from between 43°south latitude and 44°south latitude to Cape Horn, the Andes and the South Pacific meet. The continental coastline features numerous inlets and fjords, from which the mountains seem to rise straight up to great elevations; this is, for example, the case with the Cerro Macá (2,960 meters) near Puerto Aisén. The rest of the land consists of literally thousands of islands forming numerous archipelagos interwoven with sometimes-narrow channels, which provide the main routes of navigation.

In the northern part of the far south, there is still plenty of rainfall. For instance, Puerto Aisén, at 45°24' south latitude, receives

2,973.3 millimeters of rain per year. However, unlike in Valdivia, the rain falls more or less evenly throughout the year in Puerto Aisén. The summer months average 206.1 millimeters, whereas the winter months average 300 millimeters. The temperatures at sea level in Puerto Aisén average 13.6°C in the summer months and 4.7°C in the winter months. Although the area generally is chilly and wet, the combination of channels, fjords, snowcapped mountains, and islands of all shapes and sizes within such a narrow space makes for breathtaking views. The area is still heavily forested, although some of the native species of trees that grow in the central and southern parts of the country have given way to others better adapted to a generally colder climate.

The southern part of the far south includes the city of Punta Arenas, which, with about 125,000 inhabitants, is the southernmost city of any appreciable size in the world. It receives much less precipitation; its annual total is only 438.5 millimeters, or a little more than what Valdivia receives in the month of June alone. This precipitation is distributed more or less evenly throughout the year, with the two main summer months receiving a monthly average of thirty-one millimeters and the winter months 38.9 millimeters, some of it in the form of snow. Temperatures are colder than in the rest of the country. The summer months average 11.1°C, and the winter months average 2.5°C. The virtually constant wind from the South Pacific Ocean makes the air feel much colder.

The far south contains large expanses of pastures that are best suited for raising sheep. The area's other main economic activity is oil and natural gas extraction from the areas around the Strait of Magellan. This strait is one of the world's important sea-lanes because it unites the Atlantic and Pacific oceans through a channel that avoids the rough open waters off Cape Horn. The channel is perilous, however, and Chilean pilots guide all vessels through it.

The People

Formation of the Chilean People

To a traveler arriving in Santiago from Lima, Chileans will in general seem more Latin European-looking than Peruvians. By contrast, to a visitor arriving from Buenos Aires, certain native American features will seem apparent in large numbers of Chileans in contrast to Argentines. These differing perspectives can be explained by tracing the distinctive historical roots of the Chilean people.

The Cuernos del Paine (Paine Horns) and Lago Pehoe in Torres del Paine
(Paine Towers) National Park, Chilean Patagonia
Courtesy Ramón Miró and Laura Mullahy

The Spaniards who settled in the pleasant Central Valley of what is now Chile beginning in the late sixteenth century found no rich lodes of gold or silver to exploit, and therefore saw no need for employing masses of indigenous forced laborers such as those who were put to work in the Andean highlands and in the mines of Mexico. Although copper mining became an important part of the late colonial economy, even the most successful of operations employed no more than a few salaried workers. Settlers took to developing the agricultural potential of the land, which, given Chile's climate, was well suited for growing the crops they knew from the Old World. This seasonal form of farming was different from that practiced in semitropical plantations in that it required few workers except during the harvest. As a result, the Spanish settlers in Chile did not seek to force large numbers of native Americans to toil for them, and they had little use for slaves. Relatively few enslaved Africans were brought into Chile, and slavery was abolished soon after the country gained its independence from Spain in 1818.

The Spaniards encountered fierce resistance to their occupation efforts from one of the main indigenous groups, the Araucanians, who lived in the south-central part of the country. The settlers managed to take control of the land down to the Río Bío-Bío and to establish strongholds farther south, but throughout the colonial period the area that is now Chile consisted of two distinct nations: one a poor outpost of the Spanish Empire and the other an independent territory, Arauco, occupied by the Araucanians, whose territory consisted of most of south-central Chile between the Río Bío-Bío and the coastal areas around Temuco. By the end of the colonial period, the Araucanian territories had been reduced, but they had not been fully incorporated into Spanish rule. The indigenous wars lasted for more than three centuries, with a final skirmish in 1882.

Although warfare and the diseases brought by the Spaniards decimated the native population, Spain found it necessary to keep sending soldiers to protect its distant colony. They came from all regions of Spain, including the Basque country, and many of them ended up settling in Chile. The combination of an economy based on temperate-zone agriculture, native American resistance to Spanish occupation, and a continuous influx of Spaniards from the mid-sixteenth century to the end of the colonial period defined the main body of the Chilean population—a mixture of native American and Spanish blood, but one in which the Spanish element is greater than in the other Andean mestizo populations.

During the nineteenth century, the newly independent government sought to stimulate European immigration. Beginning in

1845, it had some success in attracting primarily German migrants to the Chilean south, principally to the lake district. For this reason, that area of the country still shows a German influence in its architecture and cuisine, and German (peppered with archaic expressions and intonations) is still spoken by some descendants of these migrants. People from England and Scotland also came to Chile, and some established export-import businesses of the kind that the Spanish crown previously had kept at bay. Other European immigrants, especially northern Italians, French, Swiss, and Croats, came at the end of the nineteenth century. More Spaniards and Italians, East European Jews, and mainly Christian Lebanese, Palestinians, and Syrians came in the decades before World War II. Many of these immigrants became prominent entrepreneurs or professionals, but their numbers never exceeded 10 percent of the total population at any given time. Thus, in contrast to Argentina, whose population was transformed around the turn of the century by numerous European immigrants, especially Italians, the Chilean population continued to be defined by the original Spanish and native American mixture. Acculturation was fairly rapid for all immigrant groups. Because second-generation residents saw themselves primarily as Chileans, ethnic identities had little impact on national society.

Chileans of all color gradations between the fair northern European and the darker native American complexion can be found, although most have brown hair or dark brown hair and brown eyes. There have been no really salient racial distinctions affecting daily life and politics in Chile, but there is unquestionably a strong correlation between high socioeconomic status and light skin.

The social definition of who is a native has not depended so much on phenotypical characteristics as on cultural ones. This means that Chileans generally have considered someone to be a native only if, in addition to native American features, he or she has an indigenous last name, wears native clothing, speaks a native language, or resides in a native community. Consequently, the native Americans who wish to assimilate fully into Chilean society often take Spanish surnames after moving off reservations.

The term Mapuche ("people of the land") now encompasses most of the native Chilean groups. The number of Mapuche residing on the reservations that were set up beginning in the late 1880s has declined in recent years. About 300,000 were counted as living on the reservations by the 1982 census. The 1992 census asked respondents to identify themselves ethnically as Mapuche, Aymara (the native population of northern Chile whose main trunk lies in Bolivia), Rapa Nui (the Polynesian group that lives in or originates from Easter Island), and other. The results showed that 9.6 percent of the population over age fourteen self-identified as Mapuche, 0.5 percent as Aymara, and less than 0.25 percent as Rapa Nui (see table 2, Appendix). This means that about 1.3 million Chileans are native Americans, mainly Mapuche, or the descendants of one of the fourteen or so different tribal groups that occupied what is now Chile before the Spanish conquest.

Although indigenous culture was most strongly retained on the reservations, penetration by Chilean national culture was also extensive. For example, research on a sample of Mapuche living on four reservations in the south showed that only 8.5 percent of them were monolingual Mapuche (sometimes called Mapudungu) speakers; 50.7 percent lived in homes where both Spanish and Mapuche were spoken, and 40.8 percent lived in homes where only Spanish was spoken. This situation was largely a result of the extension of primary rural education. Of all Mapuche over fifteen years of age living on the same reservations that were studied, 81 percent had gone to school for at least one year (85.5 percent of the men and 76.2 percent of the women). Significant differences in schooling by age among the Mapuche reveal how wide the reach of rural education has been in recent years. In the sampled reservation communities, the literacy rate was 81.2 percent for all residents over five years of age, and yet the rate was more than 96.2 percent for the age-group between ages ten and thirty-four. The acquisition of language and literacy skills is, of course, a principal means of acculturation.

With the partial exception of the indigenous groups, the Chilean population perceives itself as essentially homogeneous. Despite the configuration of the national territory, regional differences and sentiments are remarkably muted. Even the Spanish accent of Chileans varies only very slightly from north to south; more noticeable are the small differences in accent based on social class or whether one lives in the city or the country. The fact that the Chilean population essentially was formed in a relatively small section of the center of the country and then migrated in modest numbers to the north and south helps explain this relative lack of differentiation, which is now maintained by the national reach of radio and especially of television. The media diffuse and homogenize colloquial expressions.

Current Demographic Profile

A new decennial census was taken in 1992. Some of its data were already available officially as of this writing, but other data were still in the process of being tabulated. The total population was officially given as 13,348,401, of whom 6,553,254 were males and 6,795,147 were females (see table 3, Appendix). According to the data, the average population density in 1992 remained 17.6 inhabitants per square kilometer. Population density varied greatly, however, from the sparsely populated far north and far south to the much more densely inhabited central Chile (see table 4, Appendix). In 1993 the figure rose to eighteen inhabitants per square kilometer. The new total population figure shows that the growth of the population in the ten years between the 1982 and the 1992 censuses was about 1.7 percent per annum.

The National Statistics Institute (Instituto Nacional de Estadísticas—INE) estimated the birthrate in 1991 at 22.4 per 1,000 population, an increase over 1985, when the rate stood at 21.6 per 1,000. This has led to a corresponding widening of the base of the age pyramid of the population, which had narrowed significantly with the decline in the birthrate that began in the mid- to late 1960s (see fig. 6). The current increase in the birthrate is a slight demographic echo of the birth control programs that began in the mid-1960s. These programs reduced the fertility of women of childbearing age, causing the original drop in the birthrate, whereas the rise in the early 1990s resulted from children born to new generations of women who had reached the childbearing period of their lives. Whereas women of childbearing age (fourteen to forty-nine years) had had an average of 4.09 children in 1967, by 1992 this average had dropped to 2.39.

With the declining birthrate and no significant increase in immigration, much of the growth in the Chilean population over the 1970s and 1980s resulted from a decline in mortality. The mortality rate in 1992 was estimated at 5.6 per 1,000 population, whereas in 1960 it had been more than twice that, at 12.5 per 1,000. In 1990 life expectancy at birth was estimated at 71.0 years (sixty-eight for men and seventy-five for women), up from the 1960 figure of 57.1 years (57.6 for men and 63.7 for women). These improvements resulted in part from better health care beyond the first year of life, but they are explained primarily by a dramatic decline in infant mortality during the 1960–90 period. In 1960 infant mortality was 119.5 per 1,000 live births, and by 1991 it had declined to 14.6 per 1,000. This latter rate, one of the lowest in Latin America, indicated the success of the various health programs for expectant mothers and infants implemented since the late 1960s. In the early 1990s, the Chilean population was older than it had been in the 1960s. The 1982 census revealed for the first time ever that the population included a majority of adults over twenty-one years of age. Yet it was still a very young population: 49 percent of

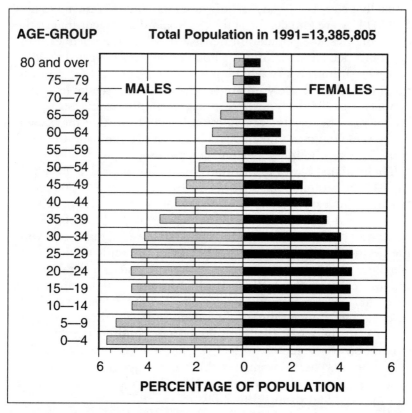

AGE-GROUP   Total Population in 1991=13,385,805

Source: Based on information from Chile, Instituto Nacional de Estadísticas, *Compendio estadístico, 1991*, Santiago, 1991, 12.

Figure 6. Estimated Population by Age and Gender, 1991

Chileans were estimated in 1991 to be less than twenty-four years of age.

Urban Areas

Since the 1930s, the majority of Chileans have lived in urban areas (defined as agglomerations of more than 2,000 inhabitants). This reflects a demographic trend of migration from rural areas that began early, according to developing world and Latin American standards. The urban population was estimated to be 86 percent of the total in 1991. A perhaps better indicator of the degree of urbanization of a country is the extent to which the population lives in agglomerations of more than 20,000. According to the 1982 census, there were fifty-one cities and towns in Chile with more than 20,000 inhabitants, and their combined population represented 65.6

percent of the total. This percentage shows that Chile is very definitely an urban country. There has continued to be a significant internal migration of the population, although mostly from one urban center to another. The 1982 census showed that a significant 8.6 percent of the population had moved to the province of current residence during the previous five years.

Central Chile is the site of the oldest urban centers, many of which were founded by the Spanish in the mid-sixteenth century. Most of the older cities are next to rivers in areas of rich soil. Santiago, founded in 1541, is typical of this pattern of settlement in a prime agricultural area. Little did its founders know that city streets and houses would occupy so much of the Santiago Valley's fertile soil in the twentieth century. Santiago was designated from its founding as the capital city of the new colony, and it has been the seat of the Chilean government ever since. Other cities, such as Valparaíso, founded in 1536, served as ports. The city of Concepción—founded in 1550 in what is now Penco and moved a bit inland to its present location in 1754—served as the center of a wheat-growing area, as a port for the southern part of the Central Valley, and as a military base on the Araucanian frontier.

Despite being continually populated for more than four centuries, Chilean cities have—unlike Lima or Cartagena, for instance—few architectural monuments from the past. This is explained in part by the poverty of the country in colonial times but also by the devastating action of the frequent earthquakes. Following the usual Spanish colonial practice, Chilean cities were planned with a central plaza surrounded by a grid of streets forming square blocks. The plazas invariably were the site of both municipal or regional government buildings and churches.

Communications between urban centers were facilitated during the colonial period by the relative proximity to the ocean of even the most Andean of locations. Except for cities in the Central Valley, between Santiago and Chillán, ocean transportation and shipping were vital to the north-south movement of people and goods until the building of railroads from the second half of the nineteenth century until the first decades of the twentieth century. Even then, the railroads only served the central and southern parts of the country to Puerto Montt, leaving sea-lanes as the main links to the extreme north and south.

The most significant feature of the development of urban centers in Chile has been the imbalance represented by the growth of Santiago, which has far exceeded that of other cities. According to the 1992 census figures, the Metropolitan Region of Santiago had about 5,170,300 inhabitants, a total equal to about 39 percent of the

Chilean population. In 1865, with a population of about 115,400, Santiago was the residence of only 6.3 percent of the nation's inhabitants. From about 1885 onward, the capital city grew at a rate between about 30 percent and 50 percent every ten to twelve years (see table 5, Appendix). The 1992 census figure showed a slight moderation of this pace, which was, nonetheless, at 3.3 percent per year significantly higher than the average national population increase.

Santiago's population growth occurred mainly as a result of migration from rural areas and provincial urban centers. Almost 30 percent of the population of the capital in 1970 had been born in areas of Chile other than Santiago, a percentage that has probably not changed much since. The only other areas of the country that have greatly increased their population in recent years are the extreme south and the extreme north. This growth has resulted from internal migration prompted by economic expansion associated with fishing and mining. However, given the much smaller populations in those areas to begin with, the fact that between 30 percent and 40 percent of their inhabitants were born elsewhere does not signify much in terms of the absolute numbers of people migrating.

Santiago is not only the seat of the national government (except for the National Congress, hereafter Congress, now located in Valparaíso) but also the nation's main financial and commercial center, the most important location for educational, cultural, and scientific institutions, and the leading city for manufacturing in terms of the total volume of production. Although sprawling Santiago has continued to absorb formerly prime agricultural areas, there are sections of town where wineries still cultivate grapes.

Historically, Santiago has been the main area of residence for the nation's wealthiest citizens, even for those with property elsewhere in the country. Unlike other Chilean cities, Santiago has always had an extensive upper- and upper-middle-class residential area. Originally near the main plaza in the center of town, this area developed toward the south and west at the end of the nineteenth century and the beginning of the twentieth century. Although neighborhoods in these areas retain some samples of the architecture of that period, by the 1990s they were occupied mainly by lower-middle-class residents. Beginning in the 1930s, Santiago's upper-class residents moved east of the center of town, toward the Andes. This transition was accompanied by an increase in the commercial use of downtown as larger and larger buildings were constructed and the public transportation system was enhanced. As use of the automobile became more common, the upper-class and upper-middle-class residential areas expanded farther up

A view from San Cristóbal Hill, Santiago
Courtesy Embassy of Chile, Washington
Children returning from school in the town of Cochamó, located
on the Seno Reloncaví in southern Chile
Courtesy Inter-American Development Bank

the foothills of the Andes. This process of suburbanization, complete with shopping malls and supermarkets with large parking lots, also has led to the development of new and faster roads to the center of the city and to the principal airport. New bus lines also were established to serve the suburbs. All of this has increased motor-vehicle traffic in the Santiago Valley, whose surrounding mountains trap particulate matter, generating levels of air pollution that are among the worst in the world. In the early 1990s, emergency restrictions on the use of motor vehicles became a routine feature of the city's life during all but the summer months, when there is more wind and the thermal inversion that traps the dirty air in the colder months no longer prevents its venting.

The large number of people migrating to Santiago and, to a lesser extent, to other major cities has led to a severe shortage of housing, especially of affordable housing for low-income people. Estimates in 1990 were that the nation as a whole needed a million more housing units to accommodate all those living in crowded conditions with relatives or friends, those with housing in poor condition, or those living in emergency housing. Since the 1960s, extensive portions of the Santiago area, especially to the south, east, and north of the center have been occupied by people who built precarious makeshift housing on lots that were often used illegally. As these areas aged, the municipal authorities extended city services to them and tried to redesign, where need be, their haphazard layout. Moreover, many people—about 28,000 between 1979 and 1984— were moved out of illegal settlements by the authorities and into low-income housing. The result was a further expansion of urbanization and an increase in the distances that people had to travel to work, look for work, or attend school. Nonetheless, by 1990 virtually all of the poorer areas of Santiago had access to electricity, running water, refuse collection, and sewerage. In fact, the country's urban population as a whole had good access to city services. By 1987, 98 percent of the population in towns and cities had running water (the great majority in their homes), 98 percent had garbage collection, and 79 percent had sewer connections.

The segregation within Chilean cities by income level has made residential areas very different from one another. In Santiago, where the differences are more sharply drawn than elsewhere, some neighborhoods are worlds apart. The upper-class areas in the eastern foothills of the Andes offer comfortable houses with neat, fenced-in gardens, or spacious apartments in sometimes attractively designed buildings, all on tree-lined streets. Restaurants, supermarkets, shopping malls, boutiques, bookstores, cinemas, and theaters add to the appeal of what is a very comfortable urban life. The area is well connected by public transportation, including the major east-west line of an excellent subway and its feeder buses. The best hospitals and clinics are within easy reach, as are the best private schools.

The poor areas of the city are not as well served. There are few supermarkets, and the usually poorly stocked corner groceries often sell their goods at higher prices. Some streets are not paved, and this, together with the lack of grass cover in the open spaces, creates dusty conditions during much of the year. Trees have been planted extensively in Santiago's poorer areas since the 1960s, but many streets are still devoid of them. Getting to the city center and to clinics and hospitals is more difficult for residents of the poorer areas. However, access to preprimary schooling and to sport facilities, especially to soccer fields, has expanded significantly since the early 1970s. Except for some very plain-looking buildings with apartments for low-income families, most housing consists of one floor. The poorest houses are made of a variety of materials, including pine boards and cardboard. Houses are generally built with brick and poured-concrete braces, and most poor people eventually try to build with such materials as well. As communities begun by land-squatters have become more settled, it has been possible to see the gradual transformation of squatter construction.

Chilean cities commonly contain relatively large housing developments (*poblaciones*), including multifamily units, single-family units, or a combination of the two. Many of these developments were constructed with loans made available to enterprises, pension funds, or savings and loan associations by the state for their employees or affiliates, usually at subsidized rates (especially before the military government). Consequently, they are often occupied by people who have the same place of employment or who belong to a specific occupational category. Such housing would not be available as easily to large numbers of people were it not for the special financial arrangements worked out for the group. Transportation to and from work is often arranged by employers. One unintended consequence of this pattern of urbanization is that it contributes to the overall segregation of housing in Chile by income level or occupation.

However, in part because of this pattern, Chile has a large proportion of homeowners. About 60 percent of housing units are owned by their occupants. As the housing developments age and many of the original occupants sell their houses and move elsewhere, the developments become more socially heterogeneous. People also begin to modify and remodel their houses; and new corner groceries, hairstyling salons, tailor shops, schools, churches, and other establishments emerge, giving the developments a more settled, urban look.

Because of a lack of jobs in the formal economy, many people need to make a living selling odds and ends on the streets. These people have not been counted as unemployed in official statistics because they are engaged in income-producing activities. During the military regime, the authorities attempted to organize this form of commerce by licensing stalls on the sidewalks of designated streets and by prohibiting sales elsewhere. However, there was greater demand for such stalls than there were available spaces, and they could not be erected in the most important commercial streets. Hence, many people defied the regulations and attempted to sell their goods where these activities were prohibited, risking confiscation of their wares by the police. The Aylwin government continued the policy in slightly modified form.

Rural Areas

Although mining, banking, and industry have been the source of the greatest Chilean fortunes since the early nineteenth century, rural society has occupied a much more central place in the nation's history. Until the 1930s, most of the population lived in rural areas, and most upper-class families, whatever the origin of their wealth, owned rural land.

Until recently, large landholdings (latifundios—see Glossary) were a characteristic feature of rural society. The *latifundia* pattern of landownership originated in the Spanish crown's early colonial practice of giving land grants, some of them huge, to soldiers involved in the conquest and to the Roman Catholic Church. By the late eighteenth century, the most important lands of the Central Valley were held in large haciendas by families with noble titles that were all inherited by the elder son under the *mayorazgo* (see Glossary) system. All such titles were abolished with Chile's adoption of a republican form of government after independence, and new laws of inheritance eventually ended the practice of primogeniture. This led to the creation of a market for rural properties and to their division as they were inherited by family members. However, by the mid-twentieth century land transfers and divisions still had not put an end to ownership of large properties.

The typical large landholding was a complex minisociety. Some of its laborers lived on the estate year-round, and they or their family members worked as needed in exchange for the right to cultivate a portion of the land for themselves and to graze their animals in specified fields. Among the rural poor, their families enjoyed better living conditions. Other workers, a majority in times of strong demand for labor, especially during the harvest, lived in rural towns and villages or on small properties they held independently (whether legally or not) at the edges of the large farms. These holdings were usually insufficient to maintain a family adequately, and its members therefore would seek employment in the large rural enterprises. When needed, other rural workers were recruited from among migrants who would come during the summer from other parts of the country. The large rural enterprises included stores where people could buy a variety of goods, chapels where priests would say mass, and dispensaries for primary medical attention. In addition to the sometimes ornate houses of the proprietors, which generally were occupied only during the summer months, there were houses for the administrators, mechanics, accountants, enologists (if wine was produced), blacksmiths, and others who constituted the professional and skilled labor forces of the enterprise.

Beginning in the 1950s, the large rural properties became the target of heightened criticism by reformist politicians and economists. They noted that the uneven distribution of land contributed to social inequality and that the large landholdings were highly inefficient agricultural producers. During the governments of presidents Eduardo Frei Montalva (1964–70), who established a reformed sector (see Glossary), and Salvador Allende Gossens (1970–73), an extensive land reform program was carried out. It basically did away with the large rural properties on prime agricultural (nonforested) lands. Thus, whereas in 1965 fully 55 percent of all agricultural lands (measured as basic irrigated hectares—BIH) were held in 4,876 properties of more than eighty hectares each, by 1973 there were only 260 such properties left, covering only 2.7 percent of all BIH. The expropriations covered 40 percent of all the nation's BIH.

The military government put an end to the agrarian reform program, as well as to the technical assistance given to the beneficiaries of the expropriations. It also returned to previous owners some of the land that had not yet been formally transferred. In addition, it distributed individual titles among residents of the peasant communities sponsored by the Allende government's agrarian reform program. Moreover, the military government permitted the sale of any rural property, including the small family farms created by the agrarian reform. This policy led to new changes in land tenancy, which did not, however, reconstitute the large landholdings to the same extent as before the agrarian reform. Instead, it favored an expansion of medium-sized holdings. After all the changes, very small holdings of fewer than five hectares still accounted for about 10 percent of the agricultural area. The largest holdings, of more than eighty hectares, were far from restored to their prior importance, at only 18 percent of the total area. If a primary purpose of the agrarian reform was to create a better distribution of the agricultural land, after much turmoil and change the data indicate that this had been achieved (see table 6, Appendix).

The remarkable transformations in land tenancy that started in the mid-1960s were accompanied by other great changes in agriculture. These led to much more intensive land use, with the accelerated incorporation of modern technologies. Labor-service tenancy and share-cropping arrangements as a source of agricultural labor have disappeared from commercial farming, replaced by wage-earning workers living mainly in towns or small rural properties. The number of self-employed workers in agriculture has also increased with the land tenancy changes.

The rural network of mainly dirt roads was expanded to permit access to new farms and logging areas. Concurrently, small-town entrepreneurs were quick to respond to new opportunities by establishing bus routes along these expanded roads, thereby facilitating the rural population's access to schools and sources of employment. By the 1980s, the peasantry was for the first time overwhelmingly literate, with attendance at primary schools by its children virtually universal (see Education, this ch.).

The Labor Force and Income Levels

With a lower rate of population growth, Chile's working-age population, which includes all those individuals more than fifteen and less than sixty-five years of age, represented 64 percent of the total population in 1992 (see table 7, Appendix). The labor force participation rate, or the ratio of those in the labor force over the working-age population, was 59 percent in August 1993; of the total population, 37 percent were employed or were seeking a job. Participation rates typically differ by age and gender. The young participate in smaller proportions and join the labor force as they leave the education system. Women have traditionally participated at lower rates also. The participation rate for men was estimated at 76 percent and that for women at 32 percent in 1992. These figures had increased since the early 1980s because of the relative aging of the overall population and a proportionately greater entry of women into the labor force. In the 1980–85 period, 74 percent of men and 26 percent of women over fifteen years of age had been active in the work force.

The rate of unemployment declined steadily throughout the 1987–91 period. The overall rate of growth in employment for the 1987–91 period was 3 percent per year. The rate was higher from 1987 to 1989 (5 percent), the period of fast recovery after the economic crisis of 1982–83. The most dynamic sectors during the 1987–89 period were construction and manufacturing, with average rates of employment growth of 20 percent and 11 percent per year, respectively. Employment creation increased by 5 percent again in 1992, and by the end of the year unemployment stood at 4.4 percent. A greater than expected increase in the size of the labor force, mainly from women seeking employment, led to a slight increase in unemployment to 4.9 percent by late 1993.

The largest single component of the Chilean employment structure in 1991 was services, which include health workers, teachers, and government and domestic employees (see fig. 7; table 8, Appendix). Next was trade and financial services, including the real estate, banking, and insurance industries. Together with transportation and communications, these categories of the services sector of the economy employed 55.6 percent of the labor force. The most important of the productive activities in terms of employment was agriculture, forestry, and fishing, which employed 19.2 percent of the labor force. If mining is included, this means that 21.5 percent of the labor force was employed in what is typically considered the economy's primary sector. The manufacturing sector employed 16 percent of the labor force, roughly the same percentage as in the mid-1960s; manufacturing's share had declined to about 12 percent during the economic crisis of 1982–83. Employment in what is often considered the secondary sector of the economy amounted to 23 percent, if the percentages engaged in construction and in electricity, gas, and water are added to that in manufacturing.

In 1991 incomes had also almost recovered, for the first time in twenty years, to their 1970 average levels (see table 9, Appendix). During 1990 and the first months of 1991, workers' wages increased more rapidly than the national average wage. This probably resulted in some measure from the return to democracy that had enabled workers to exercise their rights more freely and from labor market conditions closer to full employment. Real incomes continued to rise during 1992 and 1993, reaching levels that surpassed the previous, but then unsustainable, peak established in 1971.

Nonetheless, the monthly wages of Chileans are, when expressed in dollars, much lower than incomes in the United States (see table 10, Appendix). According to these figures, which probably understate high incomes and overstate lower ones, an unskilled worker makes less than one-tenth the amount an executive or an administrator-director makes. The purchasing power of these incomes for daily necessities is, however, higher than their dollar-denominated equivalents suggest.

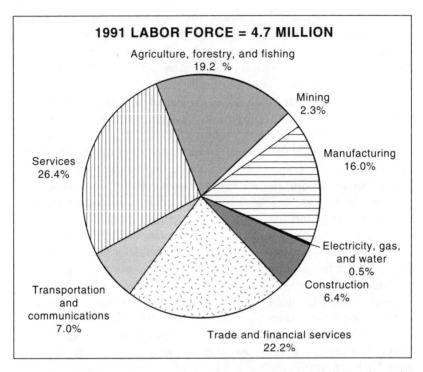

1991 LABOR FORCE = 4.7 MILLION

Agriculture, forestry, and fishing
19.2 %

Mining
2.3%

Manufacturing
16.0%

Services
26.4%

Electricity, gas,
and water
0.5%

Construction
6.4%

Transportation
and
communications
7.0%

Trade and financial services
22.2%

Source: Based on information from Chile, Instituto Nacional de Estadísticas, *Compendio estadístico, 1991*, Santiago, 1991, Table 141-02.

Figure 7. Employment by Sector, 1991

During the military government, unemployment rose well above its historical levels for the Chilean economy. There were two distinct shocks to the labor market. The first one took place around 1975 and can be related to the recessionary conditions created by anti-inflationary policies and to employment reduction in the public sector. The adjustment that followed was very slow. The second shock took place with the financial and economic crisis of 1982–83 and affected private-sector employment. From 1979 to 1981, the economy had entered into a recovery increasingly oriented toward production of nontradable goods, a pattern that was not sustainable given the speed at which international debt was being accumulated. In response to the devaluation of the Chilean peso (see Glossary) in 1982 and the macroeconomic management that followed, the economy shifted gears and reoriented production to tradable goods and services. In 1982 the unemployment rate for the country climbed to 19.4 percent, or 26.4 percent if those participating in state-financed makeshift work programs are included. Yet the adjustment that followed took place at a faster pace. By 1986 the unemployment rate totaled 13.9 percent. Chile's unemployment rate returned in the early 1990s to levels that characterized the country in the 1960s (see table 11, Appendix).

The distribution of personal income is quite regressive in Chile in general and Santiago in particular, a tendency that became more pronounced during the military government (see table 12, Appendix). The data reveal that personal income in Santiago is strongly concentrated in the highest decile, which enjoys about 40 percent of the total income. They also show that despite the great changes in the Chilean economy during this period, the distribution of personal income remains rather stable, even though a somewhat greater concentration can be seen in 1989 than in previous years. The policies on income and taxes of the Aylwin government helped to slightly reverse this trend (see Future Challenges of Democratic Consolidation, ch. 4).

The distribution of consumption by household in Santiago showed a strong tendency toward the concentration of expenditures in the higher-income groups during the military government. The figures for the first two years of the Aylwin government show a small change in direction toward a more equitable distribution of consumption, although it is still significantly more concentrated in the richest quintile than in 1969 (see table 13, Appendix). The data show that the richest quintile of households increased its consumption steadily from 1969 to 1989 but that it declined in 1990 and 1991. Moreover, by 1991 the bottom two quintiles had increased their share of consumption slightly at the expense of the fourth quintile. Hence, the distribution of household consumption was a bit more equal in 1991 than in 1988.

These results must be interpreted with caution. The distribution of household incomes is affected by the average number of income earners by household income levels, and in times of economic crisis the poorer segments may be forced to rely on the income of fewer household members. This apparently happened in Chile in 1983, when there were only 1.1 income earners in the poorest 20 percent of families; in the 30 percent of families with middle- to lower-middle incomes, there were 1.4 income earners; in the 30 percent of households in the middle- to high-income group, there were 1.7 income earners; and in the top 20 percent, there were two income earners per household. Because their incomes were also higher, the concentration of consumption in the high-income families was greater. Similarly, the expansion of secondary school enrollments during the 1980s benefited the children of poorer households, but it may have deprived them of the income derived from youth employment.

Social Organizations and Associations

Chileans have a remarkable facility for forming organizations and associations. This propensity perhaps has something to do with the fact that for more than three centuries both the Spanish-Chilean and the indigenous components of the country led a precarious life of conflict with each other, a situation that forced people to rely more than usual on collective organizing, especially, as was the case for both sides, given the weakness of the state. In contrast to North Americans, however, Chileans usually take a formal approach to creating organizations. In addition to electing a president, a treasurer, a secretary, and perhaps a few officers, they prefer to discuss and approve a statement of purpose and some statutes. This is a ritual even for organizations that need not register legally, obtaining what is called a "juridical personality" that will enable them to open bank accounts and to buy and sell properties. It is not known for certain where and how this formalism originated; it perhaps could be traced back to the densely legalistic approach adopted by Spain toward the governance of its faraway colonies and to the legalism of Roman Catholic canonical law, which applied to many aspects of society. Whatever grain of truth there is in these speculations, observers of Chilean society are rapidly struck by the density of its organizational life and the relatively high degree of continuity of its organizations and associations (see The Church, Business, Labor, and the Media, ch. 4).

In any Chilean community of appreciable size can be found sports clubs, mothers' clubs, neighborhood associations, parent centers linked to schools, church-related organizations, youth groups, and cultural clubs, as well as Masonic lodges and Rotary and Lions' clubs. Virtually all of the nation's fire fighters are volunteers, with the exception of members of a few fire departments in the largest cities. Government statistics greatly understate the number of community organizations because they refer mainly to those having some contact with one or another state office. According to the official estimate for 1991, there were about 22,000 such organizations, the main ones being sports clubs (6,939), neighborhood councils (6,289), mothers' clubs (4,243), and parent centers (1,362). Government publications do not report membership figures for these organizations.

Most of the important urban areas in Chile also include a broad sample of the local chapters of a wide variety of occupational associations. These include labor unions and federations, public

*The votive temple of Maipú,
also known as the Church
of Our Lady Carmen,
patroness of Chile
Courtesy David Shelton*

employee and health worker organizations, business and employers' associations, and professional societies of teachers, lawyers, doctors, engineers, dentists, nurses, social workers, and other occupational groups. Membership in labor unions, which declined significantly under the military government, has been growing rapidly since the late 1980s, a change directly related to the transition to democracy. Affiliation with organizations recognized as unions in labor legislation was officially estimated in 1990 at 606,800, a 20 percent increase over 1989. That figure did not include individuals affiliated with public employee associations (including health workers), who were estimated to number about 140,000, nor the members of the primary and secondary teachers' association, who numbered about 105,000. But these two groups usually have been closely tied to the labor movement through the national confederations of labor. Thus, about 19 percent of a total labor force of 4,459,600 was linked to unions or union-like associations in 1990. With the continuing increases in union affiliations, which are especially significant in rural areas, a conservative estimate is that the unionized population (in legal as well as de facto organizations) stood in 1992 at between 22 percent and 24 percent of the labor force. The most important union confederation, which encompasses the great majority of the nation's unions and union-like organizations, is the United Labor Confederation (Central Única de Trabajadores—CUT). CUT is the heir to a line of top labor

95

confederations that can be traced back through various reorganizations and name changes to at least 1936, and perhaps to 1917 (see Unions and Labor Conflicts, ch. 3; Labor, ch. 4).

There are numerous business and employer associations in Chile. Their total membership is about 190,000, although they collectively claim to speak for about 540,000 proprietors of businesses of all sizes. The most important business organization, the Business and Production Confederation (Confederación de la Producción y del Comercio—Coproco), encompasses some of the very oldest ongoing associations in Chile: the National Agricultural Association (Sociedad Nacional de Agricultura—SNA), founded in 1838, groups the most important agricultural enterprises; the Central Chamber of Commerce (Cámara Central de Comercio), founded in 1858, includes large wholesale and retail commercial enterprises; the National Association of Mining (Sociedad Nacional de Minería), founded in 1883, affiliates the main private mining companies; the Industrial Development Association (Sociedad de Fomento Fabril—Sofofa), founded in 1883, organizes the principal manufacturing industries; the Association of Banks and Financial Institutions (Asociación de Bancos e Instituciones Financieras), founded in 1943, is the main banking-industry group; and the Chilean Construction Board (Cámara Chilena de la Construcción), founded in 1951, organizes construction companies.

Another important confederation of business groups is the Council of Production, Transport, and Commerce (Consejo de Producción, Transporte y Comercio). In contrast to Coproco, this organization groups primarily medium-sized to small businesses, including many self-employed individuals who do not hire nonfamily members on a regular basis. Its main components are the 120,000-member Trade Union Confederation of Business Retailers and Small Industry of Chile (Confederación Gremial del Comercio Detallista y de la Pequeña Industria de Chile), founded in 1938, and the 24,000-member Confederation of Truck Owners of Chile (Confederación de Dueños de Camiones de Chile), founded in 1953.

Professional societies are also well established. The largest ones, aside from the teachers' organization noted previously, are those for lawyers (about 12,000 members), physicians (about 14,500), and engineers (about 11,500). Affiliation figures for most of the more than thirty professional societies were unavailable, but there are at least 100,000 members in such associations aside from teachers. If these figures are added to those for membership in business groups and unions, it appears that about a third of the labor force is involved in occupationally based associations.

The organized groups of Chilean society have long played an important role in the nation's political life. The elections in some of them—for example, in major labor federations, among university students, or in the principal professional societies—usually have been examined carefully for clues to the strength of the various national political parties. Most of the nation's university and professional institute students, totaling 153,100 in 1989, belong to student federations. The various associations also make their views known to state or congressional officials when issues of policy that affect them are debated.

Some associations traditionally have been identified with particular political parties. This was the case, to a greater or lesser extent, with Masons, fire fighters, and teachers' federations—the Radical Party (Partido Radical); union confederations—the parties of the left; employer associations—the parties of the right; and the Roman Catholic Church, as well as its related organizations—the Conservative Party (Partido Conservador), as well as, in recent decades, the Christian Democratic Party (Partido Demócrata Cristiano—PDC). Many of the most militant party members have also been active in social organizations. In addition, party headquarters in local communities often have served as meeting places for all kinds of activities. The Radical clubs of small towns in the central south are especially active, often sponsoring sports clubs as well as the formation of fire departments.

Chilean social life also has definite subcultures, with the main lines of cleavage being proximity to or distance from the Roman Catholic Church and social class. The schools that parents select for their children closely reflect these subcultural divisions. The latter are also strongly mirrored in associational life, as Chileans tend to channel their sports and leisure activities into organizations within their subculture. Schools, churches, and unions contribute to this pattern by being foci for such organizing. In addition, there are some clubs and centers related to specific ethnicities, such as Arab, Italian, or Spanish clubs, even though, as noted previously, such identities traditionally have been much less salient than religion and class. Occupational associations have been an important component of class and social status identities in Chilean society, with most of them affiliating people of like occupations regardless of their religious identities or preferences. Although this has helped diminish the significance of religiously based identities, the leadership divisions and conflicts within the nation's associations can often be traced back to those subcultural differences. People's political preferences follow the subcultural lines of cleavage as well in most cases.

Social organizations did not fare well under the military government. Those that were perceived to be linked, however loosely, to the parties of the left were subjected to sometimes severe repressive measures. This was particularly the case with labor unions, whose activities were suspended for more than six years. They were only permitted to reorganize under new legislation beginning in 1979. Moreover, most associations, including those of business groups, were hardly ever consulted on policy matters, and, in the absence of normal democratic channels for exerting influence, they found their opinions and petitions falling on deaf ears. Eventually, the most prominent social organizations joined in voicing their discontent with the military government through what was called the Assembly of Civility (Asamblea de la Civilidad), and their efforts contributed to the defeat of President Augusto Pinochet Ugarte (1973–90) in the 1988 plebiscite. The only organizations that thrived under the military government were the women's aid and mothers' clubs, which were supported by government largesse and headed at the national level by Pinochet's wife, Lucía Hiriart.

With the return to democracy, social organizations recovered the ability to pressure Congress and the national government. The new government opted for explicit solicitation of the opinions of important interest associations on some of the policies it was considering. It also fostered negotiations between top labor and business leaders over issues such as labor law reforms, minimum wage and pension levels, and overall wage increases for public employees. These negotiations led to several national agreements between state officials and business and labor leaders, thereby inaugurating a new form of top-level bargaining previously unknown in Chile.

Welfare Institutions and Social Programs

Twentieth-century Chile has had an extensive system of state-run welfare programs, including those in the social security, health, and education areas. From the mid-1970s to the early 1990s, spending on all these programs ranged from as little as 19 percent to as much as 26 percent of the gross domestic product (GDP—see Glossary), proportions that were similar to those spent in 1975 by countries belonging to the Organisation for Economic Co-operation and Development (OECD—see Glossary). In the same period, about two-thirds of the national labor force was covered by old-age pensions and other benefits. In addition, there was universal access to curative health care and programs of preventive care for all expectant mothers, infants, and children less than six years of age who did not have recourse to alternative health care. In addition, the state-run educational system, which was open to every child at primary and secondary levels but had admissions standards for higher education, was free of charge, except for nominal matriculation fees at all levels (see Education, this ch.). The state also offered low-income housing programs at heavily subsidized rates.

Spending for these various programs increasingly outpaced revenues, as the decline in the mortality rate enhanced the dependency ratio and as the programs expanded. In addition, there were numerous programs, especially in the social security area, that provided very unequal benefits. Consequently, the military government redesigned the most important welfare institutions in ways that were consistent with its market-driven ideology, and social spending was scaled down to about 17 percent of GDP by 1989.

By the end of its first year in office, the Aylwin government increased social spending by more than US$1.5 billion over the Pinochet government's budget. The revenue came from a 4 percent increase in the higher tax rate on enterprises, from 11 percent to 15 percent; a 2 percent hike in the national value-added tax (VAT—see Glossary) to 18 percent; and other sources. The objective of the Aylwin government was to enhance the purchasing power of minimum pensions, to increase the quality of educational and health services, and to provide greater assistance in the housing field. The new programs were intended to have a positive effect on the distribution of income. The military government's reforms had privatized or decentralized the administration of many welfare and social-assistance institutions. The Aylwin government did not reverse these privatizations, although it attempted to increase the quality and funding of the institutions that remained in the public sector. It also decided not to recentralize the administration of the public portions of welfare, educational, and social-assistance institutions that had been placed in the hands of local or regional governments. The Aylwin administration was committed to strengthening local and regional governments as part of a broad effort to enhance the decentralization of authority. However, in contrast to the military regime's decentralization projects that organized local and regional governments along lines of authoritarianism and corporatism (see Glossary), new constitutional and legal reforms adopted in 1992 introduced democracy to these levels of government.

Through the combination of many efforts in the social field since the 1930s, Chile has a relatively favorable overall human development index (HDI—see Glossary), as measured by the United Nations Development Programme (UNDP). The UNDP's *Human Development Report, 1993* shows Chile ranking thirty-sixth among the world's 160 countries for this indicator, eighth among all developing countries, and second only to Uruguay among all Spanish-speaking Latin American countries.

Social Security

Chile was one of the first countries in the Americas to establish state-sponsored social security coverage. In 1898 the government set up a retirement pension system for public employees. In 1924 the government approved a comprehensive set of labor laws and established a national social insurance system for workers. In large part, the authorities were responding to pressure exerted by the growing number of worker organizations and strikes. At the same time, a separate social-insurance system was set up for private white-collar employees, and the one for public employees was reorganized. The pension system for workers was known as the Workers' Security Fund (Caja del Seguro Obrero) and was modeled partly on the system pioneered by Otto von Bismarck, first chancellor of the German Empire (1871–90). The fund (*caja*) was established administratively as a semiautonomous state agency that received income from employer and worker contributions, as well as from state coffers. The systems for private and public employees provided higher benefits than the workers' *caja,* and they were financed in the same manner, except that the state acted as the employer for public employees as well. The armed forces had a separate pension system.

The Workers' Security Fund was reorganized in 1952, becoming the Social Insurance Service (Servicio de Seguro Social—SSS). Until its demise under the military government, the SSS served as the primary agency for the state-run social security system. SSS coverage expanded over the years. By the 1960s, in addition to providing old-age pensions to its main beneficiaries, it gave, at their death, pensions to their widows (but not their widowers) and to minor children, if any. It also paid flat monthly sums for each immediate family dependent, income payments for qualified illnesses and disabilities, and several months of unemployment insurance, albeit all at very low levels.

Although the fund originally was meant to meet the needs of miners and urban blue-collar and service workers, including domestics, over the years the number of occupational groups that participated in what became a system of different semiautonomous state funds increased greatly. By the early 1970s, there were thirty-five different pension funds (although three of them served 90 percent of contributors) and more than 150 social security regimes for the various occupational groups. This expansion led to many inequities because the newly incorporated groups demanded and obtained by law special treatments and new benefits that had been denied to original participants, even when these new groups' programs were added to existing funds. There was not even a standard retirement age for all groups. Funding for the various pension programs became extremely complex because the state's contributions were drawn by law from different tax bases. This pattern of growth of social security institutions is typical of countries in which the system is not conceived from the very beginning on a universal basis but rather is established for particular categories of employment. Because coverage continued to be conditioned on the employment history of the main beneficiary, it was never extended to all Chileans, even during its heyday in the early 1970s.

The military government initially hoped to rationalize what had become an unwieldy system, but eventually it changed the whole system. It decided not to continue with a basic organizational principle of most social security systems, the pay-as-you-go system, whereby benefits are paid out of funds collected from those who are still contributing. In addition, the government decided to privatize the organization and management of pension funds and to discontinue the state's own contributions to them. Thus, the military regime enacted the legal basis for the creation of privately run pension-fund companies, stipulating that all new workers entering the labor force had to establish their accounts in the new pension companies. Moreover, the government also created incentives for people in the semiautonomous, state-run system to transfer out of that system by reducing the proportion of each employee's paycheck that would be deducted under the new system to about 15 percent of gross income, instead of the prior 20 percent or 25 percent, and by permitting a transfer of funds based on the number of years individuals had paid into the system.

The new privately run pension funds are based on the notion of individual capitalization accounts. Pension amounts are set by how much there is in the individual account, which is determined by the total that has been contributed plus a proportional share of the pension fund's investments. In any event, by law no pension is allowed to fall below 70 percent of an individual's last monthly salary. If there are insufficient funds to generate the required pension levels in the account, the pension-fund company must make up the difference. If the company is unable to meet its obligations, the state, which guarantees the system, has to cover the shortfall.

Employees are allowed to choose the pension-fund company that will handle their account, and those who are self-employed may also elect to establish individual accounts. This choice is intended to stimulate competition among pension-fund companies in order to keep the administrative fees charged to account holders at a reasonable level, and to encourage the companies to invest the money they accumulate so as to generate the highest yields. Employers no longer contribute to employees' pensions under the new system. Disability and survival pensions are paid out of an account funded by a 3.8 percent share of the 15 percent the account holders contribute, leaving the remaining 11.2 percent to build up the pension-generating account. The 3.8 percent share is contracted out by the pension funds to life insurance companies, many of them newly created to meet the enormous increase in demand for their services. Individual account holders are also permitted to make payments in excess of the obligatory minimum. The retirement age is set at sixty-five years for men and sixty years for women, although individuals who accumulate enough funds to obtain a pension equal to 110 percent of the minimum pension may retire earlier.

The new system took effect in 1981, and the great majority of the contributing population opted to change to it. Deciding not to make substantial changes in the social security system, the Aylwin government increased the minimum pension paid by what remained of the state-run social security system by about 30 percent in real terms. By December 1990, there were about 3.7 million people, or 79 percent of the labor force, with accounts in fourteen pension-fund companies, called Pension Fund Administrators (Administradoras de Fondos de Pensiones—AFPs). A large proportion of the uncovered population consisted of self-employed people; only 3 percent of the total accounts came from that group. The funds gathered large sums of money relative to the size of the national economy. By the end of 1992, the pension and life insurance companies had accumulated an estimated US$15 billion. The state regulates and oversees the pension-fund companies through a newly created office that issues strict investment guidelines.

This radical departure from past institutional practices in the pension system is unique, and it drew considerable attention from experts in other Latin America countries also facing looming financial crises in their own social security systems. By generating large amounts of capital in the private sector, the new system energized the previously anemic Chilean capital markets. Because it has operated only for about a decade, however, it has yet to meet the test that will occur when the new pension funds have to pay out in benefits what would correspond to an actuarially normal load. Most of the nation's retirees and older workers have stayed in the state-run social security system, now called the Institute of Pension Fund Normalization (Instituto de Normalización Previsional—INP). By the end of 1990, the private pension companies were only paying out benefits to 2.3 percent of their affiliates (see Economic Results of the Pensions Privatization, ch. 3).

Health Programs

The state's efforts in the health field began in 1890 with the creation of an agency in charge of public hygiene and sanitation. Despite some subsequent initiatives to prevent and treat work-related accidents, it was not until 1924, with the establishment of the social security system, that the state assumed an active role in providing health care to the population. Between the mid-1920s and the early 1950s, state-run programs for health care were organized around the pension funds. During the 1940s, public health experts argued that the individual pension funds could not organize health delivery systems for their affiliates in a rational way. It was also argued that a system was needed that would provide more comprehensive coverage to the whole population, not only those who had accounts in the pension funds, if the country were to improve its overall health indexes. The eventual acceptance of these arguments by policy makers led in 1952 to the creation of the National Health Service (Servicio Nacional de Salud—SNS).

The SNS continued to provide care to all those who held accounts in the various funds, free of charge to workers and their families in the social security system and for a variable fee to others. In addition, it extended health care to the population at large regardless of ability to pay. Services to those who were poor could be slow and often inadequate if a condition was not life-threatening, but accidents and other emergencies normally were given immediate attention. Moreover, the SNS tried to identify specific health problems and focus on providing care in these areas, such as giving all women primary prenatal and postpartum care (and access since the 1960s to contraception), inoculating the population against certain diseases, and working to improve nutrition and hygiene through extension programs and publicity. It is estimated that 65 percent of the national population used the state-run system for curative medicine without paying fees. The SNS coexisted with private medical practices and hospitals, which were preferred by people who could afford them. The military developed its own system of clinics and hospitals. In the late 1960s, the government took the initiative to develop a new program for white-collar employees, permitting users to select their physicians. The program was funded by payroll deductions but required users to pay a fee equal to 50 percent of the cost of their care. The program developed its own primary- and preventive-care clinics and laboratories, although it relied on the hospitals of the SNS for backup care of the more serious cases and for hospitalizations. All but 15 percent of hospitalizations took place in SNS hospitals.

All physicians were obligated to work for the SNS for two years after graduation; they were usually sent to rural areas and small towns where there were chronic shortages of doctors. During the rest of their professional lives, physicians were also obligated to work a certain number of hours a week for the SNS, for which they received relatively small honoraria; in exchange, physicians took advantage of many of the facilities of the state system to treat and test their private patients.

By the early 1970s, the state-run health programs faced a financial crisis. Given that the SNS was intimately tied to the social security system, the military government could not change the latter without altering the former. Thus, in 1980 and 1981 policy makers redesigned the nation's health care institutions.

As a result, the Chilean health system in the early 1990s contained essentially five components. The first is the main successor of the SNS, now called the National System of Health Services (Sistema Nacional de Servicios de Salud—SNSS). In 1988 the SNSS employed about 62,000 professionals, including about 43 percent of the nation's 13,000 physicians, many fewer than had worked for the SNS because physicians no longer had any obligation to serve the public health system. The SNSS's administration was decentralized into twenty-seven regional units, and control over its clinics and primary-care centers was transferred to the nation's 340 municipal governments. However, the national government remained the main source of funding for these various units, and it continued to control their basic design, including staff size and equipment. The SNSS's funding comes from general state revenues and from a contribution of 7 percent of taxable income (up from the original 4 percent in 1981) from the employed population. Access to the SNSS is open to everyone, free of charge in the case of indigents and of those whose income falls below a certain level; a variable percentage of the cost up to 50 percent is paid by those with higher incomes.

The SNSS organizes and implements the broad public health programs in areas such as inoculations and maternal-infant care. It provides periodic preventive medical care to all children under six years of age not enrolled in alternative medical plans. Through this program, which has broad national coverage, low-income mothers can receive supplemental nutritional assistance for their children and for themselves as well if they are pregnant or nursing. As a result, the incidence of moderate to severe childhood malnutrition among those participating in the program has been reduced to negligible levels in Chile, while only about 8 percent of all children suffered mild malnutrition in 1989. The SNSS is the largest health care provider in the country. In the late 1980s, it served 8.2 million people, or about 64 percent of the total population, and its total expenditures on its participants in 1987 equaled about US$22 per person.

The second component of the health system is the National Health Fund (Fondo Nacional de Salud—Fonasa). Fonasa is part of the SNSS, except that those who register in the program may select their own primary-care physicians, as well as specialists. In this sense, Fonasa continues the modus operandi of the program initiated in the late 1960s for white-collar employees, except that anyone can register in it. Fonasa affiliates direct their payroll or self-employment contributions to the fund. Pensioners of the state-run system, the INP, may also choose to participate in Fonasa. The fund reimburses its users a variable portion of the cost of medical attention on presentation of vouchers for services that have been performed (an average 36 percent reimbursement in 1989). In 1987 Fonasa served 2.5 million people, and health expenditures in it amounted to US$79 per affiliate.

The Security Assistance Institutions (Mutuales de Seguridad— MS) constitute the third element in the health system. These consist of hospitals that deal primarily with treatment of the victims of work-related accidents. These institutions house some of the best trauma and burn centers in the country. The MS are financed out of employer contributions equivalent to about 2.5 percent of their total payrolls and completely cover the medical expenses of employees of the affiliated enterprises who are injured at work. In addition, the MS pay a temporary disability pension. The 1.96 million employees who have access to these institutions work for 52,000 different enterprises. This program is among the better funded, given that its income of US$123 million amounted to about US$62 per covered worker, while the rate of work-related accidents was only about 10.8 percent per year for all incidents, however minor. Safety experts hired by the MS system are also in charge of inspecting workplaces and suggesting improvements to prevent accidents. The MS are composed of numerous institutions administered by boards with employer and employee representatives. In 1987 they ran eight hospitals and nineteen clinics, mainly in Chile's most important urban centers. The product of initiatives taken by some of the country's largest employers in the late 1950s, the MS expanded greatly in the 1980s.

Private insurance companies that are affiliated with the Institute of Public Health and Preventive Medicine (Instituto de Salud y

Prevención—Isapre) constitute the fourth element in the health system. People enroll by asking their employers to direct their health deduction to these companies, and they pay an additional premium depending on the specific insurance policy. Medical services are reimbursed to users at a percentage of cost. In 1987 about 1.5 million people were enrolled in the Isapre, with expenditures of about US$166 per enrollee. Critics of the Isapre insurance companies note that the companies do not help mitigate the nation's highly regressive distribution of income because they channel the deductions of many people with higher incomes out of the SNSS. Moreover, as private carriers, the Isapre companies may deny enrollment to those who are at higher risk (as a result of serious illness or age), and they are prone to drop those who become excessive risks. Consequently, the SNSS must take up the burden of covering the health care of high-risk individuals.

The fifth component of the health care system is private medicine, which includes private hospitals and clinics. Most physicians, dentists, and ophthalmologists maintain a private practice even if they work for the SNSS or other systems. There are also private health insurers who do not form part of the Isapre structure because they do not collect their premiums from payroll deductions. In 1987 they insured 500,000 people drawn from the population with the highest incomes.

In 1992 Chilean health indicators were much closer to those of industrial nations than to those of the developing world (see table 14, Appendix). The four leading causes of death in Chile are circulatory diseases (27 percent), cancer (18 percent), accidents (13 percent), and respiratory illnesses (11 percent). Medical visits average about 3.5 per person per year, or about 2 to 2.5 for the general population and 1 to 1.5 for maternity and child check-ups. The SNSS handles 89.1 percent of all these visits (16.3 percent of them through Fonasa). Fully 98.4 percent of all births occur with professional assistance in hospitals or maternity clinics. In rural areas, where women might need to travel longer distances to give birth, they can spend the last ten to fifteen days of pregnancy in special hostels. Inoculations of infants and children are virtually universal for tuberculosis, diphtheria, pertussis, tetanus, poliomyelitis, and measles.

According to the Pan American Health Organization, the number of cases of acquired immune deficiency syndrome (AIDS) is gradually rising, with 3.8 per million population in 1987, 5.4 per million in 1988, 6.3 per million in 1989, 8.9 per million in 1990, and 11 per million in 1991. As of the end of 1991 in Chile, 196 individuals with AIDS in Chile had died. According to Health

Under Secretary Patricio Silva and the National AIDS Commission, of the 990 individuals who were registered as having been infected with the AIDS virus in the country, 630 had become sick and half of them had died by the end of 1992. The report stated that 93 percent of those diagnosed were men and 7 percent were women.

Although the government of President Patricio Aylwin did not make structural changes to the health system, it increased funding for the portions of the system that most benefited the poor, especially primary care services. The salaries of health workers in the public sector were increased. The government also enhanced the decentralization of authority in the public health sector by giving local and regional governments more decision-making power over the distribution and equipment of health-care resources and provisions within the limits of national government funding allotments.

Housing Policies

The state began its involvement in the construction of low-cost housing in 1906, with a law stipulating that builders of low-cost units would qualify for a complete exemption from all taxes and that their owners would be exempt from real estate taxes for twenty-five years. Subsequent housing programs in Chile have usually consisted of providing subsidies to those who built low-cost houses or to those who bought them. In addition, the programs have furnished one-time grants for the necessary down payments to permit people to obtain a loan or qualify for a housing program. Generally, all three features have been in place since the 1950s, although the emphasis on one or another means has shifted with changing governments. Subsidies to buyers have been channeled through below-market interest rates for long-term loans. These generally were made available through pension plans. Between 1955 and 1973, these subsidies mostly benefited the poorest 60 percent of the population, especially the lower-middle 30 percent (for definition of extreme poverty—see Glossary).

Starting in the 1950s, the state also assumed a major role in the construction of low-cost housing. The Housing Corporation (Corporación de la Vivienda—Corvi) was established by the national government in 1953. Between 1960 and 1972, an average of 42,000 houses per year were built in Chile, of which the state built 60 percent and the private sector with state financing built 20 percent; private companies built the remaining 20 percent with private funding.

The military government cut public spending for housing to less than half of its 1970 levels. Supporters of the regime argued that state resources were more efficiently used than before, citing a slight

107

increase, to about 43,000 units, in average annual housing construction. They also argued that attempts were made—with greater success in the late 1980s than at the beginning of the Pinochet regime—to channel state subsidies to the poorest sectors. However, on average the number of new housing units was equal to no more than 56 percent of the total number of new households created between 1974 and 1989; the result was an increase in the nation's housing deficit. A rapid acceleration of construction toward the end of the 1980s, with almost 84,000 units being built in 1989, kept the deficit from becoming even worse.

The military regime reduced the subsidies on housing loans and initiated a monthly readjustment of all such loans according to the rate of inflation as a means of retaining their real value. The government also increased the participation of the private sector in the construction of housing and municipal buildings. It also attempted to allocate houses primarily to households that met certain savings goals, an objective that proved virtually impossible for poor families to meet. As a result, toward the end of military rule the state put more resources into one-time grants to enable families to cover the down payment.

The Aylwin government increased public funds for housing by about 50 percent, although construction remained in the hands of the private sector. It changed the eligibility requirements for public housing programs to favor poorer people unable to save money. The government's intention was to freeze the housing deficit that existed in 1990 by facilitating the building of as many new houses as were needed by the new households that were being formed (see Construction, ch. 3). It also reintroduced utilities subsidies to poor neighborhoods and placed a greater emphasis on communal services for such areas.

Education

Enrollments

Despite plans dating back to 1812 to establish widespread primary education, elementary school attendance did not become compulsory until 1920. However, the government did not provide effective means to enforce this policy fully. There was considerable progress, especially in the 1920s and the 1940s, but by mid-century children of primary school age were still not universally enrolled. The principal difficulty lay in the incomplete matriculation and high dropout rate of the nation's poorest children. For this reason, in 1953 the government created the National Council for School Aid and Grants (Junta Nacional de Auxílio Escolar y Becas), which

A resident of Conchalí, a low-income district in northern Santiago, making use of a caseta, *a government-financed and government-built housing unit containing cooking and sanitation facilities*
Courtesy Inter-American Development Bank

The mayor of the low-income community of Peñalolén on the eastern side of the Santiago metropolitan area paying a visit to her constituents to inspect casetas
Courtesy Inter-American Development Bank

was charged with providing scholarships and with making school breakfasts and lunches available to all children in the tuition-free private and public schools. Through these means, policy makers hoped to encourage the very poorest parents to send their children to school and keep them there. By the early 1970s, school breakfasts were reaching 64 percent of all primary school students, and lunches were being provided to 30 percent. This strategy was apparently successful, and in the mid-1960s primary education became nearly universal. In 1966 the number of years of primary (and therefore compulsory) education was increased from six to eight; secondary education was thereby reduced to four years. In the mid-1980s, primary school attendance fluctuated between 93 percent and 96 percent of the relevant age-group—a percentage that was less than universal only because some children advanced into secondary school at the age of fourteen instead of the normal age of fifteen.

Beginning in the first half of the nineteenth century, Chile's governments made an effort to create secondary schools and led Latin America in establishing high schools for girls as well as for boys. By 1931 Chile had forty-one state-run high schools for boys and thirty-eight for girls, as well as fifty-nine private high schools for boys and sixty for girls, with a total enrollment of 20,211 boys and 15,014 girls. Reflecting French and German influences on the nation's secondary education, high schools were intended to provide a rigorous preparation for university education.

Chile had other postprimary educational channels that were meant to impart more practical or professional forms of training. Among these were normal schools for the instruction of primary school teachers (the first one for women was created in 1854), agricultural schools (that taught the rudiments of agronomy, animal husbandry, and forestry), industrial schools (with such specialties as mechanics or electricity), commercial schools (with specialties in accounting and secretarial training), so-called technical women's schools (that mainly taught home economics), and schools for painting, sculpture, and music. In 1931 there were 135 of these schools, with a total enrollment of 11,420 males and 11,391 females.

Matriculation of relevant age-groups in all forms of secondary education remained low, as can be surmised from the 1931 figures, and progress was slow. The most rapid advances occurred in the 1960s and early 1970s under the governments of presidents Frei and Allende, which increased spending for education at all levels. By 1970 about 38 percent of all fifteen- to eighteen-year olds in the country had matriculated from one form or another of secondary education; by 1974 that figure had increased to 51 percent.

Moreover, the curriculum in schools other than high schools had been enhanced significantly, and the graduates of such schools could opt to continue on to university levels. During the rest of the 1970s, under the military government's first six years in power, secondary school enrollments as a percentage of the relevant age-group stagnated. However, in the 1980s enrollments resumed their upward trend. Thus, from a level of 53 percent of the relevant age-group in 1979, secondary school matriculations rose to 75 percent in 1989.

Although the Chilean state traditionally directed about half of its education budget to universities that were either free or charged only nominal matriculation fees, the numbers of students in them had always been tiny as a proportion of the national population between nineteen and twenty-four years of age. As in other areas of education, the Frei and Allende administrations sponsored the largest expansions in postsecondary enrollments. The total numbers of students (including only those in the relevant age-group) almost doubled, from 41,801 in 1965 to 70,588 in 1970, and more than doubled from that number, to 145,663, in 1973. However, these enrollment figures were only equal to about 8 percent and 13 percent of the relevant age-group in 1970 and 1973, respectively. During the rest of the 1970s, the total number of students in universities declined, reaching a low of around 9 percent of the relevant age-group in 1980, including students enrolled in the so-called Professional Institutes (Institutos Profesionales—IPs), which had been separated from the universities by the military government. During the 1980s, the numbers of students in universities and in the IPs increased slowly and stood at about 153,100 in 1989, or 10.3 percent of the relevant age-group. However, the military government fostered the creation of Technical Training Centers (Centros de Formación Técnica—CFT) as an alternative to postsecondary education. Enrollment in these centers increased rapidly during the 1980s, to about 76,400 students by 1989. In 1991 a total of 245,875 students were in some form of higher or postsecondary education.

At the beginning of the twentieth century, under the influence of German advisers, Chile began to develop preprimary education. Matriculation in these programs also remained very small until the 1960s. In contrast to its attitude toward higher education, the military government took great interest in this form of education, and enrollments increased greatly during the Pinochet years. State-funded programs for preschoolers, which enrolled about 59,000 children in 1970, had increased their matriculation to about

109,600 by 1974. In 1989 they enrolled 213,200 children, or about 12 percent of the population under five years of age.

Administration and Reforms

Primary and Secondary Education

Until 1980, authority over all primary and secondary schools was concentrated in the national government's Ministry of Public Education. In addition to allocating funds to schools, the ministry certified the qualifications of all teachers and employed those in the state-run system. It developed all basic course content, even for private schools, and approved all textbooks to be used throughout the country.

Primary school teachers were trained mainly in normal schools, most of which were independent entities, although a few of these institutions were attached to universities. Secondary school teachers generally were graduates of pedagogical schools or university institutes, where students would be trained in the different disciplines they would later teach. Primary and secondary school teachers opting to work in the state-run system were assigned to schools during the first three years of their careers, a procedure that was meant to ensure that all rural and provincial schools had the requisite staffing. The careers of primary and secondary school teachers employed by the state were controlled by a national statute that determined promotions according to a point system and salaries according to a fixed scale. Salary supplements were given to those who taught in areas that were geographically isolated or had severe climates. Teachers also had job tenure beyond a certain probationary period. The Ministry of Public Education sponsored regular winter- and summer-vacation training programs for teachers that were designed to bring them up to date with curriculum changes and with new thinking in their disciplines. Merit increases were given to those who participated in these programs.

The Ministry of Public Education gave subsidies to private schools that did not charge tuition. These subsidies, amounting to about half the per-student cost of public education, were based on calculations of salary and other fixed costs. They were given primarily to schools sponsored by the Roman Catholic Church, as well as by Protestant churches. The teachers of these schools (except those who were in religious orders or in the clergy) were supposed to have the same salary and working conditions as teachers in the public system. Many teachers in the state-run system supplemented their salaries by taking on additional hours in the private schools, which were supposed to follow the national curriculum whether or not they received state subsidies, although they were free to add supplementary courses. All state-run primary and secondary schools were visited regularly by supervisors employed by the Ministry of Public Education, who would observe classes and monitor many final examinations. For purposes of certification, the final examinations of all private secondary schools were conducted by committees of teachers employed by the Ministry of Public Education.

Despite the successes of this education system in terms of expanding enrollments and ensuring a uniform standard of quality across the nation, the military regime's social and economic planners thought it gave the government too much influence over education, stifling parents' and local communities' freedom of choice. They also thought the administration of the system was too bureaucratic and inefficient.

The regime's education authorities decided to decentralize the administration of state schools by turning them over to the municipal governments. Presumably, the schools would thus become more responsive to local demands and needs, although the Ministry of Public Education continued to issue the basic guidelines to be followed in the curricula, to approve textbooks, and, in principle, to require the certification of teachers, although the standards became more flexible. Moreover, the national program of school breakfasts and lunches was transferred, along with the necessary resources, to the municipalities. The authorities committed the necessary funding to maintain universal primary enrollments and, after 1980, to continue to increase the size of secondary enrollments, despite the severe economic downturn of 1982–83.

With the 1980 reforms, all teachers in the state-run system became municipal employees, effectively ending the national system controlling teachers' careers. The result was new inequalities in terms of income and benefits for teachers. Despite increased education subsidies from the central government to poorer municipalities, the richer school systems were able to afford better teacher salaries and educational facilities. In addition, beginning in 1988 municipal authorities were permitted to fire teachers, ending the tenure they had enjoyed in the national career system, a measure that generated widespread manifestations of teacher discontent, including strikes.

The military government fostered the growth of privately run schools by further facilitating the process through which they could obtain subsidies. Moreover, tuition-free public and private schools were put on an equal footing in terms of access to state funding when both began to receive amounts calculated on a similar per-student basis. This amount was prorated on the basis of student attendance records, a measure that put the public systems at a disadvantage because private schools could be selective in their admissions; they could therefore draw their student body from those with more stable family backgrounds and hence could require more regular attendance and better behavior. As a result of these new incentives, enrollments in the publicly funded but privately administered system increased at the expense of the state-owned schools. In 1980, before the beginning of the reform program, the state-run schools had enrolled about 79 percent of primary and secondary students, private but state-subsidized schools enrolled 14 percent, and fully private schools (those that charged tuition) enrolled 7 percent. By the end of 1988, the proportion of students in the state-run schools (by then under municipal control) had dropped to 60 percent, the private but state-subsidized schools' proportion had increased to 33 percent, and the fully private schools continued to enroll 7 percent. Other data suggest that the number of primary and secondary students in private schools increased from 27 percent in 1981 to 56 percent in 1986 (see table 15, Appendix). The authorities also transferred administration of the state's vocational, industrial, and agricultural schools to employer associations, although the public funding of these schools continued.

The Aylwin government doubled funding for education by 1992 and began to address the new challenge the nation confronted to increase the quality of education. As part of this effort, the government examined with renewed interest the issues of teacher morale, training, and careers. It decided to reinvigorate the national continuing education programs for teachers and to reintroduce a National Statute for Teachers. This recreated in part the previous national career system, with a minimum starting salary of about US$250 per month for primary school teachers and promotions and raises based on years of service, merit, additional training, and premiums for teaching in areas that were isolated or had harsh climates. However, because of the Aylwin government's commitment to the decentralization of authority, administration of the system of primary and secondary schools remained to a significant extent in the hands of local governments, with continued efforts to provide increased funding to the poorer municipalities and regions. An initiative by the Aylwin government also committed it to increasing technical training of workers and of youth who had already left the education system. By the end of 1993, about 100,000 people, principally youth, had graduated from such training programs.

Higher Education

Chilean universities are widely recognized as being among the best in Latin America. Before the education reforms of 1980, Chile had eight universities—two state-run and six private—although all received most of their funding from the state. The two state universities consisted of the University of Chile (Universidad de Chile), founded in Santiago in 1842 as the successor to the University of San Felipe (Universidad de San Felipe; founded in 1758), and the State Technical University (Universidad Técnica del Estado), founded in Santiago in 1947. The private universities consisted of the Pontifical Catholic University of Chile (Pontífica Universidad Católica de Chile), founded in 1888; the University of Concepción (Universidad de Concepción), founded in 1919; the Catholic University of Valparaíso (Universidad Católica de Valparaíso), founded in 1928; the Federico Santa María Technical University (Universidad Técnica Federico Santa María), founded in Valparaíso in 1931; the Southern University of Chile (Universidad Austral de Chile), founded in Valdivia in 1955; and the University of the North (Universidad del Norte) in Antofagasta, founded in 1956. The nation's largest and most important university, the University of Chile, has the authority to oversee the quality of professional training programs in important fields, such as medicine, in the other universities. The University of Chile, the Pontifical Catholic University of Chile, the Federico Santa María Technical University, and, to a lesser extent, the University of Concepción all developed campuses in other cities during the expansion of university enrollments in the late 1960s and early 1970s.

As noted previously, Chilean universities did not charge tuition, aside from minimal matriculation fees that were, following changes introduced in the mid- to late 1960s, higher for students of more affluent parents. In effect, the state used general tax revenues to subsidize a higher-education system whose students were drawn disproportionately from the middle and upper classes. The regressive impact of this policy on the nation's distribution of wealth had been noted repeatedly by economists and sociologists since at least the 1950s.

The military government took a highly critical view of the nation's university system. Persuaded by the notion that state funding for lower education is more efficient in terms of generating the necessary human capital for economic development, the military decided to give priority in resource allocation to preprimary, primary, and secondary schools. In addition to politically motivated purges of faculty members and students, among the first changes the military authorities made at the higher-education level was to charge students substantially higher enrollment fees. Low-income students were supposed to continue to have access to higher education through an expanded system of student loans with generous repayment terms. Yet, as noted earlier, the expansion of higher-education enrollments that had begun in the 1960s ceased after these new policies were put into place.

With the 1980 education reforms, the military government split the two state universities apart, creating separate universities out of what had been their regional provincial campuses. In addition, taking a dim view of increases in the numbers of training programs and degree programs at these universities since the 1960s, the regime limited the degrees that could be obtained in the state-run universities to twelve of the most traditional fields, such as law, medicine, and engineering. Degrees in other areas henceforth had to be obtained from professional institutes; those sections of the state universities consequently were detached, with some attrition, and transformed into freestanding entities. The large School of Pedagogy of the University of Chile, for example, became the Pedagogical Institute.

The Pinochet government also fostered the formation of new private universities and professional institutes, allowing them to set tuition at whatever level they wished and promising to give them direct per-student subsidies, as well as funds for loans to low-income students, on an equal footing with older institutions. The education authorities hoped to stimulate competition among the universities and institutes for the best students by granting the per-student subsidies on the basis of schools' ability to attract the students with the highest scores on a national aptitude test required of all first-year applicants. This competition was thought to be an expeditious way to encourage efforts to increase the quality of higher education. Subsequently, the state subsidies did not become nearly as important as was expected because funding for universities and for student loans declined beginning with the economic crisis of 1982–83. The lower funding levels led to decreases in salaries for faculty and other personnel across the country.

As a result of the policies of breaking up the state universities and stimulating the formation of private institutions, the number of universities increased to forty-one by 1989. Only half of these received state funding that year. In addition, by 1989 there were fifty-six professional training institutes, only two of which received state funding that year. There was also a large increase in the numbers of centers for technical training. In 1989 there were 150 such centers, none of which received state support. Relying entirely on tuition payments, these centers had responded to a demand for post-secondary education that the universities and professional institutes, despite their increased number, had been unable to meet. However,

*The Department of Physical Sciences and Mathematics at the
Pontifical Catholic University of Chile in Santiago
Courtesy Inter-American Development Bank*

the quality of the training these centers provided was questionable. Most of them had two-year training programs with few facilities other than classrooms.

The changes introduced by the military government increased the number and variety of higher education institutions, but the reforms also led to much greater disparities among them, as well as to a likely decline in the overall quality of the nation's higher education system. There was an increase in part-time faculty teaching, a decline in full-time faculty salaries, and a much greater dispersion of resources needed by important facilities, such as laboratories and libraries. These changes also led to the creation of a considerable number of research institutes with no student training programs that were dependent on grants or research contracts from international or national sources for their funding. These institutes developed most prominently in the social sciences and became an important alternative source of employment for specialists who had been or would have been engaged by universities. Consequently, in contrast to the period before 1973, most of the innovative thinking and writing in these areas was no longer being done at universities, and new generations of students were having less contact with the best specialists in these fields.

The Aylwin government did not introduce fundamental changes in the higher education system handed down to it by the military regime. It continued to fund higher education in part by allocating per-student subsidies to institutions able to attract students who scored highest on the multiple-choice examination modeled on the Scholastic Aptitude Test used in the United States. However, the Aylwin government was critical of what it considered an excessive disaggregation and dispersion of higher education institutions. Consequently, it concentrated more of its direct subsidies on the traditional universities and their offshoots and attempted to enhance their quality by making more funds available for basic and applied research. The government also increased funding for low-income student loans and scholarships to pursue studies at any institution.

Religion and Churches

Religious Affiliations and Church Organization

Roman Catholicism is an integral part of Chile's history and culture, and the great majority of Chileans consider themselves Roman Catholic. However, their numbers have been declining since 1970, while the Protestant population has been increasing. The 1970 census showed that about 90 percent of the population was nominally Roman Catholic, and a little over 6 percent was Protestant. The 1982 census did not include questions on religion. The 1992 census showed that 76.9 percent of the population fourteen years of age and older declared itself Catholic, while 13.1 percent declared itself either "Evangelical" (see Glossary) or "Protestant" (see table 16, Appendix). This latter percentage reflected a moderate but steady increase with each census since 1920, when only 1.4 percent of the population was counted as Protestant. About 90 percent of Protestants belong to Pentecostal (Evangelical) denominations.

The more than doubling of the proportion of Protestants in the total population over the 1970–92 period means that a large number of them are converts. Surveys taken in December 1990 and October 1991 by the Center for Public Studies (Centro de Estudios Públicos—CEP) in collaboration with Adimark, a polling agency, showed that about 95 percent of Roman Catholic respondents have been Catholics since childhood, whereas only about 38 percent of Protestants said they have been Protestants since their early years. Moreover, fully 26 percent of Protestants noted that they had converted sometime in the previous ten years.

According to the 1992 census, there was also a significant minority of about 7 percent of Chileans who declared themselves indifferent to religion or were atheists. This group had increased from a little over 3 percent in 1970. Other religious groups, mainly Jewish, Muslim, and Christian Orthodox, accounted for 4.2 percent of the population fourteen years of age or older.

The CEP-Adimark surveys also included questions on religious practice. According to the surveys, about a quarter of all adult Chileans attend church services at least once a week, a proportion indicative of considerable secularization. A much greater proportion of Protestants (about 46 percent) than of those who said they are Roman Catholics (about 18 percent) are regular churchgoers. Thus, the authors of the CEP-Adimark report note that there is roughly one Protestant for every two Catholics among people attending church at least once a week in Chile. The proportion of nominal Catholics attending mass weekly seems to have increased slightly since the late 1970s; prior studies had shown an attendance rate between 10 and 15 percent.

The distribution of practicing Catholics and Protestants varies dramatically on the basis of socioeconomic status. In 1990–91 about half the practicing Protestant population (52.1 percent) was composed of individuals from poorer groups, while a tiny minority (2.3 percent) had high socioeconomic status. Among practicing Catholics, the proportion with high status was significant at 15 percent, whereas the poorest segment constituted about a fifth (21.8 percent) of all those who practiced. These differences are so salient that among the poor Chilean urban population, for every practicing Roman Catholic there is a practicing Protestant. The growth of Protestantism has therefore mainly been at the expense of the Catholicism of the lower socioeconomic groups, among whom Catholicism has long been weakest. Surveys taken between the late 1950s and early 1970s showed that only between 4 and 8 percent of working-class people who were nominally Catholic attended mass weekly. The 1991 survey showed that 93.4 percent of high-income respondents indicated that they are nominally Catholic; the proportions declined to 75.2 percent of middle-income people and to 69 percent of those with lower incomes. Among the latter, 22 percent consider themselves nominally Protestant. The practicing Protestants also tend to work in greater proportions in the personal service areas of the economy and to be less educated than Catholics. This is consistent with the generally lower economic status of the Protestant population.

Slightly more than half of all Chileans who declared a religious affiliation are women. However, among those who practice, the proportion of women is significantly higher. This is particularly the case for Protestants. Among urban Protestant respondents, about 70 percent of those who attend church services at least once a week are women. Among Roman Catholics, the proportion of practicing women is about 63 percent.

The Roman Catholic Church is divided into twenty-four dioceses and one armed forces chaplaincy. These are led by five archbishops and thirty bishops, some of whom serve as auxiliaries in the larger dioceses. There are also two retired cardinals. The church has long suffered from a shortage of priests. Since the 1960s, they have numbered between 2,300 and 2,500, about half of them foreign born. By 1990 there were 3,000 Catholics per priest. With about 760 parishes throughout the country, the church is unable to extend its presence to the entire Catholic population. This situation is illustrated by a comparison of the number of places of worship for Santiago's Catholic and Protestant populations: 470 Roman Catholic parishes and chapels versus about 1,150 churches and other places of Protestant (mainly Pentecostal) worship.

Religion in Historical Perspective

Independence from Spain disrupted the church-state relationship. The clergy was divided over the question of breaking the ties to Spain, although the most prominent church officials were generally royalists. As a result, the new independent governments and the leaders of the church viewed each other with distrust. The development of what would later be called the "black legend" (a highly unfavorable view of the colonial administration, of which the church was an integral part), coupled with an admiration for the progress of Protestant lands, fueled this distrust. Despite their misgivings about church attitudes toward independence, the new rulers insisted that they were entitled to exercise the *patronato real* (see Glossary), the agreement between the Spanish crown and the pope, thereby assuming this important royal power as well. This prerogative was enshrined in the 1833 constitution, which made Roman Catholicism the established church of the new Chilean state. Consequently, to oversee the goverance of the church, the authorities followed the tradition of sending church appointments to the Vatican for its formal approval. For their part, church officials expected that the government would continue to ban all other religions from the country. Moreover, they hoped to retain full authority over education, to keep all civil law subordinate to canonical law, and to continue to function as the state's surrogate civil registry, as well as to control all cemeteries. In addition, they increasingly asserted the independence of the church from the interference of state authorities.

A church in Rancagua, central Chile
Courtesy Embassy of Chile, Washington

The church-state relationship was fraught with potential for conflict, and as the nineteenth century progressed many conflicts did indeed emerge. By the late 1850s, a fundamental fault line in Chilean politics and society had developed between unconditional defenders of church prerogatives, who became the Conservatives, and those who preferred to limit the church's role in national life, who became the Liberals or, if they took more strongly anticlerical positions, the Radicals. Although most Liberals and even most Radicals were also Roman Catholics, they were in favor of allowing the existence of other churches and of limiting canonical law to church-related matters, while establishing the supremacy of the state's laws and courts over the nation as a whole, even over priests and other church officials. They also advocated the creation of non-Catholic schools and civil cemeteries, and they pressed for the establishment of a state-managed civil registry that would be entitled to issue the only legally valid birth, marriage, and death certificates. By the 1880s, a decade that saw a break in relations between the Chilean government and the Vatican, all of these points of the more secular and anticlerical agendas had been established. However, the Roman Catholic Church continued to be the established church, dependent on the state for its finances and appointments. This led periodically to new political tensions.

Emerging in the 1820s, the first source of state-church conflicts was the issue of the right of non-Catholics to practice their religion. The government favored allowing them to do so in private homes or other nonpublic places, while the Roman Catholic Church opposed this notion. The issue was a question of considerable significance for more than just civil liberties.

Independence from Spain had permitted the legal establishment of direct commercial links between Chile and other countries throughout the world. These links led to the creation, especially in Valparaíso, of wholesale commercial enterprises that brought British and other foreign nationals who were non-Catholic to the country, and they demanded the right to practice their religion. Denying them religious freedom not only created diplomatic problems with the dominant economic powers of the time but also had the potential to undermine the operations of the export-import concerns that handled much of the emerging country's foreign trade.

Beginning in the 1840s, the Chilean government sponsored the immigration of German settlers to the southern lake district. Most of them, contrary to the government's wishes, came from Protestant parts of Germany. As a result, the first Protestant services in Chile, mainly Anglican and Lutheran, began in immigrant communities. Initially, they were merely tolerated by the authorities, but in 1865 a new law interpreting the religious clause of the constitution that declared Roman Catholicism as the official state religion permitted private practice by non-Catholic denominations.

In the last quarter of the nineteenth century, Protestant missionaries of various denominations, beginning with the Presbyterians, came to Chile. Although they continued to serve mainly the immigrant communities, they also made an effort to obtain Chilean converts. The Anglicans set up missions among the Mapuche, and these are still operating in Araucanía Region. American Methodists founded schools—the well-known Santiago College, which was established in 1880, among them—that were open to middle- and upper-class Chilean children, especially girls. Parents seeking alternatives to Catholic education opted for Protestant missionary schools. By the turn of the century, a small community of local converts to Protestant denominations began to form. In 1909 a segment of the new Methodist group that had adopted charismatic rituals broke off from the main missionary body. This breakaway group became the Pentecostal Methodist Church, which itself split in 1934 when the Evangelical Pentecostal Church was formed. These two denominations remained the principal Pentecostal groups in Chile, although there were many different subdenominations.

Judaism, virtually unknown in nineteenth-century Chile, originated with the Central European Jews who arrived in the country fleeing persecution mainly between World War I and World War II. Both Jews and Protestants, as religious minorities in a predominantly Catholic country, were strongly in favor of religious freedoms and of full separation between church and state. It was therefore natural for them to identify more closely with the more secular and even anticlerical segments of Chilean society and politics; and it was natural for the latter to consider them a part of their constituency. Yet, given their religious beliefs, strict moral upbringing, and, among Chilean Protestants, generally, abstention from alcohol, these segments of the non-Catholic Chilean society had little in common with the broader anticlerical groups. In fact, on many moral issues, non-Catholics' opinions were much closer to those of practicing Roman Catholics. For this reason, although practicing Protestants and Jews tended to vote for the more secular parties in greater proportions than other groups, they generally did not have a particularly strong political identity or play important leadership roles in political or social life.

In 1925 President Arturo Alessandri Palma (1920–24, 1925, 1932–38) pressed for and obtained a separation of church and state. This resolved most sources of church-state friction, but more than a century of conflicts had already created subcultures in Chilean society that continued to leave their mark on twentieth-century educational institutions, intellectual life, social organizations, and politics. The segments most distant from and even opposed to the Catholic Church were receptive to positivism (see Glossary) and, especially after the 1930s, to Marxism. In this sense, the nineteenth-century fault line contributed indirectly to the eventual appeal among educated Chileans of the nation's communist and socialist parties.

During the interwar years, partly in response to the challenges of secular intellectuals and political leaders and partly as a result of new trends in international Catholicism, the Roman Catholic Church in Chile slowly began to espouse socially and politically more progressive positions. This more progressive Catholicism initially had its main impact among university students, who, in the mid-1930s under the leadership of Eduardo Frei, created a new party that in 1957 fused with other groups to become the Christian Democratic Party (Partido Demócrata Cristiano—PDC). This development split the subculture that was closer to the Catholic Church into politically conservative and centrist segments. By the early 1960s, a solid majority of the church hierarchy favored the Christian Democrats, and there was a significant shift of voter support from the Conservative Party (Partido Conservador) to the PDC. Following the new thinking in church circles, the hierarchy openly embraced positions favoring land reform, much to the dismay of the still-important minority of Catholics on the right.

The dominant consensus within Chilean Catholicism was much in tune with the resolutions and spirit of Vatican Council II (1962–65) in theological, ritual, and pastoral matters. Within the Latin American context, the Chilean Roman Catholic Church quickly became noted as a post-Vatican Council II church of moderately progressive positions on political and socioeconomic issues, and its representatives played an important part in the reform-minded Medellín (1968) and Puebla (1979) conferences of Latin American bishops. In the late 1960s and 1970s, the church fostered the establishment of Christian Base Communities (Comunidades Eclesiásticas de Base—CEBs; see Glossary) in poor urban neighborhoods. However, only a minority in the Chilean church subscribed to what became known as liberation theology (see Glossary).

In the wake of the military coup of September 1973, the church established, initially in association with some leaders of the nation's Protestant and Jewish communities, an office for the defense of human rights. Later reorganized under exclusive sponsorship of the archdiocese of Santiago as the Vicariate of Solidarity (Vicaría de la Solidaridad), this organization continued to receive funds from international Protestant sources and valiantly collected information on human rights violations during the nearly seventeen years of military rule. Its lawyers presented literally thousands of writs of habeas corpus, in all but a few cases to no avail, and provided for the legal defense of prisoners. The church also supported popular and labor organizations and called repeatedly for the restoration of democracy and for national reconciliation.

As the papacy of John Paul II (1978–) progressed, the Chilean Catholic Church, like other national congregations around the world, became somewhat more conservative in outlook. In the early 1990s, the episcopal conference was about evenly split between those formed in the spirit of Vatican Council II and those espousing more conservative positions. However, this shifting balance did not affect the church's advocacy of human rights and democracy during the military regime (see The Church, ch. 4).

Forms of Popular Religiosity

Anthropologists of religion would be hard-pressed to find expressions of indigenous beliefs in the ''popular'' sectors (see Glossary) of Chile. The principal exception to this is in the north, where various religious festivals honoring the Virgin Mary show bold traces of highland Andean indigenous beliefs. The most noted of these is ''La Tirana,'' held each July in Iquique and the nearby village of La Tirana. In the rest of the country, Christian and indigenous religious syncretism have been largely confined to native American communities, where faiths in various animal and bird spirits coexist with beliefs of Christian origin.

Popular religious beliefs focus to a large extent on the notion that there is a struggle between good and evil, the latter seen as a force personified by the devil. This perspective is much in line with Mapuche beliefs. Illnesses are often seen, like sin, as tied in some way to the devil's work. Catholic priests in poor parishes usually have had the experience of being called by their least educated parishioners to perform exorcisms, particularly of demons thought to be afflicting sick children, and many Pentecostal services focus on ridding body and soul of satanic influences and on faith healing. A belief in heaven and in the eternal horrors of hell is a fundamental ingredient of the popular religious imagery, with earthly life said to be a brief trial determining the soul's final destination. Much of the message of Pentecostal sermons revolves around these concepts, focusing on the weakness of the flesh and on the necessity of leading a life of constant preparation for eternal deliverance. In this respect, there is a puritan streak to the Pentecostal message that is reinforced through a liberal use of individual

125

*A dance at a religious festival held each July in Iquique and the nearby
village of La Tirana in honor of the Virgin Mary
Courtesy Embassy of Chile, Washington*

testimonies of repentance and conversion from members of the congregation. Among Catholics, this element of popular religiosity is tied intimately to a belief in the intercession of saints and, most important, of the Virgin Mary. Intercession may be invoked on behalf of deceased family members who are remembered in prayers.

The afterworld is heavily populated in popular religious imagery by errant souls atoning for their sins and seeking their final rest. Particularly in rural areas, it is common along roadsides to see niches carved into the sides of hills or shaped from clay that contain crosses, occasionally photographs, and candles. The niches are in the proximity of places where people met sudden, violent deaths, primarily from traffic accidents, without the benefit of last rites. The candles are lit mainly to plead for their souls but also in some cases to ask the deceased to intercede for those who light them. It is customary among the Chilean poor to believe that infants who die become little angels. Pilgrimages to Catholic churches that house special images of the Virgin or of saints and multitudinous processions in which these images are displayed are also part of the popular religious landscape. The faithful frequently offer penances in the hope of obtaining special favors.

A central objective of Pentecostal services is to experience a manifestation of the Holy Spirit. The leader of the service tries to cleanse the congregation of devilish influences and to prepare the way for this manifestation. Between his or her invocations stressing the necessity and possibility of redemption from sin and anointments of the sick, the congregation joins in rhythmic but often lamentational singing, sometimes to the accompaniment of guitars and tambourines, and often supplemented by the clapping of hands. While singing, some of the women who attend will frequently begin to dance, swaying back and forth, and even to "speak in tongues." Sometimes the dancing will surround certain individuals who are chosen because they need special attention for some reason. Another common practice is for members of the congregation to pray individually in a loud voice.

Attitudes Toward Family and Gender

Divorce, Abortion, and Contraception

Chile is one of the last countries in the world that has not legalized divorce. A law permits marital separation under certain conditions, but it does not terminate the conjugal bond. Despite the Catholic hierarchy's opposition to the legalization of divorce, at least half of all Chileans apparently favor enacting such a law (see table 17, Appendix). In the 1990 CEP-Adimark survey, 55.6 percent of those interviewed were in favor of legal divorce.

The differences of opinion on divorce among various categories of the population are noteworthy. Support for its legalization is slightly stronger among men than among women. It is much stronger among young adults than among the middle-aged, while only a minority of older people support it. High-income respondents constitute the group most in favor, whereas lower-income respondents largely disapprove (70.1 percent to 15.5 percent); a small majority of those with middle and lower incomes support legalization. A slight majority of self-identified Catholics are in favor, but among practicing Catholics a majority reject the notion. A small majority of those who said they are Protestant reject legalization. This rejection is stronger among weekly churchgoers. Curiously, Protestants (mainly Pentecostals, who tend to have very traditional opinions) are closer to the positions of the Catholic hierarchy than are Catholic respondents.

Although Chile does not have a divorce law, a surrogate and well-institutionalized means of severing conjugal bonds is the annulment of civil marriages. Civil marriage ceremonies are the only legally valid ones, and couples who have church weddings must also marry at the civil registry. The annulment is usually done with the assistance of attorneys who argue that there has been some procedural error in the civil marriage process. It often involves obtaining witnesses who would attest to facts, whether true or false, that vitiate the original proceedings, such as asserting that the couple does not reside where they said they did when they were married. This is enough to make a case for invalidating the action of the civil registrar who performs the ceremony and draws up the papers. To a large extent, Chile's lack of a proper divorce law can be attributed to the ability of separated couples to annul their marriage following these procedures. As a result, the political pressure to enact a divorce law is diffused. In 1991, the latest year for which there were published figures, there were 5,852 marriage annulments (and 91,732 marriages) in the country; the number of annulments showed a steady increase over seven years from a level of 3,987 in 1984. The actual number of separations of married couples is much higher, especially among those who lack the means to hire the necessary annulment lawyers. New bonds are often established outside of wedlock.

Whereas the Chilean public seems somewhat favorably inclined toward the legalization of divorce, it shows considerable resistance to legal abortion. Although survey results vary, according to the way questions on abortion are posed, the notion of permitting abortion on demand has only a small proportion of supporters. It varied from 5 percent in the CEP-Adimark December 1990 survey to a high of 22.4 percent in the July 1991 survey conducted by the Center for Contemporary Reality Studies (Centro de Estudios de la Realidad Contemporánea—CERC). However, a relatively large proportion of survey respondents favored abortion under certain circumstances. The CERC survey of July 1991 showed that 76 percent considered abortion permissible when "the mother's life is in danger or when the baby will be born with malformations"; similarly, 53.4 percent thought that abortion should be permitted in cases of rape. While nearly half of all respondents rejected abortion in all circumstances, 44.7 percent would permit it with qualifications (see table 18, Appendix).

There is a considerable degree of consensus among the various categories of respondents to a December 1991 CEP-Adimark survey, except for individuals of high socioeconomic status and practicing Catholics or Protestants. As on the issue of divorce, the first group had the most liberal views of all, with only 14 percent agreeing with the notion that abortion should not be permitted and 78 percent accepting it in qualified circumstances. Practicing Catholics rejected abortion in a somewhat greater proportion than the average, and they accepted it in qualified circumstances to a slightly lesser extent. Practicing Protestants (mainly Pentecostals) had the most restrictive views of all: more than 80 percent rejected abortion outright, 17.6 accepted it in qualified circumstances, and a tiny fraction agreed that the matter should be left up to the individual woman. Although illegal, abortions are commonly performed in Chile. Social science researchers have estimated that about a third of all Chilean women have one or more induced abortions during their childbearing years.

Birth control methods of all types find broad acceptance among the population. This is true even of practicing Catholics, 81.3 percent of whom found their use acceptable. National health programs have facilitated access to birth control since the 1960s, and the use of contraceptives is widespread. However, these programs provide easy access to birth control only to women who have already had at least one child because the programs are mainly organized to provide prenatal and postpartum primary care. Birth control is therefore more difficult to obtain for childless women, especially younger and poorer women. Thus, first pregnancies out of wedlock as well as first marriages of pregnant brides are frequent. This differential in contraceptive practices is largely responsible for the fact that the proportion of births out of wedlock over the total number of births increased with the overall decline in the birthrate (see table 19, Appendix). The number of births in wedlock has fallen almost by half since the initiation of the contraception programs, while the births out of wedlock have remained fairly constant. This means that currently a third of all births are out of wedlock, up from 17.5 percent in 1965.

Premarital sex among couples in love with each other is also broadly accepted, except among practicing Protestants, only 40 percent of whom approved, and among those age fifty-five and older, only 39 percent of whom approved. Sixty-three percent of practicing Catholics accepted this practice, despite the strong disapproval of the church hierarchy. On this issue, practicing Protestants again are closer to the Catholic hierarchy's teachings than are lay Catholics themselves. The acceptance of premarital relations compounds the problems caused by the relatively more difficult access to birth control for childless women.

Family Structure and Attitudes Toward Gender Roles

Extended-family life has occupied an important place in Chilean society. Although couples are expected to set up their own households, they remain in close contact with the members of their larger families. Children generally get to know their cousins well, as much adult leisure time, generally on weekends and holidays, is spent in the company of relatives. It is also common to find children living for extended periods of time for educational or other reasons in households headed by relatives, sometimes even cousins of their parents. These extended-family ties provide a network of support in times of nuclear family crises. It is also common for close friendships among adults to lead to links that are family-like. For example, children often refer to their parents' friends as "uncle" or "aunt."

Traditional definitions of gender roles have broken down considerably as women have won access to more education and have entered the labor force in larger numbers. By 1990 about half the students in the nation's primary and secondary schools were female; the proportion of women was lower, about 44 percent of the total enrollment in all forms of higher education. The University of Chile graduated Latin America's first female lawyers and physicians in the 1880s. However, women made faster progress in traditionally female professions than in other professions. Thus, by 1910 there were 3,980 women teachers, but there were only seven physicians, ten dentists, and three lawyers. By the 1930s, female enrollments reached significant numbers in these fields. The University of Chile in 1932 had 124 female students enrolled in law (17 percent of the total), ninety-six in medicine (9.5 percent), and 108 in dentistry (38 percent), although 55 percent of all women students at the university were enrolled in education.

Attitudes regarding the proper roles of men and women in society seemingly no longer follow a fully traditional pattern. A 1984 survey conducted in Santiago by the Diagnos polling firm found widespread support among men (more than 80 percent) and women (more than 90 percent) of high, medium, and low socioeconomic status for the notion that women benefit as individuals if they work outside the home. When asked if they agreed or disagreed with the notion that "it is better for women to concentrate on the home and men on their jobs," 43 percent of the national sample in the CERC July 1991 survey agreed, even though the term "concentrate" does not imply a denial of the right of women to work outside the home. There were some differences between the genders over this question, with 49 percent of men and 38 percent of women in agreement. The percentage in favor of this notion increased with age. Only 30 percent of those under age twenty-five agreed, while 61 percent of those over age sixty-one did so.

Men and women in the same CERC study were considerably divided over whether "women should obey their husbands." This is a sentence included in family law that is supposed to be read (although it is frequently omitted) to Chileans when they take their marriage vows in the civil registry's ceremony; 55 percent of men agreed, while only 40 percent of women did so. Again, men held the more traditional views, but considering the nature of the proposition and its long-established status in civil law, the fact that only slightly more than half of them agreed can be considered a sign of changing times.

Surveys of working-class respondents can usually be counted on to capture the more traditional views of urban society toward male and female roles because such attitudes are usually associated with lower levels of educational attainment. But working-class Chileans are in general not as tradition minded as could be expected about the issue of women working outside the home. In a 1988 survey of workers, 70 percent of the men and 85 percent of the women agreed with the notion that "even if there is no economic necessity, it is still convenient for women to work." The notion that "men should participate more actively in housework so that women are able to work" was accepted by 70 percent of men and 92 percent of women. Forty-five percent of men believed that "women who work gravely neglect their home obligations," while 21 percent of women did so. However, male support for the notion of women working outside the home varied depending on the way the question was phrased. When interviewers presented the idea that "if men were to make more money, then women should return to the home,'' 63 percent of men agreed, while only 33 percent of women did.

Nonetheless, popular beliefs hold very strongly to the notion that women reach full self-realization primarily through motherhood. This generates strong pressures on women to have children, although most take the necessary measures to have fewer children than did their mothers and especially their grandmothers. Employed working-class women usually are able to find preschools and day care for their small children, as these programs are broadly established throughout the country. The extended family also provides a means of obtaining child care.

Middle-class to upper-class households usually hire female domestic servants to do housework and take care of children. This practice facilitates the work life of the women of such households. Women can frequently be found in the professions even outside such traditionally female-dominated areas as primary and secondary education, nursing, and social work. For example, among the nation's 14,334 physicians in 1990, there were 3,811 women, or 27 percent of the total. This percentage has been increasing in recent years. Among the 7,616 physicians less than thirty-five years of age, there were 2,778 women, or 37 percent of the total. In 1991 about 48 percent of the nation's 748 judges were women; although there were none on the Supreme Court, 24.2 percent of the appellate court judges were women. A slight majority of the roughly 4,200 journalists in the country were women.

Whither Chile?

In the early 1990s, most social, economic, and political leaders are being driven by a search for consensus on pragmatic solutions to national problems. The strength of these attitudes stems in large measure from an attempt to recover from what most Chileans view, in one sense or another, as national failures. The country experienced slow and erratic growth, hyperinflation, the breakdown of its democracy, human rights abuses, the exile of many people, and a period of harsh economic adjustment under military government. Chileans hope to put these events behind them, and to do so with a new sense of unity and purpose, avoiding costly mistakes and unnecessary conflicts.

The nation's transition to democracy was a smooth one, thanks in large part to the new national mood favoring negotiations and consensus. But many challenges lie ahead. The objective of continuing rapid development while increasing equity and enhancing democratic governance is indeed a tall order. However, buoyed by high levels of growth and historically low levels of unemployment, a majority of Chileans view the future optimistically.

* * *

Since the early 1970s, Chilean social scientists have been active in studying virtually all aspects of their society. The most comprehensive, useful, and authoritative source on Chilean physical and human geography is *Geografía general y regional de Chile* by Ximena Toledo O. and Eduardo Zapater A. The book is best complemented by the latest edition of the *Compendio estadístico* of Chile's Instituto Nacional de Estadísticas, which provides a summary of the most commonly consulted statistics. The political characteristics of the various regions of the country are treated in César N. Caviedes's *The Politics of Chile.*

Consistent with the relative unimportance of ethnic divisions in the Chilean population, there are no significant studies of the nation's ethnic groups, except for the Mapuche. The best source for an examination of their culture and social organization is Louis C. Faron's *The Mapuche Indians of Chile.* A wealth of recent information on the Mapuche can be found in *Censo de reducciones indígenas seleccionadas,* edited by Jorge Martínez.

The best single work on the current situation in the countryside is Sergio Gómez and Jorge Echenique's *La agricultura chilena.* An examination of the countryside at the height of agrarian reform is Solon Lovett Barraclough and José Antonio Fernández's *Diagnóstico de la reforma agraria chilena.* A useful collection of articles covering the period from the 1950s to the early 1990s is contained in *Development and Social Change in the Chilean Countryside,* edited by Cristóbal Kay and Patricio Silva.

There is a growing body of literature on Chilean social policies, welfare institutions, and social-assistance programs. The best works are José Pablo Arellano's *Políticas sociales y desarrollo,* which provides an excellent overview of the welfare institutions since their inception; Pilar Vergara's *Políticas hacia la extrema pobreza en Chile, 1973–1988,* which examines the military government's programs to assist the poorest segments of the population; Tarsicio Castañeda's *Para combatir la pobreza,* which covers some of the same ground as Vergara but from the perspective of a supporter of the military government; Hernán Cheyre Valenzuela's *La previsión en Chile, ayer y hoy* and Augusto Iglesias P. and Rodrigo Acuña R.'s *Sistema de pensiones en América Latina, Chile,* both of which examine the new private pension system and its social and economic effects; and Jorge Jiménez de la Jara's *Chile: Sistema de salud en transición a la democracia,* which is comprehensive in its analysis of the various components of the health system.

Guillermo Campero's *Los gremios empresariales en el período 1970–1983* is the most comprehensive examination of entrepreneurial associations. A more recent analysis of entrepreneurs is Cecilia Montero's "La evolución del empresariado chileno." Alan Angell's *Politics and the Labour Movement in Chile* remains the best source for examining the composition of the twentieth-century labor movement prior to the military government. The labor movement during the 1980s is well treated in Patricio P. Frías's *El movimiento sindical chileno en la lucha por la democracia, 1973–1988.*

The best single work on the Roman Catholic Church is Brian H. Smith's *The Church and Politics in Chile.* The Catholic Church during the military regime is the object of Enrique Correa and José Antonio Viera-Gallo's *Iglesia y dictadura.* A brief but excellent examination of the growth of Protestantism, including a comparison of the social and political attitudes of practicing Protestants and Catholics, is Arturo Fontaine Talavera and Herald Beyer's "Retrato del movimiento evangélico a la luz de las encuestas de opinión pública." The development of religious life in Chile and the relations between the military regime and all religious groups, especially Protestants, is the subject of Humberto Lagos Schuffeneger's *Crisis de la esperanza.*

The most comprehensive single analysis of women in Chilean society continues to be Felícitas Klimpel's *La mujer chilena.* Paz Covarrubias and Rolando Franco's *Chile: Mujer y sociedad* covers virtually all aspects of women's involvement in society with its thirty-two separate articles. Teresa Valdés's *Venid benditas de mi padre* provides a useful in-depth look at the life of twenty-six popular-sector women. (For further information and complete citations, see Bibliography.)

Chapter 3. The Economy

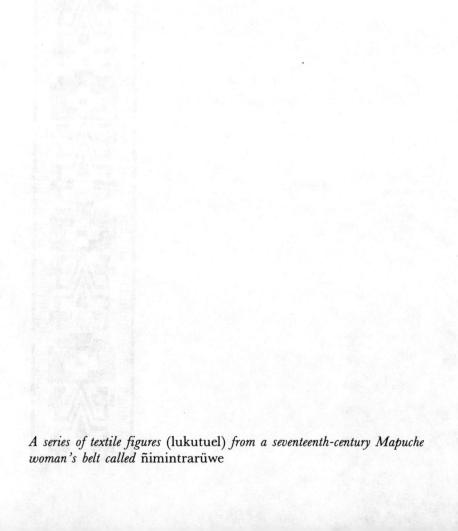

A series of textile figures (lukutuel) *from a seventeenth-century Mapuche woman's belt called* ñimintrarüwe

CHILE'S ECONOMY ENJOYED a remarkable boom in the early 1990s, the result of a comprehensive transformation that began in 1974 with the adoption of free-market economic policies. Between the 1930s and the early 1970s, the Chilean economy was one of the most state-oriented economies in Latin America. For decades, it was dominated by the philosophy of import-substitution industrialization (see Glossary). Heavily subsidized by the government, a largely inefficient industrial sector had developed. The sector's main characteristics were a low rate of job creation, a virtual absence of nontraditional exports, and a general lack of growth and development. In the early 1970s, the ruling socialist-communist Popular Unity (Unidad Popular) coalition of President Salvador Allende Gossens (1970–73) attempted to implement a socialist economic system. The Allende experiment came to an end with the military coup of September 11, 1973. From that point on, Chile's economic policies took a radical turn, as the military government undertook, first timidly and later more confidently, deep reforms aimed at creating a market economy.

In the early 1990s, politicians and analysts from around the world looked to the Chilean economy for lessons on how to open up international trade, create dynamic capital markets, and undertake an aggressive privatization process. In early 1994, Chile had the strongest economic structure in Latin America and, in large part because of the military government's reforms, was emerging as a modern economy enjoying vigorous growth. Moreover, there seemed to be a consensus among politicians of widely varying beliefs that the existing economic model should be maintained in the future.

Chile's income per capita, approximately US$2,800, placed the nation squarely in the middle of what the World Bank (see Glossary) calls "middle-income economies." Of the Latin American nations, Brazil, Uruguay, Venezuela, Mexico, and Argentina in 1990 each had a higher gross national product (GNP—see Glossary) per capita than Chile; the rest had a lower level. In the 1991–93 period, the rate at which Chile's gross domestic product (GDP—see Glossary) grew exceeded 6.5 percent per year, making Chile's GDP during these years by far the fastest growing in Latin America. In 1992 GDP grew at a record 10.3 percent pace, year-end unemployment was down to 4.5 percent, real wages were up 5 percent, inflation was down to 12.7 percent, and the public-sector surplus was equivalent to 3 percent of GDP. When a longer period is considered, Chile still comes up ahead of the rest of the Latin American nations. For instance, according to the United Nations Economic Commission for Latin America and the Caribbean (Comisión Económica para América Latina y el Caribe; see Glossary), Chile's GDP per capita increased by 32.2 percent between 1981 and 1993; Colombia was a distant second with an accumulated rate of growth during the period of 23.6 percent.

The success Chile enjoyed by the 1990s resulted largely from the boom in agricultural exports. In 1970 Chile exported US$33 million in agricultural, forestry, and fishing products; by 1991 the total had jumped to US$1.2 billion. This figure excluded those manufactured goods based on products of the agricultural, livestock, and forestry sectors. Much of the increased agricultural production in the country was the result of rapidly improving yields and higher productivity, spurred by an export-oriented policy.

There was little doubt that an exchange-rate policy aimed at encouraging exports lay behind the strong performance of the Chilean economy in the 1986–91 period. First, the liberalization of international trade substantially lowered the costs of imported agricultural inputs and capital goods, enabling the sector to become more competitive. In fact, the liberalization of international trade put an end to a long history of discrimination against agriculture. Tariffs and other forms of import restrictions throughout the 1950s and 1960s gave a relative advantage to those industries that produced importable goods, making them domestically competitive at production costs above international prices. The same policies, because they permitted an overvalued exchange rate, punished those economic activities, like agriculture, that could produce exportable goods. While those goods could be sold at international prices, the foreign-exchange earnings would be converted into domestic currency at an unfavorable exchange rate. Second, the exchange-rate policy, pursued aggressively since 1985, had provided incentives for the expansion of exports.

Third, an institutional framework that secured property rights to land and water, along with reformed labor laws, had increased the openness of factor markets (see Glossary) and established clear signals for the allocation of resources. Potential profits in new business initiatives had by then become very much tied to international prices of goods and domestic costs of resources. The likelihood of government intervention in property rights allocation, prohibitions, special permits, and so forth had been significantly reduced. Related reforms in the transportation sector, particularly in air and marine transport, had further increased access to international trade.

A fourth fundamental policy-based explanation of the increase in agricultural exports was the pursuit of a stable macroeconomic policy whose purpose was to give entrepreneurs confidence in the system and enable them to plan their activities over the longer term. Many of the export-oriented agricultural activities required sizable investments that could only be undertaken in an environment of stability and policy continuity. What is most remarkable, perhaps, is that since 1989 poverty and inequality have been reduced significantly.

Evolution of the Economy

The Colonial Era to 1950

In colonial times, the segmentation of Chile into latifundios (see Glossary) left only small parcels for native American and mestizo (see Glossary) villagers to cultivate. Cattle raised on the latifundios were a source of tallow and hides, which were sent, via Peru, to Spain. Wheat was Chile's principal export during the colonial period. From the *inquilinos* (peons), indentured to the *encomenderos* (see Glossary), or latifundio owners, to the merchants and *encomenderos* themselves, a chain of dependent relations ran all the way to the Spanish metropolis (see The Colonial Economy, ch. 1).

After Chile won its independence in 1818, the economy prospered through a combination of mercantilist and free-market policies. Agricultural exports, primarily wheat, were the mainstay of the export economy. By mid-century, however, Chile had become one of the world's leading producers of copper. After Chile defeated Bolivia and Peru in the War of the Pacific (1879–83), nitrate mines in areas conquered during the war became the source of huge revenues, which were lavished on imports, public works projects, education, and, less directly, the expansion of an incipient industrial sector (see The Liberal Era, 1861–91, ch. 1). Between 1890 and 1924, nitrate output averaged about a quarter of GDP. Taxes on nitrate exports accounted for about half of the government's ordinary budget revenues from 1880 to 1920. By 1910 Chile had established itself as one of the most prosperous countries in Latin America.

Dependence on revenues from nitrate exports contributed to financial instability because the size of government expenditures depended on the vagaries of the export market. Indeed, Chile was faced with a severe domestic crisis when the nitrate bonanza ended abruptly during World War I as a result of the invention of synthetic substitutes by German scientists. Gradually, copper replaced nitrates as Chile's main export commodity. Using new technologies that made it feasible to extract copper from lower-grade ores, United States companies bought existing Chilean mines for large-scale development.

Chile initially felt the impact of the Great Depression (see Glossary) in 1930, when GDP dropped 14 percent, mining income declined 27 percent, and export earnings fell 28 percent. By 1932 GDP had shrunk to less than half of what it had been in 1929, exacting a terrible toll in unemployment and business failures. The League of Nations (see Glossary) labeled Chile the country hardest hit by the Great Depression because 80 percent of government revenue came from exports of copper and nitrates, which were in low demand.

Influenced profoundly by the Great Depression, many national leaders promoted the development of local industry in an effort to insulate the economy from future external shocks. After six years of government austerity measures, which succeeded in reestablishing Chile's creditworthiness, Chileans elected to office during the 1938–58 period a succession of center and left-of-center governments interested in promoting economic growth by means of government intervention.

Prompted in part by the devastating earthquake of 1939, the Chilean government created the Production Development Corporation (Corporación de Fomento de la Producción—Corfo) to encourage with subsidies and direct investments an ambitious program of import-substitution industrialization. Consequently, as in other Latin American countries, protectionism became an entrenched aspect of the Chilean economy.

Import-substitution industrialization was spurred on by the advent of World War II and the loss of access to many imported products. State enterprises in electric power, steel, petroleum, and other heavy industries were also created and expanded during the first years of the industrialization process, mostly under the guidance of Corfo, and the foundations of the manufacturing sector were set. Between 1937 and 1950, the manufacturing sector grew at an average yearly real rate of almost 7 percent.

Despite initially impressive rates of growth, import-substitution industrialization did not produce a sustainable expansion of the manufacturing sector. With the industrialization process evolved an array of restrictions, controls, and often contradictory regulations. With time, consumer-oriented industries found that their markets were limited in a society where a large percentage of the population was poor and where many rural inhabitants lived at the margins of the money economy. The economic model did not generate a viable capital goods (see Glossary) industry because firms

Survivors of the March 1985 earthquake in central Chile stand among the ruins of their homes in the Santo Domingo area of Santiago.
Courtesy Inter-American Development Bank

relied on imports of often outmoded capital and intermediate goods. Survival often depended on state subsidies or state protection. In fact, it was because of these import restrictions that many of the domestic industries were able to survive. For example, a number of comparative studies have indicated that Chile had one of the highest, and more variable, structures of protection in the developing world. As a consequence, many, if not most, of the industries created under the import-substitution industrialization strategy were inefficient. Also, it has been argued that this strategy led to the use of highly capital-intensive (see Glossary) production, which, among other inefficiencies, hampered job creation. Additionally, the import-substitution industrialization strategy generated an economy that was particularly vulnerable to external shocks.

During the import-substitution industrialization period, copper continued to be the principal export commodity and source of foreign exchange, as well as an important generator of government revenues. The Chilean government's retained share of the value of copper output increased from about one-quarter in 1925 to over four-fifths in 1970, mainly through higher taxes. Although protectionist policies better insulated Chile from the occasional shocks of world commodities markets, price shifts continued to take their toll.

Economic Policies, 1950–70

Between 1950 and 1970, the Chilean economy expanded at meager rates. GDP grew at an average rate of 3.8 percent per annum, whereas real GDP per capita increased at an average yearly rate of 1.6 percent. Over this period, Chile's economic performance was the poorest among Latin America's large and medium-size countries.

As in most historical cases, Chile's import-substitution industrialization strategy was accompanied by an acute overvaluation of the domestic currency that precluded the development of a vigorous nontraditional (that is, noncopper) export sector. Although some agrarian reform was attempted, the government increasingly resorted to control-ling agricultural prices in order to subsidize the urban working and middle classes. The agricultural sector was particularly harmed by the overvaluation of Chile's currency. The lagging of agriculture became, in fact, one of the most noticeable symptoms of Chile's economic problems of the 1950s and 1960s. Over this period, manufacturing and mining, mainly of copper, significantly increased their shares in total output.

By the early 1960s, most of the easy and obvious substitutions of imported goods had already been made; the process of import-substitution industrialization was rapidly becoming less dynamic. For example, between 1950 and 1960 total real industrial production grew at an annual rate of only 3.5 percent, less than half the rate of the previous decade.

During the 1950s, inflation, which had been a chronic problem in Chile since at least the 1880s, became particularly serious; the rate of increase of consumer prices averaged 36 percent per annum during the decade, reaching a peak of 84 percent in 1955. The main source of the inflationary pressure on the Chilean economy was a remarkably lax fiscal policy. Chile's economic history has been marked by failed attempts to curb inflation. During the 1950s and 1960s, three major stabilization programs, one in each administration, were launched. The common aspect of these efforts was the emphasis placed on tackling the various consequences of inflationary pressures, such as prices, wages, and exchange-rate increases, rather than the root cause of money growth, the monetization of the fiscal deficit. In spite of the efforts of presidents Carlos Ibáñez del Campo (1927–31, 1952–58) and Jorge Alessandri Rodríguez (1958–64), inflation averaged 31 percent per annum during these two decades. In 1970, the last year of the government of President Eduardo Frei Montalva (1964–70), the inflation rate stood at 35 percent.

During the 1960s, and especially during the Frei administration, some efforts to reform the economy were launched. These included an agrarian reform, a limited liberalization of the external sector, and a policy of minidevaluations aimed at preventing the erosion of the real exchange rate. Under the 1962 Agrarian Reform Law, the Agrarian Reform Corporation (Corporación de Reforma Agraria—Cora) was created to handle the distribution, but land reform proved to be slow and expensive. In spite of these and other reforms, toward the end of the 1960s it appeared that the performance of the economy had not improved in relation to the previous twenty years. Moreover, the economy was still heavily regulated.

The Popular Unity Government, 1970–73

In September 1970, Salvador Allende, the Popular Unity candidate, was elected president of Chile. Over the next three years, a unique political and economic experience followed. Popular Unity was a coalition of left and center-left parties dominated by the Socialist Party (Partido Socialista) and the Communist Party of Chile (Partido Comunista de Chile—PCCh), both of which sought to implement deep institutional, political, and economic reforms. Popular Unity's program called for a democratic "Chilean road to socialism" (see Salvador Allende's Leftist Regime, 1970–73, ch. 1).

When Allende took office in November 1970, his government faced a stagnant economy weakened by inflation, which hit a rate of 35 percent in 1970. Between 1967 and 1970, real GDP per capita had grown only 1.2 percent per annum, a rate significantly below the Latin American average. The balance of payments (see Glossary) had shown substantial surpluses during all but one of the years from 1964 to 1970, and, at the time Popular Unity took power, the Central Bank of Chile (see Glossary) had a stock of international reserves of approximately US$400 million.

Popular Unity had a number of short-run economic objectives: initiating structural economic transformations, including a program of nationalization; increasing real wages; reducing inflation; spurring economic growth; increasing consumption, especially by poorer people; and reducing the economy's dependence on the rest of the world. The nationalization program was to be achieved by a combination of new legislation, requisitions, and stock purchases from small shareholders. The other goals—output and increased consumption, with rising salaries and declining inflation—were to be accomplished by a boost in aggregate demand, mainly generated by higher government expenditures, accompanied by strict price controls and measures to redistribute income.

Allende's macroeconomic program was based on several key assumptions, the most important being that the manufacturing sector had ample underutilized capacity. This provided the theoretical basis for the belief that large fiscal deficits would not necessarily be inflationary. The lack of full utilization was, in turn, attributed to two fundamental factors: the monopolistic nature of the manufacturing industry and the structure of income distribution. Based on this diagnosis, it was thought that if income were redistributed toward the poorer groups through wage increases and if prices were properly controlled, there would be a significant expansion of demand and output.

In regard to inflation, the Popular Unity program placed blame on structural rigidities (namely, slow or no response of quantity supplied to price increases), bottlenecks, and the role of monopolistic pricing, and it played down the role of fiscal pressures and money creation. Little attention was paid to the financial sector, given the orientation of the new regime's economic technocrats toward the import-substitution industralization, structuralist philosophy of the Economic Commission for Latin America. In fact, Allende's minister of foreign relations and vice president, Clodomiro Almeyda, relates in his memoirs how in the first postelection meeting of the economic team, these technocrats argued expressly and convincingly that monetary and financial management did not deserve too much attention. Alfonso Inostroza, the Central Bank president, stated in early 1971 that the main objective of the monetary policy was to "transform it into a key instrument . . . to achieve the complete mobilization of productive resources, and their allocation to those areas that the government gives priority to . . . ." This was consistent with the view of inflation of those espousing structuralism (see Glossary).

The Popular Unity perspective on the way the economy functioned ignored many of the key principles of traditional economic theory. This was reflected in the greatly diminished attention given to monetary policies and also in the complete disregard of the exchange rate as a key variable in determining macroeconomic equilibrium. In particular, the Popular Unity program and policies paid no attention to the role of the real exchange rate as a determinant of the country's international competitive position. Moreover, Popular Unity failed to recognize that its policies would not be sustainable in the medium term and that capacity constraints were going to become an insurmountable obstacle to rapid growth.

Economic Crisis and the Military Coup

After assuming power in November 1970, Popular Unity rapidly began to implement its program. In the area of structural reforms, two basic measures were immediately begun. First, agrarian reform were greatly intensified, and a large number of farms were expropriated. Second, the government proposed to change the constitution in order to nationalize the large copper mines, which were jointly owned by large United States firms and the Chilean state.

Government expenditures expanded greatly, and in 1971 real salaries and wages in the public sector increased 48 percent, on average. Salaries in the private sector grew at approximately the same rate. In the first two quarters of 1971, manufacturing output increased 6.2 percent and 10.6 percent, compared with the same periods in the previous year. Manufacturing sales grew at even faster rates: 12 percent during the first quarter and 11 percent during the second quarter. Overall, the behavior of the economy in 1971 seemed to vindicate Popular Unity economists: real GDP grew at 7.7 percent, average real wages increased by 17 percent, aggregate consumption grew at a real rate of 13.2 percent, and the rate of unemployment dipped below 4 percent. Also, and more important for Popular Unity political leaders, income distribution improved significantly. In 1971 labor's share of GDP reached 61.7 percent, almost ten percentage points higher than in 1970. All of this created a sense of euphoria in the government.

On June 11, 1971, Congress approved unanimously an amendment to the constitution nationalizing large copper mines. As a result, reform of the banking system and large manufacturing firms was more difficult because the government lacked the institutional means to implement nationalization. Initially, this obstacle was alleviated because the government purchased blocks of shares, especially bank shares, at high prices. These share acquisitions were complemented by a process of requisition or expropriation of foreign-owned companies based on an old, and until then forgotten, decree law promulgated during Marmaduke Grove Vallejo's short-lived Socialist Republic of 1932.

All did not remain well in the economy in 1971. Popular Unity's macroeconomic policies were rapidly generating a situation of repressed inflation. The high growth rate of GDP was largely the result of an almost 40 percent increase in imports of intermediate goods. The fiscal deficit had jumped from 2 percent of GDP in 1970 to almost 11 percent in 1971. The rate at which the money supply grew exceeded 100 percent in 1971. As a result, the stock of international reserves inherited by the Allende government was reduced by more than one-half in that year alone. A rapid reduction of inventories was another important factor in the expansion of consumption.

By the end of 1971, the mounting inflationary pressures had become evident. The economy was experiencing the consequences of an aggregate demand for goods and services well above the aggregate supply at current prices. This imbalance was aggravated by a series of labor disputes in many large establishments that resulted in the takeover of those firms by their workers. In fact, this procedure became the institutionalized way in which the government seized a large number of firms.

During 1972 the macroeconomic problems continued to mount. Inflation surpassed 200 percent, and the fiscal deficit surpassed 13 percent of GDP. Domestic credit to the public sector grew at almost 300 percent, and international reserves dipped below US$77 million.

The underground economy grew as more and more activities moved out of the official economy. As a result, more and more sources of tax revenues disappeared. A vicious cycle began: repressed inflation encouraged the informal economy, thus reducing tax revenues and leading to higher deficits and even higher inflation. In 1972 two stabilization programs were implemented, both unsuccessfully.

When evaluating the problems faced by the economy, Popular Unity economists generally held the view that the authorities had failed to impose appropriate controls in implementing Allende's program. This view guided the first, rather weak, attempt at stabilizing the economy that was launched in February 1972. Price controls were the main ingredient of the program. By mid-1972 it was apparent that the February stabilization program was a failure. The underground economy was now widespread, output had begun to fall, open inflation reached an annual rate of 70 percent in the second quarter, foreign-exchange reserves were very low, and the black-market value of the currency was falling rapidly. Parliamentary elections scheduled for March 1973 made the situation particularly difficult for the government. In August 1972, a new stabilization program was launched under the political monitoring of the PCCh. This time not only prices were officially controlled, but the distribution channels were taken over by the government in an attempt to reduce the extent of the black market.

Unlike the previous plan, the August 1972 stabilization program was based on a massive devaluation of the escudo (for value of the escudo—see Glossary). The government expected that the result would be an easing of the mounting pressures on the balance of payments. The program also called for two basic measures to contain fiscal pressures. First, nationalized firms were authorized to increase prices as a means of reducing the financing requirements of the newly formed nationalized sector. Second, the program called for a massive increase in production, especially in the recently nationalized manufacturing and agriculture sectors (large manufacturing firms and farms had been expropriated arbitrarily). The devaluation and a large number of price increases resulted in annualized inflation rates of 22.7 percent in August and 22.2 percent in September.

In mid-August 1972, the government announced that it had drafted a new wage policy based on an increase in public- and private-sector wages by a proportion equal to the accumulated rate of inflation between January and September. In addition, the new policy called for more frequent wage adjustments.

During the first quarter of 1973, Chile's economic problems became extremely serious. Inflation reached an annual rate of more than 120 percent, industrial output declined by almost 6 percent, and foreign-exchange reserves held by the Central Bank were barely above US$40 million. The black market by then covered a widening range of transactions in foreign exchange. The fiscal deficit continued to climb as a result of spiraling expenditures and of rapidly disappearing sources of taxation. For that year, the fiscal deficit ended up exceeding 23 percent of GDP.

The depth of the economic crisis seriously affected the middle class, and relations between the government and the political opposition became increasingly confrontational. On September 11, 1973, the regime came to a sudden and shocking end with a military coup and President Allende's suicide.

When the military took over, the country was divided politically, and the economy was a shambles. Inflation was galloping, and relative price distortions, stemming mainly from massive price controls, were endemic. In addition, black-market activities were rampant, real wages had dropped drastically, the economic prospects of the middle class had darkened, the external sector was facing a serious crisis, production and investment were falling steeply, and government finances were completely out of hand.

The Military Government's Free-Market Reforms, 1973–90

After the military took over the government in September 1973, a period of dramatic economic changes began. Chile was transformed gradually from an economy isolated from the rest of the world, with strong government intervention, into a liberalized, world-integrated economy, where market forces were left free to guide most of the economy's decisions. This period was characterized by several important economic achievements: inflation was reduced greatly, the government deficit was virtually eliminated, the economy went through a dramatic liberalization of its foreign sector, and a strong market system was established.

From an economic point of view, the era of General Augusto Pinochet Ugarte (1973–90) can be divided into two periods. The first, from 1973 to 1982, corresponds to the period when most of the reforms were implemented. The period ended with the international debt crisis and the collapse of the Chilean economy. At that point, unemployment was extremely high, above 20 percent, and a large proportion of the banking sector had become bankrupt. During this period, a pragmatic economic policy that emphasized export expansion and growth was implemented. The second period, from 1982 to 1990, is characterized by economic recovery and the consolidation of the free-market reforms.

Trade Policy

One of the fundamental economic goals of the military regime was to open up the economy to the rest of the world. However, this was not the first attempt at liberalizing international trade in Chile. Between 1950 and 1970, the country went through three attempts at trade liberalization without ever reaching full liberalization. Moreover, all three attempts quickly ended in frustration and in a reversion to exchange controls, the use of multiple exchange rates, and massive quantitative restrictions. A particularly interesting feature of the three attempts at liberalization is that, although they took place under three different exchange-rate systems, they all collapsed, at least in part because of a highly overvalued real exchange rate.

Starting in 1974, Chile adopted unilaterally an open trade regime characterized by low uniform import tariffs, a lack of exchange or trade controls, and minimum restrictions on capital movements. Starting in 1979, Chile's trade policy became highly liberalized; subsequently, there were no quantitative restrictions, licenses, or prohibitions. A uniform import tax varying between 10 percent and 35 percent took effect, and, until 1980, real exchange-rate overvaluation generally was avoided. By 1990 Chile was the only country, according to the World Bank, whose index of liberalization reached the maximum possible level of 20, indicating an absence of external-sector distortions.

In 1973 import tariffs averaged 105 percent and were highly dispersed, with some goods subject to nominal tariffs of more than 700 percent and others fully exempted from import duties. In addition to tariffs, a battery of quantitative restrictions were applied, including outright import prohibitions and prior import deposits of up to 10,000 percent. These protective measures were complemented by a highly distorting multiple exchange-rate system consisting of fifteen different nominal exchange rates. By August 1975, all quantitative restrictions had been eliminated, and the average tariff had been reduced to 44 percent. This process of tariff reductions continued until June 1979, when all tariffs but one (that on automobiles) were set at 10 percent. In the mid-1980s, in the midst of the debt crisis, temporary tariff hikes were implemented; by 1989, however, a uniform level of 15 percent had been established.

During the early period (1975–79) of the military regime, the opening of Chile's external sector was accompanied by a strongly depreciated real exchange rate. In 1979, however, the authorities adopted a fixed-exchange-rate policy that resulted in an acute overvaluation of the Chilean peso (for value of the Chilean peso—see Glossary), a loss in international competititiveness, and, in 1982, a deep crisis. In 1984–85 this situation was reversed, and a policy of a depreciated and highly competitive real exchange rate was implemented. The combination of these two policies—low tariffs and a competitive real exchange rate—had a significant impact on Chile's economic structure. The share of manufacturing in GNP dropped from almost 29 percent in 1974 to 22 percent in 1981. Productivity in tradable sectors grew substantially, and exports became highly diversified. Chile had also diversified its export markets, with the result that no individual market bought more than 20 percent of the country's total exports. By the early 1990s, exports had become the engine of growth, and the Chilean trade reform was winning praise from multinational institutions and observers of different ideological persuasions. Largely thanks to the boom in exports between 1986 and 1991, particularly the increasing growth in exports of fresh fruits and manufactured products, Chile experienced the highest rate of GDP growth in Latin America (the "Chilean miracle"), with an annual increase of 4.2 percent.

In what was perhaps the surest sign of the success of trade reform, the new democratic government of President Patricio Aylwin Azócar (1990–94), elected in December 1989, decided to continue the opening process and reduced import tariffs to a uniform 11 percent. Interestingly, Aylwin's economic team, including the minister of finance and the minister of economy, development, and reconstruction, had been relentless critics of the trade reform process during its implementation in the mid- and late 1970s.

Banking Reform and the Financial Sector

A major policy objective of the military regime was the liberalization and modernization of the banking sector. Until 1973 the domestic capital market had been highly repressed, with most banks being government owned. Real interest rates were negative, and there were quantitative restrictions on credit. The liberalization process began slowly, in early 1974, with the sale of banks back to the private sector, the freeing of interest rates, the relaxation of some restrictions on the banking sector, and the creation of new financial institutions. International capital movements, however, were strictly controlled until mid-1979. In June 1979, the government decided to begin to liberalize the capital account (see Glossary) of the balance of payments, lifting some restrictions on medium- and long-term capital movements.

The opening of the capital account resulted in a massive inflow of foreign capital that contributed to Chile's subsequent international debt problems. In 1980 capital inflows were more than double those of 1979—US$2.5 billion versus US$1.2 billion—and in 1981 the level of capital inflows nearly doubled again, to US$4.5 billion.

An important result of the reforms of the financial sector was that the number of financial institutions and the volume of financial intervention both increased greatly. For example, in 1981 there were twenty-six national banks, nineteen foreign banks, and fifteen savings and loan institutions (*financieras*), a number significantly higher than the eighteen national banks and one foreign bank in operation in September 1973. Furthermore, between 1973 and 1981 the real volume of total credit to the private sector increased by more than 1,100 percent.

At least in terms of increasing the degree of financial intermediation, liberalization was a success. However, it was apparent from the beginning that capital-market liberalization faced three major obstacles. First, interest rates were very high. Second, in spite of the significant growth in the extent of financial intermediation, domestic savings had not increased to the extent that the proponents of the reforms had expected. In fact, domestic savings were at one of their lowest levels in history from 1974 to 1982. There are several possible explanations for the behavior of domestic savings. One of the most popular of these relies on the notion that the appreciation of domestic assets that was taking place at the time, such as stocks and land prices, resulted in a real accumulation of assets without saving. This increase in private-sector wealth was consistent with higher levels of consumption at a given income. Third, and perhaps more important, the rapid growth of the financial sector took place in an environment in which monetary authorities exercised no supervision. As a result, many banks accumulated an unprecedented volume of bad loans, a situation that led to the financial crisis of 1982–83. As a consequence of this crisis, a number of banks went bankrupt during 1983–84, were placed temporarily under government control, and then were reprivatized. By 1992, after monetary authorities had learned the hard way the importance of bank supervision, Chile's financial sector had become highly stable and dynamic.

Rural Land Market Reform

At the time of the military coup, about 60 percent of Chile's irrigated land and 50 percent of total agricultural land was under the control of the public sector. Land reform had started in the 1960s with expropriations of large landholdings (those larger than eighty basic irrigated hectares—BIH) and the encouragement of small farms (about 8.5 BIH) managed by their owners. The Allende administration favored large-scale farms under cooperatives and state-farm management over private ownership of agricultural land. Starting in 1974, the military government began using Cora to end agrarian reform by distributing land to establish family farms with individual ownership. In a period of three years, 109,000 farmers and 67,000 descendants of the Mapuche had been assigned property rights to small farms. About 28 percent of the expropriated land was returned to previous owners, and the rest was auctioned off.

Three key legal issues were then clarified by decree law in 1978. Government authority to expropriate land was repealed, the ceilings on landholdings (the equivalent of eighty BIH) were removed, and the ban on corporate ownership of land was eliminated. At the end of 1978, all farmland owned publicly had been distributed, and Cora was legally closed.

Reforms in the legislation that regulated land rentals and land subdivisions in 1980 added flexibility to the rural land markets. But perhaps more crucial aspects of the reforms were the separation of water rights from the land itself and the legal possibility of transferring water titles independently of land transactions.

Labor-Market Reform

Immediately after the 1973 coup, many labor institutions, that is, traditional channels of influence, such as government offices, which unions used to get their voices heard, were disbanded, and some important unions were dissolved. Thus, wage adjustments became mainly a function of indexation, which, given Chile's history of inflation, had become an established element of any wage negotiation. Indexation was kept in place until 1982, through ten years of declining inflation.

Starting in October 1973, the government mandated across-the-board periodic wage adjustments tied to the rate of inflation. Lower wages were adjusted proportionally more than higher ones. From 1973 to 1979, indexation to past inflation with varying lags was the norm throughout the economy. The 1979 Labor Plan formalized this practice by requiring that collective bargaining agreements allow for wage adjustments at or above the rate of inflation. In 1982 the indexation clause of the Labor Plan was eliminated. The government continued the practice of periodically announcing wage readjustments and bonuses, with the wage increases usually not keeping pace with inflation and covering the nonunionized sector only. The dynamism of the economy in the early 1990s resulted in actual wage increases above officially announced readjustments.

The Employment Security Law established that in the absence of "just cause" for dismissal, such as drunkenness, absenteeism, or theft, a dismissed employee could be reinstated to the job by a labor court. This law was replaced by a less costly system of severance payments in 1978. Decree Law 2,200 authorized employers to modify individual labor contracts and to dismiss workers without "cause." A minimum severance payment was established that was equivalent to one month of salary per year of service, up to a maximum of five months' pay. This new system applied to all contracts signed after August 1981.

The changes introduced by Decree Law 2,200, along with the 1979 reforms, which established new mechanisms to govern union activity (Decree Law 2,756) and collective bargaining (Decree Law 2,758), became known in Chile as the Labor Plan. Decree Law 2,756 departed significantly from traditional legislation: union affiliation within a company became voluntary, and all negotiations would now have to be conducted at the company level; bargaining among many companies would be eliminated. According to the previous law, which had applied until the 1973 coup, once the majority of the workers of an enterprise chose to join an "industrial union," all workers became part of that union. That is, one union would have exclusive representation of all workers in an enterprise. The right to collective bargaining was granted to unions at the enterprise level and also to union federations and confederations. This resulted in some negotiations at the industry level with the participation of the Ministry of Labor and Social Welfare through the Labor Inspectorate. As in the past, the new law required participation of 10 percent of the workers or a minimum of twenty-five workers (whichever was greater) for creation of a union. Workers were not required to be represented by a union in collective bargaining.

Decree Law 2,758 stipulated that in the event of a strike, a firm could impose a lockout and temporarily lay off workers, which the

Farmers at work in the Maule Norte irrigation project near Talca
Courtesy Inter-American Development Bank

previous law had prohibited. At the same time, Decree Law 2,758 established norms about collective bargaining, and in its Article 26 the law established that unionized workers' nominal wages should be adjusted to at least match the rate of inflation. This article, which became a severe constraint to downward real wage flexibility during the 1982–83 crisis, can be understood only in the context of a previously existing policy of 100 percent indexation across the board. In 1982, at the onset of the debt crisis, Article 26 was amended, eliminating the downward inflexibility of real wages. This reformed law was in effect until April 1991, when some important changes proposed by the Aylwin administration were approved by the National Congress (hereafter, Congress).

Public Employment Programs

Two public employment programs affected the labor market during the period of economic reforms between 1975 and 1987. The Minimum Employment Program (Programa de Empleo Mínimo—PEM) was created in 1975 at a time when unemployment had reached record levels. The program, administered by local governments, paid a small salary to unemployed workers, who, for a few hours a week, performed menial public works. At first, the government tightly restricted entry into the program. Gradually, most of these restrictions were lifted, and a larger number of unemployed people were allowed to participate. Thus, the proportion of the labor force employed by the program remained virtually constant between 1977 and 1981, despite the economic recovery and a reduction in the real value of PEM compensation.

When Chile entered a new and more severe recession, the number of individuals employed by PEM in the Metropolitan Region of Santiago increased from about 23,000 in May 1982 to 93,000 in May 1983. An Employment Program for Heads of Household (Programa de Ocupación para Jefes de Hogar—POJH), created in October 1982, employed about 100,000 individuals in the greater Santiago area by May 1983. The two programs combined absorbed more than 10 percent of the labor force of the greater Santiago area in May 1983. These programs were also implemented in other regions of the country. The PEM program was cut back drastically in February 1984. Likewise, by December 1988, there were only about 5,000 individuals employed by the POJH in the entire country.

The Debt Crisis: Further Reforms and Recovery

The international debt crisis unleashed in 1982 hit the Chilean economy with particular severity, as foreign loans dried up and the international terms of trade (see Glossary) turned drastically against Chile. The policies implemented initially to face the 1982 crisis can best be described as hesitant. In early 1983, the financial sector was nationalized as a way to avoid a major banking crisis, and a number of subsidy schemes favoring debtors were enacted. The decision to subsidize debtors who had borrowed in foreign currency during the period of fixed exchange rates and to bail out the troubled banks resulted in heavy Central Bank losses, which contributed to the creation of a huge deficit in public-sector finance. This deficit, in turn, would become one of the underlying causes of the inflation of the early 1990s. Different exchange-rate systems were tried, including a floating rate, only to be abandoned rapidly and replaced by new plans. Policies aimed at restructuring the manufacturing sector, which had entered a deep crisis as a consequence of the collapse of some of the major conglomerates, the so-called groups (*grupos*), were implemented. In spite of this array of measures, the economy did not show a significant response; unemployment remained extraordinarily high, and the external crisis, which some had expected to represent only a temporary setback, dragged on.

In early 1985, increasingly disappointed by the economy's performance, Pinochet turned toward a group of pragmatic economists who favored free markets and macroeconomic stability. Led by newly appointed finance minister Hernán Büchi Buc, an economist who had studied business administration at Columbia University, the new economic team devised a major adjustment program aimed at reestablishing growth, reducing the burden of the foreign debt, and rebuilding the strength of the financial and manufacturing sectors. Three policy areas became critical in the implementation of the program: active macroeconomic policies, consolidation of the market-oriented structural reforms initiated in the 1970s, and debt-management policies geared toward rescheduling debt payments and making an aggressive use of the secondary market. With the help of the International Monetary Fund (IMF—see Glossary), the World Bank, and improved terms of trade, these policies succeeded in achieving their objectives.

The macroeconomic program of a group of Chilean economists known as the "Chicago boys" (see Glossary), who had guided Pinochet's early economic policies, had relied on a hands-off "automatic adjustment" strategy. By mid-1982 this approach had generated a severe overvaluation of the real exchange rate. By contrast, the new macroeconomic program relied on active and carefully monitored macroeconomic management. An active exchange-rate policy, based on large initial exchange-rate adjustments followed by periodic small devaluations, became one of the most important policies of the post-1982 period. Between 1982 and 1988, the international competitiveness of Chilean exports was increased greatly by a real exchange-rate depreciation of approximately 90 percent. This policy not only helped generate a boom in nontraditional exports but also contributed to reasonable interest-rate levels and to the prevention of capital flight.

The adjustment program that started in 1985 also had a structural adjustment component that was aimed at consolidating the market-oriented reforms of the 1970s and early 1980s, including the privatization process, the opening of the economy, and the development of a dynamic capital market. There were several structural goals of the 1985 program: rebuild the financial sector, which had been nearly destroyed during the 1982 crisis; reduce import tariffs below the 35 percent level that they had reached during 1984 to a 15 percent uniform level; and promote exports through a set of fiscal incentives and a competitive real exchange rate.

Perhaps the most important aspects of these structural reform measures were the privatization and recapitalization of firms and banks that had failed during the 1982–83 crisis. As a first step in this process, the Central Bank bought private banks' nonperforming portfolios. In order to finance this operation, the Central Bank issued domestic credit. The banks, in turn, paid a rate of 5 percent on the nonperforming portfolios and promised to repurchase them out of retained profits. This recapitalization program had as its counterpart a privatization plan that returned the ownership of those banks and firms that had been nationalized in 1983 to the private sector. Economist Rolf J. Lüders estimates that about 550 enterprises under public-sector control, including most of Chile's largest corporations, were privatized between 1974 and 1990. By the end of 1991, fewer that fifty firms remained in the public sector. The overall privatization program undertaken after 1985 has been criticized by some Chileans and also by some international economists because banks and manufacturing firms were sold too rapidly and at "very low prices."

Chile's structural adjustment of the second half of the 1980s was unique in comparison with the rest of the world. The most difficult, controversial, and costly reforms—including the bulk of privatization, trade liberalization, financial deregulation, and labor market streamlining—were undertaken in Chile in the 1975–80 period; the measures taken after 1985 were minor in comparison. The success of the post-1985 period was rooted in the early reforms. For example, the boom in nontraditional exports that took place in the second half of the 1980s was only possible because of investments begun almost ten years before. The markets' flexible and rapid response to incentives was also a direct consequence of the microeconomic reforms of the 1970s.

One of the most hotly debated issues of the Chilean recovery of the second half of the 1980s concerns the different foreign-debt conversion plans aimed at rapidly reducing foreign indebtedness. When the debt crisis erupted in 1982, Chile's foreign debt was US$17.2 billion, one of the highest debts per capita in the world. Through the aggressive use of a variety of debt-conversion plans, between 1985 and 1991 Chile retired an estimated US$10.5 billion of its debt, most of which was converted into equity in Chilean companies.

Chile's net international reserves totaled US$9 billion in 1992, enough to cover a year of imports and equivalent to roughly half of its foreign debt. The stock of foreign direct investment in Chile was estimated to be between US$10 billion and US$13 billion, roughly 30 percent of GDP. About US$4 billion of this was acquired through debt-equity conversions. The debt-swap program was ended when the growth of direct investment and the strength of the economy had done away with the need for special incentives to attract foreign capital.

The Return to Democracy, 1990

On March 11, 1990, General Pinochet handed the presidency

*A view of the Trans-Andean Highway, the most important road
link between Argentina and Chile
Courtesy Inter-American Development Bank*

of Chile to Patricio Aylwin. When Aylwin's Coalition of Parties
for Democracy (Concertación de Partidos por la Democracia—
CPD) government took over, Chile had the best performing economy in Latin America.

Continuity in Economic Policy

For years, opponents of the Pinochet government had argued
that its economic program was based on ideas alien to the Chilean
tradition. In early 1990, analysts, scholars, stockbrokers, and politicians throughout the world wondered if the new democratic
government of President Aylwin would maintain some, or for that
matter any, of the most important aspects of the military government's market-oriented policies, or if the CPD government would
reform the system along the lines of the decade-long criticisms of
the opposition. What made this question particularly interesting
was that at the time of the restoration of democracy, Chile was
considered by many, including international institutions such as
the World Bank and the IMF, as a premier example of the way
the adjustment process after the debt crisis should be carried out.
A number of analysts asked themselves how the advent of democracy would affect Chile's economic policy. In particular, analysts were

159

concerned about the new government's attitude toward the free price system and Chile's new openness to international competition.

Regarding price competition, the Aylwin program's position was stated as follows: "We affirm that within an efficient economic policy there is no role for price controls." In discussing the role of the market, the program noted: "The market cannot be replaced as a mechanism for consumers to articulate their preferences." These views were a far cry from those sustained by Frei's Christian Democratic government of the 1960s and, especially, from those of Allende's Popular Unity government of 1970–73. They were also substantially different from those of the new market critics of the 1970s and mid-1980s. Indeed, the CPD program conveyed that there had been a significant convergence of domestic views on the role of markets in the economic process.

Addressing the opening of the economy to the rest of the world, the CPD program stated: "The most important instruments of the external sector policy are the maintenance of a stable high real exchange rate and a reasonably *low import tariff*" [emphasis added]. This statement suggests that from its onset the Aylwin government was not prepared to implement major changes to one of the most fundamental features of Chile's new economics.

Emphasis on Social Programs

In seeking funding for new social programs, the Aylwin government made clear immediately that the only way of increasing social spending without generating unsustainable macroeconomic pressures was by finding secure sources of government revenue. Economists associated with Aylwin's CPD coalition calculated in 1989 that in order to implement their antipoverty social programs, annual funds on the order of 4 percent of GDP would be required. They argued that these resources could be obtained through a combination of expenditures, reallocation, foreign aid, and increased tax revenues. In order to implement these programs rapidly, in April 1990 President Aylwin submitted to the newly elected Congress a legislative proposal aimed at reforming the tax system. The main features of the package were the following: the corporate income-tax rate was to be increased temporarily from 10 percent to 15 percent for 1991–93; and the tax base, which in 1985 had been defined as distributed profits, was to be broadened to include total profits. The progressiveness of the personal income tax was to be increased by reducing the income level at which the maximum rate was applicable; and the rate of the value-added tax (VAT—see Glossary) would be increased to 18 percent from 16 percent. During most of the Pinochet government, the VAT rate had been 20 percent. It was only reduced to 16 percent prior to the electoral contest before the plebiscite on Pinochet's continuation in power. After intense and often frustrating negotiations between the Aylwin administration and the opposition, the tax reform was approved in late 1990.

Pinochet's labor reforms of 1978–79 had been, from the beginning, strongly criticized by the opponents of the military regime. Although the 1979 decrees had modernized labor relations in some areas, they had also severely limited the activities of unions and, as initially conceived, had made real wage rates unusually rigid. Reforming the labor plan was an important priority of the new democratic government.

After the support of some opposition senators was obtained, a mild labor reform was passed in 1991. An important characteristic of Chile's constitution of 1980 is that it stipulates the seating of nine nonelected senators in the legislature's upper house, as well as former presidents and former justices of the Supreme Court. The CPD coalition lacked a parliamentary majority because the nonelected senators had been appointed by Pinochet. Consequently, in order to approve legislation it had to obtain support from the opposition for some measures.

The new labor legislation restricted the causes for firing employees, increased the compensation that firms had to pay to lay off employees, and restricted employers' recourse to lockouts. Although there was little doubt that these new regulations had increased the cost of labor, it was too early to know the effect of the new legislation on job creation. It was known, however, that the reform of labor laws by a democratically elected government had greatly legitimated the modernization of labor relations. In a way, the concept of labor-market flexibility had ceased to be associated exclusively with the authoritarian military regime and had become generally accepted by the population at large.

The Current Structure of the Economy

A World Bank study shows that after the trade liberalization of the 1970s, Chile experienced a substantial increase in productivity. This study also shows that in the 1987–91 period, Chile's productivity increased much more than that of any other country in Latin America. Chile's national accounts for 1989–91 show a number of interesting features (see table 20, Appendix). First, the share of agriculture, livestock, and forestry in GDP decreased during these three years from 8.1 percent to 7.9 percent. This short-term trend, however, was somewhat misleading. In 1971 the share of GDP generated by agriculture, livestock, and forestry had been 7.4 percent.

From a historical perspective, the increase in the relative importance of the primary sector in a twenty-year span—from 7.4 percent to 7.9 percent of GDP—was somewhat of an anomaly. A well-documented trend is that in the vast majority of countries, as income and output expand and national economies become more developed, this sector generates a smaller share of GDP. In the case of Chile, the absence of this phenomenon can be explained by the drastic structural reforms implemented in the second half of the 1970s and in the 1980s. An important consequence of the market-oriented reforms of the Pinochet government was the elimination of discrimination against export agriculture that had characterized the Chilean economy during the decades of import-substitution industrialization. The level of productivity of the agricultural sector (measured as crop yields) had increased significantly by the early 1990s (see Agriculture, this ch.).

A second important feature of Chile's national accounts in 1989–91 is that the manufacturing sector represented approximately 21 percent of GDP for the period. This was significantly lower than this sector's share of total output in 1969–70, when it was almost 25 percent. The reduced participation of manufacturing also reflected the structural reforms of the 1970s and 1980s. Those policies had eliminated the protection walls that had artificially encouraged Chile's industrial sector during the 1960s.

The share of mining in GDP remained roughly constant from 1967 to 1992. However, the composition of mining production changed substantially; in particular, there was a drop in the importance of copper mining. Also, construction's share of GDP shrank from 7.7 percent of GDP in 1970 to 6.0 percent in 1992. During the same period, the share of services increased from 26 percent to 29.1 percent. Within this sector, a particularly significant increase occurred in the financial area (see fig. 8).

Industry and Manufacturing

The Chilean manufacturing sector experienced strong performance in the 1985–91 period, and the Industrial Development Association (Sociedad de Fomento Fabril—Sofofa) expected a 7 percent to 10 percent increase in industrial output in 1992. (The sector actually grew 12.3 percent during the first three quarters.) Between 1985 and 1991, the manufacturing sector grew at an average annual rate of 6.2 percent, a figure that compared favorably with the average rate for the 1960s of 5.1 percent per annum. However, in spite of the dynamic behavior of manufacturing as a whole, the development of different industries within the sector was uneven. Some industries were able to exploit Chile's comparative advantages, expanding at a rapid pace. In many cases, this expansion was the result of the development of new international markets and of rapidly growing exports. Other industries, however, were victims of drops in relative prices, caused either by trade liberalization or by loss of international buyers, and were forced to reduce their scope of operations.

The major industries of the Chilean economy in the late 1980s and early 1990s were agriculture and food products, textiles and clothing, nonelectrical machinery, transportation equipment, and industrial chemicals. As noted previously, the performance of individual industries was uneven (see table 21, Appendix). Although foodstuffs, furniture, and glass products experienced strong expansion, other industries had a lower level of output in 1991 than in 1979.

For decades, wine has been one of Chile's best-known products, and wineries were expected to experience double-digit growth in the 1990s. Exports of wine increased during the 1970s, primarily to the United States, reaching US$31.9 million in 1989. Total wine exports in 1992 were estimated at US$127 million. By that year, Chile had become the third largest exporter of wine to the United States, behind Italy and France.

Not surprisingly, those sectors that had shrunk since the early 1980s, such as footwear and transportation equipment, were those that had been hardest hit by increased foreign competition. However, the firms that finally survived in these sectors did so by adapting to the new external circumstances and by finding ways to rapidly increase productivity. In 1992 the transportation equipment sector was the most dynamic of all, increasing output at an annual rate of 46 percent.

Mining

Although copper's relative importance declined in the 1970s and 1980s, it was still the Chilean economy's most important product in 1992. The mining sector represented 6.7 percent of GDP in 1992, as compared with 8.9 percent in 1985. In 1991 copper exports represented 30 percent of the total value of exports, a substantial decline with respect to the 1960s, when it represented almost 80 percent of total exports. Mining exports in general accounted for about 48 percent of total exports in 1991.

Since the late 1970s, the production of gold and silver has increased greatly (see table 22, Appendix). The lead, iron, and petroleum industries have shrunk since the mid-1970s, the result of both adverse international market conditions and declines in the availability of some of these resources. With a combined total value

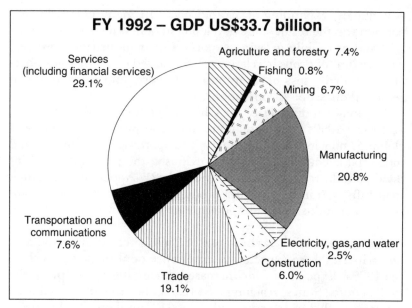

FY 1992 – GDP US$33.7 billion

Services (including financial services) 29.1%

Agriculture and forestry 7.4%

Fishing 0.8%

Mining 6.7%

Manufacturing 20.8%

Transportation and communications 7.6%

Electricity, gas, and water 2.5%

Construction 6.0%

Trade 19.1%

Source: Based on information from Economist Intelligence Unit, *Country Report: Chile* [London], No. 2, 1993, 11.

Figure 8. Gross Domestic Product (GDP) by Sector, 1992

of about US$4 billion, two of the largest investments planned in Chile in the early 1990s were designated for aluminum-smelter projects in the Puerto Aisén and Strait of Magellan areas.

Two developments in the copper sector were noteworthy. First, in the 1987–91 period there was a substantial increase in the output of refined copper, as well as a relative decline in the production of blister copper (see table 23, Appendix). Second, the state-owned Copper Corporation (Corporación del Cobre—Codelco), the world's largest copper producer, still had an overwhelmingly dominant role (accounting for 60 percent of Chile's copper output in 1991). The so-called Codelco Law of April 1992 authorized Codelco for the first time to form joint ventures with the private sector to work unexploited deposits. Thus, in a major step for Codelco, in 1992 it invited domestic and foreign mining firms to participate in four joint explorations in northern Chile. Foreign-owned private firms were to become increasingly important as new investment projects got under way. The heightened importance of these foreign private firms in large-scale copper mining also resulted from the international business community's improved perception of Chile and from a mining law enacted during the Pinochet regime that clearly established compensation rules in the case of nationalization and otherwise encouraged investment in this sector. Given this more favorable context, Phelps Dodge, a United States mining company, and the Sumitomo Metal Mining Company, a Japanese firm, signed a US$1.5 billion contract in 1992 with the Chilean government to develop La Candelaria, a copper and gold mine south of Copiapó. The mine's potential production of refined copper was equivalent to about 10 percent of Codelco's entire production.

Despite the decline in copper's importance, Chile continued to be affected by the vagaries of the international copper market. The high variability of copper prices affects the Chilean economy, particularly the external accounts and the availability of foreign exchange, in several ways. In the 1987–91 period, the international copper market was very favorable; for example, copper prices in 1989 were 50 percent higher than in 1980. By May 1992, however, the price of copper had declined to about its 1980 level. The government decided to counteract the effect of the variability of copper prices by creating the Copper Stabilization Fund, which works as follows: whenever the price of copper increases, the government directs a proportion of the increased revenues into the fund; these resources will then be used during those years when the price of copper falls below its "normal" level. This institutional development has helped Chile at least partially free itself from the volatility of the copper market.

Agriculture

As a result of land appropriations from 1970 to 1973, extensive disinvestment occurred in the agricultural sector. The Pinochet government reversed this trend by returning lands to previous owners and providing incentives for increased exports. Although Chile was basically a net importer of agricultural goods from 1960 to 1970, by 1991 agricultural exports, as well as forestry and fishing exports, were becoming increasingly important in the economy. Whereas in 1970 Chile exported US$33 million in agriculture, forestry, and fishing products, by 1991 the figure had jumped to US$1.2 billion. This figure excluded those manufactured goods based on the products of the agriculture, livestock, and forestry sectors.

In the 1989–91 period, exports of fresh fruits became increasingly important (see table 24, Appendix). Data also indicate that production of grapes, pears, lemons, and peaches was expanding rapidly (see table 25, Appendix). However, the country's virtual monopoly on grape exports during the Northern Hemisphere's winter season is likely to disappear as other potential giants, such as Argentina, begin to compete. The fruit-packing industry also expanded greatly, providing seasonal employment to thousands of workers in its refrigerated plants. Although fruit production takes place in small to medium-size landholdings, fruit-packing plants are very large operations. Indeed, six of the major fruit-packing plants generate more than half of all the boxes exported.

Chile's success in export agriculture is not confined to fruits. Also increasing significantly is production of more traditional crops, many of which are devoted primarily to domestic consumption. Much of the increased agricultural production in the country is the result of rapidly improving yields and higher productivity (see table 26, Appendix). These figures are particularly impressive if compared with historical data. For example, in the 1969–70 agricultural year, wheat's yield is 12.5 quintals per hectare, that of corn was 32.4 tons per hectare, and that of potatoes was 95.4 tons per hectare. By 1990–91 these yields had increased to 34.1 quintals of wheat per hectare, 83.9 quintals of corn per hectare, and 142.2 quintals of potatoes per hectare.

Fishing and Forestry

Chile is well endowed in fish and forest resources. Since the 1980s, output has increased rapidly in both sectors, and exports have boomed. An increasing proportion of these sectors' output is being processed, appearing in the economic statistics as manufactured products.

Fishing

The cold waters of South America's western coast are rich in fish and contain a wide variety of shellfish. For instance, about 800 varieties of mollusks are found there, including the largest abalones and edible sea urchins in the world. Some species, such as the abalones, have been depleted to the point that they cannot be harvested legally. About 750 kilometers from the mainland, the waters surrounding the Islas Juan Fernández are much warmer and contain different types of fish and shellfish, including lobster.

Fishing expanded rapidly starting in the late 1970s. By 1983 Chile was ranked fifth in the world in catch tonnage and has become the world's leading exporter of fish meal. Despite naturally caused year-to-year variations, the volume of the total fish catch has increased over the long term. For example, in 1970 the total catch was 1.2 million tons, but the figures increased to 2.9 million tons in 1980 and 6.3 million tons in 1989. The total catch was about 5.4 million tons in 1990, according to Central Bank data. Total fish caught in 1991 reached 6 million tons, and fishing exports totaled US$1.1 billion, up 21 percent from 1990 and 138 percent from 1985 (see table 28, Appendix). Of the 1991 figure, fish meal accounted

A worker pauses while unloading grapes at a packing shed in Mayoco, a farming community near Santiago. Courtesy Inter-American Development Bank

for US$466 million. Fish exports rose to 6.5 million tons in 1992.

Salmon production was expected to reach 46,000 tons in 1992, earning about US$250 million and turning the country into the third largest producer in the world (after Norway and Canada). Starting with fifty-three tons in 1981, the explosive growth in salmon production and exports reflected the combination of perfect natural conditions for its cultivation in the south with the successful adaptation of modern technology.

By the early 1990s, a lack of fishing regulations was threatening some species and giving the large fishing fleets advantages over the smaller-scale, traditional fishermen who use small boats. After long debate, Congress approved the new General Fishing Law in July 1991. The law's purpose was to encourage investment in commercial fishing by ensuring the conservation of hydrobiological resources, by protecting against overfishing, by reserving for traditional fishermen an exclusive eight-kilometer strip of coastal waters, and by promoting fishing research. The infrastructure plan also included providing resources for developing large and small ports for industrial and traditional fishing. Total output of industrialized fish products was expected to increase significantly with new investments during the 1990s. Both the good catches in the 1989–91 period and the openness of the regulations had prompted Chilean companies to invest a total of US$100 million and to build nearly twenty boats.

Forestry

Beginning in 1975, the planting and exploitation of forests was subsidized heavily by the state, which remitted 70 percent of the cost of planting new areas with trees, exempted such lands from taxes, and permitted a 50 percent deduction for tax purposes from the profits generated from cutting the forests. The forestry policy of the military government was a major exception to its free-market approach and stimulated a significant expansion of forested land.

Chile's forested land is highly concentrated in the hands of a few major companies, principally those connected with the flourishing paper industry and with the national oil company. About 90 percent of all the wood harvested comes from plantations that were established, beginning in the early 1960s, on land of poor quality that originally had been cleared of forests for the growing of wheat and other crops. Reforestation, mostly with pine but also increasingly with eucalyptus, has continued at a faster pace than the cutting of the forests, thereby ensuring ample supplies for the foreseeable future (see table 28, Appendix). It is thought that the volume of production could double 1990 levels by the year 2000.

The public sector is playing a drastically smaller role in foresttry. This diminution of the public sector's role is the result of the general tendency in the country toward reducing, and even eliminating, directly productive government activities. In 1992 the forestry industry was objecting strongly to the new powers that the Aylwin government was proposing to confer on the National Forestry Corporation (Corporación Nacional Forestal—Conaf) to protect native forests.

Whereas exports of basic—that is, nonmanufactured—forestry products had declined by the early 1990s, exports of manufactured wood products had almost doubled. This doubling of manufactured wood exports meant that instead of exporting raw logs, Chile is increasingly adding value to its forest products and is producing such items as milled boards, pulp, paper, and cardboard (see table 24, Appendix). The main market is Japan, which absorbed 25 percent of the value of exports in 1993, followed by the United States and Germany, with 8 percent each. Chile's print industry was enjoying a boom in the early 1990s, supplying books and magazines to neighboring countries, especially to Argentina (which accounted for 75 percent of overseas sales) and Brazil (12 percent). Exports of books and magazines grew by 90 percent in 1992 to about US$70 million.

Under study in 1992 was a bill to regulate Chile's shrinking but still large native old-growth forests, which totaled 7.62 million

*A team of Antofagasta fishermen repairing their nets after the
morning's catch
Courtesy Inter-American Development Bank*

hectares out of 8.86 million hectares of woodland (the remaining 1.24 million hectares are plantations). Chile's forestry industry has worked mostly on plantations of radiata pine, the raw material used for making pulp. But the country's native forests are in need of management to avoid extinction or indiscriminate harvesting of slow-growing species and the resultant erosion and loss of land for future plantations of new species. During 1991, about 107,000 hectares were planted.

Energy

Chile derives its energy mainly from petroleum and natural gas (60 percent), hydroelectric power (25 percent), and coal (15 percent) (see fig. 9). Unlike other countries in Latin America, Chile has been able to make effective plans for the development of the electricity sector. No bottlenecks are expected in this sector, and most analysts predict that it will continue to expand at a healthy pace. The country is endowed with ample hydroelectric resources and has an extensive electric net formed primarily by hydroelectric plants. For example, the Tocopilla station feeds electricity to the huge Chuquicamata and La Escondida copper mines, as well as to cities in northern Chile. An interesting feature of the system is that, although the central net is thoroughly interconnected, there are many individual producers. Since the late 1980s, there has been a marked increase in the importance of small (''other'') producers (see table 29, Appendix).

As part of the final stages in the Pinochet regime's privatization process, beginning in 1985 the two large state-owned utilities, the National Electric Company (Empresa Nacional de Electricidad—ENDESA) and the Chilean Electric Company (Compañía Chilena de Electricidad—Chilectra), both Corfo subsidiaries, were privatized. Now the entire electricity sector basically is run by private companies. The government, however, established a supervisory system that ensures electricity companies a fair return. This keeps prices under reasonable control.

Domestic petroleum production has suffered a steady decline since 1982, from 2.48 million cubic meters to 1.38 million cubic meters in 1990, a reduction of 46 percent. In an environment of fast economic growth and rising demand for energy, this decline in production has translated into a much faster decline in the share of domestic production in total consumption. Although domestic production satisfied 35 percent of domestic consumption in 1986, in 1992 it met only 13 percent of Chile's needs. Consequently, Chile's oil import bill more than doubled between 1986 and 1990. The country's

oil reserves, declining at a rate of 10 percent a year, stood at 300 million barrels in early 1992.

Petroleum exploration efforts have been unsuccessful since the 1970s. The National Petroleum Enterprise (Empresa Nacional de Petróleo—ENAP) has diversified its activities outside Chile with production contracts with Argentine, Brazilian, Colombian, and Ecuadorian companies. Exploration activities have increased in the Atacama Desert and the Strait of Magellan. In late 1992, ENAP began installing a US$18 million oil-drilling platform off Punta Arenas, the first of four that the company planned to operate in the Strait of Magellan in a joint venture with Argentina's state-owned oil company. About two-thirds of the crude oil produced in Chile came from offshore platforms in the Strait of Magellan. In 1991 domestic consumption was averaging 138,527 barrels per day (bpd) and was growing at a 5 percent annual rate.

Pipelines for crude oil products totaled about 775 kilometers in length; for refined petroleum products, about 785 kilometers; and for natural gas, about 320 kilometers. In mid-1992 Chile and Argentina agreed to build a 459-kilometer trans-Andean pipeline, designed to carry US$500 million in crude oil a year, or 94,000 bpd, from Neuquén, Argentina, and to help meet Chile's need for refined oil. Both countries also approved a US$1 billion project to build a 1,200-kilometer gas pipeline to feed Argentine natural gas to Santiago and other Chilean cities by 1997. In 1989 Chile's proven natural gas reserves totaled 46.1 billion cubic meters, of which 41.9 billion cubic meters were onshore and 4.2 billion cubic meters were offshore.

Banking and Financial Services

By the end of the Allende period, commercial banks were little more than cash vaults. The availability of credit was low, and lending patterns were highly distorted. During 1975–90, however, Chile's financial sector experienced a remarkable boom, and by 1992 it was modern and dynamic. Banks performed a variety of operations, and the stock exchange was gaining rapidly in importance. The development in the 1980s of several financial operations involved with servicing Chile's external debt helped to increase the sophistication of the system.

The road to a modern financial sector was not easy. In the process, a number of banks collapsed as a result of the credit crisis of the early 1980s, and interest rates were high. After a period of government control, the failed banks were reprivatized in the mid-1980s, and the banking sector went through an extensive consolidation process. Some banks ceased to exist, and others sought mergers. In 1989 the government made the Central Bank independent of government control by creating the Central Bank Council, a five-member group consisting of two members appointed by the government, two by the opposition, and a president selected by consensus. Beginning in the late 1980s, the number of banks became more stable: thirteen domestic banks and twenty-two foreign-owned banks. Their level of operation had risen rapidly by the early 1990s. Nevertheless, Chile's top seven banks, squeezed by growing competition from consumer finance houses and in-store credit operations, suffered a 17 percent decline in profits in 1991. As a result, the banks were looking to the mining sector for profits.

Since the economic crisis of 1982–83, a recurrent preoccupation of policy makers has been the behavior of interest rates in Chile. Many analysts argued that the near collapse of the Pinochet regime's free-market experiment in those years was the consequence of extremely high interest rates. In 1991 and the first few months of 1992, interest rates experienced a major decline; this was the case for both nominal and real interest rates. As the degree of openness in the capital account increased, domestic interest rates seemed likely to converge toward international levels.

Transportation

The heavy regulation of the transportation sector—including railroads, air transport, marine shipping, and buses—represented a tremendous barrier to international competitiveness. For all these means of transportation, reforms were enacted in the 1970s that were aimed at establishing a competitive environment and widening the participation of the private sector. Railroads were greatly affected by the imposition of self-financing discipline in the mid-1970s. With their infrastructure already failing, financial discipline forced further delays in maintenance programs. The growing demand for transportation services found a more dynamic response in the trucking industry, which developed as a more reliable and economic alternative and surpassed railroads in movement of freight.

Chile's internal transport network is basically well developed, although in need of considerable improvement. To that end, in late 1991 President Aylwin announced a US$2.4 billion public-sector investment program, designed to upgrade the neglected transport infrastructure. There are 7,766 kilometers of railroads (3,974 kilometers of 1,676-meter gauge, 150 kilometers of 1,435-meter standard gauge, and 3,642 kilometers of 1,000-meter gauge), four-fifths of which are state-owned (see fig. 10). In addition, there are 1,865 kilometers of 1,676-meter gauge and eighty kilometers of

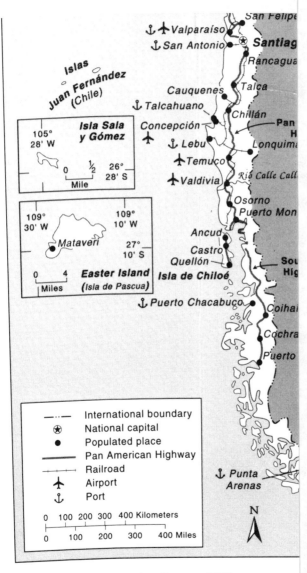

Figure 10. Transportation System, 1993

1,000-meter gauge electrified. The privately owned segment, located mostly in the desert north, totals 2,130 kilometers. A total of 8,185 kilometers of track connect the northern terminal of Iquique to Puerto Montt in the south. That trunk line is being increasingly electrified. Feeder lines run westward to the ports and seaside resorts and eastward to mines and mountain resorts. Four international railroads run to northwestern Argentina and to Bolivia and Peru; two of these lines link Chile with Bolivia between Arica and La Paz (448 kilometers) and between Antofagasta and La Paz via Calama. Except for the international routes to La Paz, passenger service to the north of Santiago has been suspended. There is no passenger service on the Chile-Argentina line.

The government plans to refurbish and modernize the State Railroad Company (Empresa de Ferrocarriles del Estado). The Aylwin government was planning to invest US$98 million in infrastructure improvements in 1993 and was considering the creation of joint ventures with private companies to run the cargo transportation services. The Santiago metro is also to be expanded.

Roads are the principal means of moving people and freight. It was only in the 1960s that a paved road had been completed, linking the extreme north with Puerto Montt at the far southern tip of the Central Valley (Valle Central), and it was only in the mid-1970s that construction began on a north-south road from Puerto Montt into the extreme south. Transversal roads run east and west from the north-south highway. These include the northern Arica-Santos Highway to Bolivia and the southern Trans-Andean Highway between Valparaíso and Mendoza (Argentina).

Chile's road network totals approximately 79,025 kilometers that can be used year-round. Of the total network, 9,913 kilometers are paved, including the Pan American Highway (Longitudinal Highway), which extends, with the opening of the Southern Highway (Gran Carretera Austral) in 1989, about 4,700 kilometers to Puerto Yungay in the south. The highway is paved only to Puerto Montt. Chile has about 10,000 kilometers of paved road, with the region around Santiago and the Central Valley being the best served. Gravel roads total 33,140 kilometers, and improved and unimproved earth roads total 35,972 kilometers. There are about 1.7 million motorized vehicles of all kinds in Chile, including more than 1 million automobiles and 176,000 trucks and buses. Chile's national bus service and Santiago's metro system are considered excellent. The 1991–94 program to improve the transportation infrastructure envisages construction of a new metro line in Santiago.

As befitting a country with such a long coastline, Chile has about eighteen ports, but the country has few good natural harbors. Only four or five ports have adequate facilities, and about ten are used primarily for coastal shipping. Shipping facilities are used to capacity, with a dozen companies engaged in coastal and international trade. Coastal shipping is restricted to Chilean flag vessels. The main ports are Antofagasta, Arica, Coquimbo, Iquique, Puerto Montt, Punta Arenas, San Antonio, Talcahuano, and, most important, Valparaíso. The state controls port organization and approximately 40 percent of the merchant marine, which had thirty-one ships totaling 756,000 deadweight tons in 1993. Chile's inland waterways are navigable for a total of only 725 kilometers, mainly in the southern lake district. The Río Calle Calle provides a waterway to Valdivia from at least one lake for ships up to 4,000 deadweight tons.

Linking the country's extremes, air transport has also become an important way of moving people and freight. Chile has 351 usable airports, forty-eight with paved runways, but none with runways longer than 3,659 meters. The international airport, in Santiago, is served by eighteen international airlines and two national ones. The state carrier, the National Airline of Chile (Línea Aérea Nacional de Chile—LAN-Chile), serves major cities in Chile and also carries passengers to other countries. Privatized in 1989, LAN-Chile merged with a new airline, Southeast Pacific, in 1992. LAN-Chile's domestic coverage is supplemented by the services of Chilean Airlines (Línea Aérea del Cobre—Ladeco), the airline of the state copper company (Ladeco is an acronym for copper airline) and Chile's second largest carrier. Ladeco has a 52 percent share of passengers, and LAN-Chile has a 46 percent share. LAN-Chile, however, controls 84 percent of the international movement of passengers, and Ladeco controls 16 percent. In 1992 Fast Air, Chile's largest air cargo carrier, incorporated the first of three DC–8 aircraft as part of a US$75 million service improvement program.

Telecommunications

Chile's Ministry of Transportation and Telecommunications oversees the telecommunications sector. The development of this natural monopoly (telecommunications) is highly influenced by the type of regulations to which it is subjected. In the mid-1980s, Chile had an estimated deficit of 300,000 telephone lines. This deficit had accumulated through years of deficient management by the public sector. It was clear that major investments were needed and that the old regulatory framework was outmoded.

Reforms that directly affected telecommunications occurred in 1982 and 1985. Before the 1982 reform, Chile's telecommunications sector had been dominated by state-owned national companies.

Santiago and the central part of the country had been served by the Telephone Company of Chile (Compañía de Teléfonos de Chile—CTC), a subsidiary of Corfo. The southern part of the country was served by two private companies, the National Telephone Company (Compañía Nacional de Teléfonos—CNT) and the Telephone Company of Coihaique (Compañía de Teléfonos de Coihaique). Another Corfo subsidiary, the National Telecommunications Enterprise (Empresa Nacional de Telecomunicaciones—Entel), controlled Chile's international telephone service and much of the domestic long-distance service (including Easter Island).

Following key pricing reforms in 1987, most of the state-owned telecommunications firms were privatized during the 1987–89 period. The National Telephone Company of Spain (Telefónica) obtained control of CTC, which has been 50 percent privatized. Entel retained its monopolies.

By 1991 Chile had 768,000 telephones. CTC plans called for installing 190,000 new lines in 1992 and investing US$500 million in 1993 in expanding and upgrading the telephone network. This would permit the installation of 280,000 new lines and the replacement of the remaining analog switching systems that were serving 320,000 lines in 1992. In April 1992, however, Chile's monopoly commission ordered Telefónica to sell its stake in one of the two Chilean telephone companies in which it owned shares—CTC and Entel. Telefónica was appealing the decision to the Supreme Court.

Chile's modern telephone system is based on extensive microwave relay facilities. The rapid development of cellular telephones, digital technology, and satellite links has put even the smallest town in Chile within reach. In 1992 telecommunications service increased 36 percent; CTC had installed more than 900,000 telephone lines by that year.

In 1991 there were 4.25 million radios in the country (see The Media, ch. 4). The United States firm Scientific-Atlantic, under contract to CTC, built a US$29 million domestic digital satellite communications receiving system. Chile was the first South American country to establish an emergency satellite rescue receiver station. A European Space Agency ERS–1 tracking and command station is located in Santiago.

Chile has 167 AM radio stations, no FM stations, 131 television stations, and 12 shortwave radio stations. Most of these units are affiliated with the Association of Chilean Broadcasters (Asociación de Radiodifusores de Chile—Archi). Chile uses two Atlantic Ocean stations and three domestic satellite ground stations of the International Telecommunications Satellite Organization (Intelsat—see Glossary).

Tourism

Another area of significant new investment is tourism, which increased significantly during the 1980s, aided by government efforts to promote it both domestically and abroad through the National Tourism Service (Servicio Nacional de Turismo—Sernatur). More than 1.5 million tourists visited the country in 1992. Sernatur reported that during 1992 a total investment of US$320 million in hotel construction had either already been made or was under consideration in Viña del Mar, Santiago, Cuenca del Sol in Coquimbo Region, and the ski resorts of La Parva and Valle Nevado. For the 1992–2007 period, more than US$2 billion is expected to be invested in tourism infrastructure projects in Chile.

One of the most important tourist destinations is Coquimbo Region, about forty-eight kilometers north of Santiago. The region is considered to have some of the best beaches and climatic and geographic conditions in Chile. A US$505 million project to develop 330 hectares with nine kilometers of beaches north of Coquimbo's capital, La Serena, was awarded competitively to a Spanish-Chilean consortium in 1992.

Construction

The relative importance of the construction sector has declined significantly since the early 1970s. In 1970 the construction share of GDP was almost 8 percent, but by 1992 it had fallen to 6 percent. This trend is largely the result of a dramatic decline in the public sector's construction activities. Whereas in 1970 the public sector was responsible for over 30 percent of the total square meters constructed, in 1991 this portion had been reduced to 3.1 percent. This trend is partially reflected in a decline in the quality of the infrastructure. In order to maintain its pace of growth, Chile must reverse this trend.

The total construction area grew during the 1987–91 period at a healthy pace of 12.5 percent per annum. However, all of this increase is attributable to the private sector. During this period, the yearly area constructed by the public sector declined (see table 30, Appendix). The sector enjoyed a robust growth of 10 percent in 1992 as a result of an increase in housing starts and other construction projects.

A significant percentage of private-sector construction is financed by the government. In fact, one of the most important innovations of the military regime was that the state's role as direct producer was greatly reduced. Since the late 1970s, the overwhelming majority

A view from the Southern Highway in southern Chile
Courtesy Inter-American Development Bank

of public works have been executed by private-sector firms under government contract. A similar major structural reform has taken place in housing for people with low income. Whereas in the 1960s and early 1970s houses in this sector were constructed by government-owned firms, in the early 1990s they were being built by private firms and sold to people with low incomes through an elaborate subsidy system (see Housing Policies, ch. 2).

Income, Labor Unions, and the Pension System

The modernization of labor-market legislation during the late 1970s played a fundamental role in the subsequent performance of the Chilean economy. Included in this modernization were: reforms in the labor code that assign individual workers the right to seek representation in collective bargaining organizations, and a reduction in the cost of dismissals. Moreover, the financial reforms in social security and health care removed a major tax burden from the labor market, as it transformed social security and health care taxes into required basic health care programs. In addition, the reforms in the financing of education had a tremendous impact on the allocation of human resources and resulted in a significant growth of privately funded technical training programs (see Welfare Institutions and Social Programs, ch. 2). The financial aspects of these reforms directly affected the efficiency of the labor market. For example, pension funds became the largest institutional investors of the capital market, representing 26.5 percent of GDP in 1990 (see Economic Results of the Pensions Privatization, this ch.).

Employment and Unemployment

According to the 1992 census, the Chilean population totaled 13,348,401 in that year. The average annual rate of population growth in the 1982–92 period was 1.6 percent, a relatively low rate in the context of Latin America. Chile and Argentina are the two countries with the lowest rates of population growth in South America (see Current Demographic Profile, ch. 2).

Chile is a highly urbanized country. According to estimates for 1991, about 85 percent of the population resides in urban areas. A large fraction of the population is in the metropolitan area, which includes the capital city, Santiago. The population share of this region was estimated at slightly more than 39 percent in 1992, which is one percentage point higher than the 1982 share. These figures indicate that the relative growth of the metropolitan area has slowed down compared with the 1970–80 decade, when the rate climbed to 38.1 percent in 1982 from 35.4 percent in 1970 (see Urban Areas, ch. 2).

With a lower rate of population growth, Chile's "working-age" population, which includes all those individuals above fifteen and below sixty-five years of age, represented 64 percent of the total population in 1992. The labor force participation rate, or the ratio of those in the labor force over the "working-age" population, was 52.6 percent in March 1992. Thus, 36.8 percent of the total population was working or seeking a job (see table 7, Appendix). The rate of unemployment has declined steadily throughout the period (see table 8, Appendix). The overall rate of growth in employment for the 1987–91 period was about 3 percent per year. The rate was substantially higher from 1987 to 1989 (5 percent), the period of fast recovery after the debt crisis. It is possible that the uncertainty regarding the final reforms on the labor legislation might have delayed employment creation, but there were other important factors, such as an increase in the interest rate. The most dynamic sectors during the 1987–89 period were construction and industry, with average rates of employment growth of 20 percent and 11 percent per year, respectively.

After years of high unemployment, in the 1990s the trend began to change. By late 1993, the rate of unemployment had plunged to 4.9 percent, a rate significantly lower that that of the rest of Latin America, and one of the lowest in Chile's modern history. Interestingly, this drastic reduction in unemployment has taken place at the same time as real wages have increased significantly. The Economic Commission for Latin America and the Caribbean estimates that average real wages increased by 13.7 percent between 1990 and 1993. This change in employment conditions has been the direct result of the emphasis that Chile's economic model has placed on the development of employment-intensive industries. The increase in employment has been so impressive that a number of analysts have argued that Chile may be running into a period of labor shortages (see The Labor Force and Income Levels, ch. 2).

Income Distribution and Social Programs

Latin America has traditionally had one of the most unequal income distributions in the world. Chile has not been an exception to this rule. Although data are scarce, existing evidence suggests that during the years of military rule income inequality increased significantly in Chile. It has been estimated that in 1985 about 25 percent of households lived in extreme poverty (see Glossary), and that 45 percent of households lived below the poverty line. During the 1990–93 period, the incidence of poverty declined substantially. In late 1993, the Ministry of Planning and Cooperation estimated that between 1990 and 1993 more than 1.3 million people moved out of poverty. This was the result of a combination of factors: the rapid rate of growth experienced by the economy; and the implementation of social programs aimed at the poorest groups in society.

The emphasis on social programs aimed at certain groups began in the mid-1970s. This approach seeks to deliver social programs directly to the poor, avoiding leakages to middle- and upper-income groups. These programs have been largely successful. It has been reported, for example, that 90 percent of the food distributed through the preschool nutritional programs went to the poorest three deciles of the population in the mid-1980s. Moreover, more than 80 percent of the food has reached the rural poor. Since the basic housing program was reformed in the early 1980s, more than 50 percent of the subsidies have been reaching the poorest three deciles of the population. In 1969, before the system was reformed, only 20 percent of subsidies were received by the poorest 30 percent of the population.

Unions and Labor Conflicts

After reluctantly accepting the Labor Plan of 1979, unions became active again in the early 1980s and were able to push for wage concessions during the economic boom of that period. A minority maintained a tough stance in opposition to the new system, but they lacked significant influence, so opposition eventually disappeared.

The most radical change experienced by the union movement with the return to democracy has been its reintegration into the national discussion of labor reforms and social policies. The reforms of 1990–91, which introduced some changes to the original Labor Plan, represented a moderate increase in workers' bargaining power in each of the three central areas of the labor law: dismissals, the right to collective bargaining, and the right of employers to hire temporary replacements or to impose lockouts during strikes.

Law 19,010, enacted in 1990, regulates individual contracts. In the area of dismissals, it introduces two important differences relative to the previous law—the size of the severance compensation and the right of the worker to appeal. Whereas the Labor Plan had introduced the practice of dismissals without cause and established a severance pay equal to one month's salary per year of service up to a maximum of five months' worth, this reform reinstates the principle of dismissal only with cause, and it increases the severance-pay ceiling to eleven months. The law considers two possible reasons for dismissal—the traditional "just cause" (serious misconduct)

A construction worker at the Río Melado Dam spillway, located about seventy kilometers southeast of Talca
Courtesy Inter-American Development Bank

and the new "economic cause." If the employee appeals and the employer fails to prove "just cause," the employer would have to pay a 50 percent penalty in addition to the usual severance. Failure to prove "economic cause" would result in a 20 percent penalty.

The previous law was also modified to provide an option to replace the normal severance with a "payment in all separations." This option is available to workers with more than seven years of service with the same employer. If this option is exercised, the employer would establish a fund in the worker's name, with monthly deposits of a minimum of 4.1 percent and a maximum of 8.3 percent of the salary (the salary base having a maximum) in a private financial institution. These contributions and the corresponding accumulated interest would be nontaxable income and would constitute a fund that would be withdrawn on separation.

Law 19,069, enacted in 1991, regulates the rights of employers and employees during collective bargaining. Under this law, enterprise-level workers' organizations have the right to negotiate with employers, and employers are obliged to negotiate with them. The law gives the employer the right to limit to thirty-five days the period of bargaining with all unions representing the enterprises' workers. Under Law 19,069, collective agreements can establish pay scales, indexation formulas, fringe benefits, and the like, but they cannot limit the sovereignty of the employer over the organization and administration of the enterprise (Article 82).

One of the important departures from the previous law is that trade unions or workers' associations are given the right to bargain with more than one employer. Yet this right can only be exercised under the following circumstances: in the case of collective bargaining affecting more than one enterprise, prior agreement of the parties is required (Article 79); submission of collective agreement by other trade union organizations (such as federations or confederations) requires approval by secret ballot of the absolute majority of the member workers of the enterprise (Article 110); and a given worker cannot be covered by more than one collective agreement (Article 83).

A strike would suspend the individual contract, give employers a conditional right to temporary replacement, and give employees a conditional right to renounce union membership and return to work. Employers can use temporary replacements from the first day of the strike if their last offer, before the strike was declared, was equivalent to the previous contract adjusted by the consumer price index (CPI—see Glossary). If the last offer was lower, employers cannot use temporary replacements within a minimum of thirty days after the strike is called. Employees have the right to renounce union membership and go back to work fifteen days after calling the strike, as long as the outstanding offer of the employer is equivalent to the last contract adjusted by the CPI. If the last offer is lower, employees must delay their walkout a minimum of thirty days after the strike is called. The law does not establish a maximum duration for strikes, but if more than half of the workers return to work, the strike must end. At that point, all workers must return to the job. In order to make use of the right to replace workers temporarily, employers must make an offer that at least adjusts wages by past inflation. If the employer also offers other fringe benefits but workers still go on strike, the employer may hire temporary replacements. However, the employer loses that right if the wage adjustment for past inflation is given but some fringe benefits are cut. That would not be a contract equivalent to the previous one adjusted by inflation. If workers go on strike, the employer cannot use temporary replacements within thirty days of the declaration of the strike.

It was unclear in 1992 what the final form would be for the new legislation on labor-management relations, labor productivity, investment, on-the-job training, and other aspects of labor markets' performance. However, workers have almost doubled their participation in labor unions since 1983, and by 1990 about 13 percent of those employed were affiliated with unions. During 1990, 25,000 workers, out of 184,000 who participated in collective contracts, used strikes as a means of pressing their demands. Most strikes during 1990 and 1991 were of short duration (see Labor, ch. 4).

Economic Results of the Pensions Privatization

Chile's pension system, which started to operate in May 1981, is based on individual capitalization of funds (see Social Security, ch. 2). This system determines a minimum basic contribution equal to 10 percent of disposable income and makes the benefit a function of an individual's contributions during his or her active life. Benefits for incapacity and survival are financed by complementary insurance with financial reserves. Decree Law 3,500 of 1981 instituted a social security system that makes contributions obligatory for dependent workers who joined the labor force after December 31, 1982, and makes them voluntary for independent workers and those who had already contributed to the traditional pension funds. The old pay-as-you-go system, which was being phased out, covered all those workers who had entered the labor force in 1982 or earlier and who chose not to transfer to the new capitalization system. The reform responds to a need that has been recognized before, when the old system entered a phase of serious financial difficulties.

In the reformed system, the state now plays a fundamental role in regulating and monitoring operations and guaranteeing "solidarity in the base" through a minimum pension. All workers, after contributing a minimum amount (15 percent of their gross income annually), have the right to a minimum pension of 85 percent of their minimum salary, even if their life-time contributions to the system result in a smaller benefit. The new system brought about an increase in coverage, with the proportion of independent workers covered increasing from 58 percent in 1985 to 79 percent in 1990. The proportion of dependent workers covered increased from 79 percent in 1985 to 92 percent in 1990.

Article 28 of Decree Law 3,500 establishes that the numerous Pension Fund Administrators (Administradoras de Fondos de Pensiones—AFPs) are authorized to charge a fee to cover their administrative costs. The most important restriction is that, with a few exceptions, fees have to be the same for all affiliates in a given AFP. After a relative increase in the fees between 1981 and 1983, competition resulted in a steady decline in the cost to individuals. In 1990 the cost for an "average contributor" was 33 percent lower in real terms than in December 1983. Commissions fell from 5 percent of taxable income in 1985 to about 3.2 percent in 1990. In 1992 the AFPs were charging about 0.9 percent of salary in insurance premiums and 1.8 percent in commissions, for a total of 2.7 percent.

Strict norms regulate the investment of pension funds. Only certain instruments may be used, and there are clear limits on the distribution of investments by type of instrument. The dynamism of the Chilean capital market since the early 1980s has forced constant revisions of these norms. Pension funds are the largest institutional investors in the capital market, representing 26.5 percent of GDP in 1990 (compared with 0.9 percent in 1981). The average real return to investment of Chilean pension funds between 1981 and 1990 was 13 percent. In 1992 AFPs were authorized to invest up to 3 percent of their portfolios abroad, double the previous maximum.

Macroeconomic Policy, Inflation, and the Balance of Payments

The Central Bank and Monetary Policy

One of the key lessons of the Chilean reforms is the importance of macroeconomic equilibrium in providing the "right" environment conducive to economic growth and stability. For all practical purposes, by 1988–89 macroeconomic equilibrium had been achieved in Chile.

One of the problems that occupied many scholars and politicians in the late 1980s was how to guarantee the continuity of macroeconomic policy after the military regime. The key issue was how to ensure that macroeconomic decisions, and in particular monetary and exchange-rate policies, would not be determined by partisan politicians with a short-term mentality. In short, a crucial point in the transition's debate was how to remove Central Bank decisions from the day-to-day urgencies of politics. This issue was seen as particularly important by those economists who argued that the politically inspired management of monetary policy was at the root of Chile's long history of inflation.

After much debate, the Pinochet government decided, in 1989, to implement a new law that would greatly enhance the independence of the Central Bank. The law made the bank autonomous and legally removed it from the area of influence of the minister of finance. According to the new legislation, the bank was to be governed by a five-member board, the Central Bank Council. Each member was to serve for ten years and could only be removed under a strict set of circumstances. The president of the republic was required to obtain Senate approval to name new members of the board.

Monkey-puzzle trees
(Araucaria araucana)
of the pine family,
valued for their beautifully
veined hardwood and
plentiful resin, near
Temuco in southern Chile
Courtesy Embassy
of Chile, Washington

When the new legislative project on Central Bank reform was announced in mid-1989, the members of the opposition denounced it as an attempt by the Pinochet regime to perpetuate itself in power. However, after some internal debate within the CPD coalition, the opposition forces decided to support the project, as long as the members of the initial board were considered unbiased technocrats. After a long process of negotiation at the highest level, it was decided that the first five members would serve for two, four, six, eight, and ten years, respectively; two of them were chosen by the opposition, two were chosen by the departing Pinochet government, and the chairperson of the board was chosen by consensus. It was also decided that the chairperson would serve for two years. In 1992 the chairperson's two years were up, and a new member of the board was chosen as chairperson, this time for ten years. On that occasion, the idea of an independent Central Bank was put into effect.

In 1991–92 the Central Bank focused on two issues: the desire to reduce the rate of inflation from double digits to single digits; and the exchange-rate policy of trying to balance the need for continuous promotion of exports with the reduction of inflation. To address these issues, the Central Bank used a number of means, including the auctioning of Central Bank bills and the acquisition of international securities. Also, the bank introduced a series of amendments to exchange-rate policy.

Exchange-Rate Policy and the Balance of Payments

There was broad agreement that the implementation of an exchange-rate policy aimed at encouraging exports had been at the center of Chile's economic success. Since at least 1985, the members of the Chilean economic team had understood that avoiding exchange-rate overvaluation was crucial to the promotion of growth and prosperity. As a result, it was decided that a policy based on small daily adjustments of the nominal exchange rate would be adopted. In this way, exporters would be compensated for any increase in their domestic costs stemming from inflation.

Although the basic elements of this "crawling peg" exchange-rate policy were maintained during the 1985–92 period, the system went through a number of changes. The first important innovation was to center the "reference" exchange rate set by the Central Bank within a 6 percent band. Market participants were allowed to transact freely within the band. A second important change was to widen the band to 10 percent and to adjust the reference rate downward. Finally, in 1992 the Central Bank decided to alter the method used to calculate the daily adjustment of the reference rate by using a basket of currencies made up of the dollar, the German deutsche mark, and the Japanese yen in a 50–30–20 ratio, instead of only the dollar.

In early 1990, Chile started to receive increasing amounts of foreign financial flows. This generated an overabundance of foreign exchange, which tended to make the exchange rate appreciate. From a practical point of view, the increased capital inflows were reflected in the fact that the exchange rate moved to the "floor" of the band, reducing the amount of real Chilean pesos that each exporter received per United States dollar exported. This development affected the profitability of a number of export projects, reducing the overall competitiveness of the Chilean economy. Also, the real appreciation of the exchange rate affected local industries that competed with imported goods, including the agricultural sector. Not too surprisingly, exporters have tried to persuade the government to alter its exchange-rate policy in a way that would increase their profits.

In 1991 the pressure of capital inflows subsided somewhat. However, this did not end the overabundance of foreign exchange, nor did it put an end to the tendency toward real exchange-rate appreciation. That year the current account of the balance of payments experienced a remarkable turnaround of almost US$1 billion (see table 31, Appendix). Consequently, during 1991 the overall result was that external accounts were once again positive, with the Central Bank accumulating more than US$1.2 billion, as compared with US$2.4 billion in 1990.

Chilean balance of payments trends for 1990–92 generally were positive, despite a current account deficit in 1992–93. Although the capital account experienced a reversal in 1991, moving from a large surplus in 1990 to a modest deficit, in 1992 this tendency appeared to be reversing itself once again, with capital inflows exceeding outflows. An important aspect of the balance of payments data for the early 1990s is the large positive figure for ''errors and omissions,'' which was US$161 million in 1991. However, there is evidence suggesting that the government's figure represents ''reversed capital flight'' entering the country in an illegal fashion. Some observers have claimed that illegal drug-related monies were moving toward Chile in the early 1990s (see Incidence of Crime, ch. 5).

Trade Policy and Export Performance

A fundamental element of the Aylwin government's economic program was the maintenance of Pinochet's foreign-trade policy. Early on, the forces of the CPD coalition pointed out that an open external sector was a fundamental component of their economic package. One of the early decisions of the Aylwin government was to open the Chilean economy further to international competition. This was done by reducing import tariffs from 15 percent to 11 percent, except for expensive luxury goods or commodities governed by a price band.

Data on exports for the 1989–91 period reveal three telling developments. First, the share of traditional mining exports showed a clear downward trend. Second, there was a significant increase in the shares of the agricultural and manufacturing sectors. (In 1991 fruits and forest products constituted 85 percent of total exports, and the agricultural sector accounted for about US$1.2 billion, or about 14 percent of total exports.) Third, an increasing proportion of manufacturing exports were going to industrial countries (see table 32, Appendix).

Exports in 1991 showed a noteworthy increase in shipments toward other Latin American countries. Chile signed a trade accord with Argentina and in 1992 was working on a trade accord with Venezuela and Colombia. In 1991 Chile signed a bilateral free-trade agreement with Mexico, under which each country would gradually reduce tariffs on three categories of products. The Chile-Mexico bilateral accord, which took effect on January 1, 1993, called for the removal of tariffs on almost all of Chile's trade with Mexico by about 1996. Chile was hesitant in the early 1990s to join the other countries in South America in participating in regional trading agreements, such as the Southern Cone Common Market (Mercado Común del Cono Sur—Mercosur; see Glossary), or the renewed Andean Group (see Glossary). By early 1994, however, Chile was ready to join Mercosur and was expected to become a member in January 1995.

Chile's exports were also moving rapidly beyond the scope of Latin America. An important goal in the area of trade diplomacy was a free-trade agreement with the United States. On October 1, 1990, Chile and the United States signed a framework agreement on trade and investment aimed at negotiation of a proposed Chile-United States free-trade accord similar to the North American Free Trade Agreement (NAFTA; see Glossary) among the United States, Mexico, and Canada. The United States remained Chile's most important trade partner, although in 1991 the value of Chilean exports to Japan surpassed the value of exports to the United States by US$10 million, and in 1992 the figure rose to at least US$52 million. Japan accounted for US$900 million of Chile's US$1.5 billion surplus in 1991.

The Future of the Economy

In early 1994, the Chilean economy stood out as one of the strongest in Latin America. Moreover, President-elect Eduardo Frei Ruiz-Tagle had stated that his administration would continue the export-oriented, market-based policies of Aylwin and Pinochet. Frei's minister-designate of finance, Harvard-educated Eduardo Aninat Ureta, publicly endorsed the main aspects of the current economic model. However, the trend in the early 1990s toward real exchange-rate appreciation clouded the future of the export sector.

However, there are still some areas of concern. Most of the growth in Chile in the early 1990s was the result of a combination of increased capacity utilization and improvements in productivity. The contribution of capital accumulation to growth has remained relatively low. Despite increases, in 1992 total capital investment barely surpassed 20 percent of GDP. Historical data from other parts of the world are emphatic in indicating that high rates of capital formation (see Glossary) are required to sustain growth in the longer run. Data for 1993 suggest that there has been a remarkable increase in savings (see table 33, Appendix). In the years to come, it will be fundamentally important to maintain (or even to increase) the savings effort.

A second and related area of concern has to do with infrastructure. Although in the case of Chile the situation is not as dire as

Buses on Avenida Bernardo O'Higgins in downtown Santiago
Courtesy Inter-American Development Bank

in other Latin American countries, Chile needs to continue to maintain and improve its infrastructure. With the already active participation of the private sector in important projects, the selective participation of the government as the main entrepreneur is clearly needed.

A third concern is the environment, where two problems are particularly acute. The first one is air pollution in Santiago. The Aylwin government decided to address this issue in a rather gradual way. Whether this is the most effective and efficient approach is unclear. The second serious problem is ocean pollution, especially in the more densely populated coastal areas.

An important fourth area to focus on in the future is the battle against poverty. President-elect Frei stated that this would indeed be a priority for his administration. The appointment of Carlos Massad Adub, a well-respected, University of Chicago-trained economist, to the Ministry of Health indeed suggests a high commitment to social services. In that regard, an increase in the aggressiveness of targeted social programs seemed to be the most promising avenue. An important question, however, is where to obtain the resources. This is not easy to answer, but creative solutions, including a possible reduction in the military budget in the years to come, are among those that might be contemplated.

* * *

A number of fine sources provide information on the recent transformation and performance of the country's economy. These include Jere Behrman's *Foreign Exchange Regimes and Economic Development: Chile,* Vittorio Corbo's *Inflation in Developing Countries,* Ricardo Ffrench-Davis's *Políticas económicas en Chile, 1952–1970,* Markos J. Mamalakis's *Historical Statistics of Chile,* and Gonzalo Martner's *El pensamiento económico del gobierno de Allende.*

The literature on the economic reforms of the mid-1970s and 1980s is extensive. Comprehensive studies include *Una década de cambios económicos: La experiencia chilena, 1973–1983* by Alvaro Bardón, Camilo Carrasco M., and Alvaro Vial G.; *Monetarism and Liberalization,* by Sebastian Edwards and Alejandra Cox Edwards; and *The National Economic Policies of Chile,* edited by Gary M. Walton. Tarsicio Castañeda's *Combating Poverty* provides a first-rate analysis of Chile's highly praised approach to social programs. In *La revolución laboral en Chile* and *El cascabel al gato,* José Piñera Echenique offers an insider's account of two of the most important and politically difficult reforms in the Chilean social and economic system: the labor decrees and the social security system.

Much of the literature on the Chilean economy appears in article form in scholarly and professional journals or in edited volumes. In Chile three journals are particularly important. One is *Colección de Estudios de CIEPLAN,* published by a Christian Democratic-leaning think tank, the Corporation for Latin American Economic Research (Corporación de Investigaciones Económicas Para América Latina—Cieplan). Early issues of this journal examine the economic thinking of many of the Aylwin government's economic officials. Other issues contain some of the more severe criticisms of the Pinochet economic policy. *Cuadernos de Economía,* published by the Catholic University of Chile, provides somewhat technical pieces on the evolution of the Chilean economy. Most of these are written by economists who sympathized with the Pinochet regime. A number of important pieces on the evolution of the Chilean economy have appeared only in the form of working papers. Although it has sometimes been difficult to gain access to these documents, a list of the most important can be found in the Bibliography. *Estudios Públicos,* published by the Centro de Estudios Públicos, is a multidisciplinary journal devoted to public policy. It has published important debates, with different positions being duly represented.

Current data on monetary variables, balance of payments, national accounts, and employment have been published periodically by the Central Bank. The National Statistics Institute (Instituto Nacional de Estadísticas—INE) is a major source of basic information. The Economic Commission for Latin America and the Caribbean, with offices in Santiago, also is a valuable source of economic and social data for Chile and all other Latin American countries. (For further information and complete citations, see Bibliography.)

Chapter 4. Government and Politics

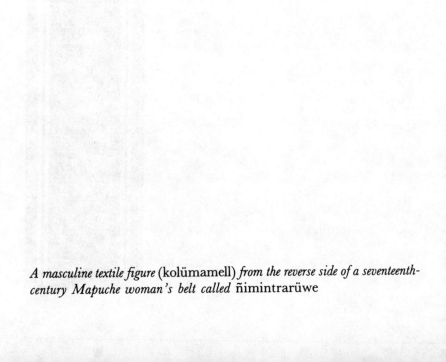

A masculine textile figure (kolümamell) *from the reverse side of a seventeenth-century Mapuche woman's belt called* ñimintrarüwe

THE REESTABLISHMENT OF DEMOCRATIC government in March 1990 once again thrust Chile into the international limelight. In the early 1970s, the long, narrow country on the west coast of South America had drawn widespread attention by electing a Marxist president, Salvador Allende Gossens (1970–73), who was intent on forging a new path to socialism. Following Allende's overthrow on September 11, 1973, Chile under military rule became notorious for some of the worst excesses of modern-day authoritarianism.

Headed by General of the Army Augusto Pinochet Ugarte (1973–90), the dictatorship was widely reviled for ending Chile's tradition of democratic politics and committing numerous violations of human rights. Although isolated politically, Chile's military government earned international acclaim for far-reaching economic and social reforms that transformed the country's state-oriented economy into one of the most open economic systems in the developing world. The economic reforms of the late 1970s and 1980s set the foundation for extraordinary investment and growth in the early 1990s. Economic progress, combined with the return of democratic politics largely devoid of the confrontation and polarization of the past, positioned Chile to enter the twenty-first century with increased prosperity in a climate of peace and freedom.

Chile's favorable situation developed because the military government's success at implementing an economic revolution was not duplicated in the political arena. From the outset, Pinochet and his colleagues had sought to displace the parties, politicians, and institutions of the past so that they might create a nation of pliant and patriotic citizens, devoted to their private pursuits under the tutelage of a strong and benevolent state with merely a facade of representative government.

However, the military commanders badly underestimated the strength of the nation's traditional political parties and failed to understand the degree to which democratic practices and institutions had become a fundamental part of Chile's national character. Indeed, Pinochet was forced to abandon his plan for virtual life-long rule after a humiliating personal defeat in a 1988 plebiscite (see Glossary) at the hands of the very civilian leaders whom he had reviled and persecuted. Their resilience made possible the transition to democracy in March 1990 and the success of Chile's first civilian government after seventeen years of authoritarian rule.

Chile's transition back to democracy encountered serious challenges. Although opposition groups had vehemently rejected the Pinochet government's constitution of 1980 as illegitimate and undemocratic, they were forced to accept the political rules and playing field as defined by the military government in order to challenge its very authority. To a greater degree than most other transitions to democracy in Latin America, Chile's was accomplished within the framework of an institutional order conceived by an authoritarian regime, one that continued to define the political game long after the return to representative government. Pinochet was unable to destroy his adversaries or project his own presidential leadership into the future, but he succeeded in imposing an institutional legacy that Chile's civilian elites would have to modify substantially if Chile were to become fully democratic.

Constitutional History

Development and Breakdown of Democracy, 1830–1973

Following the wars of independence and several failed experiments in institution building, Chile after 1830 made steady progress toward the construction of representative institutions, showing a constancy almost without parallel in South American political history. From 1830 until 1973, almost all of Chile's presidents stepped down at the end of their prescribed terms in office to make way for constitutionally designated successors. The only exceptions to this pattern occurred in 1891, after a brief civil war; in the turbulence from late 1924 to 1927, which followed the military's intervention against the populist President Arturo Alessandri Palma (1920–24, 1925, 1932–38); in 1931, when several chief executives resigned under pressure and military officers intervened directly in politics; and in 1932, when the commander of the Chilean Air Force (Fuerza Aérea de Chile—FACh), Marmaduke Grove Vallejo, proclaimed his short-lived Socialist Republic. For most of its history, Chile was governed by two charters—the constitution of 1833 and the constitution of 1925, which drew heavily on its nineteenth-century predecessor.

Under the 1833 document, Chilean presidents, notably Manuel Bulnes Prieto (1841–51) and Manuel Montt Torres (1851–61), presided over the gradual institutionalization of representative practices and a gradual expansion of suffrage, while exercising strong executive authority. By the 1870s, the president was being challenged by increasingly cohesive political parties, which, from their vantage point in the National Congress (Congreso Nacional;

hereafter, Congress), sought to limit executive prerogatives and curb presidential intervention in the electoral process.

With the assertion of congressional power, presidents were limited to one term, and their control over elections was circumscribed. However, it took the Civil War of 1891 to bring to an end the chief executive's power to manipulate the electoral process to his advantage. The victory of the congressional forces in that conflict inaugurated a long period in which Congress was at the center of national politics. From 1891 until 1924, presidents were required to structure their cabinets to reflect changing legislative majorities, and the locus of policy making was subject to the intrigues and vote trading of the legislature.

Although politics during the parliamentary period was often chaotic and corrupt, Chile enjoyed unusual prosperity based on a booming nitrate trade and relatively enlightened leadership. Political parties, whose activities had once been limited to the corridors of Congress, soon engaged the interests and energies of Chileans at every level of society. The parties thus provided the basis for an open, highly competitive political system comparable to those of Europe's parliamentary democracies. The competitiveness of Chilean politics permitted the emergence of new interests and movements, including the Communist Party of Chile (Partido Comunista de Chile—PCCh) and the Socialist Party (Partido Socialista), representing a growing and increasingly militant proletariat.

The collapse of nitrate exports and the crisis brought on by the Great Depression (see Glossary) of the 1930s discredited the politicians of Chile's oligarchical democracy and encouraged the growth of alternative political forces. From 1924 to 1931, Chile was buffeted by political instability as several presidents resigned from office and Carlos Ibáñez del Campo (1927–31, 1952–58), a military officer, rose to power on an antipolitics platform. In 1925 a new constitution was approved. Although it did not deviate substantially from previous constitutional doctrine, it was designed to shift the balance of power from Congress back to the president.

By the second and third decades of the twentieth century, Chile was facing some of the same challenges confronting the nations of Europe. Parliamentary democracy had fallen into disrepute as the machinations of corrupt elites were challenged by both fascism and socialism, doctrines that stressed social as opposed to political rights and that sought to expand the power of the state in pursuing them. Precisely because of its tradition of competitive politics and the strength of its political parties, Chile was able to withstand the challenge of alternative ideologies without experiencing the breakdown of democratic authority that swept the South American continent.

Chilean politics changed dramatically, however, as a multiparty system emerged without exact parallel in Latin America, one in which strong Marxist parties vied with conservative parties, while pragmatic centrist parties attempted to mediate. In this polarized context, presidents governed with shifting coalitions, pushing the country alternately to the right or left, depending on the particular political configuration of the moment. Although the left gained ground throughout the 1940s and 1950s, the right maintained electoral clout by blocking efforts to bring congressional representation into line with new demographic trends. This was not a period of policy stalemate, however. By encouraging a policy of import-substitution industrialization (see Glossary) and expanding social welfare programs, the Chilean state markedly increased its role in national life.

In the aftermath of the Cuban Revolution of 1959, Chilean politics changed in a qualitative sense. With the 1964 election of a Christian Democratic government under the leadership of President Eduardo Frei Montalva (1964–70), Chile embarked on an experiment in reformist politics intended to energize the economy while redistributing wealth. Frei and his colleagues were determined to modernize the country through the introduction of significant social reforms, including an extensive agrarian reform that would bring an end to the concentration of economic power in the hands of rural landlords.

Frei's government accomplished many of its objectives. In pushing for change, however, the president broke the tacit alliance with the right that had made his election possible. His attempt to co-opt part of the program of the left and mobilize followers in traditionally leftist constituencies also threatened the Marxist parties. By the end of the 1960s, the polarization of Chilean politics had overwhelmed the traditional civility of Chile's vaunted democratic institutions. The centrist agreements of the past, which had enabled presidents to navigate a difficult course of compromise and conciliation, now became more difficult to attain.

In a reflection of Chile's increased ideological polarization, Allende was elected president with 36.2 percent of the vote in 1970. Unable or unwilling to form coalitions, the left, center, and right had all nominated their own candidates in the mistaken hope of obtaining a majority. Allende's Popular Unity (Unidad Popular) government drew initially on the congressional support of the Christian Democrats, whose backing made his election possible in the congressional runoff on October 24, 1970. However, the left increasingly pushed to implement its agenda without building political bridges to the "bourgeois parties." Like Frei before him, Allende was convinced that he would be able to break the deadlock of Chile's ideologically entrenched multiparty system and create a new majority capable of implementing his revolutionary agenda. Once this effort failed, Allende's attempts to implement his program by decree only heightened opposition to his policies. Finally, the president's failure to make substantial gains from his electoral victory in the March 1973 congressional elections meant that he would be unable to obtain the necessary congressional majority to implement his legislative objectives (see table 34, Appendix). In an atmosphere of growing confrontation, in which moderates on both sides failed to come up with a regime-saving compromise, the military forces moved in to break the political deadlock, establishing the longest and most revolutionary government in the nation's history.

Imposition of Authoritarian Rule

The military commanders took power in a violent coup on September 11, 1973, accusing Allende, who committed suicide during the takeover, of having violated the constitution. Within months, however, it became apparent that the new regime blamed the breakdown of democracy not only on the parties of the left and the Marxist president but also on the institutional framework embodied in the constitution of 1925. In the military's view, Chile's constitution had encouraged the rise of venal parties and politicians preoccupied not with the broader welfare of the country but with their own interests and hunger for power. The military blamed what they viewed as self-serving politicians for allowing foreign ideologies to penetrate the nation, thereby creating an internal threat that the armed forces felt obliged to confront.

Within days of the coup, the new government appointed a commission of conservative scholars to begin crafting a new constitutional order. However, after initial enthusiasm for their work, commission members soon discovered that institutional reform was not a top priority of the authorities and that the junta was in no hurry to set a timetable for its own departure. The military's primary goal was to revitalize the economy, while destroying the parties of the left and rendering obsolete the parties and leaders of other stripes.

In 1978, however, a power struggle within the junta between Pinochet, commander of the Chilean Army (Ejército de Chile), and Gustavo Leigh Guzmán, the FACh commander, forced the military government to come to terms with its blueprint for the future of the country. Leigh resented the growing power and influence of Pinochet, his putative equal in the junta, and sought to force an early conclusion to the transition back to civilian rule in a form similar to the constitutional framework of the immediate past. Pinochet, basking in the power and authority of an executive with access to a powerful secret police network, the National Information Center (Centro Nacional de Información—CNI), which replaced the National Intelligence Directorate (Dirección Nacional de Inteligencia—DINA) in 1977, had no enthusiasm for an early return to civilian rule; rather, he hoped to institute more far-reaching transformations of Chile's institutions. The junta president was an admirer of long-time Spanish dictator Francisco Franco, whose 1975 funeral he had attended in one of his few trips abroad. Pinochet also viewed Franco's political system as a model for Chile, one in which the armed forces could play a permanent guiding role. When Leigh was forcibly dismissed from the junta in April 1978, in a veritable coup within a coup, Pinochet's position became unassailable. Within months, Pinochet instructed the constitutional commission, which had languished with no clear purpose, to produce a new constitution with a time frame more to his liking. When the Council of State (Consejo de Estado), headed by former president Jorge Alessandri Rodríguez (1958–64), softened some of the provisions of the draft and proposed a return to civilian rule by 1985, Pinochet balked and demanded a new, tougher version.

The ''permanent'' articles of the draft were designed to go into effect a decade after promulgation, and Pinochet was specifically named to preside over the country's fortunes for an eight-year ''transition'' period. Pinochet further insisted that he be named to fill the first eight-year term of the ''constitutional period'' that followed, which would begin in 1990. The president's advisers, however, were able to persuade him that ratification of the constitution in a plebiscite could be seriously jeopardized if it were too apparent that Pinochet would obtain an additional sixteen-year mandate.

To satisfy Pinochet's ambitions, the designers of the constitution provided for a plebiscite to be held in late 1988 or 1989 on a single candidate to be designated by the four commanders of the armed forces (army commander Pinochet included) to lead the country in the next eight-year term. In an obscure provision, the text specifically exempted Pinochet from the article barring presidents from reelection, a clear sign that the general had every intention of perpetuating himself in power.

With the ratification of the constitution of 1980, in a highly irregular and undemocratic plebiscite characterized by the absence of registration lists, Pinochet achieved his objectives. Chile's democratic parties had proved incapable of challenging the power of the military to impose its own blueprint for the future. After seven years of constitutional ambiguity and questionable political legitimacy, the military's sweeping control over virtually every aspect of public life had become codified and sanctioned in an elaborate "democratic" ritual, which the authorities believed finally conferred on them the legitimacy of the popular will. With the economy at last on the upswing and a majority of voters resigned to accepting military rule as the only means of ensuring order and prosperity, Pinochet seemed invincible. As if to signal the government's renewed confidence and continuing contempt for its political opponents, Andrés Zaldívar, the highly respected president of the Christian Democratic Party (Partido Demócrata Cristiano—PDC), was exiled for daring to question the plebiscite's results.

The Constitution of 1980

The constitutional document imposed by the regime in 1980 consisted of 120 "permanent" articles, which went into full effect after the transition to "constitutional government." The document also included thirty-four "transitional" articles applying to the transitional period from March 11, 1980, to March 11, 1990. The transitional articles provided the regime with sweeping powers and outlined the procedures for the 1988–89 plebiscite on constitutional amendments and the election of a legislature. The most controversial provision was Transitional Article 24, which eliminated due process of law by giving the president broad powers to curtail the rights of assembly and free speech and to arrest, exile, or banish into internal exile any citizen, with no rights of appeal except to the president himself.

The "permanent" articles of the constitution were intended to create a "modern and protected democracy," an authoritarian version of representative government that guarantees "national security" by severely circumscribing the will of the people. This was to be accomplished in three ways: through the establishment of a permanent role for the armed forces as "guarantors" of the nation's institutions; through the imposition of restrictions on political activity, including the banning of movements or ideologies hostile to democracy; and through the creation of institutional mechanisms that would limit popular sovereignty.

The cornerstone of the military regime's constitutional doctrine was, according to the 1980 document, the establishment of a permanent tutelary role for the armed forces. The principal manifestation of this "tutelage" was, according to the 1980 document, the

National Security Council (Consejo de Seguridad Nacional—
Cosena), a body composed of eleven members, eight of whom have
enjoyed full voting rights since 1989 and only two of whom were
to be elected officials (Article 95). Voting members consisted of
the president of the republic, the president of the Senate of the
Republic (Senado de la República; hereafter, Senate), the president of the Supreme Court (Corte Suprema), the commanders in
chief of the armed forces, and the director general of the Carabineros
of Chile (Carabineros de Chile). This arrangement provided military leaders with an absolute majority on any Cosena vote. Non-
voting members included the ministers of defense; economy,
development, and reconstruction; finance; foreign relations; and
interior.

The 1980 constitution prescribed that Cosena could "express
to any authority established by this constitution its opinion regarding
any deed, event, act, or subject matter, which in its judgment gravely challenges the bases of the institutional order or could threaten
national security" (Article 96). Cosena was thus empowered to ad-
monish top government leaders and institutions, including Congress and the president, on any matter Cosena deemed relevant
to the nation's security as Cosena defined it. Although the fundamental law did not specify what would transpire should an
authority ignore Cosena's opinion, the framers clearly intended
to give the armed forces constitutional authority to take matters
into their own hands should their views be ignored.

The 1980 constitution also gave Cosena significant powers of
"authorization" and "nomination." The constitution required the
president to seek approval from Cosena to impose any state of exception (see Glossary) and gave the council authority to solicit any
information it deemed necessary in "national security" matters
from any government agency. Under the 1980 charter, Cosena was
also empowered to name four of the nine designated members of
the Senate and two of the seven members of the powerful Constitutional Tribunal (Tribunal Constitucional), whereas the president and the Senate could nominate only one each. Finally, only
Cosena could remove military commanders.

Perhaps the most significant protection of military prerogatives
was provided by Article 93, which severely limits civilian control
over the armed forces. Although the president names the commanders of each of the military services and the director general
of the Carabineros, nominees must be selected from a list of the
five highest-ranking officers with greatest seniority. Once a commander is appointed, that appointee is safe from presidential

dismissal for the duration of the individual's four-year term, unless qualified charges are brought against the person.

A second set of instruments for the establishment of a "protected" democracy excluded from political life those individuals, parties, or movements whose views and objectives are judged hostile to democracy. The language of Article 8 was aimed specifically at the parties of the Marxist left, although it could be applied to other groups and movements as well. According to the article, "any act by a person or group intended to propagate doctrines that are antagonistic to the family or that advocate violence or a totalitarian concept of society, the state, or the juridical order or class struggle is illicit and contrary to the institutional order of the Republic." Furthermore, any organization, movement, or political party that supports such aims is deemed unconstitutional. Article 19 barred parties from intervening in any activities that are "foreign to them," including the labor movement and local or community politics. Finally, Article 23 and Article 57 specifically barred leaders of "intermediate groups," such as unions, community organizations, and other associations, from leadership of political parties, and vice versa; deputies or senators could lose their seats for acting directly on such groups' behalf.

Third, the military regime sought to limit the expression of popular sovereignty by placing a series of checks on government institutions whose existence derives from popular consent. The most dramatic example was the elimination of elected local governments. Since colonial times, Chileans had elected municipal governments with considerable local powers and autonomy. Although modern local governments were limited in their efficacy by the overwhelming power and financial resources of the state, participation and interest in local politics had always been high. Article 32 of the constitution called for the direct presidential appointment of regional intendants (*intendentes*), governors (*gobernadores*) of provinces, and mayors (*alcaldes*) of large cities. Other mayors could be appointed by provincial corporative bodies (see Regional and Local Government, this ch.).

Reversing Chilean democratic practice, the constitution created an exaggerated presidentialism, severely limiting the prerogatives of Congress. Article 32 was particularly dramatic, giving the president the power to dissolve the lower house, the Chamber of Deputies (Cámara de Diputados), at least once in the chief executive's term. Popular representation in Congress was to be checked through the appointment of nine "designated" senators, more than a fourth of the thirty-five-member chamber. Finally, the constitution made any reform in the basic text extremely difficult to implement by requiring the concurrence of the president and two succeeding legislatures, each of which would have to approve an amendment by a three-fifths vote.

Authoritarianism Defeated by Its Own Rules

The reversal of fortune for Chile's democratic opposition came very gradually. After massive protests in 1983, spearheaded by labor leaders buoyed by mass discontent in the wake of a sharp downturn in the nation's economy, party leaders sought to set aside their acrimonious disputes and make a collective effort to bring an end to the military government. By this point, even influential elements on the right were signaling their displeasure with the personalization of power, fearing that a prolongation of the Pinochet regime would only serve to radicalize Chilean politics further and set the stage for a popular uprising that would overwhelm the authorities.

But Pinochet seemed to relish the challenge of taking on the opposition and was determined to carry out his self-appointed mandate to reshape Chile's economic and political systems. In a strategic retreat made under pressure from regime moderates, Pinochet briefly permitted officials to open a dialogue with democratic opponents, only to refuse to make any change in the formula for transition outlined in the constitution of 1980. In response to the continuing wave of protests, Pinochet declared a state of siege in November 1984 that included a crackdown on all demonstrations.

In August 1985, after months of delicate intraparty negotiations backed by Chile's Roman Catholic cardinal Juan Francisco Fresno, a broad alliance of eleven political groups, from center-right to socialist, signed a document entitled the National Accord for Transition to Full Democracy. It called for a gradual transition to civilian rule without specifying a particular timetable; legalization of all political activity; an end to restrictions on civil liberties; and free, direct presidential elections rather than the plebiscite contemplated in the constitution of 1980. The signing of the accord by such an array of groups meant that for the first time since 1973 Pinochet could no longer claim majority support. The regime appeared vulnerable, and many Chileans began to believe that Pinochet would agree to relinquish power.

However, the accord soon lost its momentum as Pinochet and his aides worked skillfully to sow mistrust and rancor within the fragile alliance. The general refused to acknowledge the accord's existence or meet with its leaders, despite a personal plea from Cardinal Fresno.

In the face of a determined military leader, opposition forces were at a clear disadvantage. They had no coherent strategy to force the regime to accept their point of view. The far left, which had refused to endorse the accord, hoped for a Sandinista-style insurrection that would drive Pinochet from power and give the PCCh and its allies, which included clandestine armed groups, the upper hand in the formation of a "provisional" alternative government. The moderate opposition envisioned a completely different scenario: some kind of breakdown of military support for Pinochet in response to peaceful civilian discontent, followed by free elections.

With the erosion of support for the National Accord, the Chilean opposition fell back into partisan and ideological quarrels. After years without national, local, or even internal party elections, opposition leaders were frozen in past disputes, incapable of gauging popular support for various policies. Given the parties' stasis, student elections on Chile's university campuses became bellwethers of political opinion. Often, the Christian Democratic and Communist candidates for student offices proved far more willing to compromise and form working alliances than their older counterparts.

The dramatic attempt on Pinochet's life by the Manuel Rodríguez Patriotic Front (Frente Patriótica Manuel Rodríguez—FPMR) in September 1986 further weakened the general's divided opponents and temporarily strengthened his own grip on power. The elaborately planned attack by the PCCh-linked group, in which commandos stormed Pinochet's motorcade on a hillside road outside Santiago, left five bodyguards dead but the general unharmed. Conservatives rallied around the regime, Christian Democrats and moderate Socialists distanced themselves from the Communists, and the Western democracies tempered their support of the opposition movement. Over the ensuing months, several new campaigns by the democratic opposition fizzled, including a movement of prominent citizens calling for free elections. Key opposition leaders, notably Christian Democrat Patricio Aylwin Azócar, began to emphasize the wisdom of trying to take on the regime in the upcoming plebiscite, rather than pressing for free elections.

As 1987 began, Pinochet and his aides confidently started planning for the presidential plebiscite. The economy was showing signs of recovery. The Marxist left, decimated by arrests and executions following the attack on Pinochet, was discredited. The democratic opposition was torn between those who accepted the regime's transition formula and those who denounced it as illegitimate. Moderate conservatives and some regime insiders, including the chiefs of the FACh and the Carabineros, urged Pinochet to permit open elections or to allow a candidate other than himself to stand for office. But the general was surrounded by sycophants who assured him that he was the only man capable of saving Chile from anarchy and chaos. Pinochet viewed politicians as demagogues determined to reverse the accomplishments of the military regime that only he, as a patriotic, self-sacrificing soldier, could defend in the face of a life-and-death threat from the communist foe.

On August 30, 1988, Chile's four military commanders met in secret deliberation and unanimously nominated the seventy-three-year-old Pinochet to run for president in a plebiscite that would take place in just five weeks, on October 5. Any commander who might have opposed General Pinochet did not do so, apparently because of a belief in the principle of military unity, or because of intimidation by Pinochet's power. The vast resources of the regime were already mobilized to ensure Pinochet's victory. Military provincial governors and civilian mayors, all appointed by Pinochet, were acting as local campaign chiefs. A voter-registration drive had begun in early 1987, with Pinochet himself the first to register. While opposition forces were denied access to the mass media, state television aired glowing advertisements for the government's accomplishments. The regime stepped up production of low-income housing, and Pinochet presided over countless ribbon-cutting ceremonies. The general's wife, Lucía Hiriart, who headed a vast network of women's aid and mothers' clubs, organized them into a grass-roots support network for the yes vote.

The turning point for the opposition had come in 1987, when key leaders concluded that their only hope to defeat the military was to beat it at its own game. Opposition leaders accepted the reality, if not the legitimacy, of constitutional provisions they despised by agreeing to register their followers in the electoral rolls set up by the junta, legalize political parties according to the regime's own prescriptions, and prepare to participate fully in a plebiscite they viewed as undemocratic.

By early 1988, fourteen parties had joined a loose coalition for the no vote. Moderate Socialists played a key role in convincing dubious Chilean leftists to register to vote, and the more radical wing of the Socialist Party finally followed suit. With little money and only limited freedom to operate, an all-volunteer force led by Socialists and Christian Democrats registered voters, organized training sessions for poll watchers, and collected the signatures needed to legalize parties. By the cutoff date, a record 92 percent of the voting-age population had registered to vote, and four parties had collected enough signatures to register poll watchers for 22,000 voting tables.

Despite inherently unfair campaign conditions, the military government made some efforts to provide a level playing field. The

Constitutional Tribunal, to the annoyance of some hard-liners in the regime, issued a firm ruling arguing that the constitution requires the implementation of a series of measures that would guarantee an impartial vote and vote count. Ironically, these measures had not been applied in the plebiscite that had ratified the constitution itself in 1980. Although opposition leaders did not trust the government, a fair election was also in the government's interest. Pinochet and his commanders were confident that the population's fear of a return to the confrontations of the early 1970s, in combination with signs of economic recovery and a campaign run with military efficiency, would permit Pinochet to overwhelm the fractious opposition and let his detractors, both at home and abroad, know that he enjoyed broad popular legitimacy.

In the weeks before the plebiscite, the no campaign, finally granted access to television, stunned the nation with its unity and a series of upbeat, appealing advertisements that stressed harmony and joy in a reunited Chile, called for a return to democratic traditions, and hinted at the poverty and oppression average people had suffered under the dictatorship. In response, the government stepped up its official propaganda campaign, bombarding the airwaves with grim and far less appealing advertisements that reminded voters of the violence and disorder that had preceded the coup and warned that Pinochet's opponents offered only more of the same.

On October 5, 1988, the voting proceeded in a quiet, orderly fashion, with military guards at each polling place, per tradition. By 9:00 P.M., the opposition's computers had counted half a million votes and showed the no tally to be far ahead. However, the government kept delaying the release of its tallies, and state television finally switched to a comedy series from the United States.

After frantic behind-the-scenes negotiations and a failed effort by some government officials to provoke street violence as an excuse to cancel the plebiscite, government television announced, at 2:40 A.M., that with 71 percent of the vote counted, the no was far ahead. The following night, a grim-faced Pinochet appeared on television and acknowledged his defeat: 54.5 percent for the no, versus 43 percent for the yes. Pinochet's acceptance of his electoral loss was a remarkable event. Despite the general's evident ambition to remain in power, the firm discipline within Chile's military establishment and the commitment of the other junta commanders, who had pledged to guarantee the vote's outcome, prevented him from doing so.

The Constitutional Reforms of 1989

The victory of the opposition led to a period of political uncertainty.

211

The no coalition had campaigned on a platform that rejected not only Pinochet's candidacy but also the "itinerary" and proposed "institutionality" of the Pinochet government. Democratic leaders felt that their clear victory entitled them to seek significant modifications in the constitutional framework established by the armed forces. However, they firmly rejected calls for Pinochet's resignation, or the formation of a provisional government, as unrealistic. Although Pinochet and the armed forces had suffered an electoral defeat, they had, of course, not been defeated militarily, nor had they lost their iron grip on the state. Nor was there any hint that the military would be willing to disregard Pinochet's wishes and abandon the transition formula and institutional order envisioned in "their" 1980 constitution. The fact that Pinochet had received 43 percent of the popular vote, despite fifteen years in office, only strengthened his hand in military circles.

Under these circumstances, the opposition leaders understood that they could not risk upsetting the military's transition formula or giving Pinochet an excuse to renege on the constitutional provision calling for an open presidential election within seventeen months. The opposition had won the plebiscite following Pinochet's rules; it could not now turn around and fully disavow them. Yet the opposition faced a serious dilemma. The 1980 constitution would be very difficult to amend once a new government was elected; a government elected under its terms would be locked into a legal structure the coalition considered fundamentally undemocratic. Pinochet would appoint almost one-third of the Senate, and the congressional election would take place under the rules of a system designed to favor the forces of the right, which had supported the military government. Changes to the constitution could be approved much more expeditiously before the full return to democracy because they would require the approval of only four men on the military junta, subject to ratification by a plebiscite.

Moderates within the military government who were open to discussions with the opposition quickly distanced themselves from regime officials and supporters who saw any compromise as capitulation. These moderates believed that it was in the military regime's clear interest to bargain with the opposition so as to salvage the essential features of the institutional legacy of the armed forces. They wanted a "soft landing" and feared that if the regime proved inflexible, a groundswell of support for the opposition could sweep away all of what they viewed as the government's accomplishments.

The position of the moderates in the military government, whose power was not assured, was bolstered significantly by the willingness of the largest party on the right, the National Renewal (Renovación

Nacional), to sit down with the opposition parties to come to an agreement on constitutional reforms. Political leaders of the democratic right were also uncomfortable with many of the authoritarian features of the 1980 constitution and anxious to distance themselves from the more unpalatable features of the regime as the country began to move toward electoral politics. They too were committed to a spirit of dialogue that might help prevent a breakdown in the transition and a return to raw military rule. The rightists' willingness to talk to their opponents in the center and on the left placed the regime hard-liners on notice: if reforms were not accomplished before the election of a new Congress, the center-left parties of the opposition and the moderate right might yet find a way to dismantle the constitution of 1980.

The moderates within the government won the day with two additional arguments. First, they argued that any compromise with the opposition would leave the essence of the constitution intact while providing it with a legitimacy it presently lacked. The constitutional reforms finally would establish the Pinochet document as the legitimate successor to the 1925 constitution.

Second, the government soft-liners made persuasive arguments that constitutional reforms, prior to the advent of democratic politics, could improve certain features of the constitution. The constitution was designed for Pinochet's reelection, not his defeat, and the armed forces feared that the document did not sufficiently protect their institutional autonomy. By entering into a constitutional-reform agreement, the authorities could insist on an amendment that would elevate the law regulating the armed forces' internal operations, including promotions, organization, training, and finances, to the status of an ''organic constitutional law.'' This would mean that changes in the law could not be made unless approved by a majority, or four-sevenths, of all senators and deputies.

The extraordinary bargaining among the democratic opposition, the moderate right, and the regime owed much to the leadership of Patricio Aylwin, the leader of the Christian Democrats, who had become the standard-bearer of the no alliance. Aylwin understood that the hard-liners within the military government could make the transition difficult, if not impossible, if the reform process broke down. Nor did Aylwin, who expected to be the next president of Chile, relish the prospect of a confrontational transitional government in which the new authorities would endeavor vainly to implement reforms while supporters of the former military government sought to hold the line. The prospects for the first government after a long authoritarian interlude would be jeopardized by a continuous struggle to define the future of the country's institutional order. Better to agree on the playing field now, in order to avoid fatal problems later. For the regime, Carlos Cáceres, Pinochet's minister of interior, played a critical role. At one point in the talks, he threatened to resign when the general balked at key constitutional reforms, only to find strong support for his position among other commanders on the junta.

Opponents of constitutional reform on both the far left and the far right shared a curious symbiotic logic. Those on the left rejected reform because they envisioned a sharp break with the military government, which would be defeated once again in an open presidential election and would have to concede the failure of its institutional blueprint. Those on the right relished that very confrontation because they saw it as forcing the military once again to accept its "patriotic responsibility" and save the country from a citizenry still not ready for democracy.

The fifty-four reforms, approved by 85.7 percent of the voters on July 30, 1989, fell far short of the expectations of the opposition but nevertheless represented significant concessions on the part of the authorities. From the point of view of the opposition, the most important modifications were to Article 8, which in its new form penalized parties or groups that, through their actions and not simply through their objectives, threatened the democratic order. Other reforms eliminated the prohibition against party membership of labor or association leaders, required the courts to consider habeas corpus petitions in all circumstances, and prohibited exile as a sanction. The revised article also reduced the qualified majorities required for approval of organic constitutional laws and constitutional amendments in Congress; eliminated the requirement that two successive Congresses vote to enact amendments; and increased the number of elected senators to thirty-eight, thus reducing the proportion of designated senators while restoring some oversight functions to the Senate. In addition, the amended article eliminated the president's power to dissolve the lower house of Congress and reduced some of the chief executive's power to declare a state of exception; changed the mandate of Cosena by substituting the word *representar* (represent) for *hacer presente* (make known), a legal construction that the opposition interpreted from legal precedents at the Office of the Comptroller General of the Republic (Oficina de la Contraloría General de la República) as giving Cosena an advisory role, rather than an enforcement role; and increased the membership of Cosena to eight by adding another civilian member, the comptroller general (*contraloría general*). The latter modification ensured that the military members of Cosena would not enjoy a four-to-three majority.

From the perspective of the Pinochet government, the most important result of the reform process was the retention of the essential elements of its constitutional design and its ratification by an overwhelming majority of the citizenry. What the military had not achieved in 1980, it achieved with the negotiations of 1989. The constitution of the armed forces had now replaced the constitution of 1925 as the legitimate fundamental law of the land. Although it had to concede some points, the military gained a significant victory with the provision that laws dealing with the armed forces would be governed by an organic constitutional law. The Pinochet regime also succeeded in having the first elected president's term limited to four years with no option to run for reelection. Government officials were convinced that even if the opposition parties won the next election, they would be incapable of governing, a situation that would open the door in four years to a new administration more to the military's liking.

With the approval of the constitutional reforms, Chile's transition became, in political sociologist Juan J. Linz's terms, a *transición pactada* (a transition by agreement), rather than a *transición por ruptura* (a sharp break with the previous order). However, the opposition made clear that it saw the agreements as constituting only a first step in democratizing the constitution, and that it would seek further reforms of Cosena, the composition of the Constitutional Tribunal and the Senate, the election of local governments, the president's authority over the armed forces, and the powers of Congress and the courts.

With the constitutional reforms behind them, Chileans turned their attention to the December 14, 1989, elections, the first democratic elections for president and Congress in nineteen years. The fourteen opposition parties formed the Coalition of Parties for Democracy (Concertación de Partidos por la Democracia—CPD), with Aylwin as standard-bearer. His principal opponent was Pinochet's former minister of finance, Hernán Büchi Buc, who ran as an independent supported by the progovernment Independent Democratic Union (Unión Demócrata Independiente—UDI) and the more moderate rightist party, National Renewal, which ran a joint congressional coalition called Democracy and Progress (Democracia y Progreso). Independent businessman Francisco Javier Errázuriz Talavera ran as the third candidate on a populist platform supported by a heterogeneous group of small parties calling themselves Unity for Democracy (Unidad por la Democracia).

Aylwin (1990–94) won a decisive victory, improving on the no vote in the plebiscite with 55.2 percent of the 7.1 million votes cast to Büchi's 29.4 percent and Errázuriz's 15.4 percent (see table 25,

Appendix). In the congressional races, the CPD was able to beat the heavy odds imposed by the government's electoral formula and win a majority of the elected seats in both the Chamber of Deputies and the Senate. In the Chamber of Deputies, the CPD gained 49.3 percent of the vote to 32.4 percent for Democracy and Progress and 50.5 percent of the vote versus 43 percent for its opponent in the Senate (see table 36, Appendix).

Although the CPD won a majority of the contested seats in Congress, it fell short of having the numbers required to offset the designated senators to be appointed by the Pinochet government. Passage of even the simplest legislation would have required negotiations with opposition parties or individual designated senators. The military regime's electoral law had ensured an overrepresentation of the parties of the right in relation to their voting strength, making it virtually impossible for the new civilian government to adopt constitutional reforms without the concurrence of one of the main opposition groups.

Not the least of the new government's challenges was Pinochet himself, who by constitutional provision could remain as commander in chief of the army until 1997. Pinochet made it clear that he would continue to be a watchdog, ensuring that the new rules were followed and that ''none of his men were touched'' for their actions in the ''war'' to save Chile from communism.

Although Chile's authoritarian legacies clearly frustrated the new leadership, the transition probably was facilitated in the short term by the veto power that the military and the right continued to enjoy. Had the CPD pressed for an immediate modification of Pinochet's institutional edifice and attempted to dismiss many of his supporters, the armed forces would have been far more resistant to the return of civilian rule.

Chile's rightist parties, which remained suspicious of popular sovereignty and fearful that a center-left alliance with majority support could threaten their survival, would have been much more likely to conspire with the military had their ''guarantees'' been undermined. These authoritarian legacies also contributed to the success of the transition by helping the broad coalition under Aylwin's leadership achieve unity, retain it, and elaborate a common program of moderate policies. This moderation can be attributed not only to respect for a new style of politics after the traumatic years of authoritarian rule, but also to the new authorities' genuine fear of the strength of the armed forces and their rightist supporters. The danger Chile now faced was that the very provisions that made the transition possible in the short term could make the consolidation of a stable democracy more difficult in the long term.

Patricio Aylwin Azócar,
president 1990–94
Courtesy Presidency
of the Republic,
Department of
Photography

The State and Government Institutions in Chile
The State and the System of Government

Even prior to the 1970 election of Salvador Allende, the Chilean state was one of the most extensively structured in Latin America. By the end of the 1960s, direct public investment constituted over 50 percent of all gross investment. Government expenditures accounted for 14 percent of the gross national product (GNP—see Glossary), and 13 percent of the economically active population worked in the public sector. From 1940 until 1952, the budget deficit of the government averaged 0.5 percent of the gross domestic product (GDP—see Glossary). It grew to 2.4 percent between 1940 and 1952 and 4.3 percent between 1959 and 1964, a period largely conconcurrent with the administration of the conservative Jorge Alessandri.

With the growth of the state went the growth of a far-flung bureaucracy with its own dynamic and considerable independence from executive power. State expansion involved the creation of an ever larger and more bewildering array of decentralized and semi-autonomous agencies, which depended only nominally on particular ministries for control. By the mid-1960s, 40 percent of all public employees in Chile worked for more than fifty such agencies, charged with implementing most of the economic and social service responsibilities of the state.

217

Particularly important was the Production Development Corporation (Corporación de Fomento de la Producción—Corfo), created in 1939 to develop Chilean industry in accord with an import-substitution industrialization policy. By mid-century Corfo owned shares in eighty of the country's most important enterprises and held majority shares in thirty-nine of them. Utilities, ports, steel production, and other enterprises were developed by an array of state agencies. Although public ventures, these enterprises were governed by their own boards and enjoyed substantial autonomy from ministerial and executive control. Some permitted direct representation of interest groups in a quasi-corporatist scheme. Such representation was most commonly enjoyed by business organizations, which had voting rights in agencies such as the Central Bank of Chile (Banco Central de Chile; hereafter, Central Bank—see Glossary), the State Bank of Chile (Banco del Estado de Chile; hereafter, State Bank), and Corfo. During the Allende years, a policy of nationalization of private industry brought close to 500 firms into state hands, including the country's giant copper companies, which had been owned by United States interests.

The expansion of the state sector was in response to a development strategy that entrusted economic growth to public-sector initiative and regulation. State expansion was also fueled by a presidential form of government that encouraged chief executives to establish new programs as their historical legacy. Civil service laws made it difficult for incoming presidents to dismiss employees, a situation that led to the creation of new agencies to undertake new programs without dismantling old ones. In a sluggish economy, the state sector was also an important source of patronage. Political parties, particularly those that were part of the incumbent presidential coalition, became important employment centers for government agencies.

The Chilean state, however, was also notable for its general lack of corruption and its fairly efficient operation. Public employees were keenly aware that their careers could be ruined if the powerful Office of the Comptroller General caught them using funds improperly. Although tax revenues often lagged, Chile enforced tax laws with greater success than many of its neighbors. A career in public service was valued, and the Chilean state counted on many dedicated and fairly well-educated officers from Chile's middle classes. The relative efficiency and probity of the Chilean state was the result of a long history of competitive party politics, in which opposition parties and Congress kept a close watch on the conduct of public affairs.

By the 1960s, Chile's strategy of import-substitution industrialization had run its course. The country was plagued by chronic inflation as contending groups sought government subsidies or wage readjustments that would keep them ahead of their competition. The scramble for favorable state action on behalf of sectoral interests was intensified by growing polarization and confrontation in the political sphere, as increasingly mobilized social groups sought larger shares of Chile's finite resources. The system came to a breaking point during the Popular Unity government, when the authorities unabashedly used state agencies as a means of expanding political support. The Allende government swelled the rolls of government offices with regime partisans and made ample use of regulatory powers to freeze prices and increase wages, while printing unbacked money to cover an expanding government deficit. State agencies became veritable fiefdoms for the different parties, each trying to pursue its own agenda with little regard for a coordinated national policy.

Within days of toppling the Allende government, the military regime began a dramatic reduction in the size of Chile's public sector. Between 1973 and 1980, public-sector employment was reduced 20 percent, and by the latter year only forty-three firms remained in state hands. In the late 1980s, another round of privatization further reduced state control of productive enterprises. Cutbacks in state expenditures in other fields, including medical care and education, reduced deficits to the point that by the mid-1980s the state budget was in the black. Government surpluses reached 3 percent of GNP by the end of the military regime.

The civilian government of Patricio Aylwin took great pains to retain a smaller but more efficient state. By 1992 government surpluses had reached 5 percent of GNP; expansions in state expenditures for social services were financed by increased revenues generated by tax reform, rather than by deficit spending. By comparison with many developed countries, Chile still retained a powerful state sector, with utilities, railroads, and the giant copper mines that produced a significant percentage of government revenues remaining under government control. At the same time, the process of state decentralization begun by the military government continued, albeit under the aegis of democracy rather than dictatorship.

Chile's system of government was patterned after that of the United States, as were those of all of the Latin American countries. The failure of the French Revolution to produce an enduring republican model left the representative model of Philadelphia as the only viable republican system of government in the early nineteenth century. Chile thus incorporated the principle of the separation of powers into its constitutional framework, even though the country rejected in its constitution of 1833 the federal system pioneered by the United States.

Much of Chile's political history can be described as an ongoing, occasionally violent struggle for advantage among the executive and legislative branches of government. In the 1920s, the Office of the Comptroller General became a virtually coequal branch of government with the others because of its great oversight powers and its virtual autonomy. With the approval of constitutional amendments in 1970 and the adoption of the 1980 constitution, the Constitutional Tribunal, Cosena, and the Central Bank became important government organs in their own right (see The Autonomous Powers, this ch.).

The Presidency

The constitution of 1925 sought to reestablish strong presidential rule in order to offset the dominant role assumed by the legislature after the Civil War of 1891. Elected to serve a single six-year term, the president was given broad authority to appoint cabinets without the concurrence of the legislature, whose members were no longer eligible to serve in executive posts. Formal executive authority increased significantly in succeeding years as Congress delegated broad administrative authority to new presidents, who increasingly governed by decree. Constitutional reforms enacted in 1947 and in 1970 further reduced congressional prerogatives.

Although the 1925 constitution gave Chilean presidents increased power on paper, actual executive authority does not appear to have increased significantly. No president could count on gaining majority support without the backing of a broad alliance of parties. In 1932, 1938, 1942, and 1964, presidential candidates structured successful majority coalitions prior to the presidential election, promising other parties cabinet appointments and incorporation of some of their programmatic objectives. In 1946, 1952, 1958, and 1970, because presidential candidates did not attract sufficient coalition support to win a majority of the votes, the election was thrown into Congress, which chose the winner from the two front-runners. Whether elected by a majority of the voters or through compromises with opposition parties in Congress, Chilean presidents found that governing often amounted to a balancing act. Only by structuring complex majority coalitions could the president pass legislative programs and prevent the censure of key ministers by Congress.

The presidential balancing act was complicated by frequent defections from the chief executive's coalition of supporters, even by members of his own party, particularly in the waning months of

La Moneda Palace, seat of the executive branch, in Santiago
Courtesy Embassy of Chile, Washington

his constitutionally stipulated single term. One result was that the average cabinet often lasted less than a year (see table 37, Appendix). For example, in the government of Gabriel González Videla (1946–52), who was a member of the Radical Party (Partido Radical), the average cabinet lasted six and one-half months; Allende's cabinets lasted slightly less than six months. The average duration of ministerial appointments was six months and seven months in the same two governments, respectively. This pattern resulted in frustrated presidents and policy discontinuity that belied the formal powers of the chief executive.

The authors of the constitution of 1980 sought to address the government's structural problems by creating a far stronger executive. The 1980 charter increases presidential terms from six to eight years but retains the prohibition against immediate reelection, and it gives broad new powers to the president at the expense of a weakened legislature. However, prior to the transfer of power in March 1994, the constitution was amended, reducing the presidential term back to six years.

The constitution specifies that the president should be at least forty years of age, meet the constitutional requirements for citizenship, and have been born on Chilean territory. The president is elected by an absolute majority of the valid votes cast. The 1980

221

constitution did away with the traditional practice of having Congress decide between the two front-runners when no candidate receives an absolute majority of the votes. It institutes instead a second-round election aimed specifically at barring political bargaining in the legislature and ensuring the election of a president with the backing of a majority of the population.

In addition to specific prerogatives and duties, the constitution grants the president the legal right to "exercise statutory authority in all those matters that are not of a legal nature, without prejudice to the power to issue other regulations, decrees, or instructions which he may deem appropriate for the enforcement of the law" (Article 32). The president has the right to call plebiscites, propose changes to the constitution, declare states of emergency and exception, and watch over the performance of the court system. The president names ministers and, in accord with specific procedures, two senators, the comptroller general, the commanders of the armed forces, and all judges of the Supreme Court and appellate courts (*cortes de apelaciones*). Departing from previous practice, which required senatorial confirmation of diplomatic appointments, the 1980 constitution bars the legislative branch from any role in the confirmation process. Finally, it increases the legislative powers of the president dramatically, making the chief executive a virtual colegislator (Article 32, in concordance with Article 60).

Ironically, although the CPD strongly criticized the disproportionate powers given to the president in the 1980 constitution, President Aylwin moved with determination to make full use of those very powers. The son of a middle-class family whose father was a lawyer and judge and eventually president of the Supreme Court, Aylwin was born on November 26, 1918, in Viña del Mar. He studied law and had faculty appointments at the University of Chile and the Pontifical Catholic University of Chile. In 1945 he joined the National Falange (Falange Nacional), the precursor of the PDC, which he helped form in 1957. A former senator, Aylwin served seven terms as president of the PDC, a position he held when he was nominated as the PDC's presidential candidate. In his work as spokesman for the multiparty opposition coalition, he displayed great skills as a conciliator, gaining the confidence of parties and leaders on the left, who had vehemently opposed his support for the overthrow of the Allende government. A man of deep religious conviction, humble demeanor, and unimpeachable honesty, Aylwin impressed friends and foes alike when he successfully negotiated the constitutional reforms of 1989.

As president, Aylwin surprised even his closest advisers with his firm leadership, particularly his willingness to stand up to Pinochet, who remained army commander. For instance, in a crucial meeting of Cosena, Aylwin challenged Pinochet on a matter directly related to the issue of presidential authority and received backing from the other military commanders for his position. Aylwin moved cautiously but firmly in dealing with the human rights abuses of the past, appointing a commission that officially acknowledged the crimes of the security forces. Subsequent legislation provided compensation for victims or their families, even if prosecution for most of those crimes appeared unlikely ever to take place.

The Aylwin government also took great pains to assure domestic and foreign investors of its intention to maintain the basic features of the free-market economic model. The CPD was keenly aware that it needed to retain the confidence of the national and international business communities and show the world that it too could manage economic policy with skill and responsibility. Indeed, by showing that Chile could manage its economic affairs in democracy, the government could provide an even more favorable economic climate, one not clouded by the political confrontations and potential instability of authoritarianism. The Aylwin government appeared to meet this objective, as the Chilean economy grew at an average rate of more than 6 percent from 1990 through 1993.

The Aylwin government was cautious in proposing constitutional reforms for fear of alienating the military and the opposition parties of the right, which controlled the Senate. The key constitutional reform, enacted on November 9, 1991, created democratically elected local governments by reestablishing elections for municipal mayors and council members. Additional reforms of the judicial system were also approved. Although it indicated its desire to change the electoral system and the nature of civil-military relations, the Aylwin government was unable to achieve those objectives.

The executive branch in Chile is composed of sixteen ministries with portfolio and four cabinet-level agencies—the Central Bank, the Production Development Corporation (Corfo), the National Women's Service (Servicio Nacional de la Mujer—Sernam), and the National Energy Commission (Comisión Nacional de Energía) (see fig. 11). Ministers serve exclusively at the president's discretion. Each ministry is required to articulate a series of firm objectives for each fiscal year, and the president uses these ministerial goals to judge the success of a particular department and minister. Every seven months, a formal evaluation (state of progress) is conducted to ascertain the progress of each ministry. The president

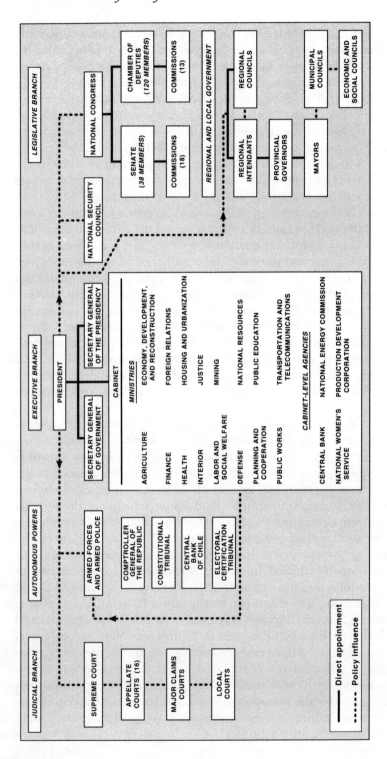

Figure 11. Government Structure, 1993

writes a formal letter to each minister in January, evaluating the accomplishments or failures of the department in question. Cabinet officers have significant authority over their own agencies.

Although important in setting the overall priorities of the government and coordinating a uniform response to issues, cabinet meetings deal primarily with general subjects. Critical policy questions, however, are often addressed at the ministerial level by interministerial commissions dealing with specific substantive areas. These include infrastructural, development, economic, socioeconomic, and political issues. If there is no unanimity on a particular matter, the question goes to "the second floor" (the president's office) for final disposition. The president is kept closely apprised of all matters under discussion at all times by the secretary general of the presidency, who has the primary responsibility of coordinating the work of ministerial commissions. Under President Aylwin, that position was held by Edgardo Boeninger Kausel, a former rector of the University of Chile. Boeninger's success resulted not from the power of his position, which in formal terms is unimportant, but from his skills as a negotiator and consensus builder and from the willingness of the cabinet, composed of individuals from different parties, to work in a collegial fashion. This style of authority might slow decisions, but it has the advantage of averting serious conflicts and sparing the president from having to micromanage policy or serve as a constant referee. Aylwin's secretary general of the government, Enrique Correa Rios, the government's chief spokesman, also played a prominent role in projecting the government's image and serving as a bridge to political parties and opposition leaders.

In addition to the office of the secretary general of the presidency and secondary general of the government, two ministries had key roles in the Aylwin administration. The Ministry of Finance had virtual autonomy in formulating and guiding overall economic and budgetary policy. The Ministry of Interior, the principal "political ministry" of the government, was charged with law enforcement and with coordinating government policy with the parties of the CPD.

The Legislative Branch

Inaugurated on July 4, 1811, the National Congress became one of the strongest legislative bodies in the world by the end of the nineteenth century. The 1925 constitution reaffirmed the commitment to a bicameral system made up of a 150-member Chamber of Deputies and a fifty-member Senate. However, that charter diminished congressional prerogatives by barring members of

Congress from occupying ministerial posts, restricting the legislature's power over budget laws, and giving the president considerable legislative powers, including the right to designate particular legislation as "urgent." Nevertheless, Congress remained a critical arena for the formulation of national policy, serving as the most important institution for cross-party bargaining and consensus building in Chile's fragmented political system. Congress produced fundamental legislation, such as laws establishing social security (1924), the Labor Code (1931), the minimum wage (1943), Corfo (1939), restrictions on the PCCh (1948), and agrarian reform (1967). Congress also had an important means of oversight in its authority to accuse ministers of wrongdoing.

Under the 1980 constitution, Chile retains a bicameral legislature composed of the Chamber of Deputies and the Senate, both of which play a role in the legislative process. However, the 1980 charter reduced the Chamber of Deputies to 120 members, two for each of sixty congressional districts. All deputies serve for four years on the same quadrennial cycle. Upon taking office, all deputies must be citizens possessing the right to vote. They must be at least twenty-one years old, must have completed secondary education, and must have lived in the district they represent for at least two years. The 1980 constitution also reduced the Senate, to thirty-eight elected members, who serve eight-year terms, with half of the body coming up for election every four years, plus nine designated senators. Senators must be citizens with the right to vote, must be at least forty years old, must have completed secondary school, and must have lived in the region they represent for at least three years. High-level government officials, including ministers, judges, and the five members of the Central Bank Council, are barred from being candidates for deputy or senator until a year after they leave their posts. Leaders of community groups or other associations also are not permitted to become candidates unless they give up their posts.

In addition to the elected senators, the Senate has nine designated senators (eight since the death of one in 1991), all of whom serve eight-year terms. The Supreme Court names two from the ranks of former members of the court and one who has served as comptroller general. Cosena designates four senators, each a former commander of each of the armed services who held that post for at least two years. Finally, the president of the republic designates two senators, one who has been a university president and the other a government minister (Article 45). All former presidents who remain in office for at least six years of the eight-year term are automatically senators for life. Pinochet, the only former president alive when the current Senate was installed in March 1990, opted instead to remain commander in chief of the army, a post that is constitutionally excluded from a senatorial position. The appointed senators played a somewhat surprising role in the Aylwin government by not always acting in unity with the rightist opposition, as the government feared they would. Indeed, these senators occasionally served as bridges between the government and the armed forces, helping to diffuse tensions and avert misunderstandings.

The Chamber of Deputies carries out its duties by means of thirteen permanent commissions, each one of which is composed of thirteen deputies. The Senate has eighteen commissions, each with five members. Most of the commissions correspond to a ministry responsible for a similar substantive area. Mixed commissions, composed of members from both houses, are charged with resolving discrepancies between the houses on particular pieces of legislation.

The constitution establishes a hierarchy of laws that must be approved by majorities of various sizes. Ordinary laws are approved by a simple majority of the members present in both chambers. Laws requiring a qualified quorum must be approved by an absolute majority of all legislators. An example would be a law redefining the boundaries of regions or provinces (see table 38, Appendix). Organic constitutional laws, designed to complement the constitution on key matters, require approval by four-sevenths of all members to be modified, repealed, or enacted into law. Finally, laws interpreting the constitution require the approval of three-fifths of all legislators for enactment.

Constitutional amendments can be initiated by the president, ten deputies, or five senators, and they require the concurrence of three-fifths of all legislators and the signature of the president to be approved. Key provisions dealing with such matters as rights and obligations, the Constitutional Tribunal, the armed forces, and Cosena require the assent of two-thirds of the members of each chamber and approval by the president. If the president rejects a constitutional reform measure that is subsequently reaffirmed by Congress by at least a three-fifths vote, he or she can take the matter to the voters in a plebiscite.

Congress has the exclusive right to approve or reject international treaties presented to it by the president before ratification, following the same procedure used in approving an ordinary law. Although the president, with the consent of Cosena, can institute a state of siege (see state of exception, Glossary), Congress, within a period of ten days, can approve or reject the state of siege by a majority vote of its members.

In case the office of the president is left vacant and there are fewer than two years left in the presidential term, Congress can select a presidential successor through a majority vote of its members. Should the vacancy occur with more than two years left in the presidential term, a new presidential election would be called. The Chamber of Deputies can also initiate a constitutional accusation by majority vote against the president, ministers, judges, the comptroller general, admirals, generals, intendants of regions, and governors of provinces for violations of the law, constitutional dispositions, or abuse of power. The Senate, in turn, acts as a jury and finds the accused either innocent or guilty as charged. If the president of the republic is accused, the conviction depends on a two-thirds majority in the Senate. The Senate is also required to give the president permission to leave the country for a period of more than thirty days or for any amount of time during the last ninety days of the presidential term. Further, the Senate can declare the physical or mental incapacity of the president or president-elect, once the Constitutional Tribunal has pronounced itself on the matter.

The original constitutional provisions of 1980 virtually barred the Senate from exercising oversight of the executive branch or expressing opinions on the conduct of government. These provisions were removed from the constitution in the 1989 amendments. The amendments also eliminate the president's power to dissolve the Chamber of Deputies. The constitution of 1980, however, severely limits the role of Congress in legislative matters relative to earlier legislatures in Chilean history. Article 62 states that "the President of the Republic holds the exclusive initiative for proposals of law related to changes of the political or administrative division of the country, or to the financial or budgetary administration of the State." Article 64 of the constitution also restricts the budgetary prerogatives of the legislative branch.

In several areas, the president is given sole authority to introduce bills. These include measures involving spending, changes in the duties and characteristics of public-sector administrative entities, modifications to the political-administrative configuration of the state, and initiatives related to collective bargaining. The president can also call the legislature into extraordinary session, at which time the legislature can only consider legislative and treaty proposals introduced by the president. The president may grant certain initiatives priority status, requiring that Congress act within three, ten, or thirty days, depending on the degree of urgency specified. In this sense, the president has the exclusive power to set the legislative agenda and, therefore, the political agenda. In a further

The Chamber of Deputies in the new parliament building in Valparaíso
The National Congress building in Valparaíso
Courtesy Embassy of Chile, Washington

229

restraint on legislators, the 1980 constitution permits the Constitutional Tribunal to remove a senator or deputy from office if he or she "permits the voting of a motion that is declared openly contrary to the political constitution of the State by the Constitutional Tribunal" (Article 57).

Finally, Congress is limited in its ability to act as a counterforce against the president's power in matters dealing with the constitutional rights of citizens. Although the president needs the approval of the majority of Congress to establish a state of siege, the president may declare a state of assembly, emergency, or catastrophe solely with the approval of Cosena (Article 40).

Important legislative initiatives approved during the Aylwin government have included, in the political sphere, constitutional changes leading to the creation of democratic local governments; laws reforming the administration of justice, including the treatment of political prisoners and terrorism; and the creation, in 1990, of a cabinet-level agency, Sernam, to pay special attention to women's issues. In the sociocultural area, changes included a revision to the National Education Law to "dignify" the teaching profession and establish a "teaching career"; a reformulation of student loan programs; and measures designed to simplify the reporting of petty crimes and robbery and increase the powers of the police in dealing with such crimes. Congress also approved measures to regulate collective bargaining and recognize labor organizations. In the economic sphere, the most important legislation enacted into law included the Industrial Patents Law, designed to ease Chile's entrance into international markets; the lowering of tariff barriers; and the creation of a price-stabilization fund for petroleum. In the international sphere, Congress approved various treaties of economic cooperation (including one with the European Economic Community) and ratified the findings of the Bryan Commission, a joint commission with the United States that settled the case of the 1977 assassination of Chilean ambassador Orlando Letelier in Washington, which had constituted a long-time source of conflict between Chile and the United States.

During the Aylwin administration, relations between the executive and Congress were conducted through an informal network of bilateral commissions composed of ministers and their top advisers and senators and deputies of the governing coalition working in the same policy area. However, these meetings proved less important than the weekly gatherings presided over by the minister of interior with party leaders of the CPD coalition, leaders of the CPD parties in the legislature, and the secretaries general of the presidency and the government. At these weekly meetings, the legislative agenda was discussed and decided upon. This pattern of decision making signified, in practice, that individual members of Congress and the legislature itself had assumed a secondary and pro forma role, following the instructions of legislative leaders in their close negotiations with government and party leaders. Nor did congressional committees or members of Congress have enough staff and expertise to deal with experts from the executive branch on complex legislative matters. Individual legislators could articulate concerns and provide important feedback, but early in the postauthoritarian period the legislature appeared to be playing a decidedly secondary role.

The Courts

Although the Republic of Chile's founders drew on the example of the United States in designing the institutions of government, they drew on Roman law and Spanish and French traditions, particularly the Napoleonic Code, in designing the country's judicial system. The judicial system soon acquired a reputation for independence, impartiality, and probity. However, the judiciary fell into some disrepute during the Parliamentary Republic (1891–1925), when it became part of the logrolling and patronage politics of the era.

The 1925 constitution introduced reforms aimed at depoliticizing and improving the judicial system by guaranteeing judicial independence. Chile's justice system established itself as one of the best on the South American continent, despite a serious lack of resources and inadequate attention to the needs of the nation's poorest citizens.

During the Popular Unity government, the Supreme Court repeatedly clashed with the president and his associates. The Allende government viewed the court as a conservative and inflexible power, obsessed with a literal definition of a law designed to protect the privileges of private property against the new logic of a revolutionary time. The Supreme Court retorted vehemently that its task was simply to follow the dictates of the law, not to change it to suit some other objective.

The courts had much less difficulty dealing with the military regime, which left the court system virtually intact. As soon as the courts accepted the legitimacy of the military junta as the new executive and legislative power, they worked diligently to adjudicate matters in conformity with the new decree laws, even when the latter violated the spirit and letter of the constitution. In particular, the courts did nothing to address the serious issue of human rights violations, continuously deferring to the military and security services. The Supreme Court saw its own jurisdiction severely eroded as the military justice system expanded to encompass a wide range of national security matters that went far beyond institutional concerns.

According to the 1925 constitution, modified somewhat by the 1980 document, the Supreme Court can declare a particular law, decree law, or international treaty "inapplicable because of unconstitutionality." This does not invalidate the statute or measure for all cases, only for the one under consideration. Another important function of the Supreme Court is the administration of the court system. The organization and jurisdiction of Chile's courts were established in the Organic Code of the Tribunals (Law 7,241) adopted in 1943. This law was modified on several occasions; two recent instances are the organic constitutional Law 18,969 of March 10, 1990, and Law 19,124 of February 2, 1992. Chile's ordinary courts consist of the Supreme Court, the appellate courts (*cortes de apelación*), major claims courts, and various local courts (*juzgados de letras*). There is also a series of special courts, such as the juvenile courts, labor courts, and military courts in time of peace. The local courts consist of one or more tribunals specifically assigned to each of the country's communes, Chile's smallest administrative units. In larger jurisdictions, the local courts may specialize in criminal cases or civil cases, as defined by law.

Chile has sixteen appellate courts, each with jurisdiction over one or more provinces. The majority of the courts have four members, although the two largest courts have thirteen members, and Santiago's appellate court has twenty-five. The Supreme Court consists of seventeen members, who select a president from their number for a three-year term. The Supreme Court carries out its functions with separate chambers consisting of at least five judges each, presided over by the most senior member or the president of the court.

Members and prosecutors of the Supreme Court are appointed by the president of the republic, who selects them from a slate of five persons proposed by the court itself. At least two must be senior judges on an appellate court. The others can include candidates from outside the judicial system. The justices and prosecutors of each appellate court are also appointed by the president from a slate of three candidates submitted by the Supreme Court, only one of whom can be from outside the judicial system. In order to be appointed, ordinary judges at the local level are appointed by the president from a slate of three persons submitted by an appellate court. They must be lawyers, must be at least twenty-five years old, and must have judicial experience. Ministers of the appellate courts must be at least thirty-two years old, and Supreme Court ministers must be at least thirty-six years old, with a specified number of years of judicial or legal experience. Judges serve for life and cannot be removed except for inappropriate behavior.

The relationship between the Aylwin administration and the Supreme Court was tense. Pinochet offered extraordinary retirement bonuses to the eldest court members to ensure the appointment of relatively young judges who were friends of the outgoing regime. The parties of the CPD were highly critical of these appointments and made no secret of their strong disapproval of the Supreme Court's behavior under the military government, particularly its complete disregard for the massive violations of human rights. Responding to these concerns, the Aylwin administration introduced constitutional reform legislation that would overhaul the nomination procedure for Supreme Court ministers, create a separate administrative structure for the judicial branch, and obligate the Supreme Court to take a more vigilant role in the protection of human rights. These reform efforts failed because the parties of the right refused to go along with change in the face of strong opposition from the Supreme Court, which was fearful that it would lose its prerogatives and concerned that the judicial system would become "politicized." Still pending as Aylwin's term neared its end were reforms of the military justice system with its authority to try civilians in areas of national security and to judge military personnel even when charged with a criminal or civil crime against civilians.

The Autonomous Powers

The Comptroller General

The Office of the Comptroller General of the Republic has been a highly visible institution since the adoption of the 1925 constitution. In 1943 it was upgraded to an autonomous government organ through an amendment to the constitution (Law 7,727) and was retained as such in the constitution of 1980. Charged with serving as the government's auditor, the agency has a large professional staff, which scrutinizes the collection and expenditure of government funds by the National Treasury, the municipalities, and other state services as determined by law. Over the years, the agency gained a reputation for insisting on strict conformity to the law, instilling respect in career officials and elected officials alike.

In addition to its preaudit and postaudit functions, the Office of the Comptroller General has significant juridical functions, as it is empowered to rule on the legality and constitutionality of decrees and laws. All supreme decrees and resolutions are routinely sent to the Office of the Comptroller General for a ruling prior to adoption. In this sense, the comptroller general's oversight functions are essentially preventive. The chief executive can overrule the comptroller general's objection to a presidential decree by issuing a so-called decree of insistence requiring the signature of every cabinet minister. Overruling the comptroller general opens the ministers to the threat of censorship by the Chamber of Deputies. In order to guarantee the comptroller general's autonomy, the official is appointed by the president, with the consent of the Senate, to serve until age seventy-five. The comptroller general has complete control over the organization and staff of the office in conformity with Law 10,336 (Law of Organization and Powers of the Comptroller General of the Republic).

The Constitutional Tribunal

Although the comptroller general serves as an effective watchdog over government officials and functionaries, definitive and binding decisions on constitutional matters are made by the Constitutional Tribunal. The tribunal was created by the constitutional reforms of 1970 (Law 17,284) to provide the country with a body that would serve as final arbiter on constitutional matters and thus prevent the adoption of unconstitutional laws or decrees. Like other "neutral" institutions, such as the military and the courts, the tribunal was highly politicized by the crisis of the Allende years. It was unable to serve as an effective arbiter as the institutional conflict—between the government and its opposition and between the presidency and Congress—as well as the political conflict escalated beyond the point of no return.

Under the 1980 constitution, the Constitutional Tribunal consists of seven members appointed on a staggered basis to eight-year terms. The Supreme Court selects three, Cosena two, and the president and Senate one each. The tribunal possesses broad powers to judge the constitutionality of laws at all points in the legislative process. It can also declare unconstitutional any decrees issued by the president of the republic and rule on the constitutionality of a plebiscite. The tribunal resolves disputes among government ministers, legislators, and the executive and can rule on complaints presented by the president or members of either of the legislative chambers, provided that at least one-fourth of the members agree to register a formal grievance. The tribunal also rules on constitutional challenges to the legality of political parties (Article 19).

The Constitutional Tribunal is the court of last resort on constitutional matters. Article 83 of the constitution provides that "no appeal whatsoever shall apply against the decisions of the Constitutional Tribunal.'' The article adds that ''once the court has decided that a specific legal precept is constitutional, the Supreme Court may not declare it inapplicable on the same grounds on which the decision was based.''

The parties represented in the Aylwin coalition were not comfortable with the tribunal's broad jurisdiction. In their view, the tribunal's far-reaching powers to determine the constitutionality of laws, presidential decrees, and other government decisions made it a highly undemocratic body, particularly given that its members are appointed almost entirely by nonelected bodies. The Aylwin government favored constitutional reforms that would give the president and Congress the right to appoint a substantial majority of the tribunal members. The government also sought to limit the tribunal's power to decide the constitutionality of laws approved by Congress and signed by the president.

Reforms seemed unlikely in the immediate future because the parties of the right argued that a tribunal designed to protect the supremacy of the constitution would be undermined, should it be constituted by those very bodies that would be scrutinized. In addition, those accepting the status of the tribunal pointed to the positive role it played in settling the dispute over the status of independent candidates in the 1992 municipal elections. They contended that the tribunal's role in settling the dispute helped avert a major political dispute that might have delayed the elections.

The Central Bank of Chile

The Central Bank of Chile, like the Office of the Comptroller General, was created in 1925 on the recommendation of the financial mission to Chile headed by United States banking official Edwin Walter Kemmerer. The Central Bank was charged with printing money and controlling its circulation. Its authority over the country's monetary policy increased gradually over the years. The 1980 constitution elevates the Central Bank to constitutional status as an ''autonomous'' state organ to be governed by an organic constitutional law (Law 18,840). The military government was concerned that the Central Bank be insulated from political pressures to ensure that sound monetary policies were followed. The regime was reacting in part to the common practice of earlier years, particularly under the Popular Unity government, when public expenditures were financed with direct and indirect loans from the Central Bank, fueling budget deficits and inflation.

The Central Bank is governed by the five-member Central Bank Council appointed by the president, with the consent of the Senate, on a staggered basis. Each member serves ten years and can be reappointed. The president of the Central Bank is selected from among the council members to serve for five years.

The Electoral Certification Tribunal

Until the adoption of the 1925 constitution, the fairness of the electoral process was determined by Congress itself. Because of widespread abuses engendered by the system, the constitutional reformers of the time created the Electoral Certification Tribunal (Tribunal de Certificación Electoral—TCE), drawn by lots from a group of distinguished public figures, primarily jurists, who would evaluate the integrity of the electoral process and rule on particular challenges. The 1980 constitution preserves the TCE, specifying that its members include three ministers or former ministers of the Supreme Court chosen by the Supreme Court through a secret ballot, a lawyer also elected by the Supreme Court, and a former president of the Senate or Chamber of Deputies who has held that post for no fewer than three years. The TCE's duties and responsibilities are defined by an organic constitutional law (Law 18,460).

The Armed Forces

The armed forces constitute an essentially autonomous power within the Chilean state. An entire chapter of the constitution (Chapter 10) is devoted specifically to the armed forces, granting them a status comparable to that of Congress and the courts. Although the opposition felt that it had reduced the tutelary role of the armed forces with the constitutional reforms of 1989 by softening the language dealing with Cosena's powers, the military continued to have a constitutionally sanctioned right to discuss politics and policy and make its views known to the democratically elected authorities.

Whether or not the commanders of the services "represent" their views "or make them known," the political fact remains that the armed forces are defined by the constitution as the "guarantors of the institutional order of the Republic." Thus, their leadership exercises tutelage over the conduct of the elected government and other state bodies. This privilege is given only to the commanding officers. The 1980 constitution lays down strict rules requiring lower-ranking officers to refrain from any political activity or expression and to conform strictly to the orders of their superiors.

The 1989 reforms did not change the provisions that insulate the commanders in chief of the armed services and the Carabineros from democratically elected leaders. Although the military commanders and the head of the Carabineros are chosen by the president from among those officers having the most seniority in their respective services, the appointment is for four years, during which time the commanders cannot be removed except by Cosena under exceptional circumstances.

The constitution also specifies that entry into the armed services can only be through the established military academies and schools that are governed exclusively by the services, without outside interference. The Organic Constitutional Law on the Armed Forces (Law 18,948 of February 1990) governs in detail military education, hierarchy, promotion, health, welfare, and retirement. It also provides the armed forces with a specific minimum budget that cannot be reduced. Other legislation provides the military with a set percentage from the worldwide sales of the state-run copper companies.

Despite seventeen years of military rule, the armed forces in 1994 were remarkably uncontaminated by factionalism or partisan politics. No major divisions within the services are apparent. However, because the military enjoyed privileged treatment during Pinochet's rule, any attempt to tamper with military prerogatives is likely to be strongly resisted.

Pinochet's insistence on retaining his position as commander in chief of the army displeased the Aylwin government. As commander of the army, the general affirmed the military's determination to resist prosecution for human rights violations. Yet the army's credibility was badly damaged by allegations of financial wrongdoing by Pinochet's son, the discovery of mass graves containing corpses of individuals who died while in military hands, and the illegal export of arms to Croatia. The report of the National Commission on Truth and Reconciliation, known as the Rettig Commission, confirmed many of the allegations of military abuses.

The Aylwin government contended that the full consolidation of democracy could not be accomplished without a fundamental change in the relationship between civil and military authority. Members of the CPD asserted that presidential control of the armed forces existed in all modern democracies and since 1822 had been an essential element in Chile's constitutional tradition.

A proposal for reform of the Organic Constitutional Law on the Armed Forces was signed by President Aylwin on March 29, 1992, and sent to Congress. Aylwin's initiative dealt specifically with Article 7 and Article 53 of the organic laws of the armed forces and police, which limit presidential prerogatives in relation to the hiring, firing, and promotion of members of the military. Among the suggested reforms was a provision providing the president with the right to choose commanders of the armed forces from among the ten most senior officers, instead of the top five. These proposals were opposed, however, by both parties of the right, making it impossible to envision any constitutional reform on this matter in the foreseeable future.

The opposition contended that the tenure of the commanders had contributed to the stability and moderation of the Chilean transition. It argued that these reforms would result in the politicization of the armed forces by undermining the hierarchy, discipline, and professionalism of military institutions. The rightist parties also contended that the reform proposals, if successful, would upset the counterweights on presidential power and would disturb the institutional balance existing among the president, the Constitutional Tribunal, Congress, and Cosena. This balance, they argued, helped guarantee the success of the Chilean transition by insulating the armed forces from overt political pressures (see Civil-Military Relations, ch. 5).

Regional and Local Government

With the adoption of the constitution of 1833, Chile abandoned earlier attempts to create a federal system and opted for a unitary form of government. As such, regional and local governments became creatures of national authority, subject to the legislative and constitutional powers vested in the central government. This did not mean that local governments did not enjoy varying degrees of self-determination and autonomy over the years. The 1833 document provided for the election of local municipal councils through direct popular vote, a practice retained by the constitution of 1925. During much of the nineteenth century, local governments were barely able to provide the minimal services they were charged with, such as the maintenance of public order and basic sanitation, given the scarcity of resources. In 1891, however, the country embarked on a bold experiment, providing significant local autonomy to the nation's elected municipalities, many of which flourished under local leadership with local resources. The center of gravity of Chilean politics shifted toward local governments and their allies in Congress.

Partly in reaction to the corrupt machine politics of the city bosses, the 1925 constitution sought greater oversight of local authorities by expanding the democratic process through the creation of elected provincial assemblies. However, enabling legislation that would have made those assemblies a reality was never adopted. Instead, the oversight functions were turned over to appointed agents of the central government. During the dramatic expansion of the national state in the wake of the Great Depression, local governments were left behind. Tax revenues, which by law were supposed to be returned to local governments, were routinely kept by the authorities of the central government. The essence of local politics became a struggle to use party and patronage networks to extract resources on a preferential basis for local development. As the nation's electorate expanded, local government officials played an increasingly important role as electoral agents. Mayors and councilors became political brokers seeking to exchange votes for a water treatment plant, a stretch of highway, or jobs for constituents. Elections for local office were as hotly contested as elections for national office and served as building blocks of party development.

The military regime viewed the somewhat fractious state of local politics as proof that parties and politicians were incapable of efficient administration. As a result, it designed a system of local administration distinctly based on corporatism (see Glossary) and heavily dependent on direct appointments from the center. According to the constitution of 1980, regional and local governments would be administered by intendants and mayors, respectively. These figures would be appointed directly by the president of the republic, although the mayors of smaller towns would be designated by regional councils created to advise the intendants. The regional councils would be formed by employees of state agencies in the locality, by military officers, and by designated representatives of interest groups with no party affiliation. This conception of regional government would be extended to the municipal level with similarly designated local councils.

Although this scheme would make local authorities highly dependent on appointments from above, the military government also took an important step to decentralize state functions by giving local administrative units greatly increased resources and autonomy to make local governments viable. A notable example was the decision to give municipal governments far more responsibility for elementary and secondary education and other local services.

The Aylwin government made the restoration of democracy at the grass-roots level a matter of high priority. Many opposition leaders on the right shared the view that the military regime had gone too far in eradicating the country's long tradition of elected local governments. After considerable debate, the government and National Renewal were able to reach consensus on a constitutional reform law, adopted in November 1991, to change Chapter 13 of the constitution dealing with local administration (Law 19,097).

The constitutional reform was followed by the adoption of a new Organic Constitutional Law on Municipalities (Law 19,130 of

March 19, 1992), which paved the way for municipal elections in June 1992. Under the law, local governments are formed by a municipal council and a mayor who serve four-year terms and are elected through a proportional representation system. Candidates must be sponsored by registered political parties that obtained at least 5 percent of the vote in previous contests. The number of councilors varies, from six in smaller municipalities to ten in the larger ones. The law establishes that the councilor who receives the most votes on the party list that receives the largest number of votes is elected mayor, provided that he or she obtains at least 35 percent of the total vote. If this requirement is not met, the mayor is elected by the municipal council from among its own number by an absolute majority of the vote. The Organic Constitutional Law on Municipalities requires that the mayor and councilors be citizens in good standing, reside in the region where they are running for office, and be literate. It bars government officials and members of Congress from running for local office. It is the mayor's responsibility to propose a communal plan, a budget, investment programs, and zoning plans to the municipal council for approval. The mayor also appoints delegates to remote areas of the community. The municipal council approves local ordinances and regulations and oversees the work of the mayor, being authorized to call to the attention of the comptroller general any irregularities.

Municipalities have sole responsibility for traffic regulation, urban planning and zoning, garbage collection, and beautification. Municipal governments work closely with state agencies on a host of other matters, ranging from public health to tourism, recreation, and education, and are authorized to create administrative units to oversee each of these activities. Most of the municipal resources come from the Common Municipal Fund, administered by the Ministry of Interior, which endeavors to favor poorer areas in the distribution of resources for local government. The law on municipalities also calls for the creation of an economic and social council in each municipality. This is an advisory body constituted by representatives of local organized groups, including neighborhood associations and functional organizations, such as parent-teacher associations and mothers' groups.

On June 23, 1992, 6.4 million Chileans (90 percent of the nation's registered voters) participated in Chile's first municipal elections since 1971. As was done in the congressional elections of 1989, joint lists designed to maximize electoral fortunes were formed by both the progovernment and the antigovernment parties. The results of the municipal contests did not deviate substantially from those observed in the earlier race. The CPD obtained 60.6 percent of the vote, to the right's 30 percent (38 percent if the independent Union of the Centrist Center [Unión de Centro Centro—UCC] is counted with the right) (see table 39, Appendix).

Nationwide elections for the country's thirteen regional councils were held in April 1993. The CPD won the majority of the thirteen regions. Of the total of 244 regional council members elected nationwide, 134 were CPD candidates and eighty-six were candidates of the opposition parties of the right. Another thirteen seats went to independent candidates or those from other parties. A tie resulted only in the sparsely populated Aisén del General Carlos Ibáñez del Campo Region in the far south, where the government and the opposition each won eight council seats.

Parties and the Electoral System

The Party System

In the early 1990s, Chile had a strong, ideologically based multi-party system, with a clear division among parties of the right, center, and left. Chile's parties traditionally have been national in scope, penetrating into remote regions of the country and structuring politics in small villages and provincial capitals. Party affiliation has served as the organizing concept in leadership contests in universities and private associations, including labor unions and professional associations. Political tendencies are passed from generation to generation and constitute an important part of an individual's identity.

By the middle of the twentieth century, each of Chile's political tendencies represented roughly one-third of the electorate. The left was dominated by the Socialist Party (Partido Socialista) and the Communist Party of Chile (Partido Comunista de Chile—PCCh), the right by the Liberal Party (Partido Liberal) and the Conservative Party (Partido Conservador), and the center by the anticlerical Radical Party (Partido Radical), which was replaced as Chile's dominant party by the Christian Democratic Party (Partido Demócrata Cristiano—PDC) in the 1960s.

Although ideological polarization characterized party politics until the 1960s, political coalitions across party lines helped to mitigate conflict. Party politics dominated both the national arena, where ideological objectives predominated, and the local arena, which focused on more clientelistic concerns. The interplay between these two levels helped moderate interparty conflict. Polarization increased markedly, however, in the wake of the 1959 Cuban Revolution as parties radicalized their programs, seeking to achieve hegemony over their rivals in an increasingly desperate attempt to control Chile's future.

The military authorities believed that their policies would fundamentally change the traditional party system. Repression, legal restrictions, and new legislation governing parties and elections, combined with profound underlying changes in the nation's social structure, would render the old parties obsolete. Although the authorities conceded by 1985, in the aftermath of national protests, that they had not destroyed the party system, they remained intent on designing rules that would change its basic physiognomy. In March 1987, the Law of Political Parties was adopted, which provided for stringent requirements that officials of the military government believed the old parties could not meet. The law requires each legal party to obtain signatures equivalent to 5 percent of the electorate in at least eight regions, or in at least three contiguous regions. It also places restrictions on party activities and regulates party financing, internal organization, and selection of leaders, specifying that top party leaders be chosen democratically by rank-and-file members.

However, Chile's parties were able to adjust well to the law. Indeed, the requirement for a large number of signatures gave party leaders a strong incentive to mobilize grass-roots support and strengthen local party organizations. The selection of party leadership through democratic means helped legitimize the leaders who fought the military government, leaders whom the authorities had often characterized as unrepresentative.

The Electoral System

The far-reaching electoral reforms implemented before the 1989 elections represented a further attempt to transform Chile's party structure into a moderate two-party system. The constitution of 1925 had established a system of proportional representation to allocate seats in multimember districts, the most widely used system in Latin America and Europe. For the elections to the Chamber of Deputies, the country was divided into twenty-eights districts, each electing between one and eighteen deputies for a total of 150, producing an average district delegation of 5.4 deputies. Although implementation of the proportional representation system was not responsible for the emergence of the country's multiparty system, it encouraged party fragmentation, particularly before 1960, when parties were allowed to form pacts with each other in constituting individual lists.

Women were granted the vote for municipal elections in 1934 and for national elections in 1949. Chile has a lively history of women's civic and political organizations that goes back to the early decades of the twentieth century, including the formation of two political parties led by women, one of which, the Feminine Civic Party (Partido Cívico Femenino), elected its main leader to the Senate before it faded from the scene in the mid-1950s. However, there are still conspicuously few women in national politics and in top government positions. Only six women were elected to Congress in 1989, and only one woman held ministerial rank in President Aylwin's government. Yet close to half of all Chileans who were affiliated with parties in 1992 were women, and slightly more than half of the electorate is composed of women.

The military government redrew electoral boundaries to create sixty legislative districts, each of which would send two representatives to the Chamber of Deputies. Redistricting favored smaller and more rural districts that were deliberately designed to favor progovernment parties. Thus, one vote in District 52, which was a government stronghold in the plebiscite, was worth three times more than one vote in District 18, in which the opposition had fared better. By reducing the electoral districts to an average representation of two deputies per district, the military authorities sought to create an electoral formula that would provide supporters of the Pinochet regime with a majority of the seats in the legislature, with a level of support comparable to Pinochet's vote in the plebiscite, or about 40 percent of the turnout.

According to the new law, parties or coalitions continue to present lists with a candidate for each of the two seats to be filled. The law considers both the votes for the total list and the votes for individual candidates. The first seat is awarded to the party or coalition with a plurality of votes. But the first-place party list must receive twice the vote of the second-place list, if it is to win the second seat. This means that in a two-list contest a party can obtain one seat with only 33.4 percent of the vote, whereas a party must take 66.7 percent of the vote to gain both seats. Any electoral support that the largest party gets beyond the 33.4 percent threshold is effectively wasted unless that party attains the 66.7 percent level.

The designers of the electoral system considered the worst-case scenario to be one that assumed a complete unity of purpose among the anti-Pinochet forces, a unity that would at best provide them with 50 percent of Congress. Government officials were convinced that another scenario was more likely: the parties of the center-left would soon fragment, unable to maintain the unity born of their common desire to defeat Pinochet. The military government envisioned multiple lists, with the list of the right being the largest, able to double the next competing list in many constituencies and thus assuring the promilitary groups at least half of all elected representation, if not a comfortable majority.

For the parties of the right, the worst-case scenario came to pass. Showing remarkable focus and discipline, the fourteen parties of the opposition structured a common list and chose a common presidential candidate, and as a result the coalition garnered a majority of the elected seats. The binomial electoral system (see Glossary) did, however, benefit the right. National Renewal obtained many more seats than it should have in light of the percentages of the vote it received nationally. The system also forced parties to coalesce into large blocs to maximize their strengths. The result was two broad coalitions, not a two-party system. Indeed, the results of the 1989 congressional elections, despite the requirements of the binomial system and the constitution that broad slates be formed by these party coalitions, reveals that the Chilean electorate split its vote for individual candidates in a manner reminiscent of traditional tendencies. Thus, the right obtained 38 percent of the vote; the center, 24 percent; and the left 24.3 percent.

Survey research corroborated that the electorate was likely to continue to identify with left-right terms of reference. In March 1993, about 22.8 percent of respondents classified themselves as politically right or center-right; 24.6 percent as center; and 33.7 percent as center-left. Only 19 percent refused to opt for an ideological identification (see table 40, Appendix). These figures differ somewhat from the electoral results reported previously but are consistent with trends indicating that the right lost some of its appeal during the Aylwin government, while the moderate left gained.

Despite attempts at political engineering, not only did Chileans continue to identify with broad ideological tendencies, but they also identified with a wide range of parties explicitly considered to embody those tendencies. In surveys, between 70 percent and 80 percent of all Chileans identified themselves with particular parties, a high level considering the many years of military rule and the experience of other democratic countries. Identification with individual parties increased during the first three years of the Aylwin government. In the March 1993 survey, more than a third of the respondents identified themselves with the Christian Democrats, 20 percent with the leading parties of the left, and 20 percent with the principal parties of the right. The rest identified themselves with smaller parties of the left, center, and right (see table 41, Appendix).

The survey findings do not mean that the ideological polarization of the past has remained constant. The Chilean electorate still segments itself into three roughly equal thirds, but the distance between its left and right extremes has narrowed substantially. With its more radical program, the PCCh was not able to win more than 6.5 percent of the vote in municipal elections. In surveys taken during the 1990–93 period, fewer than 2 percent of respondents preferred the PCCh. Right-wing nationalist parties associated with the military government had even less appeal and did not ever register on surveys. The far left of the Socialist Party had lost ground to the more moderate tendencies of the party, and the authoritarian right had developed no significant electoral following. Ideological moderation also characterized the centrist Christian Democrats, who no longer defended the ''third way'' between Marxists and capitalists that they advocated in the 1960s. Perhaps the strongest indication of programmatic moderation was the consensus in postmilitary Chile on free-market economics and the important role of the private sector in national development.

As Chile approached the twenty-first century, differences among parties were no longer based on sharply differing visions of utopias. Ideological differences now concerned more concrete matters, such as the degree of government involvement in social services and welfare or, increasingly, moral questions such as divorce and abortion. A narrowing of programmatic differences did not mean, however, that the intensely competitive, multiparty nature of Chilean politics was likely to change in the near future.

The Parties of the Left

The Communist Party of Chile (Partido Comunista de Chile—PCCh) is the oldest and largest communist party in Latin America and one of the most important in the West. Tracing its origins to 1912, the party was officially founded in 1922 as the successor to the Socialist Workers' Party (Partido Obrero Socialista—POS). It achieved congressional representation shortly thereafter and played a leading role in the development of the Chilean labor movement. Closely tied to the Soviet Union and the Third International (see Glossary), the PCCh participated in the Popular Front (Frente Popular) government of 1938, growing rapidly among the unionized working class in the 1940s. Concern over the PCCh's success at building a strong electoral base, combined with the onset of the Cold War, led to its being outlawed in 1948, a status it had to endure for almost a decade. By midcentury the party had become a veritable political subculture, with its own symbols and organizations and the support of prominent artists and intellectuals, such as Pablo Neruda, the Nobel Prize-winning poet, and Violeta Parra, the songwriter and folk artist.

As a component of the Popular Unity coalition that elected Salvador Allende to the presidency in 1970, the PCCh played a strong moderating role, rejecting the more extreme tactics of the student and revolutionary left and urging a more deliberate pace that would set the groundwork for a communist society in the future. The military government dealt the PCCh a severe blow, decimating its leadership in 1976. Although the party called for a broad alliance of all forces opposed to the dictatorship, by 1980 it moved to a parallel strategy of armed insurrection, preparing cadres of guerrillas to destabilize the regime and provide the party with the military capability to take over the state should the Pinochet government crumble.

After the attempt on Pinochet's life in 1986, the democratic parties began to distance themselves from the PCCh because the PCCh was openly opposed to challenging the regime under the regime's own rules. The PCCh's strong stand against registration of voters and participation in the plebiscite alienated many of its own supporters and long-time militants, who understood that most of the citizenry supported a peaceful return to democracy.

Particularly problematic for the party was the Manuel Rodríguez Patriotic Front (Frente Patriótica Manuel Rodríguez—FPMR), an insurrectionary organization spawned by the PCCh. The party found the FPMR difficult to rein in, and the FPMR continued to engage in terrorism after the demise of the military government. The FPMR had eclipsed Chile's better-known revolutionary group, the Movement of the Revolutionary Left (Movimiento de la Izquierda Revolucionaria—MIR), formed in the 1960s by university students, a movement that barely survived the repression of the military years. During the Aylwin administration, a group known as the Lautaro Youth Movement (Movimiento Juvenil Lautaro—MJL), an offshoot of the United Popular Action Movement-Lautaro (Movimiento de Acción Popular Unitario-Lautaro—MAPU–L), sought without success to maintain a "revolutionary" offensive (see Terrorism, ch. 5).

The dramatic failure of the PCCh's strategy seriously undermined its credibility and contributed to growing defections from its ranks. The party was also hurt by the vast structural changes in Chilean society, particularly the decline of traditional manufacturing and extractive industries and the weakening of the labor movement. The collapse of the Soviet Union and its East European allies represented a final blow. Although the PCCh obtained 6.5 percent of the vote in the 1992 municipal elections, by mid-1993 it was enjoying less than 5 percent support in public opinion surveys and did not fare well in the 1993 presidential race.

The Socialist Party (Partido Socialista), formally organized in 1933, had its origins in the incipient labor movement and working-class parties of the early twentieth century. The Socialist Party was far more heterogeneous than the PCCh, drawing support from blue-collar workers as well as intellectuals and members of the middle class. Throughout most of its history, the Socialist Party suffered from a bewildering number of schisms resulting from rivalries and fundamental disagreements between leaders advocating revolution and those willing to work within the system.

The Socialist Party's greatest moment was the election of Salvador Allende to the presidency in 1970. Allende represented the moderate wing of a party that had veered sharply to the left. The Socialist Party's radical orientation contributed to continuous political tension as the president and the PCCh argued for a more gradual approach to change and the Socialists sought to press for immediate "conquests" for the working class.

After the overthrow of Allende's Popular Unity government, the Socialist Party suffered heavy repression and soon split into numerous factions. Some joined with the Communists in supporting a more insurrectionary strategy. Another faction of "Renewed Socialists," led primarily by intellectuals and exiles in Western Europe, argued for a return to a moderate socialism for which democratic politics was an end in itself. The latter faction broke with the Marxist-Leninist line of the immediate past, embracing market economics and a far more pluralist conception of society. Guided by leaders such as Ricardo Lagos Escobar and Ricardo Núñez Muñoz, the Renewed Socialists reached an accord with the Christian Democrats to mount a common strategy to bring an end to the military government.

Prior to the 1988 plebiscite, the Socialists launched the Party for Democracy (Partido por la Democracia—PPD) in an effort to provide a broad base of opposition to Pinochet, one untainted by the labels and struggles of the past. Led by Lagos, an economist and former university administrator, the PPD was supposed to be an "instrumental party" that would disappear after the defeat of Pinochet. But the party's success in capturing the imagination of many Chileans led Socialist and PPD leaders to keep the party label for the subsequent congressional and municipal elections, working jointly with the Christian Democrats in structuring national lists of candidates.

The success of the PPD soon created a serious dilemma for the Socialist Party, which managed to reunite its principal factions—the relatively conservative Socialist Party-Almeyda, the moderate Socialist Party-Núñez "renewalists," and the left-wing Unitary

Socialists—at the Socialist Party congress in December 1990. Heretofore an instrument of the Socialists, the PPD became a party in its own right, even though many Socialists had dual membership. Although embracing social democratic ideals, PPD leaders appeared more willing to press ahead on other unresolved social issues such as divorce and women's rights, staking out a distinct position as a center-left secular force in Chilean society capable of challenging the Christian Democrats as well as the right on a series of critical issues.

As the PPD grew, leaders of the Socialist Party insisted on abolishing dual membership for fear of losing their capacity to enlarge the appeal of the Socialist Party beyond its traditional constituency. By 1993 both parties, working together in a somewhat tense relationship, had comparable levels of popular support in opinion polls. In a March 1993 survey by the Center for Public Studies (Centro de Estudios Públicos—CEP) and Adimark (a polling company), 10.6 percent of Chilean voters identified with the PPD while 8.5 percent registered a preference for the Socialist Party. As the 1993 presidential election approached, PPD leader Ricardo Lagos signaled his intention to challenge the Christian Democrats for the presidential candidacy of the CPD. His move indicated the determination of the parties of the moderate left to remain an important force in Chilean politics. However, Christian Democrat Eduardo Frei Ruiz-Tagle, son of the former president, defeated Lagos in a convention of CPD parties held on May 23, 1993, making him the strong favorite to win the presidential elections scheduled for December 11, 1993. Frei Ruiz-Tagle won by a vote of 60 percent, while Lagos received 38 percent.

Other parties that could be placed on the center-left included the Humanist-Green Alliance (Alianza Humanista-Verde) and the Social Democratic Party (Partido Social Democrático), an offshoot of the Radical Party, which managed to elect one of its leaders to the Senate. These new parties were successful in mobilizing support against Pinochet in the plebiscite but faltered in subsequent elections.

The Parties of the Center

The Christian Democratic Party (Partido Demócrata Cristiano—PDC), formally established in 1957, traces its origins to the 1930s, when the youth wing of the Conservative Party, the Conservative Falange (Falange Conservativa), heavily influenced by the progressive social doctrines of the Roman Catholic Church and the works of French Catholic philosopher Jacques Maritain, broke off to form the National Falange in 1938. Although the PDC remained small for many years, it came to prominence in the 1940s, when party leader Eduardo Frei Montalva became minister of public works. The party's fortunes gradually improved as the leadership of the Roman Catholic Church shifted from an embrace of the right toward a more progressive line that paralleled the reformist bent of the Falangist leadership. The PDC came into its own in 1957, when it adopted its present name after uniting with several other centrist groups. It elected Frei to the Senate while capturing fourteen seats in the Chamber of Deputies. The party polled 20 percent of the vote in the presidential race in 1958, with Frei as standard-bearer. In 1964, with the support of the right, which feared the election of Allende, Frei was elected president on a platform proclaiming a "third way" between Marxism and capitalism, a form of communitarian socialism of cooperatives and self-managed worker enterprises.

Although the PDC grew significantly during Frei's presidency and succeeded in obtaining the largest vote of any single party in contemporary Chilean history in the 1965 congressional race, the Christian Democrats were not able to overcome the tripartite division of Chilean politics. Its candidate in the 1970 election, Radomiro Tomic Romero, came in third with 27.8 percent of the total vote.

The PDC soon broke with Allende, rejecting measures issued by decree without legislative support and shifting to an alliance with the parties of the right. Although the PDC leadership, which by 1973 had returned to the more conservative orientation, welcomed the coup as "inevitable," a significant minority condemned it. Within months, the party began to distance itself from the military government over the new regime's strongly antipolitical cast, its human rights violations, and its clear intention of remaining in power indefinitely. By 1980 the PDC was playing a leadership role in opposition to the military regime.

In the aftermath of the military regime, the PDC emerged as Chile's largest party, with the support of about 35 percent of the electorate. The PDC had been divided internally by a series of ideological, generational, and factional rivalries. A large number of party followers identified themselves as center-left, while many viewed themselves as center-right. The PDC retained a commitment to social justice issues while embracing the free-market policies instituted by the military government. However, the communitarian ideology of the past receded in importance, and the Christian Democrats remained reluctant to take issue with the Roman Catholic Church's stands on divorce and abortion.

Although the Aylwin administration was a coalition government, the PDC secured ten of twenty cabinet seats. In the 1989 elections, the Christian Democrats also obtained the largest number of congressional seats, with fourteen in the Senate and thirty-eight in the Chamber of Deputies. In October 1991, in a major challenge to President Aylwin and the traditional leadership of the party, Eduardo Frei Ruiz-Tagle was elected PDC president, placing him in a privileged position to run for president as the candidate of the CPD.

Another party that could be classified as centrist was the Radical Party, whose political importance outweighed its electoral presence. The Radical Party owed its survival as a political force to the binomial electoral law inherited from the military government and the desire of the Christian Democrats to use the Radical Party as a foil against the left. It was to the Christian Democrats' advantage to provide relatively more space to the Radicals on the joint lists than to their stronger PPD partners. The Radicals succeeded in electing two senators and five deputies in 1989 and were allotted two out of twenty cabinet ministers, despite polls reporting that they had less than 2 percent support nationally. It remained to be seen if, over the long run, the Radical Party could compete with Chile's other major parties, particularly the PPD, which had moved closest to the Radical Party's traditional position on the political spectrum.

The Parties of the Right

In 1965, following the dramatic rise of the Christian Democrats, primarily at their expense, Chile's two traditional right-wing parties, the Liberal Party and Conservative Party, merged into the National Party (Partido Nacional). Their traditional disagreements over issues such as the proper role of the Roman Catholic Church in society paled by comparison with the challenge posed by the left to private property and Chile's hierarchical social order. The new party, energized by the presidential candidacy of Jorge Alessandri in 1970, helped the right regain some of its lost electoral ground. The National Party won 21.1 percent of the vote in the 1973 congressional elections, the last before the coup.

The National Party was at the forefront of the opposition to the Allende government, working closely with elements of the business community. National Party leaders welcomed the coup and, unlike the Christian Democrats, were content to accept the military authorities' injunction that parties go into "recess." Until 1984 the National Party remained moribund, with most of the party leaders concerning themselves with private pursuits or an occasional embassy post. With the riots of 1983 and 1984, leaders on the right began to worry about the return of civilian politics and the challenge of rebuilding party organizations. In 1987 three rightist organizations—the National Unity Movement (Movimiento de Unidad Nacional—MUN), representing many of Chile's traditional leaders of the right; the National Labor Front (Frente Nacional del Trabajo—FNT), headed by a more nationalistic group tied to small business and rural interests; and the Independent Democratic Union (Unión Demócrata Independiente—UDI), constituted by former junta advisers and officials of the military government—joined to form National Renewal as a successor to the National Party. The uneasy alliance soon broke apart as the UDI signaled its strong support for the plebiscite of 1988 and a Pinochet candidacy, while MUN indicated its preference for an open election or a candidate other than Pinochet.

With Pinochet's defeat, National Renewal's prestige rose considerably. In the aftermath of the plebiscite, National Renewal worked closely with the other opposition parties to propose far-reaching amendments to the constitution. National Renewal, however, could not impose its own party president, Sergio Onofre Jarpa, having to concede the presidential candidacy of the right to the UDI's Büchi. After the 1989 congressional race, National Renewal emerged as the dominant party of the right, benefiting strongly from the electoral law and electing six senators and twenty-nine deputies. Its strength in the Senate meant that the Aylwin government had to compromise with National Renewal to gain support for key legislative and constitutional measures. National Renewal saw much of its support wane in the wake of party scandals involving its most promising presidential candidates, whereas the UDI's positive image grew.

While National Renewal drew substantial support from rural areas and traditional small businessmen, the UDI appealed to new entrepreneurial elites and middle sectors in Chile's rapidly growing modern sector. The UDI also made inroads in low-income neighborhoods with special programs appealing to the poor, a legacy of the Pinochet regime's urban policy. The assassination of UDI founder Senator Jaime Guzmán Errázuriz on April 1, 1991, was a serious blow, depriving the party of its strongest leader.

A discussion of the parties of the right would not be complete without a mention of the Union of the Centrist Center (Unión de Centro Centro—UCC), a loose organization created by Francisco Errázuriz. Because parties of the left like to call themselves "center-left" and parties of the right "center-right" to avoid being labeled as extremist, Errázuriz coined the somewhat redundant name of the UCC to show that he is the only centrist-centrist. The UCC had no party organization and no clear programmatic orientation. Yet it regularly commanded the support of about 5 percent of the electorate, enough to place the party in a privileged position to bargain for places on the party lists of either the right or the CPD, giving Errázuriz more clout than his real support would indicate.

The advent of the 1993 presidential race underscored the continued rivalry of the parties of the right. Reformers in National Renewal failed in their effort to provide the nation with a new generation of rightist leaders as Senator Sebastian Piñera and Congresswoman Evelyn Matthei canceled themselves out in a bitter struggle. Only after months of charges and countercharges, and in the face of the CPD's remarkable capacity for unity, could National Unity, the UDI, and the UCC succeed in structuring a joint congressional list and selecting a presidential candidate.

The 1993 Presidential Election

The compromises struck in the 1980 constitutional reform discussions between the military government and the opposition led to the limitation of President Aylwin's term to four years, half of the normal term contemplated in the constitution. This meant that by mid-1992 parties and leaders were already jockeying to prepare the succession. Leaders of the Aylwin government, including prominent cabinet members, made no secret of their desire to put forth the name of Alejandro Foxley Riesco, the minister of finance, as a man who would guarantee stability and continuity. A Christian Democrat, Foxley had presided ably over the delicate task of maintaining economic stability and promoting growth.

Within the CPD, however, there was considerable disagreement over a Foxley candidacy. Christian Democrats controlling the party organization, who had not been favored with prominent governmental positions, pushed the candidacy of Eduardo Frei Ruiz-Tagle, son of the former president, as an alternative. Frei's candidacy was given an enormous boost when he succeeded in defeating several Christian Democratic factions, including the Aylwin group, by capturing the presidency of the PDC. In the first open election for party leadership among all registered Christian Democrats, Frei, drawing on the magic of his father's name, scored a stunning victory.

While most observers presumed that from his position as PDC president Frei would be able to command the nomination of the center-left alliance, elements in the Socialist Party and the PPD argued that the nomination in the second government should go

Eduardo Frei Ruiz-Tagle,
president
March 11, 1994–
Courtesy Embassy of Chile,
Washington, and
El Mercurio, *Santiago*

to a Socialist, not a Christian Democrat. This was the position of Ricardo Lagos, a minister of public education in the Aylwin cabinet and the most prominent leader of the moderate left. Lagos, who was defeated for a Senate seat in Santiago by the vagaries of the electoral law, remained one of the most popular leaders in Chile and was widely praised for his tenure in the Ministry of Public Education.

A Lagos candidacy, however, implied the serious possibility that the CPD would break up. Christian Democrats pointed to their party's significant advantage in the polls and noted that the country might not be ready for a candidate identified with the Socialist Party. Lagos faced opposition within the PPD and the Socialist Party among leaders who thought that risking the unity of the CPD could only play into the hands of forces that would welcome a victory of the right or an authoritarian reversal. Lagos, in turn, argued that the Socialists could be relegated to the position of a permanent minority force within the coalition if they did not have the opportunity to present their own candidate. The constitutional provision for a second electoral round, in case no candidate obtained an absolute majority in the first round, would permit the holding of a kind of primary. The CPD candidate that failed to go into the second round of the two finalists would simply support the CPD counterpart. Lagos, however, was not able to persuade either the Christian Democrats or his own allies to launch two center-left presidential candidacies spearheading one joint list for congressional seats. Instead, he had to settle for a national convention in which Frei handily defeated him with his greater organizational strength.

The right had even more difficulty coming up with a standard-bearer. National Renewal was intent on imposing its own candidacy this time and sought to elevate one of its younger leaders to carry the torch. Bitter opposition by the UDI and the destructive internal struggle within National Renewal precluded Chile's largest party on the right from selecting the standard-bearer of the coalition. After a bitter and highly destructive process, the parties of the right, including the UCC, finally were able to structure a joint congressional list and turn to Arturo Alessandri Besa, a senator and businessman, as presidential candidate.

Several other candidates were presented by minor parties. The PCCh, which had reluctantly supported Aylwin in 1989, endorsed leftist priest Eugenio Pizarro Poblete, while scientist Manfredo Max-Neef ran a quixotic campaign stressing environmental issues. In the election held on December 11, 1993, Eduardo Frei scored an impressive victory, exceeding the total that Aylwin obtained in 1989. Frei's victory underscored the strong support of the CPD's overall policies, bucking the Latin American trend of failed incumbent governments. Frei obtained 57.4 percent of the vote to Alessandri's 24.7 percent (see table 42, Appendix). The surprise in the race was Max-Neef, who, exceeding all expectations, obtained 5.7 percent of the vote, surpassing the vote for Pizarro, which was 4.6 percent. Max-Neef was able to translate his shoestring candidacy into the most significant protest vote against the major candidates.

The election of the fifty-one-year-old Frei marked the coming of age of a new generation of political leaders in Chile. Frei, an engineer and businessman, had avoided the political world of his father until the late 1980s when he agreed to form part of the Committee for Free Elections. Subsequently, his party faction challenged Aylwin for the leadership of the party prior to the 1989 election. Although Frei lost, he laid the groundwork for his successful bid for party leadership in 1992 and, eventually, the race for president.

Frei's election signals the intention of the CPD to remain united in a coalition government for the foreseeable future. The designation of Socialist Party president Germán Correa as minister of interior and Ricardo Lagos's acceptance of another cabinet post underscore the broad nature of the regime. Frei's challenge, however, will be to maintain unity while addressing many of the lingering social issues that still affect Chilean society without upsetting the country's economic progress.

The Church, Business, Labor, and the Media

The Church

The Roman Catholic Church has played a central role in Chilean politics since colonial days. During the nineteenth century, the question of the proper role of the Catholic Church in society helped define the differences among the country's incipient political parties. The Conservatives, in defending the social order of the colonial era, championed the church's central role in protecting that order through its control of the educational system and its tutelage over the principal rights of passage, from birth to death. They also supported the close tie between church and state based on the Spanish *patronato real* (see Glossary), which provided the president with the authority to name church officials. Liberals, and especially Radicals, drawing on the ideals of the Enlightenment, sought a secular order, a separation of church and state in which the state would take the primary responsibility for instruction and assume "civil" jurisdiction over births, marriages, and the burial of the dead. The Liberals and Radicals also promoted the liberal doctrine of the rights of man and citizenship, seeking to implement the notion of one man-one vote, unswayed by the influence of the upper class or the preaching of the clergy.

During the 1861–91 period, the Liberals were in the ascendancy, succeeding in their quest to expand the authority of the state to the detriment of that of the church. The de jure separation of church and state, however, did not occur until the adoption of the constitution of 1925. Although a few priests and Catholic laity embraced the progressive social doctrines inspired by papal encyclicals such as *Rerum Novarum* (1891) and *Quadragesimo Anno* (1931), it was not until the 1950s that the church hierarchy began to loosen its ties to the Conservative Party. Keenly aware of Marxism's challenge to their core values and the growing influence of Marxist parties, church leaders responded with an increased commitment to social justice and reform. Some of the early efforts at breaking down Chile's semifeudal land tenure system were undertaken on church lands by progressive bishops, notably Bishop Manuel Larraín Errázuriz of Talca in the 1960s.

The church's shift away from Conservative politics coincided with the development of a close alliance between the church elite and the emerging Christian Democrats, which contributed to the success of the new party, particularly among women and another previously disenfranchised group, rural voters. The church, and in particular Cardinal Raúl Silva Henriquez, the archbishop of Santiago, welcomed the election of Eduardo Frei Montalva to the presidency in 1964.

Relations between the church and Allende, however, were far less cordial. Church leaders retained correct relations with the leftist government, fearful that the new authorities would make use of the public schools for Marxist indoctrination and further undermine the waning influence of the church in society. When Allende was overthrown, all of the bishops welcomed the coup and helped legitimize the new military junta with solemn ceremonies. Several bishops, including the bishop of Valparaíso, remained staunch supporters of the military for years to come.

Other church leaders, notably Cardinal Silva, shocked by widespread human rights violations and disturbed by the growing rift between the armed forces and the church's Christian Democratic allies, soon distanced themselves from the military authorities. The church, and particularly the archdiocese of Santiago, responded by gradually assuming a critical role as a defender of human rights and providing an "umbrella" of physical and moral shelter to intellectuals and party and union leaders. Antagonizing the regime and its many supporters in upper- and middle-class sectors, the Vicariate of Solidarity (Vicaría de la Solidaridad) helped provide for the legal defense and support of victims of the dictatorship. Silva's successor, though more conservative, supported the church's work in the human rights field and, in 1985, sought to broker the National Accord for Transition to Full Democracy. As the plebiscite approached, the Episcopal Conference made clear that it did not consider the junta's plan to be democratic and urged Pinochet to step down, further aggravating the relationship between the authorities and the church.

With the restoration of democracy, the church retreated from the political arena. Following dictates from Rome and the appointment of more conservative bishops, relations between the hierarchy and the Christian Democrats cooled. Church leaders also made it clear that, in recognition of church support for the democratic opposition in the difficult years of the dictatorship, they expected support from the new government for the church's own more conservative agenda. In early 1994, Chile remained one of the few countries in the world that did not recognize divorce, and issues such as abortion and the role of women in society were not fully addressed (see Divorce, Abortion, and Contraception, ch. 2). Chile's political right made clear that it hoped to capitalize on these "moral" issues and revive an alliance between clerical authorities and the parties of the right not seen since the 1940s.

Although the challenge from the Marxist left had waned, the Roman Catholic Church appeared to be engaged in a losing struggle to stem the extraordinary growth of Protestant Evangelicals (see Glossary). Evangelical groups grew rapidly during the years of military rule, primarily as a result of severe social and economic dislocations. While the Roman Catholic Church gained adherents and supporters through its politicized Christian Base Communities (Comunidades Eclesiásticas de Base—CEBs; see Glossary) and the work of highly committed priests, tens of thousands of other Chileans were seeking a new meaning for their lives by responding to the far more flexible and spontaneous religious appeals of hundreds of storefront churches. Surveys in Santiago indicated that Evangelicals made up close to 15 percent of the population, with far larger proportions in shantytowns (*poblaciones callampas*) and other low-income neighborhoods. What is perhaps more significant is that active Evangelicals were as numerous as active Catholics (see Religion and Churches, ch. 2).

Business

Chile's business community has long played an active role in the nation's politics. During the years of import-substitution industrialization, businesses developed close links with political leaders and state agencies, seeking subsidies, tariffs, and other forms of regulation that would protect them from the rigors of market competition domestically and internationally. Indeed, the expansion of the state, in particular its decentralized semiautonomous agencies, led to the creation of semicorporatist boards whose members included formal representatives of large business associations. As the parties of the right began to decline in importance, business leaders became increasingly "apolitical," preferring "independent" candidates such as Jorge Alessandri to those with strong party ties.

In the early 1990s, most businesses in Chile employed only a handful of workers, and business trade groups probably represented less than 20 percent of all business establishments in the country. Small businesses were represented by the Council of Small and Medium Enterprises (Consejo de la Pequeña y Mediana Industria—CPMI), and large businesses were represented by the Chamber of Production and Commerce (Cámara de la Producción y Comercio—CPC). Small and medium-sized business groups were in turn divided into associations, such as the Truck Owners Association (Asociación Gremial de Dueños de Camiones) and the Federation of Retail Business of Chile (Confederación del Comercio

Detallista de Chile). The most important of the associations affiliated with the CPC were the Industrial Development Association (Sociedad de Fomento Fabril—Sofofa) and the National Agricultural Association (Sociedad Nacional de Agricultura—SNA), both of which had considerable political influence and clout.

During the Allende years, the associations of both small and large businesses played a critical role in combating the parties of the left and undermining the Allende government. Small-business associations, particularly the truck owners, brought the country to a standstill, aggravating an already difficult economic and political situation. Large-business associations also worked hard to depose the Popular Unity government. Sofofa, in particular, played an important role by supporting a highly cohesive group of economists critical of the Allende government who prepared a document that served as the basis for the military regime's shift in economic policy. Because of their prominent role in bringing down the Allende government, business leaders assumed that they would have influence over economic policy and be able to reestablish a close and mutually beneficial relationship with the state. Much to the business leaders' surprise, the far-reaching structural adjustment policies pursued by the military government proved extraordinarily disruptive, contributing to the bankruptcy of hundreds of major firms.

Business leaders, already weakened by the reform and revolutionary policies of the previous two civilian presidents, were too dispirited to oppose the determined economic advisers of the military. Small business, which had the most to lose, made some gestures toward joining the growing opposition movement after the dramatic economic downturn of 1981, only to be kept in line by the regime's strategy of using tough measures when necessary and moderating its policies at key points just enough to retain private-sector allegiance.

Overall, the lack of strenuous resistance to the regime, particularly from medium-sized and large businesses, was attributed to memories of the traumatic Allende years. Entrepreneurs and business managers feared that any strong opposition on their part might weaken the military regime and create the possibility of a return to the leftist policies that they felt had practically destroyed the private sector in the past. A weak business community, in combination with the private sector's determination not to risk a return of the left, gave the military regime wide latitude to restructure the economy as it saw fit.

Because of the weakness of the parties of the right, business groups remained influential in right-wing politics after the return to democracy. In 1989 they were instrumental in imposing an "independent" candidate of the right to run for president and actively supported one of their own in the presidential race of 1993. Yet business associations were less influential in politics in the early 1990s than previously, largely because of the changes resulting from Chile's opening to world markets and, ironically, because of the decreased importance of the state in regulating and controlling business. Political leaders and government officials, however, solicited the views of business interests on labor and environmental questions because of their common desire to encourage continued expansion of the Chilean economy (see Social Organizations and Associations, ch. 2).

Labor

For many decades, Chile had one of the most extensive labor movements in the Western Hemisphere. Large increases in unionization through the 1960s occurred in response to efforts by the authorities to organize working-class groups. Intense competition between the Christian Democrats and the left added further to the extraordinary efforts to mobilize previously disenfranchised groups in the late 1960s and early 1970s.

Under center-left administrations, Chile's workers obtained an array of workers' rights and established a collective bargaining system in which the state played a significant role as mediator. During the Popular Unity years, unions closely tied to the parties of the left played important roles in the management of enterprises taken over by the state. However, Chile's organized workers hardly constituted the revolutionary vanguard envisioned by some sectors of the far left. They were proud of their "conquests" and envisioned the policies of the Allende government as a continuation of favorable treatment for workers. Despite the size of Chile's labor movement, labor had little autonomy from party leadership. Most labor demands, outside of particular collective bargaining situations, responded to the strategies and calculations of party leaders both in and out of the government.

When the coup came, despite the rhetoric of the far left there was no independent working-class movement capable of resisting the imposition of military rule. With the arrest of labor and party leaders, any possibility of resistance vanished. The military regime was extremely harsh on organized labor because of its close ties to the parties of the left. The principal labor federation, the United Labor Federation (Central Única de Trabajadores), was disbanded, and many of its leaders were killed, imprisoned, or exiled. The authorities adopted a new labor code, which prohibited labor federations, sharply restricted the right to strike, and gave significant latitude to employers in the hiring and firing of workers and in procedures for settling disputes.

Structural changes in the Chilean economy, particularly the collapse of large traditional industries that had depended on state subsidies and tariff protection, combined with the highest levels of urban unemployment in Latin America during the 1980s, also exacted a harsh toll on the labor movement. By the mid-1980s, the number of unionized workers was only one-third of its highest level, while the growing numbers of women in the labor force, particularly in commercial agriculture, remained nonunionized. By 1987 only about 10 percent of the total work force was unionized; approximately 20 percent of industrial labor belonged to unions. Only in select areas, such as copper mining, where 60 percent of the workers were unionized, was the union movement able to hold its own.

Despite organized labor's decline, when the military authorities attempted to develop an alternative labor movement with a "renewed" leadership to their liking, they failed. Even in government-mandated elections for new union leaders at the plant level, workers tended to select union members who were hostile to the government and had close ties to opposition parties. It was this "tolerated" labor movement, spearheaded by the Confederation of Copper Workers (Confederación de Trabajadores del Cobre—CTC), that ignited the widespread protests and strikes of 1983 coordinated by the National Workers' Command (Comando Nacional de Trabajadores—CNT). Less militant was the centrist (pro-PDC) Workers' Democratic Federation (Central Democrática de Trabajadores—CDT). The government moved swiftly, however, to curb all labor activism through repressive measures and threats to fire workers, particularly in the copper mines. Party leaders soon replaced labor leaders as the principal organizers of the growing opposition to the military government.

In the early 1990s, the principal labor confederation in Chile was the Unitary Confederation of Labor (Confederación Única de Trabajadores—CUT), established in 1988 as the successor to the National Trade Union Coordinating Board (Coordinadora Nacional de Sindicatos—CNS), a grouping of industrial, professional, and mining unions led by leftist Christian Democrats and elements of the left. With the return of democracy, labor pressed for a more favorable labor code and for social policies that would improve the standard of living for the poor. Although the Aylwin government was constrained in approving new labor legislation by the opposition majority in the Senate, some modifications were made to the labor code. The strong climate of opinion in the country in favor of free markets and minimal government restrictions on labor markets, a position embraced by the Aylwin government, has hemmed in labor's room for maneuvering.

The weakness of the labor movement reflected not only the low incidence of organized labor in Chile's new economic context but also the degree to which labor continued to be controlled by Chile's principal parties, parties that were able to exert substantial "labor discipline" during Aylwin's transitional government. There were indications, however, that this discipline may have been obtained at a cost. There appeared to be dissatisfaction among rank-and-file workers with the close relationship between union and party leaders and some bitterness about the low priority the government accorded their interests, despite government success in changing some of the labor laws (see Unions and Labor Conflicts, ch. 3).

The Media

Chile has a long tradition of an active press, closely tied to the country's competitive political parties. Prior to the 1973 coup, Santiago had ten daily newspapers spanning the ideological spectrum. These included, on the left, the Communist *El Siglo,* the Socialist *Última Hora,* and the far-left papers *Puro Chile* and *Clarín.* The Christian Democrats owned *La Prensa.* Newspapers identified with the center-right or far right included *El Mercurio* (founded in 1827), *Las Últimas Noticias* (founded in 1902), *La Segunda* (founded in 1931), *La Tercera de la Hora* (founded in 1950), and *La Tribuna.*

The wide ideological range of Chile's major newspapers did not mean that circulation was evenly distributed. All of the newspapers supporting the Allende government had a combined circulation of less than 250,000, while, for instance, *La Tercera de la Hora,* a center-right paper, had a circulation of 200,000. By far the most important newspaper in Chile has been *El Mercurio,* with a Sunday circulation of 340,000 and wide influence in opinion circles. The El Mercurio Company, easily the most powerful newspaper group in Chile, also owns *La Segunda,* the sensationalist *Las Últimas Noticias,* and regional papers. With its close ties to the Chilean Navy (Armada de Chile), *El Mercurio* played a critical role in mobilizing support against the Allende government, openly supporting the military coup.

After the coup, Chile's independent press disappeared. The newspapers of the left were closed immediately, and the centrist *La Prensa* stopped publishing a few months later. Newspapers that kept publishing gave strong support to the military government and submitted to its guidelines on sensitive issues; they also developed a keen sense of when to censor themselves. The print media became even more concentrated in the hands of two groups: the Edwards family, owners of *El Mercurio,* with approximately 50 percent of all circulation nationwide, and the Picó Cañas family, owners of *La Tercera de la Hora,* with another 30 percent. Only toward the end of the military government did two opposition newspapers appear—*La Época,* founded in 1987 and run by Christian Democrats, and *Fortín Mapocho,* a publication run by groups on the left that became a daily newspaper in 1987. By 1990 Chile had approximately eighty newspapers, including thirty-three dailies.

During the years of military rule, opposition opinion was reflected in limited-circulation weekly magazines, the first being *Mensaje,* a Jesuit publication founded in 1951. Over time, magazines such as *Hoy,* a Christian Democratic weekly started in 1977; *Análisis* and *Apsi,* two leftist publications that began reaching a national audience in 1983; and the biweekly *Cauce,* established in 1983, all circulated under the often realized threat of censorship, confiscation of their publications, and arrests of reporters and staff. In perhaps the worst case of government suppression, *Cauce, Apsi, Análisis,* and *Fortín Mapocho* were all shut down from October 1984 to May 1985. After the restoration of democracy, two conservative weekly magazines were founded, opposed to the Aylwin government: the influential *¿Qué Pasa?* (founded in 1971) and *Ercilla* (founded in 1936). By 1990 Chile had more than twenty major current affairs periodicals.

The return of civilian government did not lead to an explosion of new publications. Both *La Época* and *Fortín Mapocho,* which had received some support from foreign sources, faced enormous financial challenges in competing with the established media. *Fortín Mapocho* folded, and *La Época* finally was sold to a business group, which retained the newspaper's standards of objective reporting. *El Mercurio* continued to dominate the print media and remained the most influential newspaper in the country. The El Mercurio Company remained closely tied to business groups that had supported the military regime but made efforts, particularly through *La Segunda,* to present balanced and fair reporting. The only openly pro-CPD newspaper in Chile was the government-subsidized financial newspaper, *La Nación,* which reflected the views of the authorities.

Radio traditionally has been dominated by progovernment stations, the most notable exceptions being Radio Cooperativa, run by Christian Democrats, and Radio Chilena, run by the Roman Catholic Church. At first the size of the audience for these two stations did not approach the listenership levels of Minería, Portales, and Agricultura—stations identified with the business community.

Radio Tierra, claiming to be the first all-women radio station in the Americas, has identified exclusively with women since its establishment in 1983 (see Telecommunications, ch. 3).

Although the opposition had some print outlets, it had no access to television. Not until 1987, in the months leading up to the plebiscite, did opposition leaders gain limited access to television. The medium was strictly controlled by the authorities and by network managers: the University of Chile, the Pontifical Catholic University of Chile, and the National Television Network of Chile—Channel 7 (Televisión Nacional de Chile—Canal 7).

Competitive politics transformed television news broadcasting, introducing numerous talk shows that focus on politics. Channel 7, the official station of the military government, was reorganized by the junta after Pinochet's defeat as a more autonomous entity presenting a broad range of views and striving for more impartial news presentation. The station with the widest audience in Chile in the early 1990s was the Pontifical Catholic University of Chile's Channel 13, offering a right-of-center editorial line. Other channels with a more regional focus included Channel 5 of Valparaíso, operated by the Catholic University of Valparaíso (Televisión Universidad Católica de Valparaíso—Canal 5); Channel 11, operated in Santiago by the University of Chile (Corporación de Televisión de la Universidad de Chile—Canal 11); and two commercial channels, Valparaíso's Channel 4 and Santiago's Red Televisiva Megavisión—Channel 9, owned by the Pinto Claude Group and directed by Ricardo Claro. In May 1993, the Luksic Group entered the private television market by acquiring a 75 percent share of Maxivisión (TV MAX), broadcast on UHF (ultrahigh frequency) in the Metropolitan Region of Santiago.

The National Council of Television (Consejo Nacional de Televisión) is charged with regulating the airwaves and setting broadcast standards. Its jurisdiction in matters of censorship is unclear in the wake of Supreme Court rulings challenging its decisions.

Foreign Relations

Since the early decades after independence, Chile has always had an active involvement in international affairs. In 1837 the country aggressively challenged the dominance of Peru's port of Callao for preeminence in the Pacific trade routes, defeating the short-lived alliance between Peru and Bolivia, the Peru-Bolivia Confederation (1836–39), in an international war. The war left Chile an important power in the Pacific. A second war, the War of the Pacific (1879–83), further increased Chile's regional dominance and international prestige, while adding considerably to its territory. In the twentieth century, although Chile did not become involved in an international war, it continued to maintain one of the largest standing armies per population size in the region.

Because of the prestige of Chile's democratic institutions, Chile's diplomatic service is well respected, and Chile has influence far beyond the country's size or geostrategic importance. Over the years, Chile has played an active role in promoting multilateral institutions and supporting democratic and human rights principles. Because of its strong ideologically based multiparty system, Chileans have widespread contacts with counterpart parties in Europe and are present in the international federations of Christian Democrats, Socialists, and Communists. These contacts contribute to Chile's European orientation.

During the nineteenth century, Chile's commercial ties were primarily with Britain, a country that had a decisive influence on the organization of the navy. Culturally and intellectually, Chileans felt close to France. The French influenced Chile's legal and educational systems and had a decisive impact on Chilean culture, including the architecture of the capital in the boom years at the turn of the century. German influence came from substantial German immigration to southern Chile and the organization and training of the army by Prussians. Aside from important markets for Chilean wheat in California, the United States played a decidedly secondary role.

Relations with the United States

Chile has never been particularly close to the United States. The distance between Washington and Santiago is greater than the distance between Washington and Moscow. In the twentieth century, Chile's giant copper mines were developed by United States economic interests, although Europe remained a larger market for Chilean products. Chile's democratic governments distanced themselves from European fascism during the world wars and embraced the cause of the Allies, despite internal pressures to support the Axis powers. Chile later joined with the United States in supporting collective measures for safeguarding hemispheric security from a Soviet threat and welcomed United States support in developing the Chilean Air Force. But the advent of the Cold War and the official Chilean policy of support for the inter-American system exacerbated internal conflicts in Chile. The growing presence of the Marxist left meant a sharp increase in anti-American sentiment in Chilean public opinion, a sentiment that was fueled by opposition to the United States presence in Vietnam, the United States conflict with Cuba, and increased United States intervention in domestic Chilean politics.

During the 1960s, the United States identified Chile as a model country, one that would provide a different, democratic path to development, countering the popularity of Cuba in the developing world. To that end, the United States strongly supported the candidacy of Eduardo Frei Montalva in 1964 with overt and covert funds and subsequently supported his government in the implementation of urban and rural reforms. This support spawned considerable resentment against the United States in Chile's conservative upper class, as well as among the Marxist left.

The election of Allende was viewed in Washington as a significant setback to United States interests worldwide. National Security Adviser Henry Kissinger was particularly concerned about the implications for European politics of the free election of a Marxist in Chile. Responding to these fears and a concern for growing Soviet influence in the Western Hemisphere, the United States embarked on a covert campaign to prevent Allende from gaining office and to destabilize his government after his election was ratified. Although the United States did not have a direct hand in the overthrow of Allende, it welcomed the coup and provided assistance to the military regime.

The widespread violations of human rights in Chile, combined with a strong rejection of covert activities engaged in abroad by the administration of President Richard M. Nixon, galvanized United States congressional opposition to United States ties with Chile's military government. With the election of Jimmy Carter in 1976, the United States took an openly hostile attitude toward the Chilean military government, publicly condemning human rights violations and pressing for the restoration of democracy. Particularly disturbing to the United States government was the complicity of the Chilean intelligence services in the assassination in Washington of Chilean ambassador Orlando Letelier and one of his associates, a United States citizen. That incident contributed to the isolation of the Pinochet government internationally and led to a sharp rift in relations between the two countries. The Chilean military turned elsewhere for its procurement needs and encouraged the development of a domestic arms industry to replace United States equipment (see The Defense Industry, ch. 5).

With the defeat of Jimmy Carter and the election of Ronald Reagan, the pendulum in the relations between the two countries swung the other way. Reagan argued that anticommunist authoritarian regimes should not be antagonized for fear that they might be undermined, leading to the triumph of a Marxist left, as in Nicaragua.

Chile would be pushed to respect human rights through "quiet diplomacy," while the United States government reestablished normal ties with the dictatorship.

The new policy did not last long. After the riots in Santiago in 1983, the United States began to worry that the Pinochet government was no longer a solution to a potential threat from the far left, but part of the problem. United States officials increasingly began to reflect the concerns of prominent conservatives in Chile, who believed that Pinochet's own personal ambitions could stand in the way of a successful transition back to civilian rule.

The shift in policy became far more apparent in Reagan's second term, when the Reagan administration, struggling to oppose the leftist government of Nicaragua, sought to show its consistency by criticizing the right-wing government of Chile. The United States made it clear that it did not see the Pinochet government's plebiscite as a satisfactory step toward democracy and conducive to open and competitive elections. Whereas in the early 1980s the United States government had embraced the military regime while refusing to take the democratic opposition seriously, by the end of the decade the United States was actively backing the opposition in its effort to obtain a fair electoral process so that it could attempt to defeat Pinochet at his own game. Pinochet's defeat was considered by Washington to be a vindication of its policies.

With the election of Patricio Aylwin in Chile, relations between the two countries improved greatly. The administration of George Bush welcomed Chile's commitment to free-market policies, while praising the new government's commitment to democracy. The United States also supported the Aylwin government's human rights policies and came to a resolution of the Letelier assassination by agreeing to a bilateral mediation mechanism and compensation of the victims' families.

A few issues have complicated United States-Chile relations, including the removal of Chilean fruit from United States supermarkets in 1991 by the Food and Drug Administration, after tainted grapes were allegedly discovered. The United States also objected to Chile's intellectual property legislation, particularly the copying of drug patents. However, these issues pale by comparison with the strong ties between the two countries and the admiration that United States officials have expressed for Chile's remarkable economic performance. As evidence of this "special" relationship, both the Bush and the Clinton administrations have indicated United States willingness to sign a free-trade agreement with Chile in the aftermath of the successful negotiations with Mexico on the North

President Patricio Aylwin Azócar
with President George Bush
at the White House,
May 13, 1992
Courtesy, The White House

Enrique Silva Cimma,
Aylwin's minister
of foreign relations
Courtesy Embassy of
Chile, Washington

American Free Trade Agreement (NAFTA—see Glossary). Although Chile has pressed strongly for the agreement as a way to ensure access to United States markets, the United States in 1991 was replaced by Japan as Chile's largest trading partner, with the United States accounting for less than 20 percent of Chile's world trade. Ironically, in the post-Cold War era, anti-Americanism in Chile is more prevalent in military circles and among the traditional right, still bitter about United States support for democratic parties prior to the plebiscite and concerned that the United States has hegemonic presumptions over the region.

Other Foreign Relations

With the military coup of 1973, Chile became isolated politically as a result of widespread human rights abuses. The return of democracy in 1990 opened Chile once again to the world. President Patricio Aylwin traveled extensively to Europe, North America, and Asia, reestablishing political and economic ties. Particularly significant was Chile's opening to Japan, which has become Chile's largest single trading partner.

In Latin America, Chile joined the Rio Group (see Glossary) in 1990 and played an active role in strengthening the inter-American system's commitment to democracy as a cardinal value. However, Chile has shied away from regional economic integration schemes, such as the Southern Cone Common Market (Mercado Común del Cono Sur—Mercosur; see Glossary), arguing that the country is better off opening its economy to the world, rather than building regional markets with neighboring countries. Where in the past Chile drew on the prestige of its democratic institutions to bolster its international standing, the extraordinary success of Chile's economic performance in the early 1990s has given Chile the status of a "model" country, with a global rather than regional focus.

Chile's relations with other Latin America countries have improved considerably with the return of legitimate governments in the region. However, serious border disputes still cloud relations with the country's three contiguous neighbors. Chile's victory over Peru and Bolivia in the War of the Pacific meant that Bolivia lost the province of Antofagasta and became landlocked, while Peru lost its southern province of Tarapacá. The quest to regain access to the sea became the major foreign policy objective for Bolivia and is still a source of tension with Chile. The two countries do not maintain full diplomatic relations. A treaty signed in 1929 resolved major boundary disputes with Peru that arose following the War of the Pacific, but many Peruvians do not accept the terms of the treaty. Tensions between the two countries reached dangerous levels in 1979, the centennial of the War of the Pacific.

Chile's most serious border conflict was with Argentina and concerned three islands—Picton, Lennox, and Nueva—that are located south of the Beagle Channel. The two countries agreed to submit to arbitration by Britain's Queen Elizabeth II. In May 1977, the queen ruled that the islands and all adjacent formations belonged to Chile. Argentina refused to accept the ruling, and relations between the two countries became extremely tense, moving to the brink of open warfare. In 1978 the two countries agreed to allow the pope to mediate the dispute through the good offices of Cardinal Antonio Samoré, his special envoy. The pope's ruling resulted in the ratification of a treaty to settle the dispute in Rome in May 1985. With the inauguration of democratic governments in both countries, relations improved significantly. In August 1991, presidents Aylwin and Carlos Saúl Menem signed a treaty that resolved twenty-two pending border disputes, while agreeing to

resolve the two remaining ones by arbitration. Chile continues to claim a wedge-shaped section of Antarctica, called the Chilean Antarctic Territory (Territorio Chileno Antártico), that is also claimed in part by Argentina and Britain (see fig. 12).

Future Challenges of Democratic Consolidation

In the early 1990s, Chile stood in a favorable position as it rejoined the community of democratic nations. The high rate of growth that began in 1985 continued under the Aylwin government, reaching 10.4 percent in 1992, while inflation moderated. With the exception of Colombia, Chile was the only major economy on the South American continent to finish the 1980s with a per capita GDP larger than that of 1980. High levels of foreign and domestic investment and continued improvement in Chile's export performance suggested that the country's economy would continue to improve.

Chile also made significant progress in the political sphere. Moderation of the country's political discourse permitted a return to the politics of conciliation. Paradoxically, the special guarantees given to the military and the right in the outgoing regime's institutional order, while fundamentally undemocratic, helped those sectors accept a democratic transition in the knowledge that they retained significant measures of power. The continuation of Pinochet in office also gave comfort to the supporters of the former regime, fearful of a return to popular sovereignty. Ironically, it also contributed to the strong unity and discipline of the former opposition parties that make up the government, reinforcing patterns of accommodation and compromise and contributing to the notable success of the Aylwin administration.

Although the "authoritarian enclaves" of the past may have contributed to the smooth transition process, they could endanger Chile's democratic stability over the long run. The most troubling problem appears to be the exaggerated presidentialism embodied in the 1980 constitution. The Aylwin administration performed well within the rules inherited from the military government because of the unusual collaboration among leaders who had developed a strong sense of camaraderie in opposing the dictatorship. Determined not to risk an authoritarian reversal, these leaders insisted on an extraordinary degree of unity in implementing cautious, moderate policies. Legislative leaders and middle- and lower-level activists also understood the need for discipline and consensus, deferring to their leaders within the executive branch on most matters.

This pattern of "forced consensus," however, could not continue indefinitely. As the new Frei administration was inaugurated on March 11, 1994, it was clear that members of Congress and lower-level leaders resented their lack of significant input into the policy process. The lack of authority in the legislature created the risk that Congress would become an essentially negative institution seeking to undermine the executive, with no significant role in developing arenas of accommodation and consensus that had served Chile so well in previous eras.

Particularly vexing is incompatibility between a presidentialist form of government and a highly institutionalized multiparty system, one in which the president appears unlikely to obtain majority support in the presidential race and unlikely to enjoy majority support in the legislature. Under such circumstances, Chile will need institutional rules and procedures to provide incentives to build political coalitions across party lines. Although there is consensus in 1993 among the elite on fundamental questions, there is no guarantee that consensus will remain once Chile moves away from the "heroic politics" of the immediate postauthoritarian period to the more "banal politics" of democratic normality. Among the many issues that will challenge Chile's parties and, indeed, may lead to a reconfiguration of party alliances, are, of course, poverty, as well as other matters that have not as yet reached the national policy agenda, such as divorce, abortion, the environment, and grass-roots political participation.

Chile's electoral system also poses a challenge. Rather than generate a two-party system, the electoral system has encouraged the maintenance of broad coalitions, including parties that would probably not obtain seats in a fully competitive electoral framework. The electoral system could encourage political instability if two runners-up were evenly matched. In a political system where the forces on the left, right, and center are roughly equal in size, the electoral system could lead to the disenfranchisement of one of those sectors if the politics of broad coalitions were to break down.

Finally, it remains clear that Chilean democracy will not be fully consolidated until civil-military relations are normalized. Although it is important that a democracy insulate the armed forces from partisan political meddling in the same way that the judicial system is kept "apolitical," the broad latitude given the armed forces in the 1980 constitution threatens democratic stability by shielding the military institution from civilian oversight. The task of the Frei government will be to ease this threat by completing the constitutional reforms left pending after the 1989 compromises made with the outgoing military regime.

* * *

The classic study in English of politics and government in Chile remains Federico G. Gil's *The Political System of Chile*. Paul W. Drake's *Socialism and Populism in Chile, 1932-52* and James F. Petras's *Politics and Social Forces in Chilean Development* provide valuable discussions of the politics of Chile in the pre-Allende period. There are numerous studies of the Allende years, many of which also provide background material on the political conditions in Chile leading up to the election of the Popular Unity government. These include Paul E. Sigmund's *The Overthrow of Allende and the Politics of Chile, 1964-1976*, Barbara Stallings's *Class Conflict and Economic Development in Chile, 1958-1973*, Mark Falcoff's *Modern Chile, 1970-1989*, Edy Kaufman's *Crisis in Allende's Chile*, and Arturo Valenzuela's *The Breakdown of Democratic Regimes: Chile*. Arturo Valenzuela and J. Samuel Valenzuela's *Chile: Politics and Society* provides an anthology of essays. The Allende years, from the point of view of the United States ambassador who served at the time of the coup, are described in Nathaniel Davis's *The Last Two Years of Salvador Allende*.

Studies of the Pinochet years are fewer. The first comprehensive study of the period of military rule is Pamela Constable and Arturo Valenzuela's *A Nation of Enemies*. A volume of essays providing an overview of the first decade of military rule is J. Samuel Valenzuela and Arturo Valenzuela's *Military Rule in Chile*. For coverage of civil-military relations during the 1973-88 period, see also Manuel Antonio Garretón Merino's *The Chilean Political Process*. Paul W. Drake and Iván Jaksić's *The Struggle for Democracy in Chile, 1982-1990* is an anthology covering the transition phase.

The best study of the Catholic Church in Chile is Brian H. Smith's *The Church and Politics in Chile*. Chile's party system is discussed in Timothy R. Scully's *Rethinking the Center*, Michael Fleet's *The Rise and Fall of Christian Democracy*, and Cesar N. Caviédes's *Elections in Chile*. Frederick M. Nunn's *The Military in Chilean History* provides a historical discussion of the military. A critical discussion of the military institution under Pinochet can be found in Genaro Arriagada's *Pinochet: The Politics of Power*.

United States-Chile relations in the contemporary period are treated in Michael J. Francis's *The Limits of Hegemony* and Paul E. Sigmund's *The United States and Democracy in Chile*. (For further information and complete citations, see Bibliography.)

Chapter 5. National Security

A series of masculine textile figures on a seventeenth-century Mapuche woman's belt called ñimintrarüwe

GEOGRAPHICALLY ISOLATED but not immune from occasional foreign threats over the centuries, Chileans have developed some of the strongest military and naval traditions in Latin America. The indigenous inhabitants of Chile established a formidable reputation as warriors, in no small part by warding off Incan attempts at conquest in 1460 and 1491. Even the Spanish conquerors of the sixteenth century failed to establish their dominion south of the Río Bío-Bío, which remained, in effect, the southern frontier of Chile until more than three centuries later.

Following its declaration of independence in 1810, Chile became the first Latin American country to organize its armed forces on a professional basis. Its army and navy quickly earned a reputation for effectiveness, engaging in successful wars against the Peru-Bolivia Confederation of 1836–39, against Spain in 1865–66, and again against Peru and Bolivia in 1879–83.

Chile's long coastline (6,435 kilometers) and elongated shape create major defense problems, but geographical barriers such as the Andes, the Atacama Desert, the Strait of Magellan, and the Beagle Channel have long helped discourage any thoughts of military aggression by neighboring Argentina, Bolivia, and Peru. The Chilean Army has not engaged in a foreign war since 1883. Beginning with the inauguration in 1886 of a staff school, the War Academy (Academia de Guerra), under the direction of a captain in the German army, German influence became predominant in the army, which achieved such prestige throughout Latin America that many of the other states of the region sent selected officers for postgraduate training in Chilean military schools. Several countries contracted with full-scale Chilean military and naval missions to train their armed forces, and Chilean officers taught in the military schools of several other Latin American countries.

Persistent friction with Peru since the War of the Pacific (1879–83) has been fueled by Peruvian irredentism in regard to the territories ceded to Chile following that conflict, despite the ratification in 1929 of the Treaty of Ancón (also known as the Treaty of Tacna-Arica), recognizing their loss. Bolivia also has aspired to regain its outlet to the sea through the former coastal province of Antofagasta, lost as a result of that war, but has been too weak to pursue this objective alone. In early 1994, the possibility of any escalation of tension seemed slight in the medium term.

A continuing frontier dispute with Argentina almost led to war at the turn of the twentieth century and again in 1978. Tension with Argentina led Chile to break ranks with the rest of Latin America and quietly support Britain in the 1982 Malvinas/Falklands War between Britain and Argentina, although Chile has supported Argentina's claim to the islands. The risk of outright hostilities between Chile and Argentina was removed by the Beagle Channel Treaty of May 1985, an increase in diplomatic contacts, and economic agreements since Patricio Aylwin Azócar (1990–94) took office as president. Brazil, Ecuador, and to a lesser extent Colombia have historically been Chile's natural allies, given shared disputes with Argentina and Peru. In the early 1990s, however, relations between Chile and its immediate neighbors have been generally normal. Chile has carried out joint naval exercises with both Argentina and Peru. Nevertheless, border tensions have surfaced occasionally, particularly with Peru, and the armed forces of Argentina and Chile have remained resistant to cooperation.

Despite a record of subordination to constitutional government that was almost unique in Latin America, the Chilean Armed Forces (Fuerzas Armadas de Chile) incurred international opprobrium in September 1973 when they violently overthrew the democratically elected government of Marxist president Salvador Allende Gossens (1970–73). The military regime, led by General Augusto Pinochet Ugarte (1973–90), rebuilt the country's shattered economy, but it was responsible for extensive human rights abuses. The Pinochet regime adopted a new constitution in 1980 that called for a plebiscite to renew the presidential mandate for another eight years. The candidate was Pinochet himself, having been chosen by the military junta. Bowing to domestic and international pressures, the plebiscite was held under conditions that permitted a proper test of the nation's majority will. Pinochet lost, and free presidential elections were held in December 1989 in accordance with constitutional provisions. Pinochet honored the results of the 1989 presidential elections by handing over the reins of government to a civilian coalition led by President Aylwin in March 1990. However, Pinochet was entitled by the 1980 constitution to remain as head of the army for an additional eight years, until 1998, with no possibility of removal by the president.

In 1993 the combined strength of the armed forces was at least 91,800 (including 54,000 members of the army, 25,000 members of the navy, and 12,800 members of the air force). In addition, the army reserves had about 50,000 members.

Military Tradition and the Evolution of the Armed Forces

Early History

Chile's indigenous Mapuche people established themselves as tenacious warriors in the fifteenth century. An attempted invasion by the forces of Pachacuti Inca Yupanqui (1438–71) in 1460 was held off by the Mapuche in the Valley of Coquimbo. The Incas withdrew, defeated, six years later. A second effort at invasion, this time by Huayna Cápac, son of and successor to Yupanqui, enjoyed greater success in 1491, penetrating as far as the Central Valley (Valle Central) of Chile before it, too, was turned back by the Mapuche.

The first Spanish attempt at conquest, led by Diego de Almagro in 1535–37, was undertaken by a force of 500 to 700 Spaniards and as many as 15,000 native Americans. Although this expedition penetrated as far as the Río Maule, Almagro's forces, finding no sign of hoped-for riches and constantly harassed by the Mapuche, retreated across the Atacama Desert and returned to Peru without establishing any permanent settlements. In 1540 Pedro de Valdivia launched a much smaller but longer expedition, leading some 150 Spaniards and 1,000 native Americans. Valdivia's expedition succeeded in establishing the first permanent European settlements in Chile. However, Araucanian (particularly Mapuche) resistance kept Valdivia from penetrating to any significant degree beyond the Río Bío-Bío. In a Christmas Day battle at Tucapel in 1553, Araucanian warriors, led by Lautaro, a legendary chief, slaughtered a force of Spanish cavalry commanded by Valdivia, who was executed. Lautaro had studied the Spaniards and their tactics when he was a slave for Valdivia during a period of captivity. After that initial success, the indigenous warriors adapted rapidly to European-style warfare and soon, using captured horses and weapons, fielded their own cavalry against the invader.

The Araucanians were contained only with difficulty throughout the next three centuries. The Río Bío-Bío remained the effective southern frontier throughout the colonial period. The Araucanians made frequent incursions northward, one of which threatened to destroy the Spanish settlement in Santiago in 1554. In an attempt to defeat these native Americans, Alonso de Rivera created a Chilean army of sorts in 1603. By the beginning of the eighteenth century, the Araucanian wars had already cost the lives of more than 40,000 Spaniards and untold thousands of native Americans. Throughout this period, the coastal region was also subjected to sporadic attacks by English, French, and Dutch buccaneers.

The Hispano-Amerindian society that evolved in Spanish-controlled Chile thus developed in an environment that was under a constant shadow of real or potential external threat. These circumstances produced a people for whom military defense and prowess were important attributes. During the latter years of the colonial period, Chile depended for its defense principally on a militia, which numbered 16,000 by the beginning of the nineteenth century. The Spanish colonial administration was overturned with relative ease in 1810, and a small volunteer militia, consisting of one battalion of infantry, two squadrons of cavalry, and four companies of artillery, was established.

Genesis of the Armed Forces, 1814–36

In 1814 the royalist forces, based in Peru, took advantage of internal dissensions among the various factions of the nationalist movement in Chile to mount an invasion. The 5,000-man royalist army defeated the 1,800-man nationalist force, led by Bernardo O'Higgins Riquelme and Juan José Carrera, in the Battle of Rancagua on October 2, and the remnants of the routed army (300 men) fled to Mendoza in present-day western Argentina.

The leaders of the United Provinces of the Río de la Plata, a short-lived (1813–26) federation of the provinces that had made up the Viceroyalty of the Río de la Plata, realized that their position remained insecure following independence in 1816 so long as Chile and Peru remained bastions of Spanish power. It was decided, therefore, to send an expeditionary force, named the Army of the Andes, across the mountains to confront the royalists. The combined Argentine-Chilean Army of the Andes, under the joint command of O'Higgins and José de San Martín, set out from San Juan in northern Argentina on January 12, 1817. The army consisted of 2,795 infantry, 742 cavalry, and 241 artillerymen, who carried with them twenty-one guns and sufficient arms to equip a force of 15,000. Crossing the Andes at Paso de Uspallata and Paso de los Patos, this sizable army took the royalist forces in Chile completely by surprise. With only half of the total royalist strength of approximately 4,000 available to meet the invaders (the other 2,000 were deployed mainly in defense of the southern frontier), the royalists suffered a decisive defeat at Chacabuco, northeast of Santiago, on February 12, 1817. By the end of 1817, the Chilean Army (Ejército de Chile), consisting of 5,000 soldiers and officers, had been established. Despite reverses at Talcahuano on December 16, 1817, and at Cancha Rayada on March 19, 1818, the allied army swept to final victory at Maipú on April 5, 1818. Peru, however, remained a royalist stronghold, separated from Chile by the

Atacama Desert and approachable only by sea (see Wars of Independence, 1810–18, ch. 1).

Chile had first attempted to form a navy in 1813, when the United States-built frigate *Perla* and the brigantine *Potrillo* were acquired to break the Spanish blockade of Valparaíso. However, royalist elements succeeded in bribing the mercenary crew of the *Perla,* with the result that both vessels fell into the hands of the Spaniards. The official history of the Chilean Navy (Armada de Chile) dates from February 26, 1817, when the brigantine *Águila* was acquired by the nationalists. Armed with sixteen guns, the *Águila* was commissioned as the first naval vessel of the Republic of Chile, under the command of Raimundo Morris, an Irish mercenary and former lieutenant in the British Royal Navy. Under the overall command of Manuel Blanco Encalada, the first rear admiral of the Chilean Navy, the tiny fleet rapidly tripled in size with the capture of the Spanish merchant vessel *San Miguel* and the recapture of the *Perla*. Additional vessels were added by purchase, the arming of merchant ships, and further captures from the enemy. With those acquisitions, the revolutionary fleet consisted of a small ship of the line, two large frigates, and four corvettes. In 1818 the Naval School (Escuela Naval) was established, later named the Arturo Prat Naval School (Escuela Naval Arturo Prat), after Arturo Prat Chacón, naval hero of the War of the Pacific. Then, on November 28, 1818, the famous British admiral Thomas Alexander Cochrane (Lord Dundonald), who had been forced to resign from the Royal Navy following a financial scandal, assumed command of the revolutionary fleet from Blanco Encalada. Within two years, Cochrane's fleet had established control of the sea, and it was then possible to prepare for an amphibious invasion of Peru. With the help of the Chilean fleet, the allied army, headed by San Martín, liberated Lima on July 9, 1821, and the independence of Peru was declared on July 28.

When Cochrane left Chile in 1823, Blanco Encalada reassumed command of the navy, which was reequipped in 1824. The allies—now joined by a substantial force from a republic known as Gran Colombia (consisting of present-day Colombia, Panama, and Venezuela) and led by Simón Bolívar Palacios and Antonio José de Sucre—scored successive victories at Junín and Ayacucho in August and December 1824, respectively. That year Blanco Encalada fought in Callao, Peru, under Bolívar's command. Meanwhile, despite their defeats on the Chilean mainland and in Peru, the royalists had continued to hold out on the Isla de Chiloé, off the southern Chilean coast, and were only finally defeated in 1826 after two amphibious campaigns by Blanco Encalada and several nationalist reverses.

Diego Portales Palazuelos, Chile's main political strongman from 1830 to 1837, reorganized and streamlined the army, putting it on a firm basis with three infantry battalions, two regiments of cavalry, a squadron of hussars, and a regiment of artillery. The General Bernardo O'Higgins Military Academy (Escuela Militar "General Bernardo O'Higgins"), founded by O'Higgins on March 16, 1817, was also reorganized. It provided an uninterrupted flow of professional officers from 1832 onward. Portales also reestablished the civic militias, which were important elements in the defense of cities and towns during the colonial period. Over the next decades, these militias, whose officers were appointed and removed by the ministers of interior, proved to be a significant countervailing power to that of the army. They thus contributed to the stability of the constitutional government. During the civil wars of 1851 and 1859, the authorities relied on the combination of civic militas and some army units to defeat the insurrectionists.

Peru-Bolivia Confederation War, 1836–39

Fearing a threat to Chilean commercial and shipping interests, and even sovereignty by the newly created Peru-Bolivia Confederation led by Bolivian general Andrés de Santa Cruz y Calahumana, Chile declared war on the confederation in 1836. The Chilean Navy, gradually run down since the end of the struggle for independence, consisted of only two small vessels. Nevertheless, once more it rapidly tripled its strength by captures from the larger Peruvian fleet. Within a year, the Chilean Navy had established control of the sea.

On land, a Chilean force of approximately 2,800, under the command of Blanco Encalada, landed at Islay in southern Peru in October 1837, occupying Arequipa after a long and arduous march, during which the Chileans were decimated by disease. Following an encounter at Paucarpata with an army under the command of Santa Cruz, the Chilean force concluded a peace treaty, the Treaty of Paucarpata, on November 17, before returning to Valparaíso rather ignominiously. The Chilean government repudiated the treaty in indignation and in 1838 dispatched a better-prepared Chilean force under General Manuel Bulnes Prieto. Landing at Ancón, north of Lima, on August 6, this force commenced a slow march southward toward the Peruvian capital of Lima, while the Chilean fleet blockaded the main Peruvian port of Callao.

Although their advance was delayed by harassment from small allied forces, the Chileans were finally able to lay siege to Lima. The Chilean force occupied Lima at the end of October 1838 but

*Two naval guards
at the monument
to the War of the Pacific
in front of the Naval
Headquarters, Valparaíso
Courtesy David Shelton*

abandoned it on November 3 on hearing of the approach of a large Bolivian army under General Santa Cruz. The Chileans withdrew by land and sea toward Huacho. However, Santa Cruz failed to exploit the Chilean retreat fully, despite successes in several small skirmishes culminating in a major Chilean reverse at Buín on January 6, 1839.

The resounding defeat of the Peruvian fleet at Casma by a smaller Chilean squadron under British admiral Roberto Simpson, on January 12, left Chile in absolute control of the southeastern Pacific. General Bulnes again assumed the initiative. After inflicting a crushing defeat on the Bolivian Army at Yungay on January 20, the Chileans commenced a second push southward, occupying Lima for the second time in April. Santa Cruz had already fled to Ecuador, and both the war and the short-lived Peru-Bolivia Confederation now came to an end.

After 1843, when Bulnes was president (1841–51), the Chilean Army concentrated on penetrating the area south of the Río Bío-Bío, still largely the domain of the Araucanian people. In response, the Araucanians rose in a bloody revolt, which was suppressed in 1859–61, although the southern portion of the country remained largely outside the control of the national government.

In 1865, in a last attempt to reconquer their lost South American colonies, the Spaniards blockaded Chilean and Peruvian ports, an action that led to war between Spain and an ad hoc alliance of Chile, Bolivia, Peru, and Ecuador. Hostilities were confined to the sea. Although twenty-six years of freedom from external threat had once again seen the decline of the Chilean Navy, the blockade was effectively broken by the naval victory of the allied fleet, under the Chilean admiral Juan Williams Rebolledo, at Papudo on September 17, 1866. The naval war with Spain ended shortly afterward.

War of the Pacific, 1879–83

Despite cooperation among Chile, Peru, and Bolivia in the war against Spain, friction began to develop over the mineral-rich Bolivian province of Antofagasta and the Peruvian provinces of Tarapacá, Tacna, and Arica, whose wealth was exploited largely by Chilean enterprises. In 1875 Peru seized Chilean nitrate mines in Tarapacá, and in 1878 a new Bolivian government greatly increased taxes on Chilean business interests. To protect these interests and preempt their threatened expropriation, Chile dispatched a naval squadron headed by the ironclad *Blanco Encalada* and landed 200 troops at the Bolivian port of Antofagasta on February 14, 1879, provoking a declaration of war by Bolivia on March 1, an action reciprocated by Chile on April 5. Peru, which had concluded the secret Treaty of Mutual Defense with Bolivia in 1873, was now also drawn into the conflict (see The Liberal Era, 1861–91, ch. 1).

The Bolivian Army, with 2,361 members and generally antiquated equipment, and the Peruvian Army, with 5,241 members and a mixture of modern and older equipment, opposed the comparatively well-equipped Chilean Army of 2,845 officers and enlisted personnel. The Chilean Navy, still under the command of Admiral Williams, had two new ironclads (the *Blanco Encalada* and the *Cochrane*), four unarmored steam corvettes, and two gunboats. These vessels faced a Peruvian force consisting of an ironclad frigate, a small ironclad turret ship, two monitors, an unarmored steam corvette, and a gunboat.

Neither Chile, Peru, nor Bolivia was prepared for war. While they were mobilizing their land forces, any major actions were confined to encounters between the Chilean and Peruvian navies. Bolivia lost its three warships and four Pacific Coast ports early in the war. The naval war commenced with simultaneous bombardments of Pisagua and Mollendo by the Chilean fleet, followed by blockades of Callao and Iquique.

The Chilean expeditionary force at Antofagasta, reinforced to a strength of 1,400, occupied the ports of Cobija, Tocopilla, and Mejillones, penetrating inland against weak resistance as far as Calama. No further major land actions occurred for the next five months. However, by the middle of May 1879 Bolivia and Peru, having expanded their ranks with mostly peasant conscripts, had concentrated 9,000 men at Tarapacá, 4,000 at Tacna, and an additional 7,000 in the vicinity of Arica.

Peru gained a Pyrrhic victory in the first naval action of the war. Its most powerful ships, the ironclad frigate *Independencia* and the turret ship *Huáscar,* closed in on the two Chilean ships blockading Iquique on May 21, 1879. The Peruvians broke the blockade, sinking the Chilean corvette *Esmeralda* as her captain, Arturo Prat Chacón, led a boarding party of the *Huáscar* in a heroic but futile act. However, the *Independencia* hit a reef and sank as it was pursuing the fleeing Chilean gunboat *Covadonga,* which had sought refuge in shallow waters. Despite the loss of its largest unit, the Peruvian fleet remained a great menace, mainly owing to the audacity and genius of Admiral Miguel Grau. Flying his flag on the *Huáscar,* which, together with the corvette *Unión,* broke through the Chilean blockade of Callao on three occasions, Grau wreaked havoc on Chilean shipping.

Chilean naval energies were now largely directed toward the elimination of these two Peruvian ships. On October 8, 1879, Grau's luck ran out when he skirmished with two Chilean flotillas off Punta Angamos. The *Huáscar* was captured after the heroic admiral was killed, although the *Unión* escaped. The following month, the Peruvians suffered another major setback when the gunboat *Pilcomayo,* operating as a commerce raider, was sunk by the Chileans. Chilean naval supremacy was now complete. The surviving major units of the Peruvian Navy remained blockaded at Callao and Arica, and any naval action was limited to the minor units of both fleets. These consisted mainly of torpedo boats, of which Chile acquired a total of twelve and Peru three during 1880–81.

Major land operations commenced at the end of October 1879 with the amphibious landing of more than 10,000 Chilean troops at Pisagua on what is now the Peruvian coast. After a resolute defense by its small Bolivian garrison, Pisagua was captured on November 2. The Chileans advanced rapidly southward from this beachhead. On November 19, a Chilean force of 6,000 defeated a Confederation force of 9,000 at Pozo Dolores, north of Iquique. As a result of this reverse, the Peruvians abandoned Iquique without a fight. The garrison joined the survivors of the Battle of Pozo Dolores at Tarapacá, where a total Confederation army of 5,000 assembled. Although a reconnaissance force of 2,000 Chileans was routed on November 27, the victorious Confederation forces failed to pursue their advantage, abandoning Tarapacá and retreating to

Tacna. The Chileans, now reinforced to 17,000, continued to advance toward Tacna and Arica. A Chilean force of 5,000 carried out an amphibious raid at Ilo, to the north of Tacna, on December 31, and withdrew after capturing and sacking Moquegua, the ruins of which were soon reoccupied by the Peruvians.

Another Chilean amphibious landing established a beachhead at Ilo on February 25, 1880. During the first weeks of March, most of the Chilean forces disembarked. On March 13, a force of about 10,000 men carried out another major landing, at Pacocha, and an additional 3,000 landed at Vítar on March 14. On March 22, these forces, under General Manuel Baquedano González, pushed through the defenses at Moquegua and scored a crushing victory over 2,000 Peruvians at Torata. The Chilean forces now split for a two-pronged attack on Tacna to the south.

A combination of difficult terrain and the constant harassment by Peruvian guerrillas delayed the Chilean advance. It was not until May 26 that Baquedano's forces encountered a combined force of 10,000, which the Confederation had concentrated at Alto de la Alianza, north of Tacna. Baquedano scored another spectacular victory, which split the Bolivian and Peruvian armies; the former retired toward the Altiplano (Bolivia's high plateau), and the latter retreated in the direction of Arequipa. Following this disaster, the Bolivians took no further significant part in operations.

Chilean pressure was now concentrated on Arica, whose 2,000-man garrison surrendered on June 7, 1880. Another lull in major land operations now occurred as the Chileans prepared for the final advance on Lima. At sea several minor Chilean vessels, engaged in the blockade of Callao, fell victim either to shore batteries or to the occasional sallies of Peruvian torpedo boats and armed launches.

By November the Chileans had concentrated 25,000 men at Arica. Reembarking on November 14, this force made an amphibious landing four days later and captured Pisco. During the following weeks, a series of other amphibious landings allowed the Chileans to close in on Lima. On January 13, 1881, a Chilean force under General Baquedano scored a decisive if costly victory at Chorrillos, south of Lima. Two days later, the Peruvians broke an armistice, negotiated under the auspices of the foreign diplomatic corps in Lima. The ensuing Battle of Miraflores resulted in the total rout of the Peruvians and the collapse of their army. Peru's president and his High Command fled into the interior. Lima itself surrendered to the Chileans on January 16, and Callao fell the next day. The Chilean victory was now effectively complete, although guerrilla warfare was to continue another two years.

Chile's imaginative combination of land and sea power in the war against Peru and Bolivia had introduced a highly mobile form of amphibious warfare that was without precedent in South America.

Before the victorious Chilean Army was demobilized, it was turned to the pacification of the Araucanians, who had terrorized the southern frontier after the depletion of the regular army garrisons during the war. By the mid-1880s, the authority of the Chilean government was established throughout the national territory. Chile had now emerged as the major military and naval power in Latin America, with a battle-hardened army and an impressive fleet of three ironclads, three cruising vessels, one gunboat, and ten torpedo boats. Its navy outranked all other Latin American navies, as well as the United States Navy, in terms of modern and effective seagoing warships. Thanks to its navy, Chile incorporated Easter Island (Isla de Pascua) into its national territory in 1888.

Development of the Armed Forces

French influence was perceptible in the Chilean Army from the mid-nineteenth century up to the War of the Pacific. However, following the defeat of France in the Franco-Prussian War of 1870-71, admiration of Prussian military institutions grew. This led to the appointment in 1885 of a German, Captain Emil Körner, who had fought with distinction against France, to reorganize the Chilean military instruction system. On beginning his duties in 1886, Körner reorganized the General Bernardo O'Higgins Military Academy, inaugurated a staff school (the War Academy), and quickly consolidated the growing German influence in the Chilean Army.

When most of the army sided with the winning congressional forces (Congresionalistas) in the Civil War of 1891, Körner acted as chief of the General Staff and was largely credited with the victories of the army. In that war, the majority of the navy also supported the congressional faction. However, the new torpedo gunboats, the *Lynch* and the *Condell* (the only major naval units that supported the president), scored a spectacular victory when they attacked and sank the flagship of the congressional fleet, the ironclad *Blanco Encalada,* in Valparaíso harbor on the night of April 23.

After the Civil War, Körner, now a general, was joined by thirty-six other German instructors and was confirmed as chief of staff of the army, a position he held until 1910. German instructors organized the army into four divisions and developed the General Staff. German reforms also included establishment of the Noncommissioned Officers' School (Escuela de Suboficiales y Clases) and other military schools.

The expansion of the navy continued in the decade following the Civil War, under the added impetus of an increasingly bitter boundary dispute with Argentina. The danger of war was defused as both countries agreed to mediation by King Edward VII of Britain. The mediation resulted in the General Arbitration Treaty of 1902, under which all subsequent territorial disputes with Argentina were settled until the late 1970s.

Chile's military aviation was officially inaugurated in February 1913 with the creation of the army's Captain Ávalos Prado Military Aviation School (Escuela de Aeronáutica Militar "Capitán Ávalos Prado"—EAM) at El Bosque, outside Santiago. In 1915 aircraft participated in the annual military maneuvers for the first time. The shortage of aircraft caused by World War I severely impeded the development of Chilean military aviation. With the end of the war in 1918, a dozen British fighter monoplanes were obtained to equip the First Aviation Company. As early as 1916, naval officers had also undertaken flight training at the EAM. The end of the war in Europe permitted the formation of the Naval Aviation Service (Servicio de Aviación Naval).

In 1921 the Chilean government contracted for the services of a British naval and air mission. The EAM was also reorganized, and additional aircraft were acquired. In 1924 a German air mission arrived and was entrusted primarily with the development of civil aviation. It was precluded from overt involvement in the development of the Chilean military and naval air arms by the Treaty of Versailles.

The military and naval air services were merged as the Chilean Air Force (Fuerza Aérea de Chile—FACh) on March 21, 1930, thereby becoming the world's fourth independent military air arm. The formation of the FACh coincided with a growing economic crisis that necessitated cutbacks in the armed forces, severe curtailment of procurements, and a steady attrition of fielded matériel. Demoralized as a result of pay reductions and the political chaos then rampant in the country because of the Great Depression (see Glossary), the Chilean Navy staged a work stoppage from August to November 1931. The mutiny finally collapsed after the air force bombed the fleet. Although little physical damage was done, this event significantly affected naval morale and the subsequent development of the navy by demonstrating the vulnerability of warships to air attack.

In the early 1930s, during the Great Depression, the army was reduced from four to three divisions, and its troop strength was reduced to 12,000. An improvement in the economic situation in the mid-1930s, however, permitted an expansion back to four divisions.

Chile remained officially neutral during most of World War II, although it sold its copper at a fixed price only to the United States; however, a perfunctory declaration of war on the Axis Powers was made in February 1945. As was the case for most other neutral armed forces, the war years were lean ones for the Chilean military, which was forced to rely on its own resources for the maintenance of increasingly obsolete matériel.

Despite Germany's defeat in the two world wars, German influence remained stronger in the Chilean Armed Forces as a whole than in those of any other Latin American country. However, the navy—founded largely by British, Irish, and North American mercenaries and commanded in its formative years by Thomas Cochrane, one of the most brilliant British naval officers of the day—preferred to model itself on the British Royal Navy. In the early 1990s, the Chilean Navy continued to show a strong British influence, which had been reinforced by British training missions until the eve of World War II. The navy, not immune to the German influences at work on the army for more than half a century, achieved a synthesis of the better elements of the Prussian military and British naval traditions. Yet the navy did not lose its essentially British orientation, underlined in its repeated return to British shipyards for new matériel. As in the case of the army, the influence of United States naval missions has been largely confined to the areas of tactical and operational doctrine.

The FACh also owed its early independent existence to the activities of British training missions during the 1920s. Like the Chilean Navy, the FACh retained certain Prussian influences, deriving mostly from the military and naval air services from which it had been formed. However, the FACh probably has been the most receptive of Chile's uniformed services to United States influence. A succession of United States air-training missions began in the early 1940s.

Chile has exercised a strong formative influence on the armed forces of other Latin American countries. The armed forces of Colombia, Ecuador, Venezuela, and El Salvador have come under the tutelage of Chilean military missions, in some cases for lengthy periods. Many of the smaller republics, including Nicaragua and Paraguay, have sent officer personnel for postgraduate training in Chilean military schools. The navy also has exerted considerable influence on the Colombian and Ecuadorian navies. The Ecuadorian Navy was effectively established under Chilean guidance and has continued a long-standing arrangement whereby

Ecuadorian naval cadets have received part of their training in Chile.

Growth of United States Influence

Beginning in the 1940s, United States military missions have imparted certain tactical doctrinal concepts. However, they diluted the original German influence to a markedly lesser degree than elsewhere in the region. In 1941, following the entry of the United States into World War II, a United States air mission was established in Chile and charged with reorganizing the FACh. In 1944 significant quantities of equipment for the army and air force, including 230 aircraft procured under the Lend-Lease Agreement, the legal apparatus for military equipment transfers during World War II, began to arrive in exchange for the availability of Chilean bases to the United States. However, Chile received no matériel assistance from the United States during the war period because the Chilean Navy had refused to sell the 28,000-ton battleship *Latorre*, the six destroyers of the Serrano class, and the submarine depot ship *Araucano* to the United States Navy following the Japanese attack on Pearl Harbor. Chile received only some coastal artillery equipment for the defense of the copper-mining zone, whose products were considered vital to the Allied war effort.

Following the conclusion of World War II, and with the signing of the Inter-American Treaty of Reciprocal Assistance of 1947 (Rio Treaty—see Glossary), additional United States matériel was also acquired by the army and air force. This time, acquisitions were also made by the navy. The formation of an amphibious warfare force equipped with United States war-surplus gear stimulated expansion and reorganization of the Coast Artillery (Artillería de Costas), which had been subordinate to the navy since 1904. The name of the organization was changed from Coast Artillery to the Navy Infantry Corps (Cuerpo de Infantería de la Marina—CIM), a reflection of the newly dominant role of the CIM's marine mission. Naval aviation was revived in 1953. Initially equipped with a few light transports and helicopters, the naval air force operated from a new naval air base at El Belloto, Valparaíso. In 1958 a group of frogmen commandos, modeled after the United States Navy SEALs (sea-air-land team), was also formed.

Postwar expansion of the army also brought some organizational changes. The Magallanes military district was raised to the status of a full Military Area (*área militar*—AM); its garrison was expanded into the army's Fifth Division. The Sixth Division was later established in the region adjoining the Bolivian and Peruvian borders; it also acquired the status of an AM. In 1965 the army formed a paratroop/special forces battalion, and in 1970 it regained its own aviation arm with the establishment of the Army Aviation Command (Comando de Aviación del Ejército—CAE). The CAE was initially equipped with a few light communications and observation aircraft transferred from the air force. The Seventh Brigade, raised in the southern part of AM 4 during the tension with Argentina over the Beagle Channel in the late 1970s and early 1980s, was raised to divisional status in 1990. This brought the total number of AMs and divisions to seven.

Repression and Human Rights Violations

In the immediate aftermath of the 1973 coup, there was extensive repression, including summary executions of prisoners. During this period, the number of people who were detained so exceeded the capacities of the existing penal institutions that for a time stadiums, military grounds, and naval vessels were used as short-term prisons. Subsequently, at least five prison camps were established for political prisoners, mostly in the remote south and the far north. The intelligence service that was created after the coup, the National Intelligence Directorate (Dirección Nacional de Inteligencia—DINA), also kept secret detention centers, where torture of prisoners was a routine practice. All of these places of detention had been closed down by the time of the return to civilian government in 1990.

During the four-and-one-half years following the 1973 coup, Chile was officially in a state of siege (see Glossary under state of exception) and functioned under martial law. The military tribunals expanded their jurisdictions to include all violations (including those perpetrated by civilians) of the much more encompassing security laws enacted by the government. At the end of this period, the state of siege was replaced by a state of emergency, which restored a larger degree of authority to the civilian courts, although military tribunals continued to deal with cases involving public security.

The Aylwin government reestablished the competence of the civilian courts to deal with all matters pertaining to civilians. It therefore opened the way for these courts to reexamine cases of human rights violations that had been previously dismissed by the military tribunals as lacking in evidence or as falling under the amnesty law approved by the military government in 1978. It enacted a significant constitutional amendment that reduces the power of military courts only to that of trying offenses committed by military personnel acting in the line of duty or on military bases. Military courts can no longer try civilians.

The Aylwin government also established the National Commission on Truth and Reconciliation, or Rettig Commission, to inquire into human rights abuses during the 1973–90 period of military rule. It eventually produced a voluminous report holding the security forces responsible for 2,115 deaths, including those of 957 detainees who disappeared and an additional 164 victims of political violence.

The military's reputation for apolitical professionalism was tarnished by the 1973 military coup and subsequent repression. A national survey conducted in March 1991 by the Center for Contemporary Reality Studies (Centro de Estudios de la Realidad Contemporánea—CERC), after the release of the Rettig Commission report, showed that 75.3 percent of the population assigned "much" blame to the military for violations of human rights. Another 14.4 percent thought the armed forces had at least "some" responsibility, and only 3.8 percent thought they had "none."

An amnesty law has protected military officers involved in human rights abuses committed between 1973 and 1978. However, by 1993 as many as 600 officers, mainly from the army, had been cited in 230 cases involving rights abuses. The numerous calls from civilian courts for military officers to testify regarding cases of disappearances that occurred during the military government, the decision of an independent state office that oversees cases of corruption to investigate the circumstances under which the army paid General Pinochet's sons about US$3 million for his interest in a bankrupt firm that manufactured arms, and certain delays of the Ministry of Defense in issuing decrees demanded by the army for the promotion of its officers led to a highly visible demonstration (*boinazo*) by the army in Santiago on May 28, 1993. About sixty heavily armed officers and elite troops in full battle dress mobilized to guard a meeting of the Corps of Army Generals, themselves in battle dress, in the armed forces building across the street from La Moneda, the presidential palace. The president was on an official trip to Europe, and the minister of interior, in charge of the government as vice president, thought that the events were so critical that they could well lead to a military coup. On his return to the country, President Aylwin initiated an intensive round of consultations with General Pinochet, political parties, and human rights groups, but he reaffirmed his unwillingness to back the enactment of a blanket amnesty law, such as the one approved in Uruguay. Instead, he sponsored a law that would expand the number of special civilian court judges examining the cases of the disappeared and permit the officers summoned to testify to do so in secret without their names appearing in the press. This proposed law was, however,

General Augusto Pinochet Ugarte, chief of state, 1973–90 Courtesy Embassy of Chile, Washington, and El Mercurio, *Santiago*

President Augusto Pinochet Ugarte reviewing troops at the 19th of September Armed Forces Day parade in Santiago in 1985 Courtesy David Shelton

rejected by the National Congress (hereafter, Congress), and therefore no changes resulted from the demonstration of May 28.

Civil-Military Relations

After the *boinazo* of May 1993, the international press often referred to the Aylwin administration as a co-government, in which the military and civilians shared power equally. According to this view, Chile's democracy was emasculated, with a president unable to resist the military and with a Congress acting as a rubber-stamp body. This view seemed to be supported by the fact that President Aylwin lacked the power to appoint, promote, and dismiss officers. The president cannot appoint or fire the commanders in chief of each service. Furthermore, military officers seem to be immune to prosecution for human rights abuses. In fact, the notion of "co-government" is simplistic and fails to explain some of the limited yet significant developments under the Aylwin government. In 1993 Genaro Arriagada, a leader within the Christian Democratic Party (Partido Demócrata Cristiano—PDC), referred to a civil-military opposition to Aylwin's policies. This suggests that the confrontation is not merely one between the military and civilians. Whereas the ruling center-left coalition known as the Coalition of Parties for Democracy (Concertación de Partidos por la Democracia—CPD) held an advantage in the Chamber of Deputies (seventy to forty-nine), the military was protected by a majority in the Senate, thanks to the electoral engineering of the Pinochet regime that provided for nine designated senators. Without the designated senators, the CPD would have had a majority in the Senate (twenty-two to sixteen) from 1989 until March 1994. The designated senators, appointed by Pinochet, gave the right-wing opposition a three-seat advantage in the Senate (after 1991, only a two-seat advantage, with the death of a designated senator).

The Aylwin administration was willing to raise issues in civil-military relations even when it was clear that it would not win. In mid-1992 the Aylwin government proposed a series of constitutional reforms that would have limited the prerogatives of the military by allowing the president to appoint, promote, and remove officers. In addition, the president would have the power to appoint and remove the commanders in chief of the armed forces, although this would not apply to the current commanders. The reforms were opposed by the National Renewal (Renovación Nacional) and the Independent Democratic Union (Unión Demócrata Independiente—UDI), which suffered electoral setbacks in the June 23, 1992, municipal elections and were afraid of further losses. The army also opposed the reforms in a leaked paper published by *La*

Tercera de la Hora, a leading daily. In the prosecution of military officers for human rights abuses, an unusual coalition between the right and left derailed an initiative by the Aylwin government to complete the process.

Unable to successfully carry out major constitutional reforms in relation to the military, the Aylwin administration exercised its power in other ways. The Chilean president can veto the promotions of military officers, and in late 1993 Aylwin adroitly used the threat of the veto to influence the matter of when Pinochet would step down as army commander in chief.

The Ministry of Defense lacks the power to initiate actions, but it can selectively stall army initiatives through administrative inaction. It deliberately delayed the signing of decrees on postings and promotions, in addition to the sale of armaments—one of the major causes of the May 1993 *boinazo.*

The co-government argument also fails to take into consideration the effects of time. As Eduardo Frei Ruiz-Tagle prepared to take office as president on March 11, 1994, the political right was becoming less protective of the military and the political system it had created. The largest right-wing party, the National Renewal, showed signs that it was willing to consider amendments limiting the military's prerogatives, especially after the army was involved in telephone-tapping conversations of National Renewal members in 1992. Even the extreme right-wing UDI showed signs that it was weary of some of the features of the military-sponsored system, such as the binomial electoral system (see Glossary), which hurt the party in the December 1993 elections.

Mission and Organization of the Armed Forces
Mission

The 1980 constitution, prepared and enacted by the military government, states that the armed forces "exist for the defense of the fatherland, are essential for national security, and guarantee the institutional order of the Republic" (Article 90). The military is capable of carrying out its responsibility to deter any probable enemy or group of enemies. As in most other Latin American countries, the role as guarantor of national security and institutional order is deemed to extend to the defense of national institutions against internal as well as external threats. These have been controversial notions, but the Aylwin government was unable to clarify the role of the military or to assert the principle of presidential control over the military.

The 1980 constitution and the Organic Constitutional Law of

the Armed Forces (Law 18,948 of February 1990) that was enacted at the end of the military government expanded the military's autonomy from the president and gave it a voice over national affairs through its participation in the newly created National Security Council (Consejo de Seguridad Nacional—Cosena). Presided over by the president of the republic, Cosena includes the presidents of the Senate and the Supreme Court, the commanders in chief of the armed forces, and the director general of the Carabineros of Chile (Carabineros de Chile), a national police force with a paramilitary organization (see The Security Forces, this ch.). The constitutional reforms approved in July 1989 added the comptroller general (*contraloría general*) to Cosena, bringing the total number of voting members on it to eight. Also participating as members, but without the right to vote, are the ministers of defense; economy, development, and reconstruction; finance; foreign relations; and interior. Cosena also selects four former military commanders in chief (one from each service) as designated senators and two of seven judges of the powerful Constitutional Tribunal (Tribunal Constitucional). After the 1989 constitutional reform, Cosena was given the power to represent (*representar*) its views on any matter that it deemed appropriate to the president, Congress, or the Constitutional Tribunal; to give its consent to the president to remove a top military commander (and thus a member of Cosena); and to ask any government agency for information on security matters.

In 1992 and early 1993, the Aylwin government presented constitutional reform legislation to Congress in order to reinstitute the president's right to remove military officers, including the heads of the services, at the chief executive's discretion (only Cosena has that right). Another set of proposed reforms presented in 1993 also would have eliminated the designated senators and revamped the composition of Cosena by adding the president of the Chamber of Deputies (the lower house of Congress) to it (thereby creating a civilian majority on it), and it would have changed the Constitutional Tribunal by composing it of members chosen mainly by the president and the Senate. However, the Aylwin government lacked the congressional majorities needed to enact these reforms. As a result, these changes were not instituted (see The Autonomous Powers, ch. 4).

Command Structure

Under the 1925 and 1980 constitutions, the president is the head of the armed forces, with the ability to order the disposition of the air, sea, and land forces with the advice of the military commanders. In case of war, the president may declare war and assume the supreme military command of troops directly. The minister of defense, assisted by the subsecretaries of defense for the army, navy, and air force, is responsible for the armed forces' administrative control (see fig. 13). However, since the transition to civilian government in 1990 the president has had little actual control over the military, and the Ministry of Defense has lacked any effective control of the services and the Carabineros.

The chief executive appoints, for four-year terms, commanders in chief of the army, navy, and air force and the director general of the Carabineros "from among the five senior generals who have the qualifications required as per the respective constitutional statutes for such posts" (Article 93). However, the president may not remove any of these appointees from their posts during their four-year terms, unless there are proven criminal charges against them, in which case Cosena must approve the president's disciplinary action. The president, through the minister of defense, prepares all decrees giving officers of the armed forces and Carabineros their promotions. To remove an officer, the president must refuse the officer's promotion, after the candidate has spent a maximum number of years in the current grade. Officer assignments and qualifications are made by the military command in accordance with the law and regulations of each service. The army commander, General Pinochet, has resisted all executive branch attempts to amend the constitutional article that prevents the president of the republic from removing the armed forces' commander in chief.

Although the positions of the minister of defense and the subsecretaries remained effectively unchanged under the Aylwin government, the Subsecretariat of the Carabineros and the Subsecretariat of Investigations are subordinate to the minister of defense rather than to the minister of interior, as was formerly the case. However, new laws call for the Ministry of Interior to coordinate the actions of the security forces. The Southern Military Region (Región Militar Austral), including the two provinces of Magallanes and the Chilean Antarctic Territory (Territorio Chileno Antártico), are also directly subordinate to the Ministry of Defense.

In addition to Cosena, two other bodies, whose functions are specifically limited to the advisory level, deal with matters of national defense and security: the Politico-Strategic Advisory Council (Consejo Asesor Político-Estratégico—CAPE) and the Internal Security Advisory Council (Consejo Asesor de Seguridad Interior—CASI). CAPE consists of six military and four civilian members and is entrusted with long-range planning of the defense and external security of the state. CASI, which consists of the minister

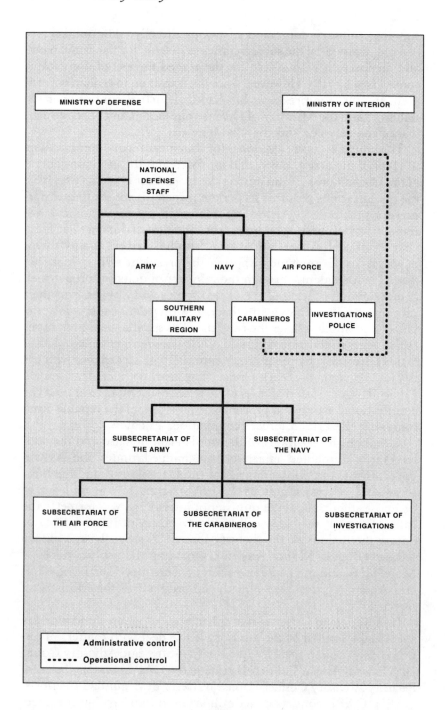

Figure 13. Organization of the Armed Forces and Security Forces, 1993

of interior and seven military members, deals with internal security planning.

A combined National Defense Staff (Estado Mayor de la Defensa Nacional—EMDN) is also largely an advisory body. The position of chief of the EMDN rotates biennially among the army, navy, and air force. Each of the armed forces also maintains its own General Staff (Estado Mayor General), which carries out standard general-staff functions with regard to its own service.

The more recently established Supreme Command of the Armed Forces (Comando Supremo de las Fuerzas Armadas—CSFA) is primarily a coordinating body, concerned with introducing the maximum possible degree of standardization in procurement policies and the elimination of duplication of effort at the administrative level. It largely superseded the Council of Commanders in Chief (Junta de Comandantes en Jefe). The latter entity, established in the late 1950s but nonoperational under the military regime, consisted of the three commanders in chief of the armed forces, together with the chief of the EMDN.

Army

The Chilean Army has long enjoyed a reputation as a creditable military force. Although it had not fought a war against a foreign enemy since the War of the Pacific, the army is still well regarded by armed forces throughout Latin America. However, it has been the most backward of the three services, having fallen behind the navy and FACh in the modernization process. Nevertheless, in 1993–94 the army was undertaking modernization measures, including the replacement of its old armored vehicles with French AMX–30 or German Leopard-1 tanks.

The army divides the country into seven military areas (AMs) headquartered in Antofagasta, Santiago, Concepción, Valdivia, Punta Arenas, Iquique, and Coihaique. AM 1 (Antofagasta) embraces the province of Antofagasta and Atacama Region. AM 2 (Santiago) includes the capital and the provinces of San Felipe de Aconcagua, Colchagua, and Valparaíso, as well as Libertador General Bernardo O'Higgins Region and Coquimbo Region. AM 3 (Concepción) encompasses the provinces of Bío-Bío, Concepción, Curicó, Linares, Malleco, Ñuble, and Talca, as well as Maule Region. AM 4 (Valdivia) contains the provinces of Cautín, Llanquihue, and Valdivia. AM 5 (Punta Arenas) shares its borders with Magallanes Province. AM 6 (Iquique) consists of Tarapacá Region. AM 7 (Coihaique) encompasses the provinces of Aisén and Chiloé.

In 1993 the army totaled about 54,000 personnel, including 27,000 conscripts. It is organized into seven divisions—one for each

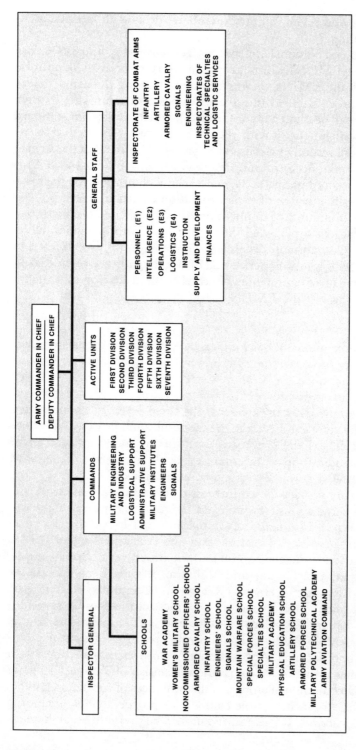

Source: Based on information from Daniel Prieto Vial, *Defensa Chile, 2000*, Santiago, 1990, 114.

Figure 14. Administrative and Operational Structure of the Army, 1993

of the seven AMs (see fig. 14). Five of the divisions are grouped under two army corps headquarters. The First Corps, based in Iquique, comprises the First Division and the Sixth Division. The Second Corps, headquartered in Punta Arenas, controls the Fourth Division, the Fifth Division and the Seventh Division. In the early 1990s, it appeared that the Second Division and the Third Division might ultimately be grouped under a third corps headquarters in keeping with the strategic doctrine developed during the 1970s, which envisaged the formation of the army into three divisions of varying sizes in time of war.

The composition of the divisions has varied considerably. The Second Division and the Third Division have between two and three times the strength of the other five. Each division essentially incorporates an artillery regiment and a regiment or battalion each of engineers, signals, and logistic troops, plus a variable number of infantry and mechanized cavalry units.

The First Division, headquartered in Antofagasta, includes a commando battalion and adds three motorized infantry regiments and one armored cavalry regiment, plus an antitank guided-weapon (ATGW) company to the basic elements. The Second Division, based in Santiago, adds three motorized regiments and five mountain infantry regiments, an armored cavalry regiment, and a motorcycle reconnaissance group to its basic support units. The Third Division, headquartered in Concepción, includes two infantry regiments, three mountain regiments, and two armored cavalry regiments. The Fourth Division, based in Valdivia, includes a commando battalion and adds two infantry regiments, one mountain regiment, and two armored cavalry regiments, plus a tank battalion to its basic support units. The Fifth Division, headquartered in Punta Arenas, also includes a commando battalion, plus two infantry regiments, two armored cavalry regiments, and an antitank battalion. The Sixth Division, based in Iquique, has a full commando regiment, plus two infantry regiments, one mountain regiment, and two armored cavalry regiments. The Seventh Division, based in Coihaique, was raised from brigade status in 1990 and comprises an infantry regiment, a reinforced mountain infantry regiment, a commando company, a horsed cavalry group, a motorcycle reconnaissance squadron, an artillery regiment, an aviation section, an engineer company, and a logistics battalion. It was scheduled to acquire a tank battalion from the Fourth Division.

Army troops include an army headquarters battalion, an aviation regiment, engineer and signals regiments, and a transport battalion. Each infantry regiment contains one to four battalions. Eight of the battalions are designated as reinforced (*reforzado*) because they have additional attached combat and logistic support elements to enable them to function as semi-independent combat teams.

The difficulty in acquiring matériel during the period of international ostracism that followed the 1973 coup resulted in an extremely varied equipment inventory likely to cause considerable logistical problems (see table 43, Appendix). In 1993 the army's aviation regiment, created in 1970, operated 111 aircraft. Each major army unit had a close defense antiaircraft artillery section.

Navy

Chile's long coast contributed to the development of a distinguished maritime tradition. The Chilean Navy accordingly has enjoyed an unusual primacy among the nation's armed forces, despite the army's formal status as the senior service. From its earliest days, the navy has operated under strong British influence.

The navy, with a strength of 25,000—including conscripts and the Navy Infantry Corps (Marines), Naval Aviation, and Coast Guard)—divides the long Chilean coastline into four naval zones, headquartered in Iquique, Punta Arenas, Talcahuano, and Valparaíso (see fig. 15). The First Naval Zone (Valparaíso) corresponds approximately to the coastal portions of AM 1 and AM 2 and contains most of the training establishments. These include the Arturo Prat Naval School, the Hydrographic Institute (Instituto Hidrográfico), the Naval War Academy (Academia de Guerra Naval), and the Supplies and Services School (Escuela de Abastecimientos y Servicios), all in Valparaíso, as well as the School of Operations (Escuela de Operaciones), the Armaments School (Escuela de Armamentos), the School of Naval Engineering (Escuela de Ingeniería Naval), and the Marine Corps School (Escuela de Infantería de Marina), all in Viña del Mar.

The Second Naval Zone (Talcahuano) corresponds approximately to the coastal portions of AM 3 and AM 4 and contains the main naval base, the Submarine School (Escuela de Submarinos), the Seamen's School (Escuela de Hombres de Mar), and the Naval Artisans' School (Escuela de Artesanos Navales), all at Talcahuano. It also includes the Chiloé Naval District (Puerto Montt). The Third Naval Zone (Punta Arenas) corresponds to the coastal portion of AM 5 and includes the Beagle Channel Naval District, which is headquartered at Puerto Williams. In the early 1990s, a new naval dockyard was under construction at Bahía Catalina. The Fourth Naval Zone (Iquique) corresponds to the former Northern Naval District, which until 1991 formed part of the First Naval Zone and covered an area corresponding to the coastal portion of AM 6.

The major operational command is the fleet, which includes four missile destroyers, two of which had been converted to helicopter carriers. The Submarine Command (La Fuerza de Submarinos) forms a separate operational command, with four submarines, a depot ship, and a subordinate group of frogmen commandos. The Transport Force (La Fuerza de Transportes) also forms an operational command. In addition, some minor patrol vessels, auxiliaries, and service craft are distributed among the naval zones and districts (see table 44, Appendix).

The 3,000 marines of the Navy Infantry Corps are organized into four detachments, based in Iquique, Viña del Mar, Talcahuano, and Punta Arenas. Each detachment consists of a reinforced infantry battalion, a commando company, a field battery, an antiaircraft battery, and logistic support units. In addition, there are some small embarked detachments, an amphibious assault battalion, and a logistics battalion, the latter two based in Valparaíso. Equipment is largely the same as that used by army infantry units. Most of the Marines' thirty LVTP–5 (landing vehicle, tracked, personnel) amphibious-landing vehicles are out of service, and their Cactus SAM systems have been disposed of. Amphibious-assault capability is confined largely to semirigid, inflatable craft.

Naval Aviation, with 750 personnel and a total of forty-five aircraft and forty-two armed helicopters, is organized into four squadrons: the General Purpose Squadron VG–1, the Helicopter Squadron VH–1, the Maritime Reconnaissance Squadron VP–1, and the Training Squadron VT–1. Naval Aviation began a modernization process in 1990 with the acquisition of new French and German helicopters and United States patrol aircraft. The principal naval air base is at Torquemada, twenty kilometers north of Viña del Mar. The Torquemada Aeronaval Base has an efficient airport of 1,750 meters and is supported by the Naval Aviation Repair Center (Centro de Reparaciones de la Aviación Naval— CRAN). There are minor bases at Punta Arenas and Puerto Williams.

The Coast Guard, a component of the General Directorate of the Maritime Territory and Merchant Marine (Dirección General del Territorio Marítimo y de la Marina Mercante), is an integral part of the navy and has 1,500 personnel. The Chilean coastline is segmented into thirteen maritime administrations (*gobernaciones marítimas*), comprising a total of forty-six port captaincies (*capitanías de puerto*). The seagoing elements of the service consist of two converted fishing vessels (employed primarily as buoy tenders), four coastal patrol craft, and ten high-speed cutters. There are also eleven inshore patrol craft, in addition to numerous small

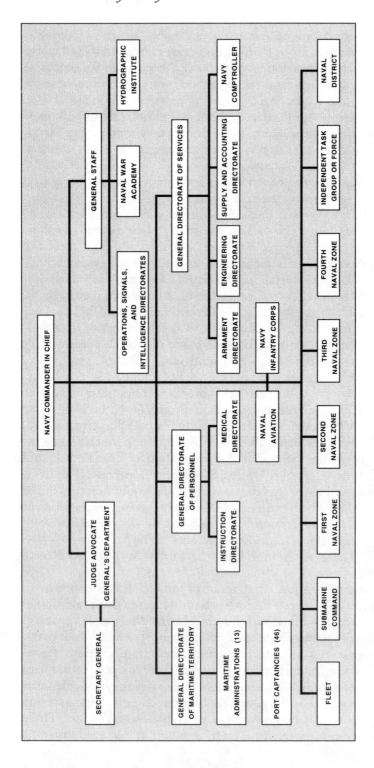

Source: Based on information from Daniel Prieto Vial, *Defensa Chile, 2000,* Santiago, 1990, 207.

Figure 15. Administrative and Operational Structure of the Navy, 1993

surface skimmers and Zodiac craft used for inshore patrol and rescue. The service also operates a floating medical-dental clinic, mainly in the coastal waters off the Isla de Chiloé, and an air-sea rescue launch, based at Easter Island.

Chile assumes responsibility for maritime search and rescue in an area extending approximately 4,000 kilometers west of its coastline. It maintains search-and-rescue coordination centers at Iquique, Valparaíso, Talcahuano, Puerto Montt, and Punta Arenas. As none of its vessels is suitable for deep-sea patrol or rescue work, the Coast Guard may call on the ships and aircraft of the navy proper, in particular its helicopters, for support when necessary. The various port captains also maintain and staff lifeboats for inshore rescue.

Air Force

The world's fourth oldest independent military air arm in existence, the Chilean Air Force (Fuerza Aérea de Chile—FACh) predated its United States counterpart by seventeen years and became the most United States-oriented of Chile's three armed forces. With a total strength of 12,800 personnel and 120 combat aircraft, the FACh is organized into the Combat Command, the Personnel Command, and the Logistical Command. FACh aircraft are deployed among four air brigades with a total of five wings (*alas*) and twelve groups (*grupos de aviación*) or squadrons. The Combat Command controls all combat units (see fig. 16). In early 1994, the FACh began studying the replacement of its fleet of thirty-two Hawker Hunter aircraft, of which only ten were operational (see table 45, Appendix).

The Air Brigade (Brigada Aérea) is the main operational formation. Each wing, an administrative unit generally concentrated at a single base wing (*ala base*), includes an Antiaircraft Artillery Group (Grupo de Artillería Antiaérea—GAA). An antiaircraft artillery regiment in La Colina serves primarily as an administrative headquarters and training school for the five dispersed antiaircraft artillery groups. The First Wing (Ala 1) and Fourth Wing (Ala 4) each also include an Electronics Communications Group (Grupo de Comunicaciones Electrónicas—GCE).

The First Air Brigade, headquartered at the Los Cóndores Air Base, Iquique, covers northern Chile from the Peruvian border to the Río Huasco in southern Atacama Region. It controls both the First Wing—based in Cerro Moreno, Antofagasta, and comprising the Seventh Group (Grupo 7) and Eighth Group (Grupo 8)—and the Fourth Wing, in Los Cóndores, which consists solely of the First Group (Grupo 1). The First Wing includes the Cerro

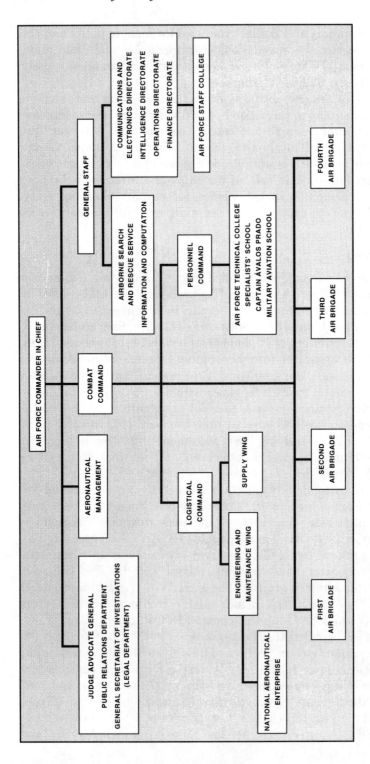

Source: Based on information from Daniel Prieto Vial, *Defensa Chile, 2000*, Santiago, 1990, 249.

Figure 16. Administrative and Operational Structure of the Air Force, 1993

Moreno Liaison Squadron (Escuadrilla de Enlace Cerro Moreno) and GCE 31. The Seventh Group and the Eighth Group are located at Cerro Moreno. The Eighth Group includes inventory that formerly equipped the now-defunct Ninth Group (Grupo 9). The Fourth Wing includes the Los Cóndores Liaison Squadron (Escuadrilla de Enlace Los Cóndores), GAA 24, and GCE 34. The First Group in Los Cóndores serves as a combined light-strike and combat-training unit. In early 1992, the First Group began replacing its Cessna A–37B Dragonflies with a mix of Enaer/CASA T–36 Halcón trainers, locally built in a joint venture between Spain's Aeronautic Constructions, S.A. (Construcciones Aeronáuticas, S.A.—CASA) and Chile's National Aeronautical Enterprise (Empresa Nacional de Aeronáutica—Enaer), and A–36 light-strike aircraft.

The Second Air Brigade, based in Los Cerrillos, Santiago, covers the region southward from the Río Huasco to the Río Bío-Bío and consists of the Second Wing (Ala 2), which combines the Second Group (Grupo 2) with the existing Tenth Group (Grupo 10) and Eleventh Group (Grupo 11). The Second Wing includes GAA 31 and GCE 32. The Second Group in Los Cerrillos is a special unit operating Canberra PR–9s in the Reconnaissance Squadron (Escuadrilla de Reconocimiento) and Beech 99As in the Electronic War Squadron (Escuadrilla de Guerra Electrónica). The Tenth Group, based at Pudahuel Airport, Santiago, is the FACh's main transport unit. The Eleventh Group, in Los Cerrillos, is primarily a refresher training unit for flying personnel previously assigned to nonflying duties. The Second Group's inventory includes the two Gates Learjet 35As of the Aerial Photogrammetric Service (Servicio Aéreo de Fotogrametría—SAF) that are based at Los Cerrillos. The Eleventh Group controls both the Piper PA–28–326 Dakotas of the FACh Specialists' School and the Extra-300s of the "Los Halcones" (The Falcons) aerobatics team.

The Third Air Brigade, headquartered at El Tepual Military Air Base, Puerto Montt, covers the region between the Río Bío-Bío and Cerro San Valentín in southern Aisén Province. It consists of the Fifth Wing (Ala 5) at Puerto Montt, which in turn consists of the recently reactivated Third Group (Grupo 3), a light-strike unit based at Temuco, and the Fifth Group (Grupo 5), a light-transport unit based in Puerto Montt. The Fifth Wing also includes GAA 25 and GCE 35.

The Fourth Air Brigade, based at the Carlos Ibáñez Military Air Base, Punta Arenas, covers the region southward from Cerro San Valentín to Cape Horn. It consists of the Third Wing (Ala 3), which is made up of the Fourth Group, the Sixth Group, and the Twelfth Group, all based at Punta Arenas. The Sixth Group (Grupo 6) is a special operations unit. This brigade also controls the Nineteenth Antarctic Exploration Group, based at Lieutenant Marsh Military Air Base on King George Island in the Chilean Antarctic Territory. The Third Wing, at Chabunco, includes GAA 23 and GCE 33.

Civic Action

All three armed forces participate in military civic-action programs, particularly in Chile's underpopulated northern and southern extremes. Engineer units of the army engage in road construction and maintenance. The navy provides lifesaving and emergency transportation services, in addition to maintaining navigational aids and regulating the activities of the Merchant Marine (Marina Mercante). The FACh provides emergency transportation and a meteorological service and plays a major role in disaster relief. It also regulates civil aviation and the administration of airports. All three of the armed forces jointly provide a comprehensive and up-to-date cartographic service covering the national territory and its coastal seas. They also provide medical services to civilians living near military bases in the less developed areas of the country.

Defense Spending

The armed forces have been entitled, under Law 18,948, to a level of funding out of the national budget at least equal to their 1989 level, which was US$640 million. From 1990 to 1993, the defense budget amounted to US$1 billion annually, according to annual *Military Balance* surveys published by London's International Institute for Strategic Studies. Personnel reportedly account for more than 70 percent of the defense budget.

According to the Copper Law enacted in 1954 by the government of Carlos Ibáñez del Campo (1952–58), the armed forces are entitled by law to 10 percent of the total copper earnings of the state-run Copper Corporation (Corporación del Cobre—Codelco). The purpose of this legislation is to provide the armed forces with stable funding and hard currency for major purchases abroad. In 1987 the military government changed the law, applying the 10 percent figure to all Codelco export earnings, including the sale of gold and molybdenum (the sale of which is insignificant compared with the copper sales). Between 1989 and 1993, Codelco provided more than US$1.2 billion to the armed forces, as follows: US$313 million in 1989, US$287 million in 1990, US$223 million in 1991, US$204 million in 1992, and US$197 million in 1993.

These figures correspond to approximately 20 percent to 30 percent of the military budget.

Under the Codelco subsidy, the armed forces are guaranteed a minimum of US$189 million annually, plus accumulated inflation (with 1987 as the base year). In 1993 the guaranteed minimum was US$210 million, but 10 percent of all Codelco sales totaled only US$197 million, or US$13 million short of the guaranteed minimum. The 1993 shortfall in Codelco revenues resulted from the drastic fall in the price of copper. Codelco managers argued that the public treasury was responsible for making up the shortfall, but there was no mechanism for such a measure.

The 1993 shortfall in Codelco revenues intensified the debate between those supporting the 1954 law (the armed forces and the political right) and those opposed to such an arrangement (Codelco, the Ministry of Mining, and many within the center-left CPD governing coalition). Those opposed to the Codelco subsidy to the armed forces argued that it was an unacceptable burden for Codelco, making it unable to compete in the world market. Total profits for Codelco in 1992 were US$920 million; in 1993 they were estimated at US$480 million. This means that 22 percent of all Codelco profit earnings in 1992 went to the armed forces and that approximately 41 percent went in 1993.

Those arguing for an end to the Codelco subsidy maintain that the armed forces should be funded through the general budget. In addition, there has been increasing pressure to privatize Codelco altogether, a measure that would probably include the abolition of the 10 percent subsidy. Those arguing against the Codelco subsidies for the armed forces have been careful to state that they are not trying to cut the resources of the armed forces but rather are giving them a more legitimate source.

The armed forces oppose an end to their Codelco funds, fearing that their budget would be politicized and reduced. Furthermore, virtually all of the resources that the armed forces receive from Codelco are already committed beyond the year 2000, mostly through the purchase of armaments on credit. Ironically, the privatization of state firms that was initiated by the military government could lead to the end of the Codelco revenues for the armed forces.

Principal beneficiaries of the increased spending in the early 1990s were the navy and air force. Their projected acquisitions include thirty British Harrier and twelve Sea-Harrier VTOL (vertical take-off and landing) aircraft, which the Chileans hope to have in service by 1997. Up to 1992, however, interservice rivalries appeared to have permitted the civilian administration, which favored cuts in military purchases, to take minimal action on this procurement.

Spending on the army, navy, and air force accounted for approximately 41 percent, 33 percent, and 21 percent, respectively, of total defense expenditures; the remaining 5 percent was accounted for by costs under the general heading of national defense.

Accusations of corruption have been made against several leading figures of the military government and certain members of their families. As a result of these problems, public attitudes toward the armed forces have been adversely affected. An October 1991 survey by CERC shows that 36.1 percent of respondents picked military spending as a target for budget cuts. However, the military government received an average score for its overall performance. The CERC's survey of March 1991 shows that 57.9 percent of respondents thought the military's performance was "neither good nor bad"; 29 percent thought it was "bad"; and 11.2 percent thought it was "good."

Manpower and Training

Recruitment and Conditions of Service

Historically, the profession of military science has been regarded as an honorable one in Chile. The army and to an even greater extent the air force have traditionally drawn their officer corps from among the middle classes, with a large portion coming from military families. Social elitism has been a traditional characteristic only of the officer corps of the navy. In 1900 military service became compulsory for all fit male citizens between the ages of eighteen and forty-five. Traditionally, only a small proportion of those eligible would actually have been drafted for one year of training in the army or air force or two years in the navy. The overwhelming majority of the approximately 30,000 conscripts selected annually served in the army. (Of the 121,000 who registered in 1993, only 29,400 were drafted.) Those not specifically exempted from service have had their names inscribed in a military register. Traditional government policy also dictates that 10 percent of the annual conscript intake should consist of illiterate citizens, who are taught to read and write during their period of military service. On completion of their period of training, conscripts are required to serve in the Active Reserve for a period of twelve years and then in the Second Reserve until the age of forty-five. However, apart from the skeleton cadres of the regular armed forces, no effective reserve organization appears to exist.

The three armed forces all have female members, who serve voluntarily. They carry out subsidiary support functions, such as nursing and administrative work.

Military personnel are well fed and well housed. The three armed forces have an education program aimed at providing enlisted personnel with useful skills for their return to civilian life. The navy and air force have relatively high educational requirements, even for compulsory enlistment, and impart technical skills to their conscripts.

Training

Each of the armed forces maintains its own complex of training establishments, which are of uniformly high quality. These centers attract large numbers of students, not only from Latin America but also from countries such as the United States, Germany, Spain, Israel, and Taiwan. In addition to the complex of training establishments maintained by each of the individual armed forces, the Ministry of Defense operates the National Defense Academy (Academia de Defensa Nacional), a triservice, university-level education establishment. Successful completion of its courses is a prerequisite to promotion to senior rank in all three services.

The army's Military Academy, the War Academy (also known as the War College, or Escuela Superior de Guerra—ESG), the Army Aviation Command (Comando de Aviación de Ejército), and the Noncommissioned Officers' School are all located in Santiago. Officer candidates must complete the five-year course of the Military Academy successfully before being commissioned and must complete an additional course at the War Academy to qualify for promotion to field rank or appointment to the General Staff. The army has a comprehensive range of specialist schools, including the Infantry School (Regimiento Escuela de Infantería) in San Bernardo (near Santiago), the Mountain Warfare School (Regimiento Escuela de Montaña) in Río Blanco (near Los Andes), the Special Forces School (Regimiento Escuela de Fuerzas Especiales y Paracaidistas) in Peldehue, the Armored Cavalry School (Regimiento Escuela de Caballería Blindada) in Quillota, a subsidiary Armored Forces School (Escuela de Fuerzas Blindadas) in Antofagasta, the Artillery School (Regimiento Escuela de Artillería) in Linares, the Engineers' School (Regimiento Escuela de Ingenieros) in Tejas Verdes, and the Signals School (Regimiento Escuela de Telecomunicaciones) in Santiago. There are also the Military Polytechnical Academy (Academia Politécnica Militar) in Santiago, the Women's Military School (Escuela Militar Femenina) in Cajón de Maipo, and the Physical Education School (Escuela de Educación Física) in Santiago.

The navy's Arturo Prat Naval School provides a five-year course for naval officer cadets. Officers must complete postgraduate courses at the Naval War Academy for promotion to flag rank or appointment to the naval General Staff. Selected petty officers may qualify for commissioned rank by completing a two-year course at the Arturo Prat Naval School but are ineligible for promotion beyond the rank of captain. Noncommissioned personnel receive their training at the navy's comprehensive range of specialist schools located in Viña del Mar or Talcahuano. The creation in Valparaíso of the Pilot Luis Pardo Villalón Antarctic Navigation School (Escuela de Navegación Antártica "Piloto Luis Pardo Villalón") was announced in August 1991 by the director of the General Directorate of the Maritime Territory and Merchant Marine.

The air force's General Staff controls the Air Force Staff College (Academia de Guerra Aérea). The FACh Personnel Command controls the other schools: the Air Force Technical College (Academia Politécnica Aérea); the Specialists' School (Escuela de Especialidades), which is equipped with Piper Dakotas; and the Captain Ávalos Prado Aviation School (Escuela de Aviación "Capitán Ávalos"). The latter offers a basic three-year course to officer cadets, followed by two years of specialized training before commissioning. It is equipped with the Enaer/CASA T-36 Halcón and the Enaer T-35 Pillán. The Logistical Command controls the non-flying Supply Wing and the Engineering and Maintenance Wing, headquartered at El Bosque.

Uniforms, Ranks, and Insignia

Army

The uniforms and insignia of the three services reflect mainly British and German influence but also United States influence. The German influence is predominant in the army's uniforms (which are gray) and insignia, whereas the navy's uniforms (which are blue) and insignia and the air force's uniforms (which are blue-gray) and insignia resemble those of their British and United States counterparts (see fig. 17; fig. 18). Noncommissioned officers' rank insignia consist of combinations of chevrons, worn point downward as in the British Army.

The army's service and dress uniforms closely resemble those of the old German Imperial Army. The uniform of the cadet corps of the Military Academy still features a *pickelhaube* (tall, plumed headgear) of the type worn by the Kaiser's Imperial Guard. The gray service uniform, with its stand-and-fall collar buttoned to the neck, worn with a plastic replica of the German "coal-scuttle" helmet, also evokes memories of the Reichsheer (a German paramilitary force).

Army rank insignia that are based on a series of gold or silver stars on shoulder straps or shoulder plaits are used for ranks up to and including that of *brigadier,* an unusual transitory grade between that of colonel and *brigadier general.* According to the Santiago newspaper *Hoy,* the rank of *brigadier* did not exist before 1981, when the reformulation of Chile's army ranks went into effect. Under the new military rank structure, *brigadier* is not a rank but a category that is assigned to senior colonels, including those slated for promotion to general. Although a *brigadier* has the rank of *coronel* and wears the three stars of a *coronel* on the shoulder boards, a *brigadier* wears a general's national coat of arms and laurel leaves on the collar. When the rank of *brigadier* was created, the names given to the generals were also changed, to include *brigadier general* (major general) and *mayor general* (lieutenant general). General officers wear rank insignia consisting of two to five gold or silver stars on shoulder boards similar to those used by general officers of the United States Army. A president may designate officers who remain on duty beyond the compulsory thirty-eight years with the quasi-rank category of lieutenant general. The rank of *capitán general* (captain general), the armed forces' highest rank (held by General Pinochet), is indicated by five stars.

In summer a white tunic is substituted for the gray one. Combat uniforms in olive-green, khaki-drab, or camouflage pattern, worn with the World War II-style United States M–1942 steel helmet, are virtually indistinguishable from those worn until the early 1980s by the United States Army. Mountain troops wear white coveralls when operating in the snow.

Navy

Naval officers' uniforms are virtually indistinguishable from their British equivalents but, like rank insignia, are also similar to those used by the United States Navy. However, officers' rank insignia, worn on the jacket cuff with the dark-blue winter service uniform and on shoulder boards with all other dress orders, follow United States practice, with a five-pointed star above various combinations of horizontal stripes. Like their army counterparts, enlisted personnel wear rank insignia based on chevrons, worn point downward. Enlisted personnel wear both a stiff white-topped dress cap, somewhat similar to that of the British Royal Navy although with a much thinner ribbon, and a working cap identical to the United States sailor's white hat. Marine enlisted personnel wear dress uniforms reminiscent of those of the United States Marine Corps (USMC), but with a stand-and-fall collar to the tunic. Marine officers wear the standard naval uniform and hold naval ranks.

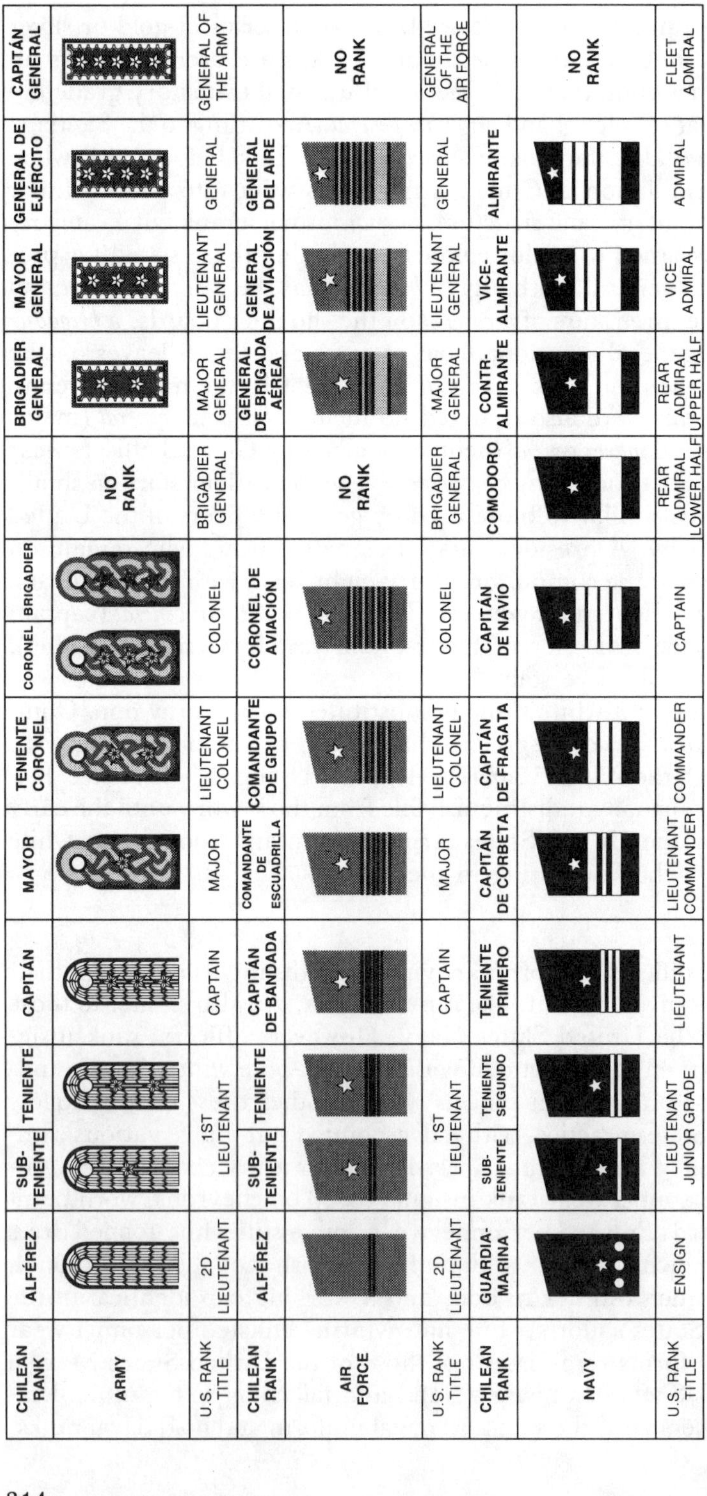

Figure 17. Officer Ranks and Insignia, 1993

	ALFÉREZ	SUB-TENIENTE	TENIENTE	CAPITÁN	MAYOR	TENIENTE CORONEL	CORONEL	BRIGADIER		BRIGADIER GENERAL	MAYOR GENERAL	GENERAL DE EJÉRCITO	CAPITÁN GENERAL
ARMY — CHILEAN RANK	ALFÉREZ	SUB-TENIENTE	TENIENTE	CAPITÁN	MAYOR	TENIENTE CORONEL	CORONEL	BRIGADIER		BRIGADIER GENERAL	MAYOR GENERAL	GENERAL DE EJÉRCITO	CAPITÁN GENERAL
ARMY — U.S. RANK TITLE	2D LIEUTENANT	1ST LIEUTENANT		CAPTAIN	MAJOR	LIEUTENANT COLONEL	COLONEL	BRIGADIER GENERAL	NO RANK	MAJOR GENERAL	LIEUTENANT GENERAL	GENERAL	GENERAL OF THE ARMY
AIR FORCE — CHILEAN RANK	ALFÉREZ	SUB-TENIENTE	TENIENTE	CAPITÁN DE BANDADA	COMANDANTE DE ESCUADRILLA	COMANDANTE DE GRUPO	CORONEL DE AVIACIÓN	NO RANK	NO RANK	GENERAL DE BRIGADA AÉREA	GENERAL DE AVIACIÓN	GENERAL DEL AIRE	NO RANK
AIR FORCE — U.S. RANK TITLE	2D LIEUTENANT	1ST LIEUTENANT		CAPTAIN	MAJOR	LIEUTENANT COLONEL	COLONEL	BRIGADIER GENERAL	NO RANK	MAJOR GENERAL	LIEUTENANT GENERAL	GENERAL	GENERAL OF THE AIR FORCE
NAVY — CHILEAN RANK	GUARDIA-MARINA	TENIENTE SEGUNDO		TENIENTE PRIMERO	CAPITÁN DE CORBETA	CAPITÁN DE FRAGATA	CAPITÁN DE NAVÍO		COMODORO	CONTR-ALMIRANTE	VICE-ALMIRANTE	ALMIRANTE	NO RANK
NAVY — U.S. RANK TITLE	ENSIGN	LIEUTENANT JUNIOR GRADE		LIEUTENANT	LIEUTENANT COMMANDER	COMMANDER	CAPTAIN		REAR ADMIRAL LOWER HALF	REAR ADMIRAL UPPER HALF	VICE ADMIRAL	ADMIRAL	FLEET ADMIRAL

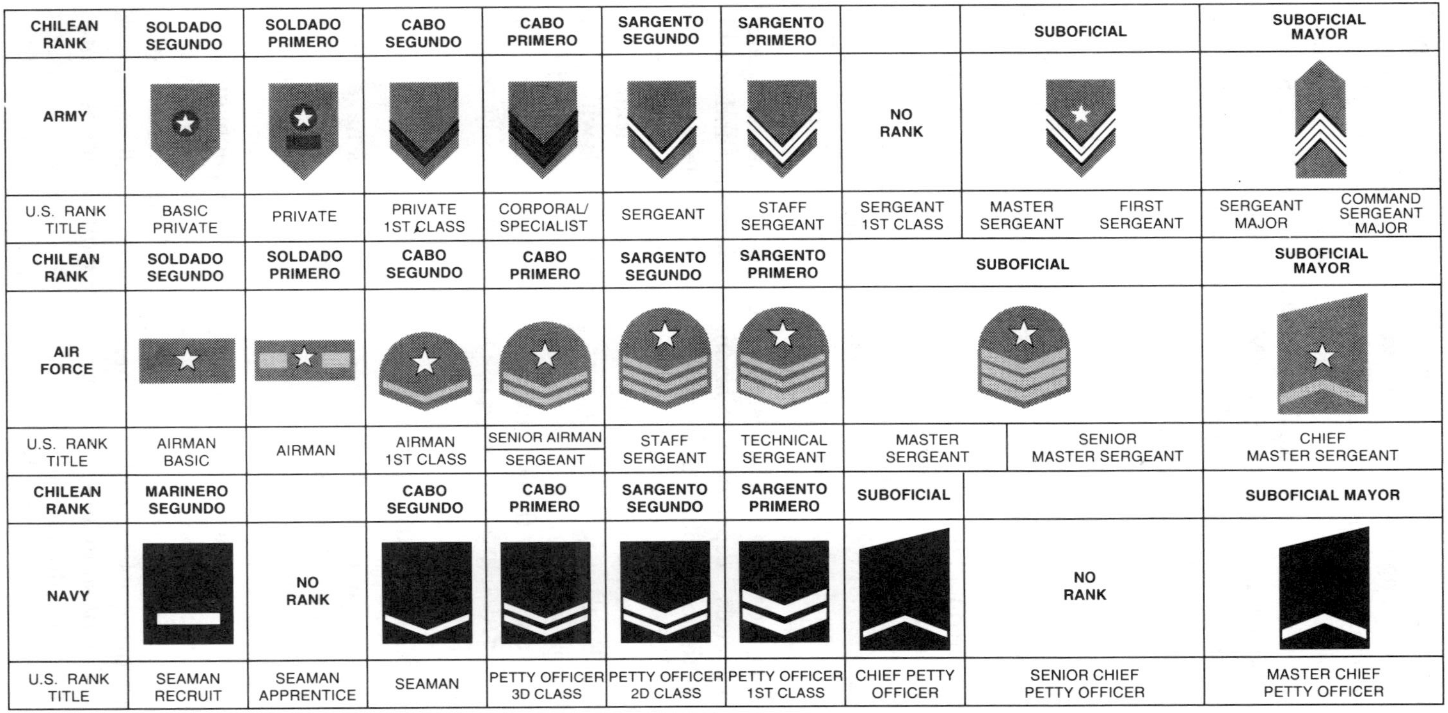

	SOLDADO SEGUNDO	SOLDADO PRIMERO	CABO SEGUNDO	CABO PRIMERO	SARGENTO SEGUNDO	SARGENTO PRIMERO	NO RANK	SUBOFICIAL	SUBOFICIAL MAYOR
CHILEAN RANK — ARMY	SOLDADO SEGUNDO	SOLDADO PRIMERO	CABO SEGUNDO	CABO PRIMERO	SARGENTO SEGUNDO	SARGENTO PRIMERO	NO RANK	SUBOFICIAL	SUBOFICIAL MAYOR
U.S. RANK TITLE	BASIC PRIVATE	PRIVATE	PRIVATE 1ST CLASS	CORPORAL/ SPECIALIST	SERGEANT	STAFF SERGEANT	SERGEANT 1ST CLASS	MASTER SERGEANT / FIRST SERGEANT	SERGEANT MAJOR / COMMAND SERGEANT MAJOR
CHILEAN RANK — AIR FORCE	SOLDADO SEGUNDO	SOLDADO PRIMERO	CABO SEGUNDO	CABO PRIMERO	SARGENTO SEGUNDO	SARGENTO PRIMERO	SUBOFICIAL	SUBOFICIAL	SUBOFICIAL MAYOR
U.S. RANK TITLE	AIRMAN BASIC	AIRMAN	AIRMAN 1ST CLASS	SENIOR AIRMAN SERGEANT	STAFF SERGEANT	TECHNICAL SERGEANT	MASTER SERGEANT	SENIOR MASTER SERGEANT	CHIEF MASTER SERGEANT
CHILEAN RANK — NAVY	MARINERO SEGUNDO	NO RANK	CABO SEGUNDO	CABO PRIMERO	SARGENTO SEGUNDO	SARGENTO PRIMERO	SUBOFICIAL	NO RANK	SUBOFICIAL MAYOR
U.S. RANK TITLE	SEAMAN RECRUIT	SEAMAN APPRENTICE	SEAMAN	PETTY OFFICER 3D CLASS	PETTY OFFICER 2D CLASS	PETTY OFFICER 1ST CLASS	CHIEF PETTY OFFICER	SENIOR CHIEF PETTY OFFICER	MASTER CHIEF PETTY OFFICER

Figure 18. Enlisted Ranks and Insignia, 1993

315

All ranks have a range of blue and white service uniforms, plus a slate-gray working uniform. A United States-style khaki-drab uniform is sometimes worn with the ordinary naval cap; the Marines also have olive-green, khaki-drab, and camouflage combat uniforms, almost indistinguishable from those of the USMC. The standard steel helmet is the United States M–1942 pattern. Naval band members wear the Germanic bird's-nest shoulder ornament on standard blue uniforms.

Air Force

FACh uniforms closely resemble those of the United States Air Force, although they are of a slightly darker shade of blue-gray. The use of lapel ornaments to supplement rank insignia imparts a Germanic flavor. Rank insignia, worn in gold on dress uniforms and light blue on all others, resemble those of the navy. However, the FACh emphasizes its status as the world's fourth oldest independent military air arm with its own peculiar rank designations. A captain is referred to as *capitán de bandada,* a major as *comandante de escuadrilla,* and a lieutenant colonel as *comandante de grupo.* The terms *coronel de aviación, general de brigada aérea, general de aviación,* and *general del aire* are used for colonels, major generals, lieutenant generals, and generals, respectively. Various permutations and combinations of the basic blue uniform are worn. Shirtsleeve order is widely used, even for semiformal occasions, in summer and other periods of hot weather. Air crew generally wear black leather flying jackets. Rank insignia are worn on shoulder boards with greatcoat, flying jacket, and shirtsleeve orders. Noncommissioned rank insignia closely follow those of the navy, although army terminology is used. FACh ground troops use the United States Fritz Kevlar ballistic helmet.

Foreign Sources of Matériel

Traditional Chilean military procurement policies have faithfully mirrored the influences at work on the individual armed forces. Thus, the army has showed a distinct preference for weapons of German design, if not necessarily German manufacture. For example, the German-designed French Hotchkiss machine gun was standard in the 1930s. For similar reasons, the navy largely confined its patronage for new construction to British yards. The FACh, again mirroring its formative influences, was initially equipped largely with British matériel. However, large quantities of United States-built aircraft, together with the products of the renascent German aircraft industry, began to appear in the mid-1930s.

During World War II, large amounts of United States matériel began to reach the army and FACh, but not the navy, as military aid. All three of the armed forces continued to receive increased quantities of United States equipment after the Rio Treaty of 1947. For almost two decades, United States war surplus dominated the inventories of the Chilean Armed Forces, as it did generally throughout the region. Between 1950 and 1977, the value of United States military assistance totaled US$97.4 million. Quantities of progressively obsolescent matériel of pre-World War II manufacture and non-United States origins were still noted in service in the early 1970s.

In the 1960s, as elsewhere in Latin America, when the United States declined to supply modern matériel because of restrictions on exports of high technology, other markets were explored. The army acquired the Swiss SG–510 rifle, which became standard, and quantities of French and Swiss armored fighting vehicles, together with Italian artillery pieces. The navy and FACh continued to favor British equipment.

With the widespread boycott of the military regime following the 1973 overthrow of Salvador Allende, Chile found many traditional sources of equipment closed. United States arms exports to Chile were formally terminated in 1976 after the adoption of the Kennedy Amendment (see Glossary) in 1974. Procurement was pursued on an ad hoc basis, and matériel was acquired from wherever available. This inevitably resulted in an increasingly heterogeneous and unbalanced equipment inventory. During this period, the navy and FACh encountered particular difficulties in the acquisition of replacements and spares. Much ingenuity was applied to prolonging the life of otherwise obsolete or worn-out matériel, and local industrial potential was expanded dramatically.

Chile managed to acquire United States arms and technology through third parties even while the United States prohibition of arms sales was in effect. In addition to spurring the Chileans to develop their own arms industry, the embargo prompted Chile to develop closer ties with arms-producing countries such as Brazil, France, Germany, Britain, and Israel. With the return of democracy in 1990, the Aylwin government assured the United States that it would continue to prosecute those responsible for the assassination of Chilean diplomat Orlando Letelier, an opponent of the military government, and his assistant, United States citizen Ronnie Moffit, in Washington in 1976. As a result of these assurances, the embargo was lifted, and United States arms sales to Chile resumed.

The return to civilian government in 1990 resolved most of the procurement problems experienced during the period of military rule (1973–90). Nevertheless, future procurements probably will continue to be broadly based. The army's main priorities are to standardize its equipment inventory and replace obsolescent weapons that are incapable of further upgrading, specifically its battle tanks and some of its artillery equipment. Missile air defense used to be the exclusive responsibility of the FACh, with its Blowpipe and Mistral and its new French Mygale vehicle-mounted antiaircraft system. However, in 1993 the army launched its own international competition program for the acquisition of a new surface-to-air missile (SAM) system. According to *Military Technology* [Bonn], the army was interested in two types of vehicle-mounted systems—existing SAM systems or procurement only of missile launchers and munitions. The latter option would entail mounting the new systems on Chilean-made Piranha 6x6 or 8x8 armored personnel carriers (APCs). The new missile system will be integrated with the army's newly adopted, Chilean-developed Lince C^2 air defense system. In May 1992, the FACh, for its part, tested its new French Mygale antiaircraft system, which has a computerized radar that seeks the target and is linked to four vehicles that carry Mistral ground-to-air missile launchers to protect air bases against supersonic aircraft attacks. Chile is the first and reportedly the only country in the region to own this system.

The navy requires at least one more Leander-class frigate, at least two more modern Oberon-class submarines, and an additional replenishment tanker. The retirement of the cruiser *O'Higgins* also left the fleet without a major command vessel. Various possibilities, including the acquisition of the British destroyer leader *Bristol,* were being considered. The *Bristol* attempt failed, however, when the British Royal Navy demanded that its Sea Dart system be removed prior to sale. The navy also hoped to establish a combat air unit equipped with Sea Harriers, although this objective was unlikely to be achieved in the foreseeable future.

The FACh requires some additional heavy-lift transport aircraft and replacements for its diminishing number of aging Hunter fighter-bombers. Possible replacements include the British Hawk 200, the United States F–16, and even the former Soviet Union's MiG-29. The FACh commander in chief stated publicly in 1992 that no immediate Hunter replacement was contemplated and that future procurements would focus on the acquisition of smaller numbers of higher-performance combat aircraft. For example, the FACh purchased ten A–37 light attack aircraft that year through an agreement with the United States.

Between sixteen and twenty Chilean Northrop F–5E Tiger III fighter aircraft were upgraded with Israeli technology by the state-owned Israeli Aircraft Industries (IAI) in Tel Aviv in 1988–93. Chile had purchased these aircraft from the United States in 1976, but they were held for many years under the regulations of a 1976 addendum to the Kennedy Amendment. The jets' avionics were greatly improved, and their electronic and navigation equipment were fully replaced by IAI. The Israeli company was also upgrading Mirage 50 aircraft purchased by Chile from France many years earlier to the Mirage 500C/Pantera standard, a configuration resembling the IAI's Kfir. In addition, the Israelis in 1993 were converting a FACh Boeing 707 to carry the Phalcon airborne early warning system developed by an Israeli electronics company.

The Defense Industry

Chile has for many years produced its own small arms, ammunition, and explosives, but it did not have a real defense industry until the 1970s. The almost universal boycott after the armed forces overthrew the Allende administration in 1973, and in particular the 1974 Kennedy Amendment, which deprived Chile of maintenance support for its large inventory of United States-manufactured defense equipment, threw the Chileans back on their own resources. At the time, war with Argentina over the Beagle Channel seemed likely, and local industrial potential was expanding dramatically. Thus, Chile became a major producer of defense equipment, the third largest in Latin America after Brazil and Argentina. In addition to small arms and ammunition, Chile manufactured infantry-support weapons, both armored and soft-skinned vehicles, artillery pieces, ballistic rocket systems, antiaircraft artillery weapons, naval vessels, military aircraft, aerial bombs and rockets, and radar and electronic warfare equipment. Nevertheless, according to defense analyst Daniel Prieto Vial, by 1991 Chile supplied no more than 3 percent of its own defense needs and purchased the remaining 97 percent elsewhere.

As Chile became a successful exporter, the biennial International Air and Space Fair (Feria Internacional del Aire y del Espacio—FIDAE) became its principal marketing event. First held in March 1980 as a modest flying display and exhibition of air defense products to celebrate the fiftieth anniversary of the FACh's formation, what was then called the International Air Fair (Feria Internacional del Aire—FIDA) was an unexpected success. It was decided to repeat what was originally conceived of as a one-time event every second year. In 1990 the name was changed to FIDAE to reflect the aerospace dimension. FIDAE continued to grow steadily both in size and in international importance and by 1992 was the major forum for the display of military equipment in the

Southern Hemisphere, attracting more than 300 exhibitors from twenty-seven countries to Los Cerrillos Air Base. These included not only other arms-producing nations in the developing world but also the major manufacturers of defense equipment in the leading industrialized nations.

Army Ordnance

Chile's major producer of ground-defense matériel, the Army Factories and Yards (Fábricas y Maestranzas del Ejército—Famae), which is subordinate to the army's Military Industry and Engineering Command (Comando de Industria Militar e Ingeniería—CIMI), had been operating for 182 years in 1994. Famae employs about 3,000 people in factories throughout the country and is in charge of maintaining and renewing the army's equipment. Since the 1960s, Famae has assembled both the Belgian FN FAL rifle and its close-support version, the FN FAP, locally known as the FN FALO. More recently, Famae has also produced under license the Swiss SG–542 assault rifle, which was replacing the SG–510 in service with the army. In addition, Famae is producing both a .32-caliber revolver and a 9mm submachine gun, together with 60mm, 81mm, and 120mm mortars, based on Brandt prototypes. An agreement with Britain's Royal Ordnance, signed in December 1989, provides for the joint development of the Rayo 160mm multiple-rocket launcher system, beginning in 1994. The Rayo was tested successfully in October 1991.

Famae produces ammunition for all these weapons, as well as hand grenades, Bangalore torpedoes, two types of antipersonnel mines, and an antitank mine, together with ammunition for the Oto Melara Model 56 105mm howitzer. Two types of antipersonnel bombs, two types of high-explosive aerial bombs, and one type of cluster bomb also have been developed, in conjunction with the FACh. These have been exported to Ecuador and Paraguay. Exports to Iran, Pakistan, and elsewhere also have been rumored. The revelation of contraband arms sales to Croatia via Hungary at the end of 1991 caused a minor political scandal early in 1992.

A new development beginning in early 1992 was the production of armored vehicles. Famae acquired a license to assemble the Swiss Mowag Piranha 8x8 APC. Prototype variations mounting either the Cockerill 90mm or the Israeli HVMS 60mm high-velocity gun also have been produced. In 1992 Famae negotiated for the local manufacture of the Cadillac-Gage Stingray light tank. In early 1993, General Pinochet headed an official delegation that visited China. During the visit, an important agreement on military cooperation and coproduction of military equipment was

A freighter navigating Chile's scenic coastal waters
Courtesy Embassy of Chile, Washington

signed between Famae and China's Northern Industrial Corporation (Norinco).

Naval Equipment

Naval Docks and Yards (Astilleros y Maestranzas de la Armada—Asmar) was established in 1895, with facilities at Talcahuano and Valparaíso. Asmar was reorganized on a commercial basis in 1960. In early 1992, Asmar Talcahuano accounted for about 80 percent of the activities of the corporation, despite the recent upgrading of repair facilities at Valparaíso and the inauguration of smaller ship repair maintenance facilities at Punta Arenas (the latter operated in collaboration with Sandok Austral of South Africa). With more than 4,500 employees, Asmar Talcahuano has become the largest and most modern shipyard on the Pacific Coast south of California. It has carried out repair and maintenance work for three foreign navies, in addition to its work for the Chilean Navy and Merchant Marine. Asmar has also performed contract work on units of the merchant fleets of such countries as Canada and Denmark.

Over the years, Asmar has built a number of minor vessels for the Chilean Navy and Coast Guard. Extensive modifications were also made to the four County-class missile destroyers purchased from Britain in the early 1980s. A combination of economic difficulties and the ready availability of suitable craft on the secondhand market had, however, prevented the construction of either a projected series of fifty-four-meter patrol craft, for which a license was obtained from Fairey Brooke Marine of Britain in 1988, or the P–400-type fast attack craft, for which a license agreement was negotiated with Chantiers de Normandie in the same year. A project to build at least four submarines was announced in 1990 but had not progressed any further. However, Asmar displayed a human-torpedo-type midget submarine, developed in association with Cosmos of Livorno, Italy, at FIDAE '92.

In early 1992, Asmar's Talcahuano facility was building four patrol boats for the navy, the first of which was scheduled to be in service in 1993. Asmar was also preparing a program for four helicopter-equipped offshore patrol vessels to police Chile's 200-nautical-mile exclusive economic zone.

In addition to its own independent electronics division, Military Manufacturers (Fabricaciones Militares—Fabmil), founded in 1982, Asmar has also established (in 1983) an electronics manufacturing and development subsidiary, Defense Systems (Sistemas Defensas—Sisdef), located in Viña del Mar. This firm, a joint venture with Britain's Feranti International, has developed a multipurpose radar system that is equally adaptable to use aboard ship or on land. Asmar itself has produced a naval gunnery control radar, which was fitted aboard the Almirante-class destroyers and other vessels of the Chilean Navy, a mortar-locating radar for the army, and a land-based air early warning radar. A newer shipyard, founded in 1974 with its facilities located at the mouth of the Río Valdivia in southern Chile, is Naval Shipyards and Services (Astilleros y Servicios Navales—Asenav).

Aircraft Equipment

In the past, several types of light aircraft were developed in Chile by the FACh-controlled National Aircraft Factory (Fábrica Nacional de Aeronaves—FNA), although none of these entered production. Starting in 1981, however, the FACh's Engineering and Maintenance Wing commenced the development of a variant of the Piper 236 Dakota light aircraft as a replacement for the Beech T–34.

The result was the T-35 Pillán two-seater primary trainer. In 1984 Enaer, the National Aeronautical Enterprise, was set up in Santiago as a state enterprise with autonomous management to handle this project. Although Enaer's main contracts have been with the FACh, by late 1991 it had sold forty Pillán training aircraft to the Spanish Air Force, fifteen to the Paraguayan Air Force, ten to the Panamanian National Air Service, and sixty to the FACh. (Those for the Spanish Air Force were built under license in Spain under the name Tamiz.) The FACh proposed ultimately to build up to 200 Pilláns, mainly in the turboprop version unveiled in 1986 and originally designated the Aucan.

In a joint venture with Spain, Enaer developed a version of the Spanish CASA 101 Aviojet fighter, called the T-36 Halcón (Falcon), to replace the Cessna T-37 in the advanced trainer/light-strike role. Fifty-six of these aircraft were in service with the FACh. A radar-equipped maritime strike version, designated the A-36M and armed with the British Aerospace Sea Eagle air-to-surface missile, was also developed; it was flown in prototype form in 1992. In 1993 Enaer and the Brazilian Aeronautics Company (Embraer) signed an agreement, as partners, to share the risks of the EMB-145 program, which will produce a minimum of 400 of these jets.

Employing about 2,000 people, Enaer has the capability to produce one aircraft per week, although the plant was not working to full capacity in early 1992. The engines for the Pillán and the Halcón are imported from the United States and Spain, respectively. The airframes and most other parts, including such sophisticated items as ejection seats, are produced in Chile. Enaer also manufactures parts for the CASA 235 and the BAe 146.

Enaer's Electronics Division has developed and produced the Caiquen I and II early warning radars, which are in full production. Enaer has also developed the Itata airborne electronic intelligence-gathering system, the Medusa radio interception and jamming system, and the Eclipse chaff/infrared decoy launcher.

Cardoen Industries

Despite the spectacular expansion of the public sector of the Chilean defense industry since the mid-1970s, the privately owned Cardoen Industries (Industrias Cardoen), owned by Carlos Cardoen Cornejo, is the most successful Chilean defense manufacturer in the export field. In less than eight years, this firm developed from a modest operation manufacturing demolition charges for the mining industry into a diversified industrial empire. In the early 1990s, it employed more than 800 persons in six separate factory complexes producing a variety of defense equipment, together with nondefense-related products, and had subsidiaries in Ecuador, Italy, Spain, and Greece. Under a 1989 agreement with the Guatemalan government, Cardoen Industries agreed to establish a plant for the manufacture of explosives, grenades, and mines in Guatemala.

In 1979 Cardoen Industries took over the project of rebuilding the Chilean Army's World War II-vintage M–3A1 half-track APCs, which Famae had commenced five years earlier but had been forced to drop for lack of funds. This venture resulted in the development of an entirely new vehicle, the BMS–1 Alacrán, a number of which were acquired by the Chilean Army.

Building on the experience gained in the Alacrán project, the Cardoen company commenced the assembly, under license, of the Swiss Mowag Piranha 6x6 APC in the early 1980s. In 1993 there were 180 of these in service with the Chilean Army as the Cardoen/Mowag Piranha. Several variants of this vehicle, including a mortar carrier and a fire-support version, with the turret-mounted 90mm Cockerill gun, were also developed.

Simultaneously with the Piranha project, Cardoen Industries also developed the VTP–1 Orca 6x6 APC/armored load carrier, the world's largest vehicle of its kind, capable of carrying sixteen men with their equipment. The Chilean Army eventually ordered 100 Orcas. Limited numbers of another tracked infantry vehicle, the VTP–2 4x4 Escarabajo light APC, were in service with the FACh for airfield defense. With Chinese collaboration, the company also produced a 6x6 all-terrain truck for both civilian and military purposes and a light two-seater hovercraft.

In keeping with its origins as a manufacturer of explosives, Cardoen produces three types of demolition charges and a series of detonators and Bangalore torpedoes, in addition to three types of hand grenades, two types of antipersonnel mines, and an antitank mine. The company also produces 70mm ballistic rockets, 300-kilogram fragmentation bombs, and three types of general-purpose aircraft bombs. Experiments with fuel-air bombs were reported to have been carried out at the corporation's testing area in the Atacama Desert.

The most successful of all Cardoen products, however, and one used extensively by Iraq against coalition forces in the Persian Gulf War of January–February 1991, is the patented Cardoen cluster bomb, a 227-kilogram bomb whose 240 "bomblets" create a lethal zone of up to 50,000 square meters. The company reportedly sold more than US$200 million worth of cluster bombs to Iraq between 1984 and 1988 and was described in early 1991 as the world's leading producer of this type of bomb.

Cardoen Industries has also developed a low-cost combat helicopter, based on the Bell 206. A demilitarized version of this gained a United States Federal Aviation Administration license in 1990. Nevertheless, in 1992 the prototype remained impounded in the United States on the grounds of the company's known involvement with Iraq, and Cardoen's contract to service Bell helicopters was revoked.

In early 1992, Cardoen Industries and its various subsidiaries were finding the previously close association with Iraq, particularly the illegal export of zirconium for use in armor-piercing cluster bombs, highly embarrassing in the wake of the 1991 Persian Gulf War. Consequently, the company was assiduously emphasizing its nonmilitary activities at the expense of the defense sector, on which the prosperity of Cardoen Industries had been built. Following a two-year investigation of Carlos Cardoen, United States officials brought civil charges against him and moved to confiscate Cardoen-owned properties in Florida valued at more than US$30 million. These problems prompted Cardoen Industries to change its name to Metalnor.

Minor Defense Manufacturers

Several Chilean companies not primarily engaged in the production of military matériel also have dabbled in this field. Longest established of these is the General Society of Commerce (Sociedad General de Comercio—Sogeco). Founded in 1941, Sogeco did not enter the arms business until 1974. It was initially concerned with the production of bomb trolleys for the FACh. Sogeco also developed the ejection seat for the Pillán and, through its subsidiary Famil, has produced two models of a towed twin 20mm antiaircraft artillery gun, known as the FAM–2 and based on either the Oerlikon KAD 20 or the Hispano-Suiza 820. The firm of Makina, which produces the armored bodies of the Cardoen vehicles, itself developed the Carancho 180, a 4x4 airfield defense armored vehicle, for the FACh. Ferrimar Limitada, a firm engaged mainly in the construction of steel-hulled fishing craft and with no previous experience in the defense field, developed an artillery computer, designated Carmo, a light landing craft, and projects for modularized mobile command centers, in addition to its own Avispa cluster bomb in the mid-1980s. Despite some success on the export market, the Avispa appeared to be out of production in 1992, following litigation with Cardoen, which claimed infringement of copyright. The interest of Ferrimar in the field of military production appeared subsequently to have lapsed.

The Security Forces

Under the 1980 constitution, the police are referred to as the Forces of Order and Public Security, their role being defined as the maintenance of law and order. There are two separate law enforcement forces: the Carabineros and the Investigations Police, both under the operational control of the Ministry of Interior. The Carabineros constitute a national police force that forms a potential reserve for the army and has a paramilitary organization. The Investigations Police is a national plainclothes organization comparable in some respects to the United States Federal Bureau of Investigation (FBI).

The Carabineros

During the colonial period, there existed a fifty-man police unit known as the Queen's Dragoons, which was responsible for law enforcement in the Santiago area. This force changed its name to Dragons of Chile (Dragones de Chile) in the early years of the republic and, by 1850, had increased in strength to 300. It was subsequently incorporated into the army as a cavalry regiment. By that time, civil police forces had also been set up in the major population centers. In 1881 the Rural Police Law created a separate rural police force in each province, and six years later each municipality was authorized to set up its own local police force.

In 1902 four of the army's seven cavalry regiments were ordered to detach a squadron apiece to form a new entity to be known as the Border Police (Gendarmes de la Frontera) and to be engaged primarily in the suppression of banditry in the less developed regions of the country. Despite being administratively and operationally subordinate to the Ministry of Interior, this unit remained ultimately under the jurisdiction of the minister of war. Five years later, it acquired a larger establishment and changed its name to the Carabineros Regiment (Regimiento de Carabineros).

Although still lacking a formal permanent institutional existence, in 1909 the Carabineros established an Institute of Instruction and Education, which admitted its first class of police cadets in August of that year. Five years later, the responsibilities of the force were extended to railroad security. Finally, in 1919, the force acquired a formal independent existence under the Ministry of Interior, and its title was changed again to the Carabineros Corps (Cuerpo de Carabineros). Six years later, by which time the corps consisted of 204 officers and 3,760 enlisted personnel, the Carabineros acquired a new organization that combined their various independent squadrons into five Rural Service Regiments, together with

Two members of the Carabineros patrolling during the 19th of September Armed Forces Day parade in Santiago in 1985
Courtesy David Shelton

a Railway Regiment, Training Regiment, and Customs Squadron, the latter based at Valparaíso.

The strength, resources, and qualities of the various municipal and rural police forces varied enormously. In 1924, in an effort to provide a degree of uniformity, the country was divided into five police zones, with their headquarters at Antofagasta, Valparaíso, Santiago, Talca, and Concepción. The same law divided the police functionally into three divisions: the Public Order Division, entrusted with general peacekeeping on a relatively passive level; the Security Division, with a role of active law enforcement; and the Identification Division, which embraced record keeping and general crime detection. This arrangement provided for the coordination of the activities of the various existing law enforcement agencies, on a zonal basis, with the General Directorate of Police (Dirección General de Policía) at the national level. At that time, in the mid-1920s, the various police forces numbered 728 officers and 8,628 enlisted personnel.

Although now downgraded in importance, the provinces and the municipalities continued to maintain their individual police forces. Only the municipal police of Santiago and Valparaíso seem to have been effective, however, and in 1927 all law enforcement agencies were incorporated in a single national force, the Carabineros of Chile. The force had a total strength of 1,123 officers and 15,420 enlisted personnel in 1929.

In 1993 the Carabineros numbered 31,000, including officers, noncommissioned officers (NCOs), and a significant women's element. Although normally under the jurisdiction of the Ministry of Interior, the Carabineros were put under the Ministry of Defense during the period of national emergency following the overthrow of the Allende regime. Despite the return of civilian government in 1990, the Carabineros remain subordinate to the Ministry of Defense, but their operations are coordinated by the Ministry of Interior. The Aylwin administration authorized an increase in strength of 1,100 annually over the 1991–94 period.

Organization

The Carabineros are commanded by a director general and organized geographically into three main zones—the Northern Zone, the Central Zone, and the Southern Zone. Each of these zones is in turn subdivided into prefectures (*prefecturas*), subprefectures (*subprefecturas*), commissariats (*comisarías*), subcommissariats (*subcomisarías*), lieutenancies (*tenencias*), reserves (*retenes*), and outposts (*puestos avanzados*).

The Carabineros also include marine and air sections. The Air Police, which ranks as a separate prefecture, dates from 1946, when it was formed with a single Aeronca Champion aircraft. The Air Police acquired its first helicopter in 1968; by 1993 its inventory of helicopters had increased to fourteen (see table 46, Appendix).

Operationally, the Carabineros are divided into seventeen departments: analysis and evaluation, armaments and munitions, borders and boundaries, civic action, data processing, drug control and prevention of offenses, finance, forestry, internal security, legal, minors, police services, public relations, social action, supply, traffic control, and transport. In addition to their normal law enforcement and allied functions, the Carabineros perform extensive civic action, including the provision of medical and dental services to the populations of the less developed regions of the country and the protection of forests and wildlife. The Carabineros are also responsible for customs control and the Presidential Guard. Separate prefectures deal with the Air Police, the Radio Patrol, and the Special Forces.

The largest single concentration of Carabineros is in Santiago, where apart from headquarters and administrative personnel, the schools, and the Presidential Guard, there are five geographical prefectures: the Central Prefecture, North Prefecture, South Prefecture, East Prefecture, and West Prefecture. These are in turn subdivided into twenty-six territorial and nine operational commissariats.

Recruitment and Training

Service in the Carabineros is voluntary, and admission standards are high. Applicants are required to have completed secondary school and to have passed exacting physical examinations and psychological tests. A highly professional organization, the Carabineros have enjoyed a prestige and universal respect that are almost unique among Latin American police forces. The force's principal problem at the beginning of the 1990s was the lack of adequate resources to combat crime. Although budget appropriations for the Carabineros had risen steadily in the early 1990s (from US$37 million in 1990 to US$78 million in 1993), low pay and even inadequate clothing were a source of discontent within the ranks. The force has its own cadet, NCO, and staff officer schools, in addition to a specialists' training center, all of which are located in Los Cerrillos, Santiago.

Uniforms

The Carabineros wear an olive-drab uniform with green trim, a high-crowned cap with brown leather visor, and brown leather apparel. Motorcycle police wear white crash helmets and gauntlets with the standard service uniform. Riot helmets and shields are used by special units. Female members wear a version of the male uniform with skirt and hard-crowned, kepi-type cap. Officers' rank insignia are identical to those of the army but are worn on silver rather than gold shoulder straps and plaits. NCO rank insignia are in silver lace and worn on the upper sleeve.

The Investigations Police

The Investigations Police, numbering about 4,000, is a plainclothes civilian agency engaged primarily in the detection and investigation of crime. Headquartered in Santiago, the force has seven substations in other parts of Chile. It functions throughout the country in support of the Carabineros. Operationally, its chain of command runs from the director general through a deputy director to the inspectors in charge of the provincial substations. Functionally, it is divided into a number of departments, including administration, foreign and internal police, health, justice, personnel, and welfare. The force also includes the Air Police Brigade, responsible for airport surveillance; the National Identification Bureau, which keeps records of all adult citizens and foreign residents and issues identification cards that must be carried at all times; and the Forensic Medicine Laboratory. In addition, the Special Units

Prefecture comprises six brigades dealing with fraud, murder, robberies, vehicle theft, vice, and women's affairs.

The Investigations Police functions in close collaboration with the International Criminal Police Organization (Interpol) and with the intelligence services of the army, navy, and air force. During the military government, some Investigations Police agents became involved in criminal activities. By early 1992, its new director, Horácio Toro, a retired army general appointed by the Aylwin government, had withdrawn more than 200 officers from duty because of their alleged involvement in drug trafficking.

Internal Security Intelligence Organizations

In the immediate aftermath of the 1973 coup, a semiformal umbrella group, the National Intelligence Directorate (Dirección Nacional de Inteligencia—DINA), was formed, ostensibly to coordinate the activities of the intelligence services of the army, navy, air force, Carabineros, and Investigations Police. From the beginning, DINA functioned as a secret police and was engaged in the repression of dissidence within the state and the exaction of revenge on its enemies without. So notorious were its activities that of 957 identified "disappearances" of enemies of the Pinochet regime, DINA was blamed by the Rettig Commission on human rights abuses for perpetrating 392.

DINA has also been linked by prosecutors in the United States, Italy, Argentina, and Chile to the murder of General Carlos Prats, the former commander in chief of the army, in Buenos Aires in 1974; the attempted murder of Bernardo Leighton, the Christian Democratic leader, in Rome in 1974; and the assassination of Orlando Letelier, a former member of the Allende administration and ambassador to the United States under the Popular Unity (Unidad Popular) regime, in Washington in 1976. DINA was abolished in 1977 and replaced by a new organization known as the National Information Center (Centro Nacional de Información—CNI).

The functions of the CNI combined those functions carried out by the United States Central Intelligence Agency (CIA), FBI, and Secret Service. Although human rights abuses abated significantly after the abolition of DINA, its successor continued to draw criticism and was disbanded upon the return of civilian government in 1990. Most of its approximately 2,000 operatives were absorbed either by army intelligence or by a new coordinating body for military intelligence, operating under the aegis of the National Defense Staff and known as the Directorate of National Defense Intelligence (Dirección de Inteligencia de la Defensa Nacional—DIDN). The

DIDN concerns itself primarily with defense rather than with internal intelligence.

The Aylwin government relied mainly on the Investigations Police to combat terrorist groups. Technical assistance has been obtained from Italy and Germany. The Carabineros created a new countersubversive intelligence body in May 1990, the Directorate of Carabineros Political Intelligence (Dirección de Inteligencia Política de Carabineros—Dipolcar). Its previous unit was implicated in human rights violations. In early 1993, the government was finally able to enact new legislation, after more than a year of congressional delays in approving the project, creating the Directorate of Public Security and Information (Dirección de Seguridad Pública e Informaciones). The new directorate is under the Ministry of Interior and allows the ministry to coordinate the intelligence and anticrime and antiterrorist activities of the Carabineros and Investigations Police.

Public Order and Internal Security

Incidence of Crime

Crime rates in the early 1990s remained far below those of the United States. However, the notion that common crime was rare in Chile until the 1970s and 1980s is a myth. Chile's rural areas were plagued with outlaw gangs in the early nineteenth century. The most notorious gang, Los Pincheira, operated during the 1817–32 period, purportedly in defense of the cause of the king of Spain. Based in the Andes and the heights of Chillán, the four brothers who headed the gang—Antonio, Santos, Pablo, and José Pincheira—wreaked death and destruction in the provinces of Ñuble and Concepción. Nineteenth-century historian Benjamín Vicuña Mackenna described their rural terror, and Los Pincheira became the subject of novels as well. The gang grew to the size of an army, requiring the government of Joaquín Prieto Vial (1831–36, 1836–41) to mobilize the army to eradicate the group. General Manuel Bulnes was put in charge of combating Los Pincheira in its own territory. At the command of 1,000 soldiers, Bulnes surprised Los Pincheira near the Palaquén lagoons, killing more than 200 bandits in a pitched battle. With the defeat of Los Pincheira in 1832, the government was able to establish its authority in all of the national territory.

The crime situation was confusing to analyze under the military regime in the 1970s and 1980s because the government and media tended to lump ordinary criminal behavior together with dissident violence. In the early 1980s, officials were prone to attribute bank robberies, assassinations, and shootouts with police to left-wing extremist organizations, although skeptics often pointed to rightist provocateurs or to government agents themselves as being responsible for at least some of the incidents. Figures on crime and criminals released by the National Statistics Institute (Instituto Nacional de Estadísticas—INE) are not very enlightening as to the actual status of crime in the country. There are no breakdowns of figures according to gender in either the juvenile or the adult category, and there are no statistics on prison populations.

News media have also contributed to a perception that crime had increased in the early 1990s, but crime statistics are still difficult to obtain. Few, if any, published sources provide general crime statistics, with the main exception of figures for arrests, readily available in the INE's *Compendio estadístico*. According to sociologist J. Samuel Valenzuela, the general crime pattern did not appear to have changed markedly in 1992 from 1980–91. However, violent crime was reported to have increased, and the average age of those committing crimes had declined.

Available figures for 1980–91 show a mixed picture because some forms of crime remained stable or declined, while others had increased (see table 47, Appendix). Of those that had increased, the biggest jump occurred in the mid-1980s. Crime during the period of democratic transition from 1989 to 1991 did not fall into a single pattern. The biggest jump in the rate of robberies occurred in the mid-1980s. The average rate increased by 82.5 percent between 1986 and 1988, compared with the first three years of the decade. Between 1989 and 1991, the rate increased by 7 percent over the average in the previous three years. The trend between 1989 and 1991, however, was steadily upward. There was no overall increase or decrease in the rate of burglaries. The average for the 1980–91 years was a 17 percent decrease over 1986–88. However, the rate of burglaries was higher between 1989 and 1991 than it was between 1980 and 1982. Like robberies, murders had increased significantly in the mid-1980s. In 1986–88 the average rate increased by 27 percent over the 1980–82 years. In 1989–91 the average rate was a 9.1 percent increase over the previous three years.

A poll conducted by the Center for Public Studies (Centro de Estudios Públicos—CEP) and the Adimark Company in March 1993 in Osorno reveals the existence of a very real fear of crime in the country. According to the CEP/Adimark survey, 59 percent of those polled perceived more crime than a year earlier. Only 13 percent felt that crime had dropped. Moreover, 76 percent said that crime was more violent, whereas only 8 percent said it was less violent. In a retrospective analysis, the study revealed that citizen concern about crime rose sharply between December 1989 and March 1991, with the figure approaching 65 percent in 1991. The study also reveals that 59 percent of those polled thought that the Carabineros provided the needed assistance. Nevertheless, some 43.3 percent said they were dissatisfied with police protection in their neighborhood; only 37.2 percent were satisfied.

Narcotics Trafficking

Chile long remained relatively unaffected either by drug trafficking or by extensive drug abuse. Some expansion, both of drug trafficking and of narcotics abuse, occurred during the late 1960s and early 1970s, reflecting an international trend. By the early 1970s, Chile had become an important regional center for cocaine processing. The problem had become sufficiently acute to occasion the passage of the country's first antinarcotics law by Allende's Popular Unity government early in 1973. Later that year, the military government formed a special narcotics unit within the Carabineros and began a big crackdown. This was highly effective, bringing the narcotics problem under control within a year. The Carabineros also pioneered the introduction of antinarcotics-oriented, youth education programs. A pilot project was set up in 1976, eight years before any comparable program was initiated in the United States. Toward the end of the period of military rule, a new form of drug-related crime was noted in the northern Chilean provinces adjoining the Bolivian and Peruvian frontiers: the illicit exporting to Peru and Bolivia of chemicals used in the processing of cocaine.

Since the early 1980s, drug trafficking has been growing in Chile. The country has become more prone to drug trafficking not only because of its geographic configuration and location, bordering on the world's two leading producers of coca—Peru and Bolivia— but also because of its economic stability. With its open-market economy and bank-secrecy laws, Chile is an attractive haven for money laundering. A number of drug traffickers who were expelled by the military regime after the 1973 coup cultivated contacts with drug-trafficking groups while living in exile in the United States and Europe. On returning to Chile to reside, these traffickers, acting as finance men and heads of operations, profited from their international contacts. Chile served as a good transit country also because of its booming export activities. In mid-1992 an operational director of the Carabineros reported that money obtained through drug trafficking was being laundered through the construction industry in central Chile and the fishing industry in the far south.

In order to enhance the country's antidrug capabilities, the Aylwin government signed several antidrug agreements in 1992, including one with Italy in October (which also included antiterrorist cooperation) and one with Bolivia in November. Chile's most serious drug-related problems by 1992 reportedly involved transit through the country along the northern corridor to Arica. In early 1993, a new cocaine/cocaine paste drug route reportedly came from Bolivia through the Azapa Valley, an area with a sizable Bolivian and Peruvian population located to the east of the city of Arica. At that time, the Investigations Police began implementing a new drug enforcement plan, with the aid of a turbo Cessna 206 for patrolling the area along the Bolivian and Peruvian borders, in coordination with motor vehicles and twenty powerful all-terrain Cagiva motorcycles, donated by Italy.

After 1989 drug-related crime increased dramatically, particularly in the northern part of the country, to the extent that police reportedly estimated in 1990 that 20 percent of the population of the city of Arica between the ages of fifteen and thirty-four were habitual drug users. Of 385 homicides (or 0.3 per 10,000) in Chile during 1990, nearly 20 percent were classified as drug related. By comparison, eight were classified as resulting from acts of terrorism. During 1990 about 30 percent of robberies were also said to be drug related. The size of drug seizures varied considerably. In 1991 some 220,000 kilograms of cocaine were seized, compared with 36,500 in 1988 and 798,000 in 1989. Police estimated that only 10 percent of the drug traffic was getting intercepted. Most of the cocaine seizures occurred in the northern port of Arica.

Criminal Justice

The 1980 constitution establishes the independence of the judiciary from the executive and legislative arms of government (see The Courts, ch. 4). The legal system is based on Roman law. There is no provision for trial by jury, and heavy reliance is placed on police evidence in criminal cases. Judges are required to be qualified not only in law but also in criminology and psychology. There is provision for an annual review by the Supreme Court of the fitness of the members of the judiciary to continue to hold office.

The Criminal Code of Chile, first drafted in 1870 after two unsuccessful attempts, was promulgated in 1874 and modified in 1928. Its models were the criminal codes of Austria, Belgium, France, and Spain. In 1930 extensive modifications were made, including the abolition of the death penalty, although capital punishment was reinstituted for certain crimes in 1937.

The Criminal Code is divided into general and special sections. The former enumerates the general principles of criminal law relating to jurisdiction, the concept of crime, attempted crime, second party participation in the commission of crime, habitual criminals, penalties, circumstances that exclude criminal responsibility, and circumstances that extinguish criminal responsibility. The latter section defines specific offenses and their appropriate penalties. In this respect, the courts are charged with ensuring that the penalty is not merely appropriate to the crime but that it is also appropriate to the criminal's ability to discharge it.

Crimes are divided into three basic categories: serious crimes (*crímenes*), minor crimes (*delitos*), and misdemeanors (*faultas*). Crime is defined as a voluntary act or omission for which the law imposes punishment. Criminal responsibility is specifically excluded in cases in which defendants are insane or less than ten years of age. The responsibility of minors ten to sixteen years of age is also excluded unless it can be proven that they acted with full understanding of their acts. Criminal responsibility is also excluded for violent acts committed in the defense of one's own person, property, or rights and in defense of those of one's spouse or those of a third party. Also excluded are violent acts committed accidentally in the exercise of a legal act, violent acts committed in the exercise of public duty, violent acts committed under duress or fear, and the killing or wounding of the accomplice of an adulterous spouse. Criminal responsibility is also excluded in the case of crimes of omission owing to a legal or irresistible cause. Suicide and attempted suicide are specifically decriminalized.

The Penal System

The penal system also has been standardized since 1930, coming under the jurisdiction of the minister of justice. The system emphasizes the rehabilitation of the offender as its primary goal. The normal prison regime is humane; the degree of confinement is reduced progressively throughout the duration of the prisoner's sentence and ends, subject to good behavior, in conditional release for periods up to 50 percent of the total sentence. The lengths of the successive stages in the relaxation of the prison regime are varied and are implemented on the basis of semiannual judicial review, which takes into account behavior and perceived progress toward rehabilitation.

Under the Criminal Code, all persons sentenced for periods between sixty-one days and five years are obligated to work. Prisoners are remunerated for their work on a rising scale as they progress through the penal system and are eligible for the benefits of social insurance on the same basis as those in voluntary employment. However, a percentage of prisoners' earnings is deducted to cover their keep and the maintenance of the penal service and as a contribution toward the discharge of civil responsibility arising from their offenses. Work can be either directly for the state, on contract, or on lease. Examples of work for the state include manufacture of such items as road signs or automobile license plates, or public road construction and maintenance. Work on contract to private firms or individuals is still carried out within the penal institution, but with tools and materials supplied by the contractor. Work on lease differs inasmuch as the private contractor is responsible for the housing and maintenance of the prisoner in secure conditions. Prisoners may also undertake additional discretionary work of a gainful nature within certain limitations laid down by the prisons administration.

There are some 140 penal institutions of various types with a capacity for approximately 15,000 inmates. Of these about sixty-five are intended to house short-term (sixty-day maximum) or remand prisoners; six are intended for long-term prisoners; twenty-three are correctional institutions for females and are supervised by a Catholic order of nuns; one is an open prison, located on Isla Santa María, southwest of Concepción; one is a special institution for juvenile offenders; and the remainder house prisoners serving sentences of between sixty-one days and five years. These are administered by the Gendarmerie, or Judicial Police of Chile (Gendarmería de Chile), which reports to the Ministry of Justice and numbers approximately 4,000 members.

A combination of social and political factors have inflated the prison population relative to its capacity; in 1990 it exceeded 25,000 inmates. Some 60 percent of these were on remand awaiting trial. After the riots of 1980, the military regime was widely condemned for crowding 1,800 inmates into Santiago's San Bernardo Prison. However, the same institution, designed to hold 800, housed 3,300 inmates during the third quarter of 1990.

Terrorism

During the first five years of the Pinochet regime (1973–78), the armed forces and security forces successfully contained left-wing resistance against the government. Many members of Chile's oldest left-wing extremist group, the Movement of the Revolutionary Left (Movimiento de la Izquierda Revolucionaria—MIR), which was founded in 1965 and had close ties to Cuba, were killed or exiled. Nevertheless, the MIR remnants, under the leadership of the late Salvador Allende's nephew, Andrés Pascal Allende, continued to operate a small underground network in Chile. The MIR's principal leader, Miguel Enríquez, returned clandestinely to Chile in 1978 to revitalize the movement and organize for armed struggle and was soon joined by newly infiltrated cadres who had been trained in Cuba and Nicaragua. The security forces kept the MIR off balance, however, and Enríquez was killed in September 1983.

Several new left-wing terrorist groups emerged in the early 1980s. One was the United Popular Action Movement-Lautaro (Movimiento de Acción Popular Unitario-Lautaro—MAPU-L), a splinter of the United Popular Action Movement (Movimiento de Acción Popular Unitario—MAPU), a party founded in 1969 by a breakaway group from the Christian Democrats. Many MAPU leaders embraced Marxist positions, but the party was not a terrorist group. In December 1982, the MAPU–L established a youth group, the Lautaro Youth Movement (Movimiento de Juventud Lautaro—MJL), and a group dedicated to the overthrow of the military government, the Lautaro Popular Rebel Forces (Fuerzas Rebeldes Populares Lautaro—FRPL). The Manuel Rodríguez Patriotic Front (Frente Patriótica Manuel Rodríguez—FPMR), an armed group affiliated with the Communist Party of Chile (Partido Comunista de Chile—PCCh), was formed in 1983. In response to increased armed attacks, the regime promulgated the 1984 Antiterrorist Law, which greatly expanded the list of crimes that could be categorized as terrorism.

In the second half of the 1980s, the FPMR became the dominant terrorist group, emerging as a sophisticated, well-trained, and well-supported terrorist organization. Just how strong it was became evident in August 1986 when the security forces captured a huge FPMR arms cache that was traced to Cuba. That September FPMR commandos nearly succeeded in assassinating Pinochet with M–16 assault rifles and antitank rockets. In response to these two events, Pinochet declared a state of siege and mounted an offensive against the FPMR and MIR.

Intensified police and security-service pressure on the FPMR and MIR continued throughout 1987, inhibiting the groups' activities. That year the FPMR splintered as a result of the PCCh's denunciation of violence; the breakaway Maoist-oriented FPMR-Autonomous (FPMR-Autónomo—FPMR–A) became the most active left-wing terrorist group, whereas the FPMR followed the PCCh's line and laid down its arms after the restoration of democracy in 1990. Mainly as a result of FPMR–A activities, terrorist attacks increased in the late 1980s.

Meanwhile, the security forces failed to apprehend any members of right-wing extremist groups, such as the Chilean Anti-Communist Action Group (Acción Chilena Anticomunista—AChA) and the Nationalist Combat Front (Frente Nacionalista de Combate—FNC). The ability of these groups to operate with apparent impunity led to speculation in the late 1980s that their actions were unofficially sanctioned by some officials in the security forces.

The rationale for continued left-wing subversion and right-wing counterterror effectively vanished with the return of civilian government in 1990. Many left-wing extremists who had fled the country following the 1973 coup were allowed to return in 1990. Nevertheless, left-wing terrorism did not disappear. Within a few months after President Aylwin's accession to power, the FPMR–A and MJL showed that they remained committed to armed struggle and were responsible for most of the increased number of terrorist incidents in the early 1990s. The total number of documented terrorist actions during the first year of the Aylwin government was 207 (including 148 attacks on buildings and other properties), compared with 465 similar actions during 1984 and 401 in 1985—two peak years for terrorist activity during the latter half of the period of military rule.

The Aylwin government's attempts to control terrorism were quite successful. In 1991 it expanded training and increased efforts by the Investigations Police and the Carabineros. Police improved their counterterrorism capabilities, surpassing the effectiveness of the military government. This was made evident by their success in arresting numerous leaders and in uncovering several safe houses and training sites used by Chilean terrorists. By early 1993, more than 200 terrorist militants were under indictment. The capture of many top leaders of the MAPU–L and FPMR–A crippled these organizations, and terrorist incidents declined. The Aylwin government appointed special investigating judges to try the more serious cases of terrorism, such as the assassination of Senator Jaime Guzmán Errázuriz on April 1, 1991.

National Security Outlook

Neither terrorism nor foreign military aggression posed a significant threat to Chilean national security in early 1994. The establishment of democratic governments in both Argentina and Chile has resulted in unprecedented economic, political, and even military cooperation between the two countries. By early 1994, both countries had ratified the Tlatelolco Treaty, which bans the development of nuclear weapons.

Nevertheless, many Chileans believe there is a constant threat from neighboring countries. Consequently, Chile is attempting to maintain a credible deterrent force. Occasional border disputes still occur, so Argentina, Chile, and Peru attempt to be prepared to use military force, if necessary, in defense of their perceived national interests. The overall situation of the Chilean Armed Forces in early 1994 was positive, but modernization of their forces had become a priority. Despite the lifting of the arms embargo, modernization was continuing to a significant extent within the framework of the national arms industry and indigenous technology. At the same time, the armed forces were looking to the European and United States arms markets for more advanced equipment to compete, for example, with the sale of thirty-six United States-made A–4M Skyhawk bombers to Argentina. It would be ironic, however, if the democratic governments in Argentina and Chile were to become involved in an arms race over mutual fears that the other side had a slight military supremacy.

* * *

Agustín Toro Dávila's *Síntesis histórico militar de Chile* provides a good summary of Chile's military history from the earliest times to the 1891 Civil War. Frederick M. Nunn's *The Military in Chilean History* and *Chilean Politics, 1920–1931* are highly recommended. Despite its unwieldy title, Theodorus B.M. Mason's *The War on the Pacific Coast of South America Between Chile and the Allied Republics of Peru and Bolivia, 1879–81* (published in 1883) provides a concise history of the War of the Pacific. A much more recent and well-documented study is William F. Sater's *Chile and the War of the Pacific*. Roberto Querejazu Calvo's weighty *Guano, salitre, y sangre* is probably the best single-volume history of the War of the Pacific, despite a slight pro-Bolivian bias.

Daniel Prieto Vial's *Defensa Chile, 2000* provides an interesting insight into at least one geostrategist's views of the direction that Chile's defense policies should take. A somewhat conflicting view of the subject from an ostensibly economic viewpoint is Fernando Bustamente, Miguel Navarro, and Guillermo Patillio's *¿Cual debe ser el gasto militar en el Chile de los 90?* The best global treatment of the contemporary Chilean defense structure is Raúl Sohr's *Para entender a los militares*. The same author's study of Chile's defense industry in *La industria militar chilena* is also definitive.

On the subject of the Chilean Army, the "Chile" section of John Keegan's *World Armies* is useful, and *Cuatro siglos de uniformes en Chile* by Alberto Márquez Alison and Antonio Márquez Alison, in addition to being the definitive work within its own field, provides a wealth of historical information beyond the limitations implied by its title. The same may be said of R.J. Bragg and Roy Turner's *Parachute Badges and Insignia of the World* and, to a lesser degree, of Bert Campbell and Ron Reynolds's *Marine Badges and Insignia of the World*. Emilio Meneses Ciuffardi's *El factor naval en las relaciones entre Chile y los Estados Unidos, 1881–1951* is essential reading on modern Chilean naval history and is much broader in scope than its title implies. Rodrigo Fuenzalida Bade's four-volume historical work, *La armada de Chile desde la alborada al sesquicentenario, 1813–1968,* is unmatched by any comparable history of the army or air force. The history of the Carabineros remains to be written.

Even the English-language professional and technical press tends to ignore the subject of Latin American defense, and the best sources of current and relatively objective information on the subject are the Spanish monthly journal *Defensa Latinoamericana* and the German-published, Spanish-language journal *Tecnología Militar,* which also has an English version, *Military Technology.* (For further information and complete citations, see Bibliography.)

Appendix

Table

Table 1. Metric Conversion Coefficients and Factors

When you know	Multiply by	To find
Millimeters	0.04	inches
Centimeters	0.39	inches
Meters	3.3	feet
Kilometers	0.62	miles
Hectares (10,000 m²)	2.47	acres
Square kilometers	0.39	square miles
Cubic meters	35.3	cubic feet
Liters	0.26	gallons
Kilograms	2.2	pounds
Metric tons	0.98	long tons
....	1.1	short tons
....	2,204	pounds
Degrees Celsius	1.8	degrees Fahrenheit
(Centigrade)	and add 32	

Table 2. Population by Selected Native American Group, 1992 *
(in thousands of persons age fourteen and over)

Age-Group	Mapuche		Aymara		Rapa Nui		Total	
	Males	Females	Males	Females	Males	Females	Males	Females
14-24	125.2	119.0	6.8	5.9	2.6	3.413	4.7	128.3
25-39	176.5	166.5	8.4	7.9	3.3	4.318	8.2	178.7
40-49	73.9	70.1	4.0	4.0	1.3	1.77	9.2	75.8
50-64	65.7	67.0	3.7	3.7	1.4	2.0	70.8	72.7
65 and over	29.5	34.7	1.9	2.2	0.7	1.03	2.1	37.9
TOTAL	470.7	457.3	24.9	23.6	9.4	12.5	505.0	493.4

* Figures may not add to totals because of rounding.

Source: Based on information from Chile, Instituto Nacional de Estadísticas, *Resultados oficiales: Censo de población, 1992,* Santiago, 1993, 69.

Table 3. Population by Region, Gender, Urban-Rural Breakdown,
and Persons of Foreign Birth, 1992

Region		Males	Females	Total
I	Tarapacá	171,356	168,223	339,579
II	Antofagasta	206,786	203,938	410,724
III	Atacama	117,835	113,038	230,873
IV	Coquimbo	249,578	254,809	504,387
V	Valparaíso	670,889	713,447	1,384,336
VI	Libertador General Bernardo O'Higgins	353,379	342,990	696,369
VII	Maule	420,800	415,341	836,141
VIII	Bío-Bío	857,343	876,962	1,734,305
IX	La Araucanía	389,074	392,168	781,242
X	Los Lagos	475,758	473,051	948,809
XI	Aisén del General Carlos Ibáñez del Campo	42,410	38,091	80,501
XII	Magallanes y La Antártica Chilena	74,669	68,529	143,198
—	Metropolitan Region of Santiago	2,523,377	2,734,560	5,257,937
TOTAL		6,553,254	6,795,147	13,348,401
Urban		5,364,760	5,775,645	11,140,405
Rural		1,188,494	1,019,502	2,207,996
Persons of foreign birth		58,204	56,393	114,597

Source: Based on information from Chile, Instituto Nacional de Estadísticas, *Resultados oficiales: Censo de población, 1992,* Santiago, 1993, 68.

Table 4. *Area and Population Density of the Regions, Selected Years, 1980–93*

Region		Area [1]	Population Density [2]					
			1980	1983	1986	1988	1989	1993
I	Tarapacá	58,073	4.5	5.0	5.4	5.8	6.0	6.4
II	Antofagasta	125,306	2.7	2.8	2.9	3.0	3.1	3.1
III	Atacama	78,268	2.3	2.4	2.5	2.5	2.5	2.7
IV	Coquimbo	39,647	10.4	10.9	11.4	11.8	12.0	12.2
V	Valparaíso	16,378	72.9	76.6	80.2	82.6	83.5	87.7
—	Metropolitan Region of Santiago	15,782	266.1	285.0	304.4	18.4	25.3	355.4
VI	Libertador General Bernardo O'Higgins	15,950	36.6	37.7	39.0	39.7	40.2	40.4
VII	Maule	30,518	23.6	24.7	26.0	26.7	27.1	28.7
VIII	Bío-Bío	36,007	42.1	43.3	44.7	45.6	46.0	46.3
IX	La Araucanía	32,472	21.3	22.0	22.9	23.7	24.1	25.4
X	Los Lagos	69,039	12.3	12.6	13.0	13.2	13.2	14.1
XI	Aisén del General Carlos Ibáñez del Campo	107,153	0.6	0.6	0.7	0.7	0.7	0.8
XII	Magallanes y La Antártica Chilena	132,034 [3]	0.9	1.0	1.1	1.1	1.2	1.3
CHILE		756,627	14.7	15.5	16.3	16.8	17.6	18.0

[1] In square kilometers.

[2] In inhabitants per square kilometer.

[3] Mainland; calculation excludes the 1,250,000-square-kilometer area of the Chilean Antarctic.

Source: Based on information from Banco Central de Chile, Dirección de Estudios, *Indicadores económicos y sociales regionales, 1980–1989*, Santiago, 1991, 151; and Chile, Instituto Nacional de Estadísticas, *Compendio estadístico, 1993*, Santiago, 1993, 1, Table 121–02.

Table 5. Growth of Santiago's Population, Selected Years, 1865–1992

Year	Population	Percentage Increase	Percentage of Total Population
1865	115,377	n.a.	6.3
1875	129,807	12.5	6.3
1885	189,332	45.8	7.6
1895	256,403	35.5	9.5
1907	332,724	29.8	10.3
1920	507,296	52.5	13.7
1930	712,533	40.5	16.6
1940	952,075	33.6	19.0
1952	1,350,409	41.8	22.8
1960	1,907,378	41.2	25.9
1970	2,730,895	43.2	30.7
1980	3,899,495	42.8	35.1
1992 *	5,170,293	32.6	39.0

n.a.—not available.
* Preliminary census figures.

Source: Based on information from Ximena Toledo O. and Eduardo Zapater A., *Geografía general y regional de Chile,* Santiago, 1989, 183; and Chile, Instituto Nacional de Estadísticas, Santiago (various publications).

Table 6. Distribution of Agricultural Landownership,
1965, 1973, and 1987
(in percentages)

Area [1]	1965	1973	1987 [2]
0–5	9.7	9.7	10.0
5–20	12.7	15.7	29.0
20–40	9.4	12.7	15.0
40–80	12.8	19.7	26.0
More than 80	55.4	2.7	18.0
Reformed sector [3]	0.0	39.9	0.0

[1] In number of basic irrigated hectares.
[2] Estimated.
[3] For definition of reformed sector—see Glossary.

Source: Based on information from Sergio Gómez and Jorge Echenique, *La agricultura chilena,* Santiago, 1991, 101, 106.

Table 7. Composition of the Population and Labor Force, 1987-91 [1]
(in thousands of persons)

	1987	1988	1989	1990	1991
Population					
Under 15 years	3,812	3,853	3,896	3,939	3,984
15 years or older	8,520	8,663	8,809	8,958	9,114
Total population [2]	12,333	12,516	12,704	12,897	13,098
Working-age population					
Labor force	4,354	4,552	4,675	4,729	4,794
Inactive	4,166	4,111	4,134	4,229	4,320
Total working-age population ..	8,520	8,663	8,809	8,958	9,114
Labor force					
Employed	4,011	4,266	4,425	4,460	4,540
Unemployed	344	286	250	269	254
Total labor force	4,355	4,552	4,675	4,729	4,794
Unemployed					
Laid-off	285	231	204	229	220
Seeking employment for the first time	59	55	46	40	34
Total unemployed	344	286	250	269	254
Unemployment rate [3]	7.9	6.3	5.3	5.7	5.3
Lay-off rate [3]	6.5	5.1	4.4	4.9	4.6

[1] Surveys conducted in October–December periods.
[2] Figures may not add to totals because of rounding.
[3] In percentages.

Table 8. Employed Population by Sector, 1987-91 [1]
(in thousands of persons)

Sector	1987	1988	1989	1990	1991 [2] Number	1991 [2] Percentage
Agriculture, forestry, and fishing	837	865	857	866	881	19.2
Mining	n.a.	n.a.	n.a.	101	n.a.	2.3
Manufacturing	607	670	746	716	753	16.0
Electricity, gas, and water	25	25	23	21	21	0.5
Construction	208	276	299	286	321	6.4
Trade	690	731	756	788	774	n.a.
Financial services	177	182	192	202	228	22.2
Transportation and communications	253	274	301	309	308	7.0
Services	1,132	1,155	1,150	1,178	1,173	26.4
Unspecified	1	1	0	0	1	0.0
TOTAL	3,930	4,179	4,324	4,467	4,460	100.0

n.a.—not available.
[1] Surveys conducted in October–December periods.
[2] Figures for number of employees and for percentages of employees are taken from different sources.

Source: Based on information from Banco Central de Chile, *Boletín Mensual* [Santiago] (various issues); and Chile, Instituto Nacional de Estadísticas, *Compendio estadístico, 1991*, Santiago, 1991, Table 141-02.

Table 9. *Index of Real Wages and Salaries, 1978–93*
(1970 = 100)

Year	December Index	Year	December Index
1978	76.0	1986	84.9
1979	82.2	1987	84.7
1980	89.3	1988	90.3
1981	97.3	1989	92.0
1982	97.6	1990	93.7
1983	86.9	1991	98.3
1984	87.1	1992	102.8
1985	83.2	1993 *	106.4

* April.

Source: Based on information from Corporación de Investigaciones Económicas para Latinoamérica, "Set de estadísticas económicas," *Colección Estudios de CIEPLAN* [Santiago], No. 92, July 1992, Table 11; and Corporación de Investigaciones Económicas para Latinoamérica, "Set de estadísticas económicas," *Colección Estudios de CIEPLAN* [Santiago], January 1994, Table 12.

Table 10. *Average Monthly Wage by Wage-Earning Group, 1989*
(in United States dollars) *

Wage-Earning Group	Wage
Executives and top administrators	2,327
Professionals and technicians	858
Retail sales people	565
Specialized employees	526
Administrative personnel	444
Skilled workers	325
Unskilled workers	251
Domestic and other personal service workers	250

* Exchange rate 297 Chilean pesos = US$1.

Source: Based on information from Chile, Instituto Nacional de Estadísticas, *Compendio estadístico, 1990,* Santiago, 1990, 42–43.

Table 11. Evolution of Unemployment, 1960–92
(in percentages)

Years	Unemployment	Rate of Unemployment [1]
1960–69	6.4	6.4
1970–74	5.3	5.3
1975–79	13.4	17.6
1980–84	14.3	22.3
1985–89	8.1	11.6
1990	6.0	6.0
1991	6.5	6.5
1992 [2]	4.8	4.8

[1] Includes the Minimum Employment Program (Programa de Empleo Mínimo—PEM) and the Employment Program for Heads of Household (Programa de Ocupación para Jefes de Hogar—POJH), which are makeshift work programs financed by the state to help the jobless.
[2] Average for the first four months.

Source: Based on information from Programa Economía del Trabajo, *Serie de indicadores económico sociales: Series anuales,* Santiago, 1990, 51; and Corporación de Investigaciones Económicas para Latinoamérica, "Set de estadísticas económicas," *Colección Estudios de CIEPLAN* [Santiago], No. 92, July 1992, Table 9.

Table 12. Distribution of Personal Income by Decile in Metropolitan Region of Santiago, 1969, 1979, and 1989
(in cumulative percentages)

Decile	1969	1979	1989
1	1.3	1.4	1.2
2	3.7	3.8	3.5
3	7.0	7.0	6.6
4	11.3	11.1	10.6
5	16.7	16.1	15.7
6	23.4	22.6	22.0
7	32.0	31.0	30.0
8	43.6	42.8	41.0
9	61.0	60.9	58.4
10	100.0	100.0	100.0

Source: Based on information from Programa Economía del Trabajo, *Serie de indicadores económico sociales: Series anuales,* Santiago, 1990, 68.

Table 13. Distribution of Household Consumption by Quintile
in Metropolitan Region of Santiago, Selected Years, 1969-91
(in percentages)

Quintile	1969	1978	1988	1989	1990	1991
1	7.7	5.2	4.4	4.6	4.9	5.5
2	11.8	9.3	8.2	8.0	8.4	9.2
3	15.6	13.6	12.7	11.3	11.5	12.4
4	20.6	21.0	20.1	16.6	17.2	18.2
5	44.5	51.0	54.6	59.5	58.0	54.7

Source: Based on information from Joaquín Vial, Andrea Butelmann, and Carmen Celedón
Cariola, ''Fundamentos de las políticas macroeconómicas del gobierno democrático
chileno (1990-1993),'' *Colección Estudios de CIEPLAN* [Santiago], No. 30, December 1990, 60; and *La Nación* [Santiago], December 27, 1992, 15.

Table 14. Health Indicators, Selected Years, 1960-91

Indicator	1960	1970	1980	1985	1991
Life expectancy at birth [1]	57.1	63.6	71.0	71.5	72.0
Birthrate [2]	37.5	26.4	22.2	21.6	22.4
Mortality rate [2]	12.5	8.7	6.6	6.1	5.6
Infant mortality [3]	119.5	82.0	33.0	19.5	14.6
Under age 5 mortality [4]	n.a.	n.a.	40.0	26.0 [5]	23.0
Maternal mortality [3]	2.99	1.68	0.73	0.47 [5]	0.35
Infant diarrhea mortality [3]	n.a.	14.6	1.9	0.7 [5]	0.2
Infant bronchopneumonia mortality [3]	n.a.	23.6	3.8	2.6 [5]	1.6
Percentage of dwellings with running water	59	67	72	n.a.	n.a.

n.a.—not available.
[1] In years.
[2] Per 1,000 population.
[3] Per 1,000 live births.
[4] Per 1,000 in 0-4 age-group.
[5] Figure for 1986.

Source: Based on information from Chile, Instituto Nacional de Estadísticas, *Compendio
estadístico, 1993,* Santiago, 1993, Tables 122-03, 122-04, and 162-07; Chile, Instituto Nacional de Estadísticas, *Informe demográfico de Chile: Censo 1992,* Santiago,
1993, 12, Table 2; and Ernesto Medina Lois, ''Situación de salud en Chile,'' in
Jorge Jiménez de la Jara (ed.), *Chile: Sistema de salud en transición a la democracia,*
Santiago, 1991, 32, Table 16.

Table 15. Public and Private Education
by Education Level, 1981 and 1986 [1]
(in thousands of students)

Year and Education Level	Public	Private	Total
1981			
Pre-basic [2]	91	37	128
Basic (regular)	1,756	451	2,208
Basic (special)	18	1	20
Secondary (science and humanities)	354	99	454
Secondary (technical and professional)	141	46	187
Higher	73	5	119
Total 1981	2,434	680	3,114
1986			
Pre-basic	115	95	210
Basic (regular)	1,378	705	2,083
Basic (special)	17	13	30
Secondary (science and humanities)	370	232	602
Secondary (technical and professional)	80	63	142
Higher	79	129	208
Total 1986	2,039	1,236	3,275

[1] Figures may not add to totals because of rounding.
[2] Basic is equivalent to primary.

Source: Based on information from David E. Hojman, *Chile: The Political Economy of Development and Democracy in the 1990s*, Pittsburgh, 1993, 38.

Table 16. Population by Gender and Declared Religious Affiliation, 1992
(persons over fourteen years of age)

Religious Affiliation	Males	Females
Catholic	3,660,367	3,864,016
Evangelical *	530,369	668,016
Protestant	39,299	40,960
Other religion	196,198	213,712
No religion	364,582	197,703
TOTAL	4,790,815	4,984,407

* For definition of Evangelical—see Glossary.

Source: Based on information from Chile, Instituto Nacional de Estadísticas, *Resultados oficiales: Censo de población, 1992*, Santiago, 1993, 29.

Table 17. *Opinions Regarding the Legalization of Divorce, December 1990* *
(in percentages agreeing or disagreeing with
the following statement: "In your opinion,
should Chile have a law permitting
divorce?")

Sector	Yes	No
Males	59.2	36.9
Females	52.8	44.1
Ages 18 to 34	64.1	32.3
Ages 35 to 54	50.7	44.8
Age 55 or more	43.8	54.9
High socioeconomic status	70.1	15.5
Middle socioeconomic status	55.8	41.7
Low socioeconomic status	52.1	45.4
All Catholics	54.6	41.1
All Protestants	47.2	51.0
Practicing Catholics	39.5	57.1
Practicing Protestants	35.5	62.9
CHILE	55.6	40.9

* Poll conducted by Centro de Estudios Públicos and Adimark. Percentages do not add to 100.0 because remainder had no opinion.

Source: Based on information from Centro de Estudios Públicos, "Estudio social de opinión pública, diciembre 1990," *Documento de trabajo* [Santiago], No. 151, February 1991, 61; and Arturo Fontaine Talavera and Herald Beyer, "Retrato del movimiento evangélico a la luz de las encuestas de opinión pública," *Estudios Públicos* [Santiago], No. 44, Spring 1991, 95.

Table 18. *Opinions Regarding Abortion, December 1990* *
(in percentages responding to the following
question: "There are different opinions
regarding abortion. Which of
these corresponds best with
what you think?")

| | Should Be Permitted | | |
| | To All Women Who Want It | Only in Special Qualified Cases | Should Not Be Permitted |
Sector			
Males	5.8	45.3	47.4
Females	4.4	44.3	50.7
Ages 18 to 34	6.0	46.7	46.5
Ages 35 to 54	3.9	41.8	53.3
Age 55 or more	4.5	45.0	48.5
High socioeconomic status	8.0	78.0	14.0
Middle socioeconomic status	5.7	47.1	45.8
Low socioeconomic status	3.2	33.5	62.5
All Catholics	4.4	48.6	46.3
All Protestants	1.9	27.7	69.3
Practicing Catholics	0.7	40.9	58.2
Practicing Protestants	0.1	17.6	82.3
CHILE	5.0	44.7	49.2

* Poll conducted by Centro de Estudios Públicos and Adimark. Percentages may not add to 100.0 because remainder had no opinion.

Source: Based on information from Centro de Estudios Públicos, "Estudio social de opinión pública, diciembre 1990," *Documento de trabajo* [Santiago], No. 151, February 1991, 63; and Arturo Fontaine Talavera and Herald Beyer, "Retrato del movimiento evangélico a la luz de las encuestas de opinión pública," *Estudios Públicos* [Santiago], No. 44, Spring 1991, 96.

Table 19. *Birthrates in and out of Wedlock, Selected Years, 1965–88*

| | Births per 1,000 Population | | Percentage of Births out of Wedlock |
Year	In Wedlock	Out of Wedlock	
1965	29.3	6.2	17.5
1970	21.5	5.3	19.8
1975	19.6	5.0	20.3
1980	16.3	5.9	26.6
1985	14.8	6.9	31.8
1988	15.6	7.8	33.5

Source: Based on information from Ernesto Medina Lois, "Situación de salud en Chile," in Jorge Jiménez de la Jara (ed.), *Chile: Sistema de salud en transición a la democracia,* Santiago, 1991, 30.

Table 20. Gross Domestic Product (GDP) by Sector, 1989, 1990, and 1991
(in millions of 1977 Chilean pesos) [1]

Sector	1989	1990	1991
Agriculture, livestock, and forestry	37,902	39,737	40,194
Fishing	4,418	3,964	4,294
Mining	35,629	35,378	37,060
Manufacturing	98,983	99,043	104,451
Electricity, gas, and water	11,575	11,920	12,847
Construction	25,559	28,247	29,581
Trade	84,622	86,701	94,196
Transportation and communications	30,286	33,430	37,419
Services [2]	139,269	141,903	149,111
TOTAL	468,243	480,323	509,153
Rate of growth of GDP (in percentages)	10.0	2.1	6.0

[1] For value of the Chilean peso—see Glossary.
[2] Includes financial, education, and other services.

Source: Based on information from Banco Central de Chile, Dirección de Estudios, Santiago (various publications).

Table 21. Index of Manufacturing Production in Selected Sectors, 1988-92
(1979 = 100)

Sector	1988	1989	1990	1991	1992
Foodstuffs	139.5	149.8	142.1	144.7	169.3
Textiles	120.8	122.4	116.4	126.4	121.0
Footwear	71.4	79.7	75.5	89.6	92.7
Furniture	279.6	319.7	329.6	329.8	322.0
Chemicals	118.2	119.8	120.1	129.7	138.6
Glass products	122.1	172.9	171.8	187.3	214.8
Machinery (nonelectric)	85.2	107.8	119.4	114.6	170.9
Transportation equipment	59.4	75.3	65.6	70.2	81.7
ALL MANUFACTURING	126.4	137.2	136.3	144.5	165.5

Source: Based on information from Chile, Instituto Nacional de Estadísticas, Santiago (various publications); and Chile, Instituto Nacional de Estadísticas, Compendio estadístico, 1993, Santiago, 1993, Table 233-01.

Table 22. Mining Output, 1991 and 1992
(in thousands of tons unless otherwise indicated)

Mineral	1991	1992	Percentage Change
Copper (fine content)	1,363.7	1,445.0	6.0
Molybdenum (fine content)	11.1	10.4	-6.3
Zinc (fine content)	22.7	23.2	2.2
Manganese	33.2	37.4	12.7
Iron	6,238.1	5,230.5	-16.2
Gold (tons, fine content)	19.6	25.3	29.1
Silver (tons, fine content)	431.7	783.2	81.4
Lead (tons, fine content)	817.0	251.0	69.2

Source: Based on information from "Business Outlook: Chile," *Business Latin America*, December 21, 1992, 3.

Table 23. Copper Production, 1987–92
(in thousands of tons, refined)

	1987	1988	1989	1990	1991	1992
Refined	970.3	1,012.8	1,071.0	1,191.6	1,228.3	1,101.3
Blister	136.6	176.6	195.6	136.9	67.8	61.6
In bulk	311.2	261.6	342.7	259.9	518.2	781.0
TOTAL *	1,418.1	1,451.0	1,609.3	1,588.4	1,814.3	1,943.8

* Figures may not add to totals because of rounding.

Source: Based on information cited by Sebastian Edwards from Comisión Chilena del Cobre, Santiago; and Chile, Instituto Nacional de Estadísticas, *Compendio estadístico, 1993*, Santiago, 1993, Table 232-02.

Table 24. Agricultural and Forestry Exports, 1989, 1990, and 1991
(in millions of United States dollars)

Product	1989	1990	1991
Agriculture			
Fresh fruits			
Grapes	273.9	379.3	49.5
Other	69.6	361.5	941.5
Total fresh fruits	343.5	740.8	991.0
Other	153.1	142.7	144.9
Total agriculture	496.6	883.5	1,135.9
Forestry			
Basic forestry			
Pine trees	34.9	50.6	38.5
Pulp	39.2	16.5	25.8
Other	1.3	9.3	3.0
Total basic forestry	75.4	76.4	67.3
Paper products	422.5	423.2	445.6
Wood products	291.5	370.3	427.5
Total forestry	789.4	869.9	940.4
TOTAL	1,286.0	1,753.4	2,076.3

Source: Based on information cited by Sebastian Edwards from Banco Central de Chile, Santiago.

Table 25. Fruit Production, Crop Years 1987-88 to 1990-91
(in thousands of tons)

Fruit	1987-88	1988-89	1989-90	1990-91
Apples	630.0	660.0	690.0	750.0
Apricots	14.5	16.0	19.5	11.2
Avocados	28.0	39.0	37.6	39.0
Grapes	516.0	547.0	660.0	650.0
Lemons	60.0	72.5	86.0	88.0
Oranges	96.0	99.0	97.2	99.0
Peaches	92.4	97.4	112.0	113.0
Pears	99.0	119.0	139.6	165.0
Plums	85.0	98.5	110.0	100.0

Source: Based on information cited by Sebastian Edwards from Chile, Instituto Nacional de Estadísticas, Santiago.

Table 26. Yields of Principal Agricultural Products, Crop Years
1986-87 to 1990-91
(in quintals per hectare)

Crop	1986-87	1987-88	1988-89	1989-90	1990-91
Barley	29.5	33.9	34.6	34.8	33.7
Beans	9.5	13.2	11.5	12.7	13.2
Corn	71.2	73.2	75.3	81.4	83.9
Peas	8.6	7.8	8.9	n.a.	n.a.
Potatoes	126.0	149.8	140.6	150.3	142.2
Rice	39.3	41.7	43.1	41.7	39.4
Sugar beets	493.6	511.6	544.5	537.5	554.6
Sunflowers	21.0	21.0	21.2	23.4	23.9
Wheat	27.1	30.1	32.7	29.5	34.1

n.a.—not available.
Source: Based on information cited by Sebastian Edwards from Chile, Instituto Nacional
de Estadísticas, Santiago.

Table 27. Fishing Industry Exports, 1987-91
(in millions of United States dollars)

Product	1987	1988	1989	1990	1991
Agar	14	19	22	32	28
Crustaceans (canned)	4	6	29	28	26
Crustaceans (fresh and frozen)	31	25	3	3	2
Fish (canned)	29	32	42	42	36
Fish (fresh and frozen)	110	163	209	325	407
Fish meal	359	459	515	380	466
Fish oil	16	23	23	14	26
Mollusks (canned)	49	49	41	41	58
Mollusks (fresh and frozen)	24	37	24	17	20
Seaweed	9	10	12	19	18
Other	6	13	11	15	17
TOTAL *	652	837	932	915	1,104

* Figures may not add to totals because of rounding.
Source: Based on information from Chile, Ministry of Foreign Affairs, General Directorate
of International Economic Relations, Export Promotion Department, *ProChile* [San-
tiago], No. 43, September–October 1992, 6.

Table 28. Forest Area Planted by Public Sector and Private Sector, 1982–90
(in hectares)

Year	Public Sector	Private Sector	Total
1982	41	68,545	68,586
1983	21,811	54,469	76,280
1984	40,302	53,300	93,602
1985	24,193	72,084	96,277
1986	n.a.	66,193	66,193
1987	n.a.	66,441	66,441
1988	n.a.	72,944	72,944
1989	n.a.	86,704	86,704
1990	n.a.	94,130	94,130

n.a.—not available.

Source: Based on information from Banco Central de Chile, Dirección de Estudios, *Indicadores económicos y sociales regionales, 1980–89,* Santiago, 1991, 58.

Table 29. Electric Energy Production by Producer, 1988–92
(in millions of kilowatts)

Company	1988	1989	1990	1991	1992
Chilectra [1]	2,210.4	3,886.6	4,243.0	2,516.4	n.a.
Colbun	2,510.7	2,005.4	1,926.4	2,818.3	n.a.
ENDESA [2]	7,420.0	6,648.9	6,607.5	6,434.1	n.a.
Pilmaiguen	202.4	231.4	269.2	2,315.0	n.a.
Pullingue	169.1	170.0	228.8	209.8	n.a.
Other	4,384.0	4,785.2	5,046.5	5,514.0	n.a.
TOTAL	16,896.6	17,727.5	18,321.4	19,807.6	22,167.3

n.a.—not available.
[1] Compañía Chilena de Electricidad (Chilean Electric Company).
[2] Empresa Nacional de Electricidad (National Electric Company).

Source: Based on information cited by Sebastian Edwards from Chile, Instituto Nacional de Estadísticas, Santiago; and Chile, Instituto Nacional de Estadísticas, *Compendio estadístico, 1993,* Santiago, 1993, Table 234–01.

Table 30. Public-Sector and Private-Sector Construction, 1987–91
(in square meters)

Sector	1987	1988	1989	1990	1991
Public sector					
Housing	91,677	98,797	72,550	13,396	35,357
Industry	14,512	6,347	9,125	24,696	24,581
Services	168,337	148,439	145,188	139,929	177,772
Total public sector ...	274,526	253,583	226,863	178,021	237,710
Private sector	4,498,966	5,331,605	6,309,495	6,065,258	7,404,551
TOTAL	4,773,492	5,585,188	6,536,358	6,243,279	7,642,261

Source: Based on information cited by Sebastian Edwards from Chile, Instituto Nacional de Estadísticas, Santiago.

Table 31. Key Economic Indicators, 1988-92

	1988	1989	1990	1991	1992
Gross domestic product (GDP; in millions of United States dollars)	29,698	32,289	33,297	35,297	33,700
Real GDP growth (in percentages)	7.4	10.0	2.1	6.0	10.4
Consumer price inflation (average annual percentage)	12.7	21.4	27.3	18.7	12.7
Population (in millions)	12.8	13.0	13.0	13.2	13.4
GDP per capita (in United States dollars)	2,330	2,520	2,527	2,637	2,515
Exports, f.o.b. (in millions of United States dollars) [1]	7,052	8,080	8,310	8,929	9,986
Imports, f.o.b. (in millions of United States dollars)	4,833	6,502	7,037	7,353	9,237
Current account (in billions of United States dollars)	-0.17	-0.77	-0.82	0.09	-0.50
Reserves, excluding gold (in billions of United States dollars)	3.16	3.60	6.07	7.04	9.17
Total external debt (in billions of United States dollars)	19.0	17.4	18.6	17.4	18.9
Debt-service ratio (in percentages)	26.9	27.7	25.9	21.5	18.6
Exchange rate (average, Chilean pesos to United States dollar) [2]	245.1	267.2	305.1	349.4	362.6
Investment (as a percentage of GDP, in constant Chilean pesos)	17.0	18.6	19.5	18.2	23.0

[1] f.o.b.—free on board.
[2] For value of the Chilean peso—see Glossary.

Source: Based on information from Economist Intelligence Unit, *Country Report: Chile* [London], No. 2, 1993, 3; Inter-American Development Bank, *Economic and Social Progress in Latin America: 1992 Report,* Washington, October 1992, 286; and Inter-American Development Bank (various other sources).

Table 32. Direction of Trade, 1989–92
(in millions of United States dollars)

Country	1989	1990	1991	1992
Exports, f.o.b. [1]				
Argentina	110	114	257	462
Belgium and Luxembourg	179	243	235	172
Brazil	523	487	448	451
Britain	499	559	408	572
China	53	31	79	262
France	n.a.	402	390	396
Germany [2]	914	941	709	604
Hong Kong	53	40	58	135
Italy	410	402	345	388
Japan	1,121	1,388	1,644	1,707
Netherlands	n.a.	315	363	334
Peru	n.a.	74	146	173
South Korea	258	259	263	243
Spain	223	268	346	367
Taiwan	400	280	395	491
United States	1,456	1,469	1,596	1,649
Imports, c.i.f. [3]				
Argentina	399	503	554	634
Brazil	703	564	698	996
Britain	152	180	163	187
Canada	107	224	157	149
China	n.a.	n.a.	n.a.	146
France	223	297	241	282
Gabon	33	203	169	152
Germany [2]	483	523	498	630
Italy	153	193	177	273
Japan	737	568	646	965
Mexico	117	101	138	178
Nigeria	141	259	199	324
South Korea	165	123	168	250
Spain	157	159	148	224
Taiwan	83	82	112	160
United States	1,348	1,373	1,582	1,985

n.a.—not available.
[1] f.o.b.—free on board.
[2] Includes only West Germany until July 1990; then includes former East Germany.
[3] c.i.f.—cost, insurance, and freight.

Source: Based on information from Economist Intelligence Unit, *Country Report: Chile* [London], No. 3, 1993, 7; and *Business Latin America*, April 1993, 11.

Table 33. Public-Sector Finance, 1990-93
(in percentages of GDP) [1]

	1990	1991	1992	1993 [2]
Central government				
Revenues				
Current				
Tax revenues	14.5	16.9	17.5	18.5
Copper revenues (net)	1.6	1.1	1.3	0.8
Other	4.5	4.6	4.6	5.0
Total current	20.6	22.6	23.4	24.3
Capital	1.4	1.2	1.1	1.0
Total revenues	22.0	23.8	24.5	25.3
Expenditures				
Current	18.2	19.0	18.2	19.2
Capital	3.1	3.3	4.0	4.3
Total expenditures	21.3	22.3	22.2	23.5
Overall surplus	0.7	1.5	2.3	1.8
Savings	2.4	3.6	5.2	5.1
Public enterprises, overall surplus	2.8	0.6	0.7	0.5
Nonfinancial public sector, overall surplus	3.5	2.1	3.0	2.6
Operational deficit of Central Bank (cash basis) [3]	-2.2	-1.1	-1.2	-1.0
Consolidated public sector, overall balance	1.3	1.0	1.8	1.3

[1] GDP—gross domestic product.
[2] Preliminary.
[3] For explanation of Central Bank—see Glossary.

Source: Based on information provided by Sebastian Edwards from World Bank, Washington.

Table 34. Electoral Results for the Chamber of Deputies, March 1973 [1]

Ideological Orientation and Party	Number of Votes	Percentage of Total Votes	Number of Deputies Elected
Right			
National Party [2]	777,084	21.1	32
Center			
Radical Party [3]	133,751	3.6	19
Christian Democratic Party [4]	1,049,676	28.5	55
Total center	1,183,427	32.1	74
Left			
Socialist Party [5]	678,674	18.4	15
Communist Party of Chile [6]	595,829	16.2	22
Total left	1,274,503	34.6	37
TOTAL	2,535,014	87.8	143

[1] Parties listed are those that obtained more than 5 percent of the total vote in more than one congressional election.
[2] Partido Nacional (PN). In 1973 the National Party was the principal right-wing party.
[3] Partido Radical (PR).
[4] Partido Demócrata Cristiano (PDC).
[5] Partido Socialista (PS).
[6] Partido Comunista de Chile (PCCh).

Source: Based on information from Chile, Dirección del Registro Electoral, Santiago.

Table 35. *Electoral Results of the Presidential Elections of December 14, 1989*
(in percentages)

Region	Patricio Aylwin Azócar	Hernán Büchi Buc	Francisco Javier Errázuriz Talavera
I .... Tarapacá	49.7	31.5	18.8
II .... Antofagasta	57.6	24.8	17.5
III .... Atacama	60.7	30.3	9.0
IV .... Coquimbo	57.2	30.7	12.1
V .... Valparaíso	52.6	28.9	18.4
VI .... Libertador General Bernardo O'Higgins	51.6	29.5	18.9
VII .... Maule	55.5	29.4	15.0
VIII .... Bío-Bío	55.8	25.4	18.8
IX .... La Araucanía	47.1	29.1	23.8
X .... Los Lagos	51.0	29.2	19.7
XI .... Aisén del General Carlos Ibáñez del Campo	54.7	31.0	14.3
XII .... Magallanes y La Antártica Chilena	60.3	29.6	10.1
— Metropolitan Region of Santiago	56.2	31.2	12.6
CHILE	55.2	29.4	15.4
Total votes	3,850,571	2,052,116	1,077,172

Source: Based on information from Chile, Servicio Electoral, Santiago.

363

Table 36. Electoral Results for the Chamber of Deputies and Senate, December 14, 1989

	Democracy and Progress [1]				Coalition of Parties for Democracy [2]					Unity for Democracy [3]
	RN [4]	UDI [5]	Independents	Total	PDC [6]	PPD [7]	PR [8]	Other	Total	PAIS [9]
Chamber of Deputies [10]	29	11	6	46	38	17	5	6	66	8
Senate [11]	6	2	8	16	14	3	2	3	22	0

[1] Democracia y Progreso, a coalition.
[2] Concertación de Partidos por la Democracia, a coalition.
[3] Unidad por la Democracia, a coalition.
[4] Renovación Nacional (National Renewal).
[5] Unión Demócrata Independiente (Independent Democratic Union).
[6] Partido Demócrata Cristiano (Christian Democratic Party).
[7] Partido por la Democracia (Party for Democracy).
[8] Partido Radical (Radical Party).
[9] Partido Amplio de la Izquierda Socialista (Broad Socialist Left Party). PAIS was the only party in the coalition to win seats.
[10] The Chamber of Deputies has a total of 120 deputies, two from each of sixty districts.
[11] The Senate consists of thirty-eight elected senators (two from each of nineteen electoral regions) and nine designated senators. The table shows only the elected senators.

Source: Based on information from Chile, Servicio Electoral, Santiago.

*Table 37. Presidencies, Cabinet Changes, and Ministerial Turnovers, 1932–41 and 1946–73 ***

President	Number of Interior Ministers	Number of Partial Cabinet Changes	Number of Major Cabinet Changes	Total Number of Ministers	Average Length of Cabinet	Average Length of Ministerial Service
Arturo Alessandri Palma (1932–38)	6	2	3	59	10 months	12 months
Pedro Aguirre Cerda (1938–41)	7	2	2	44	9 months	11 months
Gabriel González Videla (1946–52)	8	3	5	84	6.5 months	6 months
Carlos Ibáñez del Campo (1952–58)	8	3	5	75	7 months	12 months
Jorge Alessandri Rodríguez (1958–64)	2	1	1	20	29 months	43 months
Eduardo Frei Montalva (1964–70)	3	2	1	22	31 months	40 months
Salvador Allende Gossens (1970–73)	9	1	5	65	5.2 months	7 months

* Data for the presidencies of Jerónimo Méndez Arancibia (1941–42) and Juan Antonio Ríos Morales (1942–46) not available.

Source: Based on information from Luis Valencia A., *Anales de la república*, Santiago, 1951; *Hispanic American Reports* (various issues); and *El Mercurio Edición Internacional* [Santiago] (various issues).

Table 38. Administrative Divisions and Their Capitals, 1993

Region		Region Capital	Province	Province Capital
I	Tarapacá	Iquique	Arica	Arica
			Iquique	Iquique
			Parinacota	Putre
II	Antofagasta	Antofagasta	Antofagasta	Antofagasta
			El Loa	Calama
			Tocopilla	Tocopilla
III	Atacama	Copiapó	Chañaral	Chañaral
			Copiapó	Copiapó
			Huasco	Vallenar
IV	Coquimbo	La Serena	Choapa	Illapel
			Elqui	Coquimbo
			Limarí	Ovalle
V	Valparaíso	Valparaíso	Isla de Pascua	Hanga Roa
			Los Andes	Los Andes
			Petorca	La Ligua
			Quillota	Quillota
			San Antonio	San Antonio
			San Felipe de Aconcagua	San Felipe
			Valparaíso	Valparaíso
—	Metropolitan Region of Santiago	Santiago	Área Metropolitana de Santiago	Santiago
			Chacabuco	Colina
			Cordillera	Puente Alto
			Maipo	San Bernardo
			Melipilla	Melipilla
			Talagante	Talagante
VI	Libertador General Bernardo O'Higgins	Rancagua	Cachapoal	Rancagua
			Cardenal Caro	Pichilemu
			Colchagua	San Fernando

Table 38.—Continued

	Region	Region Capital	Province	Province Capital
VII	Maule	Talca	Cauquenes	Cauquenes
			Curicó	Curicó
			Linares	Linares
			Talca	Talca
VIII	Bío-Bío	Concepción	Arauco	Lebu
			Bío-Bío	Los Ángeles
			Concepción	Concepción
			Ñuble	Chillán
IX	La Araucanía	Temuco	Cautín	Temuco
			Malleco	Angol
X	Los Lagos	Puerto Montt	Chiloé	Castro
			Llanquihue	Puerto Montt
			Osorno	Osorno
			Palena	Chaitén
			Valdivia	Valdivia
XI	Aisén del General Carlos Ibáñez del Campo	Coihaique	Aisén	Puerto Aisén
			Capitán Prat	Cochrane
			Coihaique	Coihaique
			General Carrera	Chile Chico
XII	Magallanes y La Antártica Chilena	Punta Arenas	Antártica Chilena	Puerto Williams
			Magallanes	Punta Arenas
			Tierra del Fuego	Porvenir
			Última Esperanza	Puerto Natales

Source: Based on information from Ana María Errázuriz Korner (ed.), *Manual de Geografía de Chile*, Santiago, 1987, 23–26.

Table 39. National-Level Results of the Municipal Elections of June 23, 1992

Coalitions, Subpacts, and Parties	Number of Votes	Percentage
Concertación por la Democracia [1]		
Subpact PDC–PR–PSD–AHV		
Partido Demócrata Cristiano (PDC) [2]	1,855,137	28.9
Partido Radical (PR) [3]	314,759	4.9
Partido Social Democrático (PSD) [4]	26,788	0.4
Alianza Humanista-Verde (AHV) [5]	52,481	0.8
Total Subpact PDC–PR–PSD–AHV	2,249,165	35.1
Subpact PPD–PS		
Partido por la Democracia (PPD) [6]	590,547	9.2
Partido Socialista (PS) [7]	547,079	8.5
Independents	31,106	0.5
Total Subpact PPD–PS	1,168,732	18.2
Total Concertación por la Democracia .	3,417,897	53.3
Partido Comunista de Chile [8]	419,478	6.5
Partido Liberal [9]	15,505	0.2
Participación y Progreso [10]		
Renovación Nacional [11]	860,808	13.4
Partido Nacional [12]	4,145	0.1
Unión Demócrata Independiente [13]	652,668	10.2
Independents	383,066	6.0
Total Participación y Progreso	1,900,687	29.7
Unión de Centro Centro [14]	519,017	8.1
Independent candidates	136,826	2.1
TOTAL [15] •............................	6,409,410	100.0

Number of voting tables: 25,211 (each voting table contains approximately 350 voters)
Number of voting sites: 1,626
Registered males: 3,791,364
Registered females: 4,048,644
Total registered: 7,840,008

[1] Coalition for Democracy, an alliance of left-of-center parties.
[2] Christian Democratic Party.
[3] Radical Party.
[4] Social Democratic Party.
[5] Humanist-Green Alliance, a party.
[6] Party for Democracy.
[7] Socialist Party.
[8] Communist Party of Chile, running under the Allendista Movement of the Democratic Left (MIDA).
[9] Liberal Party.
[10] Participation and Progress, an alliance of right-of-center parties.
[11] National Renewal.
[12] National Party.
[13] Independent Democratic Union, a party.
[14] Union of the Centrist Center, a party.
[15] Figures may not add to totals because of rounding.

Source: Based on information from Chile, Ministry of Interior, Santiago.

Table 40. Ideological Orientation of Electorate, June 1990 to March 1993
(in percentages of respondents to survey)

Ideological Orientation	June 1990	December 1990	July 1991	December 1991	April 1992	December 1992	March 1993
Right or center-right	14.3	13.4	13.4	21.9	19.0	26.9	22.8
Center	25.3	29.9	23.2	30.8	24.9	22.4	24.6
Left or center-left	28.5	23.7	24.2	23.3	24.1	36.7	33.7
Independent, none, or do not know ..	32.0	33.1	39.1	24.1	32.1	13.9	19.0
TOTAL *	100.0	100.0	100.0	100.0	100.0	100.0	100.0

* Figures may not add to totals because of rounding.

Source: Based on information from Centro de Estudios Públicos and Adimark, Santiago, March 1993.

Table 41. Party Orientation of Electorate, December 1990 to March 1993
(in percentages of respondents to survey)

Party	December 1990	July 1991	December 1991	April 1992	December 1992	March 1993
PDC [1]	37.5	29.5	41.3	35.4	40.4	36.2
PPD [2]	6.8	8.7	5.4	8.4	9.9	10.6
PS [3]	6.6	5.0	6.7	7.6	7.0	8.5
RN [4]	8.1	6.0	8.2	5.3	8.9	6.5
UDI [5]	3.5	5.8	9.3	7.2	7.7	6.0
UCC [6]	n.a.	4.1	3.7	6.4	6.8	5.2
PC [7]	1.7	1.8	1.5	1.8	1.8	2.0
PR [8]	0.9	2.1	0.4	0.9	1.1	1.9
AHV [9]	n.a.	0.8	0.6	0.6	1.3	1.3
PSD [10]	n.a.	0.7	0.4	0.5	0.6	0.6
Other	1.1	0.8	0.8	1.7	0.6	1.0
None	33.8	34.3	21.4	22.6	13.8	20.2
TOTAL [11]	100.0	100.0	100.0	100.0	100.0	100.0

n.a.—not available.
[1] Partido Demócrata Cristiano (Christian Democratic Party).
[2] Partido por la Democracia (Party for Democracy).
[3] Partido Socialista (Socialist Party).
[4] Renovación Nacional (National Renewal).
[5] Unión Demócrata Independiente (Independent Democratic Union).
[6] Unión de Centro Centro (Union of the Centrist Center).
[7] Partido Comunista (Communist Party).
[8] Partido Radical (Radical Party).
[9] Alianza Humanista-Verde (Humanist-Green Alliance).
[10] Partido Social Democrático (Social Democratic Party).
[11] Figures may not add to totals because of rounding.

Source: Based on information from Centro de Estudios Públicos and Adimark, Santiago, March 1993.

Table 42. *Regional-Level Electoral Results of the Presidential Elections of December 11, 1993* [1]

(in percentages)

	Region	Alessandri [2]	Frei [3]	Piñera [4]	Pizarro [5]	Max-Neef [6]	Reitze [7]
I	Tarapacá	26.87	53.42	7.97	6.18	4.70	0.86
II	Antofagasta	21.92	55.48	7.07	7.80	6.82	0.91
III	Atacama	22.32	58.33	5.37	8.36	4.64	0.98
IV	Coquimbo	20.91	61.79	5.53	6.83	3.85	1.09
V	Valparaíso	25.32	55.46	7.84	4.74	5.75	0.90
VI	Libertador General Bernardo O'Higgins	21.99	61.69	5.26	5.02	4.84	1.20
VII	Maule	26.34	60.81	3.98	3.81	3.49	1.56
VIII	Bío-Bío	22.48	60.14	4.94	4.76	6.12	1.56
IX	La Araucanía	29.95	57.11	4.15	3.09	3.89	1.81
X	Los Lagos	29.20	57.29	3.84	3.79	4.47	1.41
XI	Aisén del General Carlos Ibáñez del Campo	32.17	54.39	3.98	4.55	3.61	1.30
XII	Magallanes y La Antártica Chilena	22.38	60.46	6.92	3.86	5.36	1.02
—	Metropolitan Region of Santiago	24.06	55.84	8.17	4.38	6.66	0.89
CHILE		24.65	57.37	6.54	4.64	5.67	1.14

[1] According to the second official count of 53.7 percent of the votes delivered at 10:00 P.M. Total number of voters registered in April 1993 was 8,783,123.

[2] Arturo Alessandri Besa (Union for the Progress of Chile), 1,685,584 votes.

[3] Eduardo Frei Ruiz-Tagle (Coalition of Parties for Democracy), 4,008,654 votes.

[4] José Piñera Echenique (independent), 427,286 votes.

[5] Eugenio Pizarro Poblete (Allendista Movement of the Democratic Left), 324,121 votes.

[6] Manfredo Max-Neef (ecologist), 383,847 votes.

[7] Cristián Reitze (Humanist-Green Alliance), 81,095 votes.

Source: Based on information from Chile, Servicio Electoral, Santiago.

Table 43. Major Army Equipment, 1993

Type and Description	Country of Origin	In Inventory
Light tanks		
AMX-13	France	47
M-41	United States	50
M-24	-do-	60
Medium battle tanks		
AMX-30	France	21
M4A3/M51 Israeli-modified Super-Sherman	United States/Israel	150
Armored personnel carriers		
EE-9 Cascavel	Brazil	200
EE-11 Urutu	-do-	300
M-113A1	United States	60-100
Famae-Mowag Piranha 8x8	Chile/Switzerland	50
Cardoen-Mowag Piranha 6x6	-do-	180
Armored infantry fighting vehicles		
Mowag Piranha with 90mm gun	-do-	20
Mortar carriers		
Cardoen-Mowag Piranha 120mm	-do-	50
Mortars		
60mm M-19	United States	n.a.
81mm M-29	-do-	300
Famae 60mm	Chile	n.a.
Famae 81mm M-1	-do-	n.a.
Famae 107mm	-do-	15
Famae 120mm (50 self-propelled)	-do-	110
Hotchkiss-Brandt MO-120-M65	France	n.a.
Recoilless launchers (150 total)		
57mm M-18	United States	n.a.
75mm M-18	-do-	n.a.
89mm M-20 3.5-inch	-do-	n.a.
M40A1 106mm recoilless launcher	-do-	n.a.
Light antitank guided weapons (3,000 total)		
Milan 120mm	France/Germany	n.a.
Mamba	Germany/South Africa	n.a.
Armbrust 300 80mm	Germany	n.a.
Air defense weapons		
HSS-639 single 20mm gun	Switzerland	100
Oerlikon K 63 twin 20mm gun	-do-	100
35mm twin	n.a.	24
L/70 40mm (in storage)	n.a.	6
Blowpipe SAM missile launchers	Britain	50

Table 43.—Continued

Type and Description	Country of Origin	In Inventory
Fire-support vehicles		
Cardoen-Mowag Piranha with 90mm gun	–do–	20
Artillery		
M-101 105mm	United States	74
Oto Melara Model 56 105mm	Italy	36
Soltam M-68 155mm towed howitzer	Israel	30
Mk F3 SPH 155mm	France	10
LFH-18 105mm towed howitzer	Germany	n.a.
Fixed-wing aircraft		
CASA CN-235	Spain	3
CASA C-212 Aviocar	–do–	6
PA-31 Piper Navajo	United States	3
PA-28 Piper Dakota	–do–	8
Cessna O-1	–do–	4
Cessna 337G	–do–	3
Cessna Citation (VIP)	–do–	1
Cessna R172K	–do–	16
Cessna R172 (training)	–do–	16
Dassault-Breguet Falcon 200	France	1
DHC-6	Canada	4
Helicopters		
Bell UH-1H	United States	3
Bell 206B	–do–	2
Hughes 530F (armed training)	–do–	5
Aérospatiale AS-332B Super Puma	France	3
Aérospatiale SA-330 Puma	–do–	9
Aérospatiale SA-315B Lama	–do–	10
Enstrom 280 FX	n.a.	14

n.a.—not available.

Source: Based on information from *The Military Balance, 1993–1994,* London, 1993, 179–80; and "World Defence Almanac, 1992-93: The Balance of Military Power," *Military Technology* [Bonn], 18, No. 1, January 1993, 44.

Table 44. Major Naval Equipment, 1993

Type and Description	Country of Origin	In Inventory
Navy		
Missile destroyers		
County-class	Britain	4
Almirante Williams-class		
(soon to be retired)	–do–	2
Missile frigates		
Leander-class	–do–	4
Submarines		
Oberon-class	–do–	2
IKL Type 209/1400	Germany	2
Fast transports		
Charles Lawrence-class	United States	1
Missile attack craft		
Reshev (Sa'ar IV)-class	Israel	2
Sa'ar III-class	–do–	2
Torpedo attack craft		
Guacolda (Lürssen)-class	Germany	4
Large patrol boats		
PC–1638-class submarine chaser	United States	1
Dabur-class	Israel	6
Project Taitao Micalvi-class	Chile	4
Corvettes		
Abnaki-class former fleet tug	United States	1
Amphibious		
Maipo (French Batral) medium		
landing ship (LSM)	France	3
Elicura-class LSMs	Chile	2
Sail training ships		
Four-masted schooner	Spain	1
Submarine depot ships		
2,600 tons	Germany	1
Transports		
2,600 tons	Chile	1
Armed tugs		
Cherokee-class ATF	United States	2
Surveying vessels		
Cherokee-class ATF	–do–	1

Table 44.—Continued

Type and Description	Country of Origin	In Inventory
Naval Aviation		
Aircraft		
EMB-111 AN Bandeirante	Brazil	6
EMB-110 CN Bandeirante	-do-	3
CASA-212 Aviocars	Spain	3
A-36 Halcón (C-101)	Chile/Spain	10
Piper PA-31 Navajo	United States	1
Pilatus PC-7	Switzerland	10
Dassault-Breguet Falcon 200	France	2
P-3 Orion	n.a.	8
IAI-1124	Israel	2
Helicopters		
AS-332 Super Puma	France	3
AS-365 Dauphins	-do-	4
Alouette-III	-do-	10
SA-316	-do-	6
SA-319B Alouette III	-do-	7
MBB Bo-105	Germany	3
Bell 206B Jet Ranger	United States	3
Bell 476	-do-	6
EMB-111AN	Brazil	6
Marines		
Small patrol craft	n.a.	10
Amphibious		
Transport landing vehicle, tracked, personnel (LVTP-5)	n.a.	30
Armored personnel carriers		
Mowag Roland with Blowpipe SAMs	France	40
Towed artillery		
M-101 105mm howitzers	United States	16
M-114 155mm	-do-	36
Coast guns		
GPFM-3 155mm	-do-	16
Mortars		
50mm	-do-	50
80mm	-do-	50
Service craft	n.a.	3
Rescue craft	n.a.	13
Coast Guard		
Large patrol boats		
Protector-class	Britain/Chile	4
Small patrol vessels		
Anchova-class	Brazil	10

Table 44.—Continued

Type and Description	Country of Origin	In Inventory
Ona-class	Chile	2
Service launch for search-and-rescue at Easter Island	–do–	1
Service launch	–do–	1
Fast launch	–do–	1
Small trawler-type buoy tenders	Brazil	2
Search-and-rescue craft	Chile	10

n.a.—not available.

Source: Based on information from *The Military Balance, 1993–1994*, London, 1993, 179–80; *Combat Fleets of the World, 1993*, Ed., Bernard Prézelin, Annapolis, 1993, 79–86; and *Jane's Fighting Ships, 1993–94*, London, 1993, 103–13.

Table 45. *Major Air Force Equipment, 1993*

Type and Description	Country of Origin	In Inventory
Fighters		
Northrop F-5E	United States	13
Northrop F-5F	-do-	3
Dassault Mirage 50CH	France	6
Dassault Mirage DCH	-do-	1
Dassault Mirage FCH (Panteras)	-do-	8
Enaer/Dassault Pantera 50C	Chile/France	6
Hawker Hunter FGA-9	Britain	8
Hawker Hunter F-71	-do-	18
Hawker Hunter FR-71	-do-	4
Hawker Hunter T-72	-do-	3
Strike aircraft		
Enaer/CASA T-36 Halcón trainers and A-36 light-strike aircraft	Chile/Spain	20
Cessna A-37B	United States	30
Reconnaissance aircraft		
Canberra PR-9	Britain	2
Gates Learjet 35A	United States	2
King Air A-100	-do-	1
Airborne early warning		
Boeing 707 Phalcon AEW system	Israel/Chile	1
Transports		
Boeing 707-320, 707-321, 707-331	United States	4
Lockheed C-130B	-do-	3
Lockheed C-130H	-do-	2
Beech King E 99	-do-	9
King Air, 2 B 200	-do-	n.a.
Super King Air	-do-	3
DHC-6-300 Twin Otter	Canada	14
CASA 212	Spain	2
Helicopters		
Aérospatiale SA-315B Lama	France	5
Aérospatiale AS-330 Puma	-do-	1
Bell UH-1D, UH-1H	United States	14
Bell 212	-do-	n.a.
MBB BK-117	Germany	1
MBB Bo-105CB	-do-	6
Trainers		
Enaer/CASA T-36	Chile/Spain	20
Enaer T-35A, T-35B Pillán	Chile	48
Cessna T-37B, T-37C	United States	26
Support		
Beech Baron	-do-	1
Beech 99A Petrel	-do-	3
Cessna L-19	-do-	3
Piper PA-28-326 Dakota	-do-	13
Extra-300	Germany	5

Table 45.—Continued

Type and Description	Country of Origin	In Inventory
Air defense		
20mm S-639/-665	n.a.	n.a.
20mm GA1-CO1 twin	n.a.	n.a.
35mm Oerlikon K-63 twin	Switzerland	36
Oerlikon K63 twin 35mm gun systems ..	–do–	n.a.
Samantha/Mistral/Mygale systems	France	12
Sogeco SOG-1,SOG-3 cannons	–do–	n.a.
20mm Famil FAM-2M twin	Chile	n.a.
AS-11/-12 air-to-surface	n.a.	n.a.
AIM-90 Sidewinder, Shafir	United States/Israel	n.a.
Airfield defense vehicles		
VTP-2	Chile	n.a.
Carancho 180	–do–	n.a.

n.a.—not available.

Source: Based on information from *The Military Balance, 1993-1994,* London, 1993, 179–80; and *International Military and Defense Encyclopedia,* 2, Washington, 1993, 489.

Table 46. Major Carabineros Equipment, 1993

Type and Description	Country of Origin	In Inventory
Armored personnel carriers		
Mowag Roland (6x6)	Chile/Switzerland	20
Mortars		
60mm	n.a.	n.a.
80mm	n.a.	n.a.
Fixed-wing aircraft		
Swearingen SA-226TC Metro	United States	4
Piper Navajo twin	–do–	4
Cessna 182Q	–do–	4
Cessna 206	–do–	2
Cessna 210-M Centurion II	–do–	2
Helicopters		
MBB Bo-105C, Bo-106CB, and Bo-105LS	Germany	12
Bell 206L3	United States	2

n.a.—not available.

Source: Based on information fron *The Military Balance, 1993-1994,* London, 1993, 181; and "World Defence Almanac, 1992-93: The Balance of Military Power," *Military Technology* [Bonn], 17, No. 1, January 1993, 47.

Table 47. National Crime Statistics, Selected Years, 1980–91

Year	Robberies	Burglaries	Rapes	Murders
1980	31,679	15,514	694	213
1981	29,896	13,927	709	190
1982	36,570	14,292	820	290
1986	71,150	22,066	783	288
1987	67,775	22,949	829	285
1988	60,659	19,789	765	292
1989	61,018	17,646	582	269
1990	76,709	19,118	753	385
1991 *	87,546	20,132	735	339

* Annualized projections made in early November 1991.

Source: Unpublished report submitted by the Carabineros to the government of Chile, November 1991.

Bibliography

Chapter 1

Agor, Weston. *The Chilean Senate.* Austin: University of Texas Press, 1971.

Alexander, Robert J. *Arturo Alessandri: A Biography.* Ann Arbor: University Microfilms International for Latin American Institute, Rutgers University, 1977.

_____. *The Tragedy of Chile.* Westport, Connecticut: Greenwood Press, 1978.

Angell, Alan. *Politics and the Labour Movement in Chile.* London: Oxford University Press for Royal Institute of International Affairs, 1972.

Arriagada, Genaro. *Pinochet: The Politics of Power.* Boston: Unwin Hyman, 1988.

Aylwin, Mariana, Carlos Bascuñán, Sofía Correa, Christián Gazmuri, Sol Serrano, and Matías Tagle. *Chile en el siglo XX.* Santiago: Editorial Emisión, 1983.

Barbier, Jacques A. *Reform and Politics in Bourbon Chile, 1755–1796.* Ottawa: University of Ottawa Press, 1980.

Bauer, Arnold J. *Chilean Rural Society from the Spanish Conquest to 1930.* New York: Cambridge University Press, 1975.

Behrman, Jere. *Macroeconomic Policy in a Developing Country: The Chilean Experience.* New York: Elsevier/North-Holland, 1977.

Bergquist, Charles. *Labor in Latin America: Comparative Essays on Chile, Argentina, Venezuela, and Colombia.* Stanford: Stanford University Press, 1986.

Blakemore, Harold. *British Nitrates and Chilean Politics, 1886–1896.* London: Athlone Press, 1974.

Bonilla, Frank, and Myron Glaser. *Student Politics in Chile.* New York: Basic Books, 1970.

Boorstein, Edward. *Allende's Chile: An Inside View.* New York: International, 1977.

Bouvier, Virginia M. *Alliance or Compliance: Implications of the Chilean Experience for the Catholic Church in Latin America.* Syracuse: Maxwell School of Citizenship and Public Affairs, Syracuse University, 1983.

Bowers, Claude G. *Chile Through Embassy Windows, 1939–1953.* New York: Simon and Schuster, 1958.

Branch, Taylor, and Eugene M. Propper. *Labyrinth.* New York: Viking Press, 1982.

Burnett, Ben G. *Political Groups in Chile: The Dialogue Between Order and Change.* Austin: University of Texas Press, 1970.

Burr, Robert N. *By Reason or Force: Chile and the Balancing of Power in South America, 1830-1905.* Berkeley: University of California Press, 1965.

Campero, Guillermo. *Los gremios empresariales en el período 1970-1983: Comportamiento sociopolítico y orientaciones ideológicas.* Santiago: Instituto Latinoamericano de Estudios Transnacionales, 1984.

Campero, Guillermo, and José A. Valenzuela. *El movimiento sindical en el régimen militar chileno, 1973-1981.* Santiago: Instituto Latinoamericano de Estudios Transnacionales, 1984.

Campos Harriet, Fernando. *Historia constitucional de Chile: Las instituciones políticas y sociales.* (6th ed.) Santiago: Editorial Jurídica de Chile, 1983.

Carriere, Jean. *Landowners and Politics in Chile: A Study of the Sociedad Nacional de Agricultura, 1932-1970.* Amsterdam: Centrum voor Studie en Documentatie van Latijns-Amerika, 1981.

Cavallo, Ascanio, Manuel Salazar, and Oscar Sepúlveda. *La historia oculta del régimen militar.* Santiago: Ediciones La Época, 1988.

Caviedes, César N. *Elections in Chile: The Road Toward Redemocratization.* Boulder, Colorado: Rienner, 1991.

————. *The Politics of Chile: A Sociogeographical Assessment.* Boulder, Colorado: Westview Press, 1979.

Chavkin, Samuel. *Storm over Chile: The Junta under Siege.* Westport, Connecticut: Hill, 1985.

Cleaves, Peter. *Bureaucratic Politics and Administration in Chile.* Berkeley: University of California Press, 1975.

Clissold, Stephen. *Bernardo O'Higgins and the Independence of Chile.* New York: Praeger, 1969.

Collier, Simon. *Ideas and Politics of Chilean Independence.* New York: Cambridge University Press, 1967.

Constable, Pamela, and Arturo Valenzuela. *A Nation of Enemies: Chile under Pinochet.* New York: Norton, 1991.

Davis, Nathaniel. *The Last Two Years of Salvador Allende.* Ithaca: Cornell University Press, 1985.

Dennis, William Jefferson. *Tacna and Arica: An Account of the Chile-Peru Boundary Dispute and of the Arbitration by the United States.* Hamden, Connecticut: Archon Books, 1931.

de Ramón, Armando, and José Manuel Larraín. *Orígenes de la vida económica chilena, 1659-1808.* Santiago: Centro de Estudios Públicos, 1982.

de Shazo, Peter. *Urban Workers and Labor Unions in Chile, 1902-1927.* Madison: University of Wisconsin Press, 1983.

de Vylder, Stefan. *Allende's Chile: The Political Economy of the Rise and Fall of the Unidad Popular*. Cambridge: Cambridge University Press, 1976.

Dinges, John, and Saul Landau. *Assassination on Embassy Row*. New York: Pantheon, 1980.

Drake, Paul W. "Allende, Salvador." Pages 18-20 in Joel Krieger (ed.), *The Oxford Companion to Politics of the World*. New York: Oxford University Press, 1993.

_____. *The Money Doctor in the Andes: The Kemmerer Missions, 1923-1933*. Durham: Duke University Press, 1989.

_____. *Socialism and Populism in Chile, 1932-52*. Urbana: University of Illinois Press, 1978.

Drake, Paul W., and Iván Jaksić. *The Struggle for Democracy in Chile, 1982-1990*. Lincoln: University of Nebraska Press, 1991.

Dunkerley, James. *Political Suicide in Latin America and Other Essays*. New York: Verso, 1992.

Edwards, Sebastian, and Alejandra Cox Edwards. *Monetarism and Liberalization: The Chilean Experiment*. Cambridge: Ballinger, 1987.

Edwards Vives, Alberto. *La fronda aristocrática*. Santiago: Editorial del Pacífico, 1928.

Ellsworth, P.T. *Chile: An Economy in Transition*. New York: Macmillan, 1945.

Espinosa, Juan G., and Andrew S. Zimbalist. *Economic Democracy: Workers' Participation in Chilean Industry, 1970-73*. New York: Academic Press, 1978.

Evans, Henry Clay. *Chile and Its Relations with the United States*. Durham: Duke University Press, 1927.

Falcoff, Mark. *Modern Chile, 1970-89: A Critical History*. New Brunswick, New Jersey: Transaction Books, 1989.

Faron, Louis C. *The Mapuche Indians of Chile*. New York: Holt, Rinehart, and Winston, 1968.

Farrell, Joseph P. *The National Unified School in Allende's Chile*. Vancouver: University of British Columbia Press, 1986.

Faúndez, Julio. *Marxism and Democracy in Chile: From 1932 to the Fall of Allende*. New Haven: Yale University Press, 1988.

Fermandois, Joaquín. *Chile y el mundo, 1970-1973: La política exterior del gobierno de la Unidad Popular y el sistema internacional*. Santiago: Ediciones Universidad Católica de Chile, 1985.

Ffrench-Davis, Ricardo. *Políticas económicas en Chile, 1952-1970*. Santiago: Ediciones Nueva Universidad, 1973.

Fischer, Kathleen. *Political Ideology and Educational Reform in Chile, 1964-1976*. Los Angeles: Latin American Center, University of California at Los Angeles, 1979.

Fleet, Michael. *The Rise and Fall of Chilean Christian Democracy*. Princeton: Princeton University Press, 1985.

Foxley Riesco, Alejandro. *Latin American Experiments in Neoconservative Economics.* Berkeley: University of California Press, 1983.

Francis, Michael J. *The Limits of Hegemony: United States Relations with Argentina and Chile During World War II.* Notre Dame: University of Notre Dame Press, 1977.

Furci, Carmelo. *The Chilean Communist Party and the Road to Socialism.* London: Zed Books, 1984.

Galdames, Luis. *A History of Chile.* New York: Russell and Russell, 1964.

Garretón, Manuel Antonio. *The Chilean Political Process.* Boston: Unwin Hyman, 1989.

Gil, Federico G. *The Political System of Chile.* Boston: Houghton Mifflin, 1966.

Gil, Federico G., Ricardo Lagos, and Henry A. Landsberger. *Chile at the Turning Point: Lessons of the Socialist Years, 1970–1973.* Philadelphia: Institute for the Study of Human Issues, 1979.

Góngora, Mario. *Origen de los inquilinos de Chile central.* Santiago: Editorial Universitaria, 1960.

————. *Studies in the Colonial History of Spanish America.* New York: Cambridge University Press, 1975.

Grayson, George. *El Partido Demócrata Cristiano chileno.* Buenos Aires: Editorial Francisco de Aguirre, 1968.

Halperin, Ernst. *Nationalism and Communism in Chile.* Cambridge: MIT Press, 1965.

Handelman, Howard, and Thomas G. Sanders. *Military Government and the Movement Toward Democracy in South America.* Bloomington: Indiana University Press, 1981.

Hauser, Thomas. *The Execution of Charles Horman: An American Sacrifice.* New York: Harcourt, Brace, Jovanovich, 1978.

Heise González, Julio. *Historia de Chile: El período parlamentario, 1861–1925.* (2 vols.) Santiago: Editorial Universitaria, 1974, 1982.

Herrick, Bruce H. *Urban Migration and Economic Development in Chile.* Cambridge: MIT Press, 1965.

Hojman, David E. *Chile after 1973: Elements for the Analysis of Military Rule.* Liverpool: Centre for Latin American Studies, University of Liverpool, 1985.

Jaksić, Iván. *Academic Rebels in Chile: The Role of Philosophy in Higher Education and Politics.* Albany: State University of New York Press, 1989.

Jara, Alvaro. *Guerra y sociedad en Chile.* Santiago: Editorial Universitaria, 1971.

Jarvis, Lovell S. *Chilean Agriculture under Military Rule: From Reform to Reaction, 1973–1980.* (Research Series No. 59.) Berkeley: Institute of International Studies, University of California Press, 1985.

Jobet, Julio César. *Ensayo crítico del desarrollo económico-social de Chile.* Santiago: Editorial Universitaria, 1955.

Kaufman, Edy. *Crisis in Allende's Chile: New Perspectives.* New York: Praeger, 1988.

Kaufman, Robert R. *The Politics of Land Reform in Chile, 1950–1970: Public Policy, Political Institutions, and Social Change.* Cambridge: Harvard University Press, 1972.

Kinsbruner, Jay. *Bernardo O'Higgins.* New York: Twayne, 1968.

————. *Chile: An Historical Interpretation.* New York: Harper and Row, 1973.

————. *Diego Portales: Interpretive Essays on the Man and Times.* The Hague: Martinus Nijhoff, 1967.

Kirsch, Henry W. *Industrial Development in a Traditional Society: The Conflict of Entrepreneurship and Modernization in Chile.* Gainesville: University Press of Florida, 1977.

Korth, Eugene H. *Spanish Policy in Colonial Chile: The Struggle for Social Justice, 1535–1700.* Stanford: Stanford University Press, 1968.

Korth, Eugene H., and Della M. Flusche. *Forgotten Females: Women of African and Indian Descent in Colonial Chile, 1553–1800.* Detroit: B. Ethridge Books, 1983.

Lomnitz, Larissa, and Ana Melnick. *Chile's Middle Class: A Struggle for Survival in the Face of Neoliberalism.* Boulder, Colorado: Rienner, 1991.

Loveman, Brian. *Chile: The Legacy of Hispanic Capitalism.* (2d ed.) New York: Oxford University Press, 1988.

————. *Struggle in the Countryside: Politics and Rural Labor in Chile, 1919–1973.* Bloomington: Indiana University Press, 1976.

McBride, George. *Chile: Land and Society.* New York: Octagon Books, 1936.

McCaa, Robert. *Marriage and Fertility in Chile: Demographic Turning Points in the Petorca Valley, 1840–1976.* Boulder, Colorado: Westview Press, 1983.

Mamalakis, Markos J. *The Growth and Structure of the Chilean Economy: From Independence to Allende.* New Haven: Yale University Press, 1976.

Mamalakis, Markos J., and Clark W. Reynolds. *Essays on the Chilean Economy.* Homewood, Illinois: Irwin, 1965.

Mellafe, Rolando. *La introducción de la esclavitud negra en Chile.* Santiago: Editorial Universitaria, 1959.

Monteón, Michael. *Chile in the Nitrate Era: The Evolution of Economic Dependence, 1880–1930.* Madison: University of Wisconsin Press, 1982.

Moran, Theodore H. *Multinational Corporations and the Politics of Dependence: Copper in Chile.* Princeton: Princeton University Press, 1974.

Moreno, Francisco José. *Legitimacy and Stability in Latin America: A Study of Chilean Political Culture.* New York: New York University Press, 1969.

Morris, James O. *Elites, Intellectuals, and Consensus: A Study of the Social Question and the Industrial Relations System in Chile.* Ithaca: Cornell University, 1966.

Muñoz, Heraldo. *Las relaciones exteriores del gobierno militar de Chile.* Santiago: PROSPEL and Centro de Estudios de la Realidad Contemporánea, Las Ediciones del Ornitorrinco, 1986.

Muñoz, Heraldo, and Carlos Portales. *Elusive Friendship: A Survey of U.S.-Chilean Relations.* (Latin American and Caribbean Center Studies on Latin America and the Caribbean.) Boulder, Colorado: Rienner, 1991.

Muñoz, Oscar. *Crecimiento industrial de Chile, 1914–1965.* Santiago: Universidad de Chile, 1968.

Mutchler, David. *The Church as a Political Factor in Latin America, with Particular Reference to Colombia and Chile.* New York: Praeger, 1971.

Nunn, Frederick M. *Chilean Politics, 1920–1931: The Honorable Mission of the Armed Forces.* Albuquerque: University of New Mexico Press, 1970.

_____. *The Military in Chilean History: Essays on Civil-Military Relations, 1810–1973.* Albuquerque: University of New Mexico Press, 1976.

_____. *Yesterday's Soldiers: European Military Professionalism in South America, 1890–1940.* Lincoln: University of Nebraska Press, 1983.

O'Brien, Philip, and Jackie Roddick. *Chile: The Pinochet Decade.* London: Latin America Bureau, 1983.

O'Brien, Thomas F. *The Nitrate Industry and Chile's Crucial Transition, 1870–1891.* New York: New York University Press, 1982.

Orrego Vicuña, Francisco (ed.). *Chile: The Balanced View.* Santiago: Institute of International Studies, University of Chile, 1975.

Petras, James F. *Politics and Social Forces in Chilean Development.* Berkeley: University of California Press, 1969.

Petras, James F., and Morris Morley. *The United States and Chile: Imperialism and the Overthrow of the Allende Government.* New York: Monthly Review Press, 1975.

Pike, Fredrick B. *Chile and the United States, 1880–1962.* Notre Dame: University of Notre Dame Press, 1962.

Pinochet Ugarte, Augusto. *The Crucial Day, September 11, 1973.* Santiago: Editorial Renacimiento, 1982.

Pocock, Hugh R.S. *The Conquest of Chile.* New York: Stein and Day, 1967.

Politzer, Patricia. *Fear in Chile: Lives under Pinochet.* New York: Pantheon Books, 1989.

Pollack, Benny, and Herman Rosenkrantz. *Revolutionary Social Democracy: The Chilean Socialist Party.* London: Pinter, 1986.

Ramírez Necochea, Hernán. *Balmaceda y la contrarevolución de 1891.* (2d ed.) Santiago: Editorial Universitaria, 1969.

Ramos, Joseph R. *Neoconservative Economics in the Southern Cone of Latin America, 1973-1983.* Baltimore: Johns Hopkins University Press, 1986.

Remmer, Karen L. *The Chilean Military under Authoritarian Rule, 1973-1987.* Albuquerque: University of New Mexico Press, 1988.

_____. *Military Rule in Latin America.* Boston: Unwin Hyman, 1989.

_____. *Party Competition in Argentina and Chile: Political Recruitment and Public Policy, 1890-1930.* Lincoln: University of Nebraska Press, 1984.

Roxborough, Ian, Philip O'Brien, and Jackie Roddick. *Chile: The State and Revolution.* New York: Holmes and Meier, 1977.

Sater, William F. *Chile and the United States: Empires in Conflict.* Athens: University of Georgia Press, 1990.

_____. *Chile and the War of the Pacific.* Lincoln: University of Nebraska Press, 1986.

_____. *The Heroic Image in Chile: Arturo Prat, Secular Saint.* Berkeley: University of California Press, 1973.

_____. "A Survey of Recent Chilean Historiography, 1965-1976," *Latin American Research Review,* 14, No. 2, 1979, 55-88.

Scully, Timothy R. *Rethinking the Center: Party Politics in Nineteenth- and Twentieth-Century Chile.* Stanford: Stanford University Press, 1992.

Sideri, Sandro (ed.). *Chile, 1970-73: Economic Development and Its International Setting: Self-Criticism of the Unidad Popular Government's Policies.* The Hague: Martinus Nijhoff, 1979.

Sigmund, Paul E. *The Overthrow of Allende and the Politics of Chile, 1964-1976.* (Pitt Latin American Series.) Pittsburgh: University of Pittsburgh Press, 1977.

Silva, Patricio. *Estado, neoliberalismo, y política agraria en Chile, 1973-1981.* Amsterdam: Centrum voor Studie en Documentatie van Latijns-Amerika, 1987.

Smith, Brian H. *The Church and Politics in Chile: Challenges to Modern Catholicism.* Princeton: Princeton University Press, 1982.

Solberg, Carl. *Immigration and Nationalism: Argentina and Chile, 1890-1914.* Austin: University of Texas, 1970.

Stallings, Barbara. *Class Conflict and Economic Development in Chile,*

1958-1973. Stanford: Stanford University Press, 1978.

Steenland, Kyle. *Agrarian Reform under Allende: Peasant Revolt in the South.* Albuquerque: University of New Mexico Press, 1977.

Stevenson, John Reese. *The Chilean Popular Front.* Westport, Connecticut: Greenwood Press, 1970.

Talbott, Robert D. *A History of the Chilean Boundaries.* Ames: Iowa State University Press, 1974.

Thiesenhusen, William. *Chile's Experiments in Agrarian Reform.* Madison: University of Wisconsin Press, 1966.

Tulchin, Joseph S., and Augusto Varas. *From Dictatorship to Democracy: Rebuilding Political Consensus in Chile.* Boulder, Colorado: Rienner, 1991.

Valenzuela, Arturo. *The Breakdown of Democratic Regimes: Chile.* Baltimore: Johns Hopkins University Press, 1978.

_____. *Political Brokers in Chile: Local Government in a Centralized Polity.* Durham: Duke University Press, 1977.

Valenzuela, Arturo, and J. Samuel Valenzuela (eds.). *Chile: Politics and Society.* New Brunswick, New Jersey: Transaction Books, 1976.

_____. "Visions of Chile," *Latin American Research Review,* 10, No. 3, 1975, 155-76.

Valenzuela, J. Samuel. *Democratización vía reforma: La expansión del sufragio en Chile.* Buenos Aires: Ediciones del IDES, 1985.

Valenzuela, J. Samuel, and Arturo Valenzuela (eds.). *Military Rule in Chile: Dictatorship and Oppositions.* Baltimore: Johns Hopkins University Press, 1986.

Valenzuela, María Elena. *La mujer en el Chile militar.* Santiago: Ediciones Chile y América, 1987.

Varas, Augusto. *Los militares en el poder: Régimen y gobierno militar en Chile, 1973-1986.* Santiago: Pehuén, 1987.

Vergara, Pilar. *Auge y caída del neoliberalismo en Chile.* Santiago: Facultad Latinoamericana de Ciencias Sociales, 1983.

Vernon, Ida W. *Pedro de Valdivia: Conquistador of Chile.* Austin: University of Texas Press, 1946.

Walton, Gary M (ed.). *The National Economic Policies of Chile.* Greenwich, Connecticut: Jai Press, 1985.

Werlich, David P. *Peru: A Short History.* Carbondale, Illinois: Southern Illinois University Press, 1978.

Wilgus, A. Curtis. *Historical Atlas of Latin America: Political, Geographic, Economic, Cultural.* New York: Cooper Square, 1967.

Winn, Peter. *Weavers of Revolution: The Yarur Workers and Chile's Road to Socialism.* New York: Oxford University Press, 1986.

Woll, Allen. *A Functional Past: The Uses of History in Nineteenth Century Chile.* Baton Rouge: Louisiana State University Press, 1982.

Worcester, Donald E. *Sea Power and Chilean Independence.* Gainesville: University of Florida Press, 1962.

Wright, Thomas C. *Landowners and Reform in Chile: The Sociedad Nacional de Agricultura, 1919-40.* Urbana: University of Illinois Press, 1982.

Yeager, Gertrude Matoyka. *Barros Arana's Historia General de Chile: Politics, History, and National Identity.* Fort Worth: Texas Christian University Press, 1981.

Zeitlin, Maurice. *The Civil Wars in Chile, 1851 and 1859.* Princeton: Princeton University Press, 1984.

Zeitlin, Maurice, and Richard Earl Ratcliff. *Landlords and Capitalists: The Dominant Class of Chile.* Princeton: Princeton University Press, 1988.

Chapter 2

Angell, Alan. *Politics and the Labour Movement in Chile.* London: Oxford University Press for Royal Institute of International Affairs, 1972.

Arellano, José Pablo. *Políticas sociales y desarrollo: Chile, 1924-1984.* (2d ed.) Santiago: Corporación de Investigaciones Económicas para Latinoamérica, 1988.

Banco Central de Chile. Dirección de Estudios. *Indicadores económicos y sociales regionales, 1980-1989.* Santiago: 1991.

Barraclough, Solon Lovett, and José Antonio Fernández. *Diagnóstico de la reforma agraria chilena.* Mexico City: Siglo Veintiuno, 1974.

Brunner, José Joaquín. *Chile: Transformaciones culturales y modernidad.* Santiago: Facultad Latinoamericana de Ciencias Sociales, 1989.

Campero, Guillermo. *Los gremios empresariales en el período 1970-1983: Comportamiento sociopolítico y orientaciones ideológicas.* Santiago: Instituto Latinoamericano de Estudios Transnacionales, 1984.

Campero, Guillermo, and José A. Valenzuela. *El movimiento sindical en el régimen militar chileno, 1973-1981.* Santiago: Instituto Latinoamericano de Estudios Transnacionales, 1984.

Castañeda, Tarsicio. *Para combatir la pobreza: Política social y descentralización en Chile durante los ochenta.* Santiago: Centro de Estudios Públicos, 1990.

Caviedes, César N. *The Politics of Chile: A Sociogeographical Assessment.* Boulder, Colorado: Westview Press, 1979.

Centro de Estudios de la Realidad Contemporánea. ''Informe encuesta nacional CERC.'' Santiago: July 1991.

Centro de Estudios Públicos. ''Estudio social de opinión pública, diciembre 1990," *Documento de trabajo* [Santiago], No. 151, February 1991.

Cheyre Valenzuela, Hernán. *La previsión en Chile, ayer y hoy: Impacto de una reforma.* Santiago: Centro de Estudios Públicos, 1991.

Chile. Instituto Geográfico Militar. *Atlas Geográfico de Chile.* Santiago: 1988.

_____. Instituto Nacional de Estadísticas. *Compendio estadístico, 1990.* Santiago: 1990.

_____. Instituto Nacional de Estadísticas. *Compendio estadístico, 1991.* Santiago: 1991.

_____. Instituto Nacional de Estadísticas. *Compendio estadístico, 1993.* Santiago: 1993.

_____. Instituto Nacional de Estadísticas. *Informe demográfico de Chile: Censo 1992.* Santiago: 1993.

_____. Instituto Nacional de Estadísticas. *Resultados oficiales: Censo de población, 1992: Población total país, regiones, comunas, por sexo y edad.* Santiago: 1993.

_____. Instituto Nacional de Estadísticas and Centro de Estudios Latinoamericanos de Demografía. *Chile: Proyecciones y estimaciones de población por sexo y edad: Total del país económicamente activa urbana y rural.* Santiago: Instituto Nacional de Estadísticas, 1991.

Corporación de Investigaciones Económicas para Latinoamérica. *Colección Estudios de CIEPLAN* [Santiago], No. 30, December 1990.

_____. "Set de estadísticas económicas," *Colección Estudios de CIEPLAN* [Santiago], No. 92, July 1992.

_____. "Set de estadísticas económicas," *Colección Estudios de CIEPLAN* [Santiago], January 1994.

Correa, Enrique, and José Antonio Viera-Gallo. *Iglesia y dictadura.* Santiago: Centro de Estudios Sociales [1986].

Cortázar, René. *Política laboral en el Chile democrático: Avances y desafíos en los noventa.* Santiago: Ediciones Dolmen, 1993.

Covarrubias, Paz, and Rolando Franco (eds.). *Chile: Mujer y sociedad.* Santiago: Fondo de la Naciones Unidas para la Infancia, 1978.

Dubet, François, and Eugenio Tironi, with Vicente Espinoza and Eduardo Valenzuela. *Pobladores: Luttes sociales et démocratie au Chili.* Paris: Editions L'Harmattan, 1989.

Echeverría, Fernando. "Perfiles del sindicalismo: La opinión de los trabajadores," *Proposiciones* [Santiago], No. 17, July 1989, 161–62.

Encina, Francisco. *Nuestra inferioridad económica: Sus causas, sus consecuencias.* Santiago: Editorial Universitaria, 1955.

Faron, Louis C. *The Mapuche Indians of Chile.* New York: Holt, Rinehart, and Winston, 1968.

Fontaine Talavera, Arturo, and Herald Beyer. "Retrato del movimiento evangélico a la luz de las encuestas de opinión pública," *Estudios Públicos* [Santiago], No. 44, Spring 1991.

Foxley Riesco, Alejandro. *Chile y su futuro: Un país posible.* Santiago: Corporación de Investigaciones Económicas para Latinoamérica, 1987.

Frías, Patricio P. *El movimiento sindical chileno en la lucha por la democracia, 1973-1988.* Santiago: Programa Economía del Trabajo, 1989.

Gómez, Sergio, and Jorge Echenique. *La agricultura chilena: Las dos caras de la modernización.* (3d ed.) Santiago: Facultad Latinoamericana de Ciencias Sociales, 1991.

Hojman, David E. *Chile: The Political Economy of Development and Democracy in the 1990s.* Pittsburgh: University of Pittsburgh Press, 1993.

Hurtado, Alberto. *¿Es Chile un país católico?* Santiago: Editorial Splendor, 1941.

Iglesias P., Augusto, and Rodrigo Acuña R. *Sistema de pensiones en América Latina, Chile: Experiencia con un régimen de capitalización, 1981-1991.* Santiago: Comisión Económica para América Latina and Programa de las Naciones Unidas para el Desarrollo, 1991.

Jiménez de la Jara, Jorge (ed.). *Chile: Sistema de salud en transición a la democracia.* Santiago: Editorial Atena, 1991.

Kay, Cristóbal, and Patricio Silva (eds.). *Development and Social Change in the Chilean Countryside: From the Pre-Land Reform Period to the Democratic Transition.* Amsterdam: Center for Latin American Research and Documentation, 1992.

Klimpel, Felícitas. *La mujer chilena: El aporte femenino al progreso de Chile, 1910-1960.* Santiago: Editorial Andrés Bello, 1962.

Lagos Schuffeneger, Humberto. *Crisis de la esperanza: Religión y autoritarismo en Chile.* Santiago: Programa Evangélico de Estudios Socio-Religiosos and Ediciones Literatura Americana Reunida, 1988.

Levy, Daniel C. "Chilean Universities under the Junta: Regime and Policy," *Latin American Research Review,* 21, No. 3, 1986, 95-128.

Martínez, Jorge (ed.). *Censo de reducciones indígenas seleccionadas: Análisis sociodemográfico.* Santiago: Instituto Nacional de Estadísticas, 1991.

Medina Lois, Ernesto. "Situación de salud en Chile." In Jorge Jiménez de la Jara (ed.), *Chile: Sistema de salud en transición a la democracia.* Santiago: Editorial Atena, 1991.

Meller, Patricio. "Revisión del empresariado chileno: ¿Surge un nuevo actor?" *Colección Estudios de CIEPLAN* [Santiago], No. 30, December 1990, 5 54.

Montero, Cecilia. "La evolución del empresariado chileno: ¿Surge un nuevo actor?" *Colección Estudios de CIEPLAN* [Santiago], No. 30, December 1990, 91-122.

Mujica, Patricio, and Osvaldo Larrañaga. "Social Policies and Income Distribution in Chile." Pages 17-51 in Ricardo Hausmann and Ricoberto Rigobón (eds.), *Government Spending and Income Distribution in Latin America.* Washington: Inter-American Development Bank, 1993.

Piñera, José. *El cascabel al gato: La batalla por la reforma previsional.* (3d ed.) Santiago: Zig-Zag, 1991.

Programa Economía del Trabajo. *Economía y trabajo en Chile: Informe anual.* Santiago: 1993.

_____. *Serie de indicadores económico sociales: Series anuales.* Santiago: 1990.

Ruiz-Tagle P., Jaime. *Una mirada crítica: Los trabajadores en democracia.* Santiago: Programa Economía del Trabajo, 1993.

Sánchez, Alfredo, and Roberto Morales. *Las regiones de Chile: Espacio físico, humano, y económico.* Santiago: Editorial Universitaria, 1990.

Smith, Brian H. *The Church and Politics in Chile: Challenges to Modern Catholicism.* Princeton: Princeton University Press, 1982.

Stewart-Gambino, Hannah W. *The Church and Politics in the Chilean Countryside.* Boulder, Colorado: Westview Press, 1992.

Subercaseaux Zañartu, Benjamín. *Chile, o una loca geografía.* (20th ed.) Santiago: Editorial Universitaria, 1989.

Tironi, Eugenio. *Autoritarismo, modernización, y marginalidad: El caso de Chile, 1973-1989.* Santiago: Ediciones SUR, 1990.

Tironi, Eugenio, and Javier Martínez. *Las clases sociales en Chile.* Santiago: Ediciones SUR, 1986.

Toledo O., Ximena, and Eduardo Zapater A. *Geografía general y regional de Chile.* Santiago: Editorial Universitaria, 1989.

United Nations Development Programme. *Human Development Report, 1993.* New York: Oxford University Press, 1993.

Valdés, Teresa. *Venid benditas de mi padre: Las pobladoras, sus rutinas y sus sueños.* Santiago: Facultad Latinoamericana de Ciencias Sociales, 1988.

Valenzuela, Arturo, and J. Samuel Valenzuela (eds.). *Chile: Politics and Society.* New Brunswick, New Jersey: Transaction Books, 1976.

Valenzuela, Eduardo. *La rebelión de los jóvenes.* Santiago: Ediciones SUR, 1985.

Valenzuela, J. Samuel. "Sindicalismo, desarrollo económico, y democracia: Hacia un nuevo modelo de organización laboral en Chile," *Economía y Trabajo* [Santiago], 1, No. 2, 1993, 65–97.

Valenzuela, J. Samuel, and Arturo Valenzuela (eds.). *Military Rule in Chile: Dictatorship and Oppositions,* Baltimore: Johns Hopkins University Press, 1986.

Venegas Leiva, Sylvia. *Una gota al día . . . Un chorro al año: El impacto social de la expansión frutícola.* Santiago: Grupo de Estudios Agro-Regionales and Universidad Academia de Humanismo Cristiano, 1992.

Vergara, Pilar. *Políticas hacia la extrema pobreza en Chile, 1973–1988.* Santiago: Facultad Latinoamericana de Ciencias Sociales, 1990.

Vial, Joaquín, Andrea Butelmann, and Carmen Celedón Cariola. "Fundamentos de las políticas macroeconómicas del gobierno democrático chileno (1990–1993)," *Colección Estudios de CIEPLAN* [Santiago], No. 30, December 1990.

Winn, Peter. *Weavers of Revolution: The Yarur Workers and Chile's Road to Socialism.* New York: Oxford University Press, 1986.

Zapata, Francisco (ed.). *Clases sociales y acción obrera en Chile.* Mexico City: El Colegio de México, 1986.

(Various issues of the following periodicals were also used in the preparation of this chapter: Banco Central de Chile, *Boletín Mensual* [Santiago]; *El Mercurio* [Santiago]; and *La Nación* [Santiago].)

Chapter 3

Ahumada, C. Jorge. *En vez de la miseria.* (10th ed., rev.) Santiago: Ediciones BAT, 1990.

Alaluf, David. *La economía chilena en 1971.* Santiago: Instituto de Economía y Planificación, Universidad de Chile, 1972.

Allende, Salvador. *El pensamiento económico del gobierno de Allende.* Santiago: Editorial Universitaria, 1971.

Almeyda, Clodomiro. *Reencuentro con mi vida.* Santiago: Ediciones del Ornitorrinco, 1987.

Aranda, Sergio, and Alberto Martínez. "Estructura económica: Algunas características fundamentales." Pages 55–172 in Aníbal Pinto (ed.), *Chile hoy.* Mexico City: Siglo Veintiuno, 1970.

Arellano, José Pablo (ed.). *Modelo económico chileno: Trayectoria de una crítica.* Santiago: Editorial Aconcagua, 1982.

Asociación Latinoamericana de Integración. "Elementos de juicio para el establecimiento de un programa para la eliminación de restricciones no arancelarias." Caracas: 1984.

Balassa, Bela. "Exports, Policy Choices, and Economic Growth in Developing Countries after the 1973 Oil Shock," *Journal of Development Economics*, 18, 1985, 23–35.

_____. "The Interaction of Domestic Distortions with Development Strategies." (Discussion Paper No. 249.) Washington: World Bank, February 1987.

_____. "Policy Experiments in Chile, 1973–1983." Pages 203–38 in Gary M. Walton (ed.), *The National Economic Policies of Chile*. Greenwich, Connecticut: Jai Press, 1985.

Balassa, Bela, Gerardo M. Bueno, Pedro Pablo Kuczynski, and Mario Henrique Simonsen. *Toward Renewed Economic Growth in Latin America*. Washington: Institute for International Economics, 1986.

Ballesteros, M., and Tom Davis. "The Growth of Output and Employment in Basic Sectors of the Chilean Economy, 1908–1957," *Economic Development and Cultural Change*, 12, March 1963, 152–76.

Banco Central de Chile. Dirección de Estudios. *Indicadores económicos y sociales regionales, 1980–89*. Santiago: 1991.

_____. Dirección de Política Financiera. *Cuentas nacionales de Chile, 1960–1983*. Santiago: 1984.

_____. Dirección de Política Financiera. *Indicadores económicos y sociales, 1960–1982*. Santiago: 1983.

Barandiarán, Edgardo. "Nuestra crisis financiera." (Documento de Trabajo No. 6.) Santiago: Centro de Estudios Públicos, 1985.

Bardón, M. Alvaro, and Felix Bacigalupo. "Algunos puntos referentes al manejo monetario en Chile," *Boletín del Banco Central de la República* [Santiago], 53, July 1980, 1947–54.

Bardón, M. Alvaro, Camilo Carrasco M., and Alvaro Vial G. *Una década de cambios económicos: La experiencia chilena, 1973–1983*. Santiago: Editorial Andrés Bello, 1985.

Bechelli, Carlos M., and Roberto D. Brandt. "Six Latin American Countries Could Join in New Gas Market," *Oil and Gas Journal*, October 21, 1991, 46–52.

Behrman, Jere. *Foreign Trade Regimes and Economic Development: Chile*. Cambridge, Massachusetts: Ballinger, 1976.

_____. *Macroeconomic Policy in a Developing Country: The Chilean Experience*. New York: Elsevier/North-Holland, 1977.

Bennathan, Esra, with Luis Escobar and George Panagakos. "Deregulation in Shipping: What Is to Be Learned from Chile." (Discussion Paper No. 67.) Washington: World Bank, 1989.

Berg, Archie, and Jeffrey Sachs. "The Debt Crisis: Structural Explanations of Country Performance," *Journal of Development Economics*, 29, No. 3, November 1988, 271–306.

Bianchi Andrés, Roberto Devlin, and Joseph Ramos. "The Adjustment Process in Latin America, 1981–1986." (Paper presented at World Bank-IMF Symposium on Growth Oriented Adjustment Programs, Washington, D.C., ECLA/CEPAL WP, February 1987.) [A version in Spanish is published in *El Trimestre Económico*, 54, No. 216, October 1987, 855–911.]

Bitar, Sergio. *Chile: Experiment in Democracy.* Philadelphia: Institute for the Study of Human Issues, 1986.

_____. *Transición, socialismo, y democracia.* Mexico City: Siglo Veintiuno, 1979.

Boorstein, Edward. *Allende's Chile: An Inside View.* New York: International, 1977.

Bosworth, Barry P., Rudiger Dornbusch, and Raúl Labán (eds.). *The Chilean Economy: Policy Lessons and Challenges.* Washington: Brookings Institution, 1994.

Bruno, Michael. "Real Versus Financial Openness under Alternative Exchange Rate Regimes." Pages 131–49 in Pedro Aspe Armella, Rudiger Dornbusch, and Maurice Obstfeld (eds.), *Financial Policies and the World Capital Market: The Problem of Latin American Countries.* Chicago: University of Chicago Press, 1983.

"Business Outlook: Chile," *Business Latin America,* December 21, 1992, 3.

Castañeda, Tarsicio. *Combating Poverty: Innovative Social Reforms in Chile During the 1980s.* (An International Center for Economic Growth Publication.) San Francisco: ICS Press, 1992.

_____. *Evolución del empleo y desempleo y el impacto de cambios demográficos sobre la tasa de desempleo en Chile, 1960–1983.* (Documento serie investigación, No. 64.) Santiago: Departamento de Economía, Universidad de Chile, August 1983.

Chile. Instituto Nacional de Estadísticas. *Compendio estadístico, 1993.* Santiago: 1993

_____. Ministry of Foreign Affairs. General Directorate of International Economic Relations. Export Promotion Department. *ProChile* [Santiago], No. 43, September–October 1992, 6.

Choksi, Armeane M., and Demetris Papageorgiou (eds.). *Economic Liberalization in Developing Countries.* Oxford: Basil Blackwell, 1986.

Cline, William R. "Latin American Debt: Progress, Prospects, and Policy." Pages 31–64 in Sebastian Edwards and Felipe Larrain (eds.), *Debt, Adjustment, and Recovery in Latin America.* Oxford: Basil Blackwell, 1989.

Cline, William R., and Sidney Weintraub (eds.). *Economic Stabilization in Developing Countries.* Washington: Brookings Institution, 1981.

Comisión Económica para la América Latina. *Anuario estadístico de la CEPAL.* Santiago: 1986.

_____. *Balance preliminar de la economía latino americana, 1986.* Santiago: 1986.

————. "Banco de datos sobre inversiones extranjeras directas en América Latina y el Caribe." Santiago: September 1986.

————. "Cooperación comercial y negociaciones regionales." Santiago: July 28, 1986.

————. *Origen y destino del comercio exterior de los países de la Asociación Latinoamericana de Integración y del Mercado Común Centroamericano.* (Cuadernos Estadísticos, No. 9.) Santiago: 1985.

————. "Origen y destino del comercio exterior en 1983." Santiago: August 28, 1986.

————. *Panorama económico de América Latina, 1986.* Santiago: 1986.

————. "Relaciones económicas y cooperación de América Latina y el Caribe." Santiago: September 1986.

————. "Reorientación del comercio exterior de productos básicos hacia América Latina." Santiago: June 25, 1986.

Corbo, Vittorio. "Chilean Economic Policy and International Economic Relations since 1970." Pages 107–44 in Gary M. Walton (ed.), *The National Economic Policies of Chile.* Greenwich, Connecticut: Jai Press, 1985.

————. "Inflación en una economía abierta: El caso de Chile," *Cuadernos de Economía* [Santiago], No. 56, April 1982, 5–16.

————. *Inflation in Developing Countries: An Econometric Study of Chilean Inflation.* Amsterdam: North-Holland, 1974.

————. "Problems, Development Theory, and Strategies of Latin America." (DRD Working Paper No. 190.) Washington: World Bank, 1986.

————. "Reforms and Macroeconomic Adjustment in Chile during 1974–1983," *World Development,* 13, No. 8, August 1985, 839–916.

Corbo, Vittorio, and Jaime de Melo. "Lessons from the Southern Cone Policy Reforms," *World Bank Research Observer,* 2, No. 2, July 1987, 111–42.

————. "Liberalization and Stabilization in the Southern Cone of Latin America: Overview and Summary," *World Development,* 13, August 1985.

Corbo, Vittorio, Jaime de Melo, and James Tybout. "What Went Wrong with the Recent Reforms in the Southern Cone," *Economic Development and Cultural Change,* 34, No. 3, April 1986, 607–40.

Cortázar, René. "Distribución del ingreso, empleo, remuneraciones reales en Chile, 1970–1978," *Colección Estudios de CIEPLAN* [Santiago], June 3, 1980, 5–24.

Cortázar, René, and Jorge Marshall. "Indice de precios al consumidor en Chile, 1970–1978," *Collección Estudios de CIEPLAN* [Santiago], November 4, 1980, 159–201.

Cortés, Hernán, and Larry A. Sjaastad. "Protección y empleo," *Cuadernos de Economía* [Santiago], August–December 1981, 54–55.

de Castro, Sergio. *Exposición de la Hacienda Pública.* Santiago: Ministerio de Hacienda, 1981.

de la Cuadra, Sergio. "Política cambiaria y deuda externa," *Boletín Mensual* [Santiago], May 1981, 1021–26.

de Vylder, Stefan. *Allende's Chile: The Political Economy of the Rise and Fall of the Unidad Popular.* Cambridge: Cambridge University Press, 1976.

Díaz-Alejandro, Carlos Federico. "Comment on Harberger." Pages 371–414 in Sebastian Edwards and Liquad Ahamad (eds.), *Economic Adjustment and Exchange Rates in Developing Countries.* Chicago: University of Chicago Press, 1986.

_____. "¿Economía abierta y política cerrada?" *El trimestre económico* [Santiago], 50, No. 197, January–March 1983, 207–44.

_____. "Goodbye Financial Repression, Hello Financial Crash," *Journal of Development Economics,* 19, January 1985, 1–24.

_____. "Latin America in Depression, 1929–1939." Pages 334–55 in Mark Gersocitz, Carlos F. Díaz-Alejandro, Gustav Ranis, and Mark Rosenzweig (eds.), *The Theory and Experience of Economic Development.* London: Allen and Unwin, 1982.

_____. "Southern Cone Stabilization Plans." Pages 121–26 in William R. Cline and Sidney Weintraub (eds.), *Economic Stabilization in Developing Countries.* Washington: Brookings Institution, 1981.

_____. "Stories of the 1930s for the 1980s." Pages 5–35 in Pedro Aspe Armella, Rudiger Dornbusch, and Maurice Obstfeld (eds.), *Financial Policies and the World Capital Market: The Problem of Latin American Countries.* Chicago: University of Chicago Press, 1983.

Dornbusch, Rudiger. "Stabilization Policies in Developing Countries: What Have We Learned?" *World Development,* 10, No. 9, 1981, 701–8.

Dornbusch, Rudiger, and Sebastian Edwards. *The Macroeconomics of Populism in Latin America.* Chicago: University of Chicago Press, 1992.

Economist Intelligence Unit. *Country Report: Chile* [London], No. 2, 1993.

_____. *Country Report: Chile* [London], No. 3, 1993.

_____. *Country Report: Chile* [London], No. 4, 1993.

Edwards, Alejandra Cox. "The Chilean Labor Market, 1970–1983: An Overview." (Discussion Paper No. DRD152.) Washington: World Bank, 1986.

_____. "Economic Reform, External Shocks, and the Labor Market: Chile, 1974–83." (Paper presented at World Bank

Conference on Adjustment of Labor Markets in LDCs to External Shocks, June 1986.)

――――. "Labor Market Adjustment with Wage Indexation: The Case of Chile between 1974 and 1980." Pages 133-52 in Philip Brock, Michael B. Connoly, and Claudio González-Vega (eds.), *Latin American Debt and Adjustment.* New York: Praeger, 1989.

――――. "Mercado laboral chileno durante la década de 1974-1984: Problemas de ajuste," *Cuadernos de Economía* [Santiago], 24, No. 72, August 1987, 165-95.

――――. "Three Essays on Labor Markets in Developing Countries." (Ph.D. dissertation.) Chicago: University of Chicago, 1984.

Edwards, Alejandra Cox, and Sebastian Edwards. "Markets and Democracy: Lessons from Chile," *World Economy*, 15, No. 2, March 1992, 203-19.

Edwards, Sebastian. "LDCs, Foreign Debt, and Country Risk," *American Economic Review*, 74, September 1984.

――――. "Minimum Wages and Trade Liberalization: Some Reflections Based on the Chilean Experience." (Working Paper No. 230.) Los Angeles: Department of Economics, University of California at Los Angeles, 1982.

――――. "Monetarism in Chile, 1973-1983: Some Economic Puzzles?" *Economic Development and Cultural Change*, 34, No. 3, April 1986, 535-59.

――――. "The Order of Liberalization of the External Sector in Developing Countries," *Princeton Studies in International Finance*, No. 156, December 1984.

――――. "Stabilization with Liberalization: An Evaluation of Ten Years of Chile's Experience with Free Market Policies, 1973-1983," *Economic Development and Cultural Change*, 33, January 1985, 223-54.

――――. "Structural Reforms and Labor Market Adjustment." (Working Paper.) Los Angeles: Department of Economics, University of California at Los Angeles, 1989.

――――. "Terms of Trade, Tariffs, and Labor Market Adjustment in Developing Countries," *World Bank Economic Review*, 2, 1988, 165-85.

Edwards, Sebastian, and Alejandra Cox Edwards. *Monetarism and Liberalization: The Chilean Experiment.* Chicago: University of Chicago Press, 1991.

Edwards, Sebastian, and Felipe Larrain. "Debt, Adjustment, and Recovery in Latin America: An Introduction." Pages 1-30 in Sebastian Edwards and Felipe Larrain (eds.), *Debt, Adjustment, and Recovery in Latin America.* Oxford: Basil Blackwell, 1989.

Falcoff, Mark. *Modern Chile, 1970–1989: A Critical History.* New Brunswick, New Jersey: Transaction Books, 1989.

Ffrench-Davis, Ricardo. "Debt-Equity Swaps in Chile," *Cambridge Journal of Economics* [Cambridge], 14, No. 1, March 1990, 109–26.

———. "Una estrategia de apertura externa selectiva." Pages 237–98 in Alejandro Foxley Riesco (ed.), *Reconstrucción económica.* Santiago: Editorial Aconcagua, 1983.

———. *Políticas económicas en Chile, 1952–1970.* Santiago: Ediciones Nueva Universidad, 1973.

Ffrench-Davis, Ricardo, and Ernesto Tironi (eds.). *El cobre en el desarrollo económico nacional.* Santiago: Ediciones Nueva Universidad, 1974.

Fontaine, Juan Andrés. "The Chilean Economy in the 1980s: Adjustment and Recovery." Pages 208–33 in Sebastian Edwards and Felipe Larrain (eds.), *Debt, Adjustment, and Recovery in Latin America.* Oxford: Basil Blackwell, 1989.

Foxley Riesco, Alejandro. *Latin American Experiments in Neoconservative Economics.* Berkeley: University of California Press, 1983.

———. "Stabilization Policies and Their Effects on Employment and Income Distribution: A Latin American Perspective." Pages 191–225 in William R. Cline and Sidney Weintraub (eds.), *Stabilization in Developing Countries.* Washington: Brookings Institution, 1981.

———. "Towards a Free Market Economy: Chile, 1974–1975," *Journal of Developing Economics,* 10, No. 1, February 1982, 3–29.

Foxley Riesco, Alejandro, and Oscar Múñoz. "Income Redistribution, Economic Growth, and Social Structure: The Case of Chile," *Oxford Bulletin of Economics and Statistics* [Oxford], 36, No. 1, 1974, 21–44.

Furtado, Celso. *La economía latinoamericana.* Santiago: Editorial Universitaria, 1969.

Geller, Lucio, and Jaime Estévez. "La nacionalización del cobre." Pages 557–78 in Fidel Azócar (ed.), *La economía chilena en 1971.* Santiago: Instituto de Economía, Universidad de Chile, 1972.

Guardia, Alexis. "Structural Transformations in Chile's Economy and Its System of External Economic Relations." Pages 45–102 in Sandro Sideri (ed.), *Chile, 1970–1973: Economic Development and Its International Setting: Self-Criticism of the Unidad Popular Government's Policies.* The Hague: Martinus Nijhoff, 1979.

Guzmán, José Florencio (ed.). *La reforma tributaria: Sus efectos económicos.* Santiago: Departmento de Economía, Universidad de Chile, 1975.

Hachette, Dominique. "Aspectos macroeconómicos de la economía chilena 1973–1976." (Documento de Trabajo No. 55.)

Santiago: Instituto de Economía, Universidad Católica, 1978.

Hachette, Dominique, and Rolf Lüders. *Privatization in Chile: An Economic Appraisal.* (An International Center for Economic Growth publication.) San Francisco: ICS Press, 1993.

Harberger, Arnold. "The Chilean Economy in the 1970s: Crisis, Stabilization, Liberalization, Reform." Pages 115–52 in Karl Brunner and Alan H. Meltzer (eds.), *Economic Policy in a World of Change.* (Carnegie-Rochester Conference Series on Public Policy, No. 17.) Amsterdam: North-Holland, 1982.

_____. "Comment on Foxley." Pages 226–28 in William R. Cline and Sidney Weintraub (eds.), *Economic Stabilization in Developing Countries.* Washington: Brookings Institution, 1981.

_____. "Observations on the Chilean Economy, 1973–1983," *Economic Development and Cultural Change,* 33, April 1985, 451–62.

_____. "A Primer on the Chilean Economy." Pages 73–83 in Armeane M. Choksi and Demetris Papageorgiou (eds.), *Economic Liberalization in Developing Countries.* Oxford: Basil Blackwell, 1986.

_____. "The Real Exchange Rate of Chile: A Preliminary Survey." (Paper presented at Conference on Economic Policy, Viña del Mar, Chile, April 1981.) Viña del Mar, Chile: 1981.

Hojman, David E. *Chile: The Political Economy of Development and Democracy in the 1990s.* Basingstoke: Macmillan Press, 1993.

Iglesias P., Augusto, Rodrigo Acuña R., and Claudio Chamorro. *10 años de historia del sistema de AFP: Antecedentes estadísticos, 1981–1990.* Santiago: AFP Habitat, 1991.

Inostroza, Alfonso. "El programa monetario y la política de comercio exterior de la Unidad Popular," *Panorama económico* [Santiago], March 1979, 7–21.

Inter-American Development Bank. *Economic and Social Progress in Latin America: 1992 Report.* Washington: October 1992.

Jarvis, Lovell S. *Chilean Agriculture under Military Rule: From Reform to Reaction, 1973–1980.* (Research Series No. 59.) Berkeley: Institute of International Studies, University of California Press, 1985.

Krueger, Anne O. "Problems of Liberalization." Pages 403–23 in Arnold Harberger (ed.), *World Economic Growth.* San Francisco: Institute for Contemporary Studies Press, 1984.

Lagos, Ricardo A. "Debt Relief Through Debt Conversion: A Critical Analysis of the Chilean Debt Conversion Programme," *Journal of Development Studies* [London], 28, No. 3, 473–99.

Larrain B., Felipe. *Democracia en Chile.* Santiago: Universidad Católica, 1989.

_____. "Desarrollo económico para Chile en democracia." Pages 21–84 in *Desarrollo económico en democracia: Proposiciones para una sociedad libre y solidaria*. Santiago: Ediciones Universidad Católica de Chile, December 1987.

Larrain B., Felipe, and Marcelo Selowsky. "Public Sector Behavior in Latin America's Biggest Debtors." Washington: World Bank, December 1987.

Larrain B., Felipe, and Andrés Velasco. "Can Swaps Solve the Debt Crisis? Lessons from the Chilean Experience," *Princeton Studies in International Finance*, No. 69, November 1990.

Larroulet, V. Cristian (ed.). *Soluciones privadas a problemas públicos*. Santiago: Instituto Libertad y Desarrollo, 1991.

López, Julio. "La economía política de la Unidad Popular: Una evaluación de su primer año de gobierno." Pages 319–54 in Fidel Azócar (ed.), *La economía chilena en 1971*. Santiago: Instituto de Economía, Universidad de Chile, 1972.

Lüders, Rolf J. "Massive Divestiture and Privatization: Lessons from Chile," *Contemporary Policy Issues*, 9, No. 4, 1991, 1–19.

McKinnon, Ronald. *Financial Control in the Transition to a Market Economy*. (2d ed.) Baltimore: John Hopkins University Press, 1992.

_____. "The Order of Economic Liberalization: Lessons from Chile and Argentina." Pages 159–86 in Karl Brunner and Alan H. Meltzer (eds.), *Economic Policy in a World of Change*. (Carnegie-Rochester Conference Series on Public Policy, No. 17.) Amsterdam: North-Holland, 1982.

Maddison, Angus. *Two Crises: Latin America and Asia, 1929–38 and 1973–1983*. Paris: Development Centre of the Organisation for Economic Co-operation and Development, 1988.

Mamalakis, Markos J. *Historical Statistics of Chile*. Westport, Connecticut: Greenwood Press, 1978.

Mamalakis, Markos J., and Clark W. Reynolds. *Essays on the Chilean Economy*. Homewood, Illinois: Irwin, 1965.

Mamalakis, Markos J., Oscar Múñoz, and Juan A. Fontaine. "Los últimos diez años de historia económica," *Estudios Públicos* [Santiago], 15, Winter 1984, 191–206.

Martino, Orlando D. (ed.). *Mineral Industries of Latin America*. Washington: GPO, 1988.

Martner, Gonzalo (ed.). *El pensamiento económico del gobierno de Allende*. Santiago: Editorial Universitaria, 1971.

Mathieson, Donald J. "Estimating Models of Financial Market Behavior During Periods of Extensive Structural Reform: The Experience of Chile," *IMF Staff Papers*, No. 30, June 1983, 350–93.

Matte, Patricia, and Antonio Sancho. "Sector educación básica y media." Pages 93–118 in Cristian Larroulet V. (ed.), *Soluciones privadas a problemas públicos.* Santiago: Instituto Libertad y Desarrollo, 1991.

Meller, Patricio. *Adjustment and Equity in Chile.* Paris: Development Centre of the Organisation for Economic Co-operation and Development, 1992.

Méndez, Juan Carlos (ed.). *Chilean Economic Policy.* Santiago: Calderon, 1979.

Múñoz, Oscar. *Crecimiento industrial de Chile, 1914-1965.* Santiago: Universidad de Chile, 1968.

National Bureau of Economic Research. "Labor Market Distortions and Structural Adjustment in Developing Countries." (Working Paper No. 3346.) Washington: May 1990.

Nove, Alec. "The Political Economy of the Allende Regime." Pages 51-78 in Philip O'Brien (ed.), *Allende's Chile.* New York: Praeger, 1976.

Oppenheim, Lois Hecht. "The Chilean Road to Socialism Revisited," *Latin American Research Review,* 24, No. 1, 1989, 155-83.

Orrego Vicuña, Francisco (ed.). *Chile: The Balanced View.* Santiago: Institute of International Affairs, University of Chile, 1975.

Parkin, Vincent. "Economic Liberalization in Chile, 1973-1982: A Model of Growth and Development or a Recipe for Stagnation and Impoverishment?" *Cambridge Journal of Economics* [Cambridge], No. 7, June 1983, 101-24.

Piñera Echenique, José. *El cascabel al gato: La batalla por la reforma previsional.* Santiago: Zig-Zag, 1991.

_____. *La revolución laboral en Chile.* (2d ed.) Santiago: Zig-Zag, 1991.

Rabkin, Rhoda. "How Ideas Become Influential: Ideological Foundations of Export-Led Growth in Chile, 1973-1990," *World Affairs,* 156, No. 1, Summer 1993, 3-25.

Ramos, Joseph R. "The Economics of Hyperstagflation," *Journal of Economic Development,* 7, No. 4, 1980, 467-88.

_____. *Neoconservative Economics in the Southern Cone of Latin America, 1973-1983.* Baltimore: Johns Hopkins University Press, 1986.

Selowsky, Marcelo, and Herman van der Tak. "The Debt Problem and Growth," *World Development,* 14, No. 9, September 1986.

Sideri, Sandro (ed.). *Chile, 1970-1973: Economic Development and Its International Setting: Self-Criticism of the Unidad Popular Government's Policies.* The Hague: Martinus Nijhoff, 1979.

Sistema Económico Latinoamericano. *El FMI, el Banco Mundial, y la Crisis Latino Americana.* Mexico City: Siglo Veintiuno, 1986.

Sjaastad, Larry. "Failure of Economic Liberalism in the Cone of Latin America," *World Economy,* 6, March 1983, 5-26.

Solimano, Andrés. "Política de remuneraciones en Chile: Experiencia pasada, instrumentos y opciones a futuro," *Colección Estudios de CIEPLAN* [Santiago], No. 25, December 1988, 159–90.

Stallings, Barbara. *Class Conflict and Economic Development in Chile, 1958–73.* Stanford: Stanford University Press, 1978.

Sunkel, Osvaldo. "Inflation in Chile: An Unorthodox Approach," *International Economic Papers*, 10, 1960, 107–31.

Unidad Popular. *Programa básico de gobierno.* Santiago: 1969.

United Nations. Economic Commission for Latin America. *Balance preliminar de la economía latinoamericana, 1986.* Santiago: 1986.

_____. Economic Commission for Latin America. *Panorama económico de América Latina, 1987.* Santiago: September 1987.

Valdés, Alberto. "Mix and Sequencing of Economywide and Agricultural Reforms: Chile and New Zealand." Washington: World Bank, June 1992.

Vogel, Robert. "The Dynamics of Inflation in Latin America, 1950–1969," *American Economic Review*, 64, No. 1, 1974, 102–14.

Vuskovic, Pedro. "Distribución del ingreso y opciones de desarrollo," *Cuadernos de la realidad nacional* [Santiago], No. 5, September 1970, 41–60.

_____. "Dos años de política económica del gobierno popular." Pages 9–37 in *El golpe de estado en Chile.* Mexico City: Fondo de Cultura Económica, 1975.

_____. "The Economic Policy of the Popular Unity Government." Pages 49–56 in J. Ann Zammit (ed.), *The Chilean Road to Socialism.* Austin: University of Texas Press, 1973.

Walton, Gary M. (ed.). *The National Economic Policies of Chile.* Greenwich, Connecticut: Jai Press, 1985.

Wisecarver, Daniel. "Economic Regulation and Deregulation in Chile, 1973–1983." Pages 145–202 in Gary Walton (ed.), *The National Economic Policies of Chile.* Greenwich, Connecticut: Jai Press, 1985.

Yáñez, Jorge. "Una corrección del indice de precios al consumidor durante el período 1971–73." Pages 205–57 in Francisco Contreras (ed.), *Commentarios sobre la situación económica.* Santiago: Universidad de Chile, 1978.

Zammit, J. Ann (ed.). *The Chilean Road to Socialism: Proceedings of an ODEPLAN-UDS Round Table.* Austin: University of Texas Press, 1973.

Zhaler, Roberto. "The Monetary and Real Effects of the Financial Opening Up of National Economies to the Exterior," *CEPAL Review* [Santiago], 10, April 1980, 127–54.

_____. "Recent Southern Cone Liberalization Reforms and Stabilization Policies: The Chilean Case, 1974–1982," *Journal of Interamerican Studies and World Affairs,* 25, November 1983, 509-62.

Zorrilla, Américo. "Exposición de la hacienda pública, 27 de noviembre de 1970." Pages 11-36 in Gonzalo Martner (ed.), *El pensamiento económico del gobierno de Allende.* Santiago: Editorial Universitaria, 1971.

(Various issues of the following periodicals were also used in the preparation of this chapter: Banco Central de Chile, *Boletín mensual* [Santiago]; *Business Latin America;* Comisión Nacional del Cobre, various publications; *El Mercurio* [Santiago]; *Latin American Integration Process;* and *Situación Latinoamericana* [Madrid].)

Chapter 4

Ahumada, Eugenio, and Rodrigo Atria. *Chile, la memoria prohibida: Las violaciones a los derechos humanos, 1973-1983.* Santiago: Pehuén, 1989.

Americas Watch. *The Vicaría de la Solidaridad in Chile.* New York: 1987.

Amnesty International. "Chile: Evidence of Torture." London: 1983.

Arellano Iturriaga, Sergio. *Mas allá del abismo.* Santiago: Proyección, 1985.

Arriagada, Genaro. *Pinochet: The Politics of Power.* Boston: Unwin Hyman, 1988.

Arteaga Alemparte, Ignacio. *Partido Conservador XVI-convención nacional—1947.* Santiago: Imprenta Chile, 1947.

Banco Central de Chile. Dirección de Estudios. *Indicadores económicos y sociales, 1960-1988.* Santiago: 1989.

Barahona Urzúa, Pablo, and Tomás P. MacHale. *Visión crítica de Chile.* Santiago: Edición Portada, 1972.

Bardón, A., C. Carrasco, and A. Vial. *Una década de cambios económicos.* Santiago: Andrés Bello, 1985.

Basso, Lelio. *Transición al socialismo y la experiencia chilena.* Santiago: CESO-CEREN, 1972.

Becker, David. *La experiencia terapéutica con víctimas de represión política en Chile y el desafío de reparación social.* Santiago: Instituto Latinoamericano de Salud Mental y Derechos Humanos, 1989.

Bitar, Sergio. *Isla 10.* Santiago: Pehuén, 1987.

_____. *Transición, socialismo, y democracia: La experiencia chilena.* Mexico City: Siglo Veintiuno, 1979.

Branch, Taylor, and Eugene M. Propper. *Labyrinth.* New York: Viking Press, 1982.

Brodsky, Ricardo (ed.). *Conversaciones con la FECH.* Santiago: CESOC, 1988.

Brunner, José Joaquín. *La cultura autoritaria en Chile.* Santiago: Facultad Latinoamericana de Ciencias Sociales, 1981.

―――. *Informe sobre la educación superior en Chile.* Santiago: Facultad Latinoamericana de Ciencias Sociales, 1986.

Bulnes Aldunate, Luz. *Constitución de la República de Chile: Concordancias, anotaciones, y fuentes.* Santiago: Editorial Jurídica de Chile, 1981.

Campero, Guillermo. *Los gremios empresariales en el período 1970-1983: Comportamiento sociopolítico y orientaciones ideológicas.* Santiago: Instituto Latinoamericano de Estudios Transnacionales, 1984.

Cánovas Robles, José. *Memorias de un magistrado.* Santiago: Editorial Emisión, 1987.

Carrasco Delgado, Sergio. *Génesis y vigencia de los textos constitucionales chilenos.* Santiago: Editorial Jurídica de Chile, 1980.

Castillo Velasco, Jaime. *Las fuentes de la democracia cristiana.* Santiago: Editorial del Pacífico, 1965.

Cavallo, Ascanio, Manuel Salazar, and Oscar Sepúlveda. *La historia oculta del régimen militar.* Santiago: Ediciones La Época, 1989.

Caviédes, Cesar N. *Elections in Chile: The Road Toward Redemocratization.* Boulder, Colorado: Rienner, 1991.

Chavkin, Samuel. *The Murder of Chile.* New York: Everest House, 1982.

Chelen Rojas, Alejandro. *Trayectoría del socialismo.* Buenos Aires: Editorial Austral, 1967.

Chile. *Constitución de la República de Chile, 1980.* Santiago: Editorial Jurídica de Chile, 1981.

―――. Instituto Geográfico Militar. *Atlas Geográfico de Chile.* Santiago: 1988.

Comisión Nacional de Verdad y Reconciliación. *Informe Rettig.* (2 vols.) Santiago: La Nación and Ediciones Ornitorrinco, 1991.

―――. *Report of the Chilean National Commission on Truth and Reconciliation.* (2 vols.) Notre Dame: Center for Civil and Human Rights, University of Notre Dame Press, 1993.

Comité de Defensa de los Derechos del Pueblo. *Hermanos Vergara Toledo: Asesinados el 29 de marzo de 1985.* Santiago: 1986.

Constable, Pamela, and Arturo Valenzuela. "Chile's Return to Democracy," *Foreign Affairs,* 68, Winter 1989-90, 169-86.

―――. "Is Chile Next?" *Foreign Policy,* 63, Summer 1986, 58-75.

―――. *A Nation of Enemies: Chile under Pinochet.* New York: Norton, 1991.

Contreras, Victoria. *Sobrevivir en la calle: El comercio ambulante en Santiago.* Geneva: Programa Empleo de América Latina y el Caribe, 1988.

Correa, Raquel, and Elizabeth Subercaseaux. *Ergo sum Pinochet.* Santiago: Zig-Zag, 1989.

Cortes, Lia, and Jordi Fuentes. *Diccionario político de Chile.* Santiago: Editorial Orbe, 1967.

Cristi, Renato, and Carlos Ruiz. *El pensamiento conservador en Chile: Seis ensayos.* Santiago: Editorial Universitaria, 1992.

Cusack, David. "The Politics of Chilean Private Enterprise under Christian Democracy." (Ph.D. dissertation.) Denver: University of Denver, 1970.

Dahse, Fernando. *Mapa de la extrema riquesa.* Santiago: Editorial Aconcagua, 1979.

Davis, Nathaniel. *The Last Two Years of Salvador Allende.* Ithaca: Cornell University Press, 1985.

Delano, Manuel, and Hugo Traslaviña. *La herencia de los Chicago boys.* Santiago: Las Ediciones del Ornitorrinco, 1989.

de Vylder, Stephan. *Allende's Chile: The Political Economy of the Rise and Fall of the Unidad Popular.* Cambridge: Cambridge University Press, 1976.

Díaz, Florencio Infante. *Escuela militar del libertador Bernardo O'Higgins.* Santiago: Dirección de Bibliotecas, Archivos y Museos, 1985.

Dinges, John, and Saul Landau. *Assassination on Embassy Row.* New York: Pantheon, 1980.

Drake, Paul W. *Socialism and Populism in Chile, 1932-52.* Urbana: University of Illinois Press, 1978.

Drake, Paul W., and Iván Jaksić. *The Struggle for Democracy in Chile, 1982-1990.* Lincoln: University of Nebraska Press, 1991.

Durán Bernales, Florencio. *El Partido Radical.* Santiago: Editorial Nascimiento, 1958.

Echeverría, Andrés B., and Luis Frei B. *1970-1973: La lucha por la juridicidad en Chile.* (3 vols.) Santiago: Editorial del Pacífico, 1974.

Edwards, Alberto, and Eduardo Frei. *Historia de los partidos políticos chilenos.* Santiago: Editorial del Pacífico, 1949.

Edwards, Sebastian, and Alejandra Cox Edwards. *Monetarism and Liberalization: The Chilean Experiment.* Cambridge, Massachusetts: Ballinger, 1987.

Errázuriz Korner, Ana María (ed.). *Manual de Geografía de Chile.* Santiago: Editorial Andrés Bello, 1987.

Facultad Latinoamericana de Ciencias Sociales and Centro de Estudios del Desarrollo. *Opinión pública y cultura política.* Santiago:

Facultad Latinoamericana de Ciencias Sociales, August 1987.

Falcoff, Mark. "The Coming Crisis in Chile: Pinochet Is Playing into the Communist Hands," *Policy Review,* No. 34, October 1985, 18–24.

_____. *Modern Chile, 1970–1989: A Critical History.* New Brunswick, New Jersey: Transaction Books, 1989.

Falcoff, Mark, Arturo Valenzuela, and Susan Kaufman Purcell. *Chile: Prospects for Democracy.* New York: Council on Foreign Relations, 1988.

Fleet, Michael. *The Rise and Fall of Christian Democracy.* Princeton: Princeton University Press, 1985.

Fontaine Aldunate, Arturo. *Los economistas y el presidente Pinochet.* Santiago: Zig-Zag, 1988.

Francis, Michael J. *The Limits of Hegemony: United States Relations with Argentina and Chile During World War II.* Notre Dame: University of Notre Dame Press, 1967.

Furci, Carmelo. *The Chilean Communist Party and the Road to Socialism.* London: Zed Books, 1984.

Garretón Merino, Manuel Antonio. *The Chilean Political Process.* Boston: Unwin Hyman, 1989.

Garretón Merino, Manuel Antonio, and Tomás Moulian. *Análisis coyuntural y proceso político: Las fases del conflicto en Chile, 1970–73.* San José, Costa Rica: Editorial Universitaria Centroamericana, 1978.

Garretón Merino, Manuel Antonio, et al. *Cronología del período 1970–73.* (9 vols.) Santiago: Facultad Latinoamericana de Ciencias Sociales, 1978.

Gil, Federico G. *The Political System of Chile.* Boston: Houghton Mifflin, 1966.

Godoy, Oscar (ed.). *Hacia una democracia moderna: La opción parlamentaria.* Santiago: Ediciones Universidad Católica de Chile, 1990.

Gonzáles Camus, Ignacio. *El día que murió Allende.* Santiago: CESOC, 1988.

Grayson, George. *El Partido Demócrata Cristiano chileno.* Buenos Aires: Editorial Francisco de Aguirre, 1968.

Gross, Leonard. *The Last Best Hope: Eduardo Frei and Chilean Christian Democracy.* New York: Random House, 1967.

Guilisasti Tagle, Sergio. *Partidos políticos chilenos.* Santiago: Editorial Nascimiento, 1964.

Guzmán, Jaime. "El camino político de Chile," *Realidad* [Santiago], 1, No. 7, December 1979.

Halperin, Ernst. *Nationalism and Communism in Chile.* Cambridge: MIT Press, 1965.

Hauser, Thomas. *The Execution of Charles Horman: An American*

Sacrifice. New York: Harcourt, Brace, Jovanovich, 1978.

Hojman, Eugenio. *Memorial de la dictadura.* Santiago: Editorial Emisión, 1989.

Huneeus, Carlos. *Los chilenos y la política: Cambio y continuidad bajo el autoritarismo.* Santiago: Centro de Estudios de la Realidad Contemporánea and Academia de Humanismo Cristiano, 1987.

Huneeus, Carlos, and Jorge Olave. "La Partecipazione dei Militari nei Nuovi Autoritatismi il Cile in una Prospettiva Comparata," *Rivista Italiana di Scienza Politica* [Rome], 17, No. 1, April, 1987.

Jobet, Julio Cesar. *Ensayo crítico del desarrollo económico-social de Chile.* Santiago: Editorial Latinoamericana, 1965.

_____. *El Partido Socialista de Chile.* (2d ed.) (2 vols.) Santiago: Ediciones Prensa Latinoamericana, 1971.

Kaufman, Edy. *Crisis in Allende's Chile: New Perspectives.* New York: Praeger, 1988.

Kaufman, Robert R. *The Politics of Land Reform in Chile, 1950–1970: Public Policy, Political Institutions, and Social Change.* Cambridge: Harvard University Press, 1972.

Kinsbruner, Jay. *Diego Portales: Interpretative Essays on the Man and Times.* The Hague: Martinus Nijhoff, 1967.

Larrain B., Felipe (ed.). *Desarrollo económico en democracia: Proposiciones para una sociedad libre y solidaria.* Santiago: Ediciones Universidad Católica de Chile, 1988.

Lavín, Joaquín. *Chile: Revolución silenciosa.* Santiago: Zig-Zag, 1987.

Linz, Juan J., and Arturo Valenzuela (eds.). *The Failure of Presidential Democracy.* Baltimore: Johns Hopkins University Press, 1994.

López Pintor, Rafael. "Development Administration in Chile: Structural Normative and Behavioral Constraints to Performance." (Ph.D. dissertation.) Chapel Hill: University of North Carolina, 1972.

_____. *Una explicación sociológica del cambio administrativo: Chile, 1812–1970.* (Documentación Administrativa No. 168.) Madrid: n. pub., 1975.

Loveman, Brian. *Struggle in the Countryside: Politics and Rural Labor in Chile, 1919–1973.* Bloomington: Indiana University Press, 1976.

Marras, Sergio. *Confesiones.* Santiago: Ornitorrinco, 1988.

Martner, Gonzalo (ed.). *El pensamiento económico del gobierno de Allende.* Santiago: Editorial Universitaria, 1971.

Menges, Constantine. "Public Policy and Organized Business in Chile: A Preliminary Analysis," *Journal of International Affairs,* 2, No. 2, 1966, 343–65.

Mericq, Luis S. *Antarctica: Chile's Claim.* Washington: National Defense University Press, 1987.

Meza, María Angélica (ed.). *La otra mitad de Chile*. Santiago: CESOC, Instituto para el Nuevo Chile [1986].

Morales, Eduardo, Hernán Pozo, and Sergio Rojas. *Municipio, desarrollo local y sectores populares*. Santiago: Facultad Latinoamericana de Ciencias Sociales, 1988.

Moulian, Tomás. *Democracia y socialismo en Chile*. Santiago: Facultad Latinoamericana de Ciencias Sociales, 1983.

Muñoz, Heraldo. *Las relaciones exteriores del gobierno militar de Chile*. Santiago: PROSPEL and Centro de Estudios de la Realidad Contemporánea, Las Ediciones del Ornitorrinco, 1986.

Muñoz, Heraldo, and Carlos Portales. *Elusive Friendship: A Survey of U.S.-Chilean Relations*. (Latin American and Caribbean Center Studies on Latin America and the Caribbean.) Boulder, Colorado: Rienner, 1991.

Nunn, Fredrick M. "Emil Körner and the Prussianization of the Chilean Army: Origins, Process, and Consequences, 1885–1920," *Hispanic American Historical Review*, 2, May 1970, 300–322.

_____. *The Military in Chilean History: Essays on Civil-Military Relations, 1810–1973*. Albuquerque: University of New Mexico Press, 1970.

Oppenheim, Lois Hecht. *Politics in Chile: Democracy, Authoritarianism, and the Search for Development*. Boulder, Colorado: Westview Press, 1993.

Orellana, Patricio. *Violación de los derechos humanos e información*. Santiago: Fundación de Ayuda Social de Iglesias Cristianas, 1989.

Organización de Estados Americanos. Comisión Inter-Americana de Derechos Humanos. *Informe sobre la situacion de los derechos humanos en Chile*. Washington: 1985.

Ortega R., Eugenio, and Ernesto Tironi B. *Pobreza en Chile*. Santiago: Centro de Estudios del Desarrollo, 1988.

Palma Zuñiga, Luis. *Historia del Partido Radical*. Santiago: Editorial Andrés Bello, 1967.

Petras, James F. *Politics and Social Forces in Chilean Development*. Berkeley: University of California Press, 1969.

Petras, James F., and Morris Morley. *The United States and Chile: Imperialism and the Overthrow of the Allende Government*. New York: Monthly Review Press, 1975.

Piedrabuena Richards, Guillermo. *La reforma constitucional*. Santiago: Ediciones Encina, 1970.

Pinochet Ugarte, Augusto. *El día decisivo, 11 de septiembre de 1973*. (5th ed.) Santiago: Editorial Andrés Bello, 1984.

_____. *Pinochet: Patria y democracia*. Santiago: Editorial Andrés Bello, 1983.

————. *Política, politiquería, demagogia.* Santiago: Editorial Renacimiento, 1983.

Politzer, Patricia. *Altamirano.* Santiago: Melquíades, 1990.

————. *La ira de Pedro y los otros.* Santiago: Planeta, 1988.

Prado Valdes, José Miguel. *Reseña histórica del Partido Liberal.* Santiago: Imprenta Andina, 1963.

Prats González, Carlos. *Memorias: Testimonio de un soldado.* Santiago: Pehuén, 1985.

Programa Interdisciplinario de Investigaciones en Educación. *Las transformaciones educacionales bajo el régimen militar.* (2 vols.) Santiago: 1984.

Quiroga, Patricio (ed.). *Salvador Allende: Obras escogidas, 1970–1973.* Barcelona: Editorial Crítica, 1989.

Ramírez Necochea, Hernan. *Historia del movimiento obrero en Chile: Antecedentes siglo XIX.* Santiago: Editorial Austral, 1956.

————. *Origen y formación del Partido Comunista de Chile.* Santiago: Editorial Austral, 1965.

Ramos, Joseph R. *Neoconservative Economics in the Southern Cone of Latin America, 1973–1983.* Baltimore: Johns Hopkins University Press, 1984.

Razeto, Luis, et al. *Las organizaciones económicas populares.* Santiago: Programa Economía del Trabajo, 1986.

Reyes Matta, Francisco, Carlos Ruiz, and Guillermo Sunkel (eds.). *Investigación sobre la prensa en Chile, 1974–1984.* Santiago: Centro de Estudios de la Realidad Contemporánea and Instituto Latinoamericano de Estudios Transnacionales, 1986.

Rojas, Robinson. *The Murder of Allende.* New York: Harper and Row, 1976.

Rosenkranz, Hernán, and Benny Pollack. *Revolutionary Social Democracy: The Chilean Socialist Party.* London: Frances Pinter, 1986.

Roxborough, Ian, Philip O'Brien, and Jackie Roddick. *Chile: The State and Revolution.* New York: Holmes and Meier, 1977.

Ruiz-Tagle P., Jaime. *Sindicalismo y estado en el régimen militar chileno.* Santiago: Programa Economía del Trabajo, 1986.

Salinas, Luis Alejandro. *Sursum corda.* Santiago: Todos, 1984.

Sanfuentes Carrion, Marcial. *El Partido Conservador.* Santiago: Editorial Universitaria, 1957.

Schkolnik, Mariana. *Sobrevivir en las poblaciones José María Caro y en Lo Hermida.* Santiago: Programa de Economía del Trabajo, Academia de Humanismo Cristiano, 1988.

Schkolnik, Mariana, and Berta Teitelboim G. *Pobreza y desempleo en poblaciones: La otra cara del modelo neoliberal.* Santiago: Programa Economía del Trabajo, Academia de Humanismo Cristiano, 1988.

Scully, Timothy R. *Rethinking the Center: Party Politics in Nineteenth-and Twentieth-Century Chile.* Stanford: Stanford University Press, 1992.

Sesnic, Rodolfo. *Tucapel: La muerte de un dirigente.* Santiago: Bruguera, 1986.

Siavelias, Peter M. "The Chilean Legislative Branch and Democratic Stability: The Institutional Dimensions of Legislative Performance." (Ph.D. dissertation.) Washington: Department of Political Science, Georgetown University, work in progress, 1994.

Sigmund, Paul E. *The Overthrow of Allende and the Politics of Chile, 1964-1976.* (Pitt Latin American Series.) Pittsburgh: University of Pittsburgh Press, 1977.

_____. *The United States and Democracy in Chile.* (A Twentieth Century Fund Book.) Baltimore: Johns Hopkins University Press, 1993.

Signorelli, Aldo, and Wilson Tapia. *Quien mató a Tucapel.* Santiago: Ariete, 1986.

Silva Bascuñán, Alejandro. *Tratado de derecho constitucional.* (3 vols.) Santiago: Editorial Jurídica de Chile, 1963.

Silva Cimma, Enrique. *Derecho administrativo chileno y comparado.* (2d ed.) Santiago: Editorial Jurídica de Chile, 1969.

Silvert, Kalman H. *Chile: Yesterday and Today.* New York: Holt, Rinehart, and Winston, 1965.

Smith, Brian H. *The Church and Politics in Chile: Challenges to Modern Catholicism.* Princeton: Princeton University Press, 1982.

Sobel, Lester A. (ed.). *Chile and Allende.* New York: Facts on File, 1974.

Soto Kloss, Eduardo. *Ordenamiento constitucional.* Santiago: Editorial Jurídica de Chile, 1980.

Stallings, Barbara. *Class Conflict and Economic Development in Chile, 1958-1973.* Stanford: Stanford University Press, 1978.

Tironi, Eugenio. *Los silencios de la revolución.* Santiago: Puerta Abierta, 1987.

Turner, Joan. *Víctor Jara: Un canto no truncado.* Concepción: Editorial LAR, 1988.

United States. Congress. 92d, 1st Session. House of Representatives. Committee on Foreign Affairs. Subcommittee on Inter-American Affairs. *United States and Chile During the Allende Years, 1970-1973.* Washington: GPO, 1975.

_____. Congress. 92d, 1st Session. Senate. Select Committee to Study Governmental Operations with Respect to Intelligence Activities. *Covert Action in Chile, 1963-1973.* (Staff report.) Washington: GPO, 1975.

411

Urzúa Valenzuela, Germán. *Evolución de la administración pública chilena, 1818-1968.* Santiago: Editorial Jurídica, 1970.

_____. *Los partidos políticos chilenos.* Santiago: Editorial Jurídica de Chile, 1968.

Valdés, Juan Gabriel. *La escuela de Chicago: Operación Chile.* Buenos Aires: Grupo Zeta, 1989.

Valencia A., Luis. *Anales de la república.* Santiago: 1951.

Valenzuela, Arturo. *The Breakdown of Democratic Regimes: Chile.* Baltimore: Johns Hopkins University Press, 1978.

_____. "The Chilean Political System and the Armed Forces, 1830-1925." (Master's thesis.) New York: Department of Public Law and Government, Columbia University, 1967.

_____. "Parties, Politics, and the State in Chile: The Higher Civil Service." Pages 254-75 in Ezra Suleiman (ed.), *Bureaucrats and Policy Making: A Comparative Overview.* New York: Holmes and Meier, 1984.

_____. "Party Politics and the Failure of Presidentialism in Chile: A Proposal for a Parliamentary Form of Government." In Juan J. Linz and Arturo Valenzuela (eds.), *The Failure of Presidential Democracy.* Baltimore: Johns Hopkins University Press, 1994.

_____. *Political Brokers in Chile: Local Government in a Centralized Polity.* Durham: Duke University Press, 1977.

Valenzuela, Arturo, and J. Samuel Valenzuela. *Chile: Politics and Society.* New Brunswick, New Jersey: Transaction Books, 1976.

_____. "Los orígenes de la democracia: Reflexiones teóricas sobre el caso de Chile," *Estudios Públicos* [Santiago], No. 12, Spring 1982, 5-39.

Valenzuela, Estéban. *Fragmentos de una generación.* Santiago: Editorial Emisión, 1988.

Valenzuela, J. Samuel. *Democratización vía reforma: La expansión del sufragio en Chile.* Buenos Aires: Ediciones del IDES, 1985.

Valenzuela, J. Samuel, and Arturo Valenzuela (eds.). *Military Rule in Chile: Dictatorship and Oppositions.* Baltimore: Johns Hopkins University Press, 1986.

Varas, Florencia. *Conversaciones con Viaux.* Santiago: Eire, 1972.

_____. *Gustavo Leigh: El general disidente.* Santiago: Editorial Aconcagua, 1979.

Varas Lonfat, Pedro. *Chile: Objetivo del terrorismo.* Santiago: Instituto Geográfico Militar, 1988.

Velasco L., Eugenio. *Expulsión.* Santiago: Sociedad Editora Copygraph, 1986.

Verdugo, Patricia. *Los zarpazos del puma.* Santiago: Ediciones Chile-America and CESOC, 1989.

Verdugo, Patricia, and Cármen Hertz. *Operación Siglo Veinte.* Santiago: Ediciones Ornitorrinco, 1990.

Vergara, Pilar. *Auge y caída del neoliberalismo en Chile.* Santiago: Facultad Latinoamericana de Ciencias Sociales, 1983.

Vicaría de la Solidaridad. *El Comité de Cooperación por la Paz en Chile: Chronología de dos años de labor.* Santiago: 1975.

_____. *Donde están.* (7 vols.) Santiago: 1979.

Vicuña, Manuel Rivas. *Historia política y parlamentaria de Chile.* (3 vols.) Santiago: Editorial Nascimiento, 1964.

Vitale, Luis. *Interpretación marxista de la historia de Chile.* Frankfurt: Verlag Jugend und Politik, 1975.

Weinstein, Eugenia, and Fundación de Ayuda Social de las Iglesias Cristianas. *Trauma, duelo, y reparación: Una experiencia de trabajo psicosocial en Chile.* Santiago: Fundación de Ayuda Social de las Iglesias Christianas and Editorial Interamericana, 1987.

Whelan, James. *Allende: Death of a Marxist Dream.* Washington: Council for Inter-American Security, 1981.

Zammit, J. Ann (ed.). *The Chilean Road to Socialism: Proceedings of an ODEPLAN–UDS Round Table.* Austin: University of Texas Press, 1973.

Zeitlin, Maurice. *The Civil Wars in Chile: 1851 and 1859.* Princeton: Princeton University Press, 1984.

(Various issues of the following periodicals were also used in the preparation of this chapter: *Hispanic American Reports;* and *El Mercurio Edición Internacional* [Santiago].)

Chapter 5

Americas Watch. *Human Rights and the "Politics of Agreements": Chile During President Aylwin's First Year.* New York: 1991.

Andrade, John. "Chile." Pages 94–134 in John Andrade (ed.), *Latin American Military Aviation.* Earl Shilton, United Kingdom: Midland Counties Publications, 1982.

Bragg, R.J., and Roy Turner. *Parachute Badges and Insignia of the World.* Poole, United Kingdom: Blandford Press, 1979.

Bustamente, Fernando, Miguel Navarro, and Guillermo Patillio. *¿Cual debe ser el gasto militar en el Chile de los 90?* Santiago: Editorial Atena, 1991.

Campbell, Bert, and Ron Reynolds. *Marine Badges and Insignia of the World.* London: Blandford Press, 1983.

Cavalla Rojas, Antonio. *Fuerzas armadas y defensa nacional.* Culiacán, Mexico: Universidad Autónoma de Sinaloa, 1981.

Chile. Armada de Chile. *Orientación profesional.* Valparaíso: 1979.

_____. Ejército de Chile. *Historia militar de Chile.* Santiago: Estado Mayor General del Ejército, 1984.

"Chile." Pages 103-113 in *Jane's Fighting Ships, 1991-94.* (Ed., Richard Sharpe.) London: Jane's, 1993.

"Chile." Pages 46-48 in "World Defence Almanac 1992-93: The Balance of Military Power," *Military Technology* [Bonn], 17, No. 1, January 1993.

Combat Fleets of the World, 1993: Their Ships, Aircraft, and Armament. (Ed., Bernard Prézelin.) Annapolis: Naval Institute Press, 1993.

Conway's All the World's Fighting Ships, 1860-1905/1922-1982. (5 vols.) London: Conway Maritime Press, 1979-83.

"Edición especial: La creación de la Fuerza Aérea de Chile," *Revista Fuerza Aérea de Chile* [Santiago], 39, No. 152, January-March 1980.

English, Adrian J. "Chile." Pages 132-63 in Adrian J. English (ed.), *Armed Forces of Latin America: Their Histories, Development, Present Strength, and Military Potential.* London: Jane's, 1984.

_____. "Chile." Pages 76-100 in *Regional Defence Profile: Latin America.* London: Jane's, 1988.

_____. "¿Chile: Pariah o martir?" *Defensa Latinoamericana* [Maidenhead, United Kingdom], June 1986, 6-9.

_____. "The Chilean Coast Guard," *Navy International* [Haskmere, United Kingdom], 91, No. 11, November 1986, 675.

_____. "Chilean Forces Are Among Latin America's Best," *Jane's Defence Weekly* [London], 4, No. 18, November 1985, 972-73.

_____. "The Chilean Navy," *Navy International* [Newdigate, United Kingdom], 87, No. 4, 1982, 966-70.

_____. "Defence in Chile," *International Defence Review* [Geneva], No. 2, February 1988, 135-38.

_____. "La industria de equipos de defensa de Chile," *Defensa Latinoamericana* [Maidenhead, United Kingdom], June 1986, 10-12.

_____. "Perfil: Chile—sus fuerzas armadas y su defensa," *Tecnología Militar* [Bonn], June 1990, 30-37.

_____. "Los 60 años de la Fuerza Aérea de Chile," *Iberoamericana de Tecnologías* [Bonn], February 1990, 42-45.

Faúndes Merino, Juan Jorge. *Cardoen: ¿Industrial o traficante?* Buenos Aires: Grupo Editorial Zeta, 1991.

Fauriol, Georges (ed.). *Latin American Insurgencies.* Washington: National Defense University, 1985.

Fuentes, Claudio, and Augusto Varas. *Defensa Nacional: Chile, 1990-94.* Santiago: Facultad Latinoamericana de Ciencias Sociales Serie Libros, 1994.

Fuenzalida Bade, Rodrigo. *La armada de Chile desde la alborada al sesquicentenario, 1813–1968.* (2d ed.) (4 vols.) Santiago: Talleres Empresa Periodística "Aquí Está," 1978.

Galuppini, Gino. *Warships of the World.* New York: Military Press, 1989.

García Ziemsen, Gustavo. "La Fuerza Aérea de Chile," *Tecnología Militar* [Bonn], No. 5, 1980, 30–36.

Green, William, and John Fricker. *The Air Forces of the World.* London: Macdonald, 1958.

Gumucio, Mariano Baptista. *Historia gráfica de la Guerra del Pacífico.* La Paz: Biblioteca Popular Boliviana de Última Hora, 1978.

Hillmon, Tommie. *A History of the Armed Forces of Chile.* Syracuse: Syracuse University Press, 1966.

Hunter, Brian (ed.). "Chile." Pages 349–54 in *The Statesman's Year-Book, 1993–94.* (130th ed.) New York: St. Martin's Press, 1993.

Ingleton, Roy D. *Police of the World.* Shepperton, United Kingdom: Ian Allen, 1979.

International Military and Defense Encyclopedia, 2. Washington: Brassey's, 1993.

Jane's Armour and Artillery, 1990–1991. London: Jane's, 1990.

Jane's Fighting Ships, 1993–94. London: Jane's, 1993.

Jarpa Gerhard, Sergio. "Campaña marítima de 1879," *Revista de Marina* [Valparaíso], 98, No. 744, 1981, 553–62.

Keegan, John. "Chile." Pages 105–9 in John Keegan (ed.), *World Armies.* London: Macmillan, 1983.

Kurian, George Thomas. "Chile." Pages 61–63 in George Thomas Kurian (ed.), *World Encyclopaedia of Police Forces and Penal Systems.* New York: Facts on File, 1989.

López, Jacinto. *Historia de la guerra del guano y el salitre.* Lima: Editorial Universo, 1980.

Marambio, Cristián. "La Armada de Chile," *Tecnología Militar* [Bonn], No. 6, 1991, 26–33.

_____. "La Fuerza Aérea de Chile," *Tecnología Militar* [Bonn], No. 1, 1992, 41–51.

_____. "In Defence of Chile," *Military Technology* [Bonn], No. 2, 1992, 72–82.

Márquez Alison, Alberto, and Antonio Márquez Alison. *Cuatro siglos de uniformes en Chile.* Santiago: Editorial Andrés Bello, 1976.

Mason, Theodorus B.M. *The War on the Pacific Coast of South America Between Chile and the Allied Republics of Peru and Bolivia, 1879–81.* Washington: Office of Naval Intelligence, 1883.

Meneses Ciuffardi, Emilio. *El factor naval en las relaciones entre Chile y los Estados Unidos, 1881–1951.* Santiago: Ediciones Pedagógicas Chilenas, Librería Francesa, 1989.

———. "Maintaining a Regional Navy with Very Limited Resources: The Chilean Case, 1900–1990," *Defence Analysis* [London], 7, No. 4, 1991, 345–62.

Meneses Ciuffardi, Emilio, and Miguel Navarro Meza. "Antecedentes, problemas, y perspectivas de las adquisiciones militares chilenas en la década de los años noventa," *Fuerzas Armadas y Sociedad* [Santiago], 5, No. 1, 1990.

The Military Balance, 1992–1993. London: International Institute for Strategic Studies, 1992.

The Military Balance, 1993–1994. London: International Institute for Strategic Studies, 1993.

Moss, Robert. *Chile's Marxist Experiment.* Newton Abbott, United Kingdom: David and Charles, 1973.

Nunn, Frederick M. *Chilean Politics, 1920–1931: The Honorable Mission of the Armed Forces.* Albuquerque: University of New Mexico Press, 1970.

———. *The Military in Chilean History: Essays on Civil-Military Relations, 1810–1973.* Albuquerque: University of New Mexico Press, 1976.

Pike, Fredrick B. *Chile and the United States, 1880–1962.* Notre Dame: University of Notre Dame Press, 1962.

Pinochet Ugarte, Augusto. *La Guerra del Pacífico: Campaña de Tarapacá.* Santiago: Editorial Andrés Bello, 1972.

Prenafeta, Alejandro. *La Armada de Chile.* Santiago: Departamento de Relaciones Públicas, Armada de Chile, 1985.

Prieto Vial, Daniel. *Defensa Chile, 2000: Una política de defensa para Chile.* Santiago: Facultad Latinoamericana de Ciencias Sociales, 1990.

Querejazu Calvo, Roberto. *Guano, salitre, y sangre: Historia de la Guerra del Pacífico.* La Paz: Los Amigos del Libro, 1979.

Rouquié, Alain. *The Military and the State in Latin America.* Berkeley: University of California Press, 1989.

Sater, William F. *Chile and the War of the Pacific.* Lincoln: University of Nebraska Press, 1986.

Scheina, Robert L. *Latin America: A Naval History, 1810–1987.* Annapolis: Naval Institute Press, 1987.

Sohr, Raúl. *La industria militar chilena.* Santiago: Comisión Sudamericana de Paz, 1990.

———. *Para entender a los militares.* Santiago: Comisión Sudamericana de Paz, 1989.

Toro Dávila, Agustín. *Síntesis histórico militar de Chile.* (3d ed.) Santiago: Editorial Universitaria, 1988.

Walters, Brian. "La prefectura aeropolicial de Chile," *Iberoamericana de Tecnologías* [Bonn], 6, January 1991, 50–51.

Worchester, Donald E. *Sea Power and Chilean Independence.* Gainesville: University of Florida Press, 1962.

"World Defence Almanac. 1992–93: The Balance of Military Power," *Military Technology* [Bonn], 17, No.1, January 1993, 47.

Glossary

Alliance for Progress—Established in 1961 at a hemispheric meeting in Punta del Este, Uruguay, under the leadership of President John F. Kennedy as a long-range program to help develop and modernize Latin American states through multisectoral reforms, particularly in health and education. Involved various forms of foreign aid, including development loans offered at very low or zero interest rates, from the United States to all states of Latin America and the Caribbean, except Cuba.

Andean Group—An economic group, also known as the Andean Pact or the Andean Common Market, created in 1969 by Bolivia, Chile, Colombia, Ecuador, and Peru (Venezuela joined in 1973) as a subregional market to improve its members' bargaining power within the Latin American Free Trade Association (LAFTA—*q.v.*). Its commission meets three times a year to encourage increased trade and more rapid development and to plan and program economic subregional integration. Chile left the Andean Group in 1976.

Andean Pact—*See* Andean Group.

audiencia—A high court of justice, exercising some administrative and executive functions in the colonial period.

balance of payments—An annual statistical summary of the monetary value of all economic transactions between one country and the rest of the world, including goods, services, income on investments, and other financial matters, such as credits or loans.

binomial electoral system—In this unique system, which governs Chile's congressional elections, political parties or groupings form pacts and permit slates (two candidates per slate), from which two senators and two deputies are elected from each district. By requiring each party to obtain two-thirds of the vote in each district for the successful election of its two candidates to the legislature, this system gives the opposition disproportionate representation in Congress.

capital account—A section of the balance of payments accounts that records short-term and long-term capital flows.

capital formation—Creation of new capital or the expansion of existing capital, during a fiscal period, normally financed by savings.

capital goods—A factor-of-production category consisting of manufactured products used in the process of production.

capital-intensive—A high ratio of capital to labor and other resources used in the production process.

capital market—An institutional system of communications, vested largely in the security exchanges, where lenders and borrowers interact with a view to transacting or trading.

Central Bank of Chile—Chile's Central Bank, as is usually the case with central banks in general, is a federal, government-related institution entrusted with control of the commercial banking system and with the issuance of the currency. Responsible for setting the level of credit and money supply in an economy and serving as the bank of last resort for other banks. Also has a major impact on interest rates, inflation, and economic output. Under Article 97 of the constitution, the Central Bank of Chile is an autonomous institution.

"Chicago boys"—A pejorative expression coined in the early years of the Pinochet regime to refer to those University of Chicago-trained or -affiliated economists, including Milton Friedman and Arnold Harberger, who recommended and implemented the liberalization and stabilization policies of the military government. However, because many other respected economists have since advocated free-market policies, the term has become misleading. Furthermore, economist David E. Hojman has pointed out that the model advocated by the "Chicago boys" characterized Chilean policy making for many decades and thus was not particularly extraneous to Chilean institutions and traditions.

Chilean peso (Ch$)—Chile's currency. Replaced escudo on September 29, 1975, at a rate of 1,000 escudos per peso. Peso notes are for 500, 1,000, 5,000, and 10,000 pesos; coins are for 1, 5, 10, 50, and 100 pesos. Official exchange rate of Chilean peso was pegged to United States dollar until July 3, 1992, at a rate adjusted at daily intervals and determined by monthly rates of national and world inflation. On January 26, 1992, the Central Bank of Chile (*q.v.*) revalued the peso, reducing the official dollar exchange rate by 5 percent, which meant it dropped from 395 to 375 pesos. On July 3, 1992, the Central Bank, in a move designed to halt currency speculation, announced the peso would no longer be measured exclusively against the United States currency, but rather would use a basket of the United States dollar, the German deutsche mark, and the Japanese yen in a 50–30–20 ratio. On September 13, 1994, Ch$405.9 = US$1.

Christian Base Communities (Comunidades Eclesiásticas de Base—CEBs)—Groups consisting of mostly poor Christian lay people through which advocates of liberation theology (*q.v.*) mainly work. Members of CEBs meet in small groups to reflect on Scripture and discuss the Bible's meaning in their lives. They are introduced to a radical interpretation of the Bible, one employing Marxist terminology to analyze and condemn the wide disparities between the wealthy elite and the impoverished masses in most underdeveloped countries. This reflection often leads members to organize and improve their living standards through cooperatives and civic-improvement projects.

Communist International (Comintern)—The Russian Communist Party founded the Communist International (Comintern) in Moscow in March 1919 for the purpose of rallying socialists and communists. The Comintern adopted Leninist principles and rejected reformism in favor of revolutionary action against capitalist governments. Disbanded in May 1943 and replaced by the Communist Information Bureau (Cominform) in September 1947.

communitarianism—The Christian Democrats supported unionization of the peasantry through communitarianism rather than Marxism. According to political scientist Paul E. Sigmund, whereas in the early decades of their party Chile's Christian Democrats preferred to describe their program simply as communitarian instead of as socialist, after the election of Salvador Allende Gossens as president in 1970 they described it as "communitarian socialism," as opposed to Allende's statist socialism.

consumer price index (CPI)—A statistical measure of sustained change in the price level weighted according to spending patterns.

corporatism—A sociopolitical philosophy that is antithetical to both Marxist and liberal democratic political ideals. It found its most developed expression in Italy under Benito Mussolini. A corporatist would organize society into industrial and professional corporations that serve as organs of political representation within a hierarchical, centralized polity controlled by the state. A corporatist society is elitist, patrimonialist, authoritarian, and statist. Some social science theorists have argued that Latin American political tradition has had a fundamentally corporatist nature, but others argue that it is but one of many cultural influences in the region.

Economic Commission for Latin America (ECLA)—*See* Economic Commission for Latin America and the Caribbean (ECLAC).

Economic Commission for Latin America and the Caribbean (ECLAC)—A United Nations regional economic commission established on February 25, 1948, as the Economic Commission for Latin America (ECLA). More commonly known in Latin America as the Comisión Económica para América Latina (CEPAL). In 1984 it expanded its operations and name to include the Caribbean. Its main functions are to initiate and coordinate policies aimed at promoting economic development. In addition to the countries of Latin America and the Caribbean, ECLAC's forty-one members in 1992 included Britain, Canada, France, the Netherlands, Portugal, Spain, and the United States. There were an additional five Caribbean associate members.

encomenderos—Colonial grantees, usually large landowners, to rights over native American labor and tribute in exchange for assuming responsibility to protect and Christianize these native subjects.

encomienda—A system or legal arrangement adopted by Spain in 1503 whereby the Spanish crown assigned rights over native American labor and tribute in the Spanish American colonies to individual colonists (*encomenderos—q.v.*) in return for protecting and Christianizing their subjects. However, most native Americans ended up as virtual slaves with no recognized rights. Not to be confused with the landed estate (latifundio—*q.v.*), the *encomienda* system was not ended until late in the eighteenth century.

escudo—*See* Chilean peso.

Evangelical—Term used in Chile to refer to all non-Catholic Christian churches with the exception of the Orthodox Church (Greek, Serbian, and Armenian) and the Mormon Church. Most Evangelicals are Pentecostal. Some would say "Protestant" refers to non-Pentecostal churches of the Reformation, but they themselves (i.e., the Methodists and Presbyterians) also identify with the term "Evangelical." The 1992 census used both "Protestant" and "Evangelical" to ask about religion, but the difference is meaningless. Pastors of all denominations urged people to say they were "Evangelicals."

extreme poverty—The Chilean government defines poor people as those who do not earn enough in a year to cover twice the cost of the *canasta básica* (basic basket). The extremely poor are those who simply cannot buy the *canasta básica*.

factor markets—Producer goods markets in which factors of production—inputs such as land, labor, capital, entrepreneurship, and other material instruments used in the production of goods and services—are procured.

Gini coefficient—A measure of inequality in a country's wealth distribution. It contrasts actual income and property distribution with perfectly equal distribution. The value of the coefficient, or index, can vary from 0 (complete equality) to 1 (complete inequality).

Great Depression—The 1929–34 economic slump in North America and other industrialized areas of the world, precipitated by the collapse of the United States stock market in October 1929. The term "depression" denotes, in its economic sense, a cyclical phase of the economy with high unemployment of labor and capital, business and consumer pessimism, accumulated inventories, minimal investment, and, in some sectors, falling prices.

gross domestic product (GDP)—The broadest measure of the total value of goods and services produced by the domestic economy during a given period, usually a year. GDP has mainly displaced a similar measurement, the gross national product (GNP—*q.v.*). GDP is obtained by adding the value contributed by each sector of the economy in the form of profits, compensation to employees, and depreciation (consumption of capital). The income arising from investments and possessions owned abroad is not included, hence the use of the word *domestic* to distinguish GDP from GNP. Real GDP adjusts the value of GDP to exclude the effects of price changes, allowing for measurement of actual yearly increases or decreases in output.

gross national product (GNP)—Total market value of all final goods (those sold to the final user) and services produced by an economy during a year, plus the value of any net changes in inventories. Measured by adding the gross domestic product (GDP—*q.v.*), net changes in inventories, and the income received from abroad by residents, less payments remitted abroad to nonresidents.

human development index (HDI)—A measurement of human progress introduced by the United Nations Development Programme (UNDP) in its *Human Development Report, 1990.* By combining indicators of real purchasing power, education, and health, the HDI provides a more comprehensive measure of development than does GNP alone.

import-substitution industrialization—An economic development strategy and a form of protectionism that emphasizes the growth of domestic industries by restricting the importation of specific manufactured goods, often by using tariff and nontariff measures, such as import quotas. Theoretically, capital thus would be generated through savings of foreign-exchange earnings. Proponents favor the export of industrial goods over primary products and foreign-exchange considerations. In the post-World War II period, import-substitution industrialization was most prevalent in Latin America. Its chief ideological proponents were the Argentine economist Raúl Prebisch and the Economic Commission for Latin America (*q.v.*). The main weaknesses in Latin America are as follows: the domestic markets in the region are generally too small; goods manufactured domestically are too costly and noncompetitive in the world market; most states in the region have an insufficient variety of resources to build a domestic industry; and most are also too dependent on foreign technology.

Inter-American Treaty of Reciprocal Assistance of 1947 (Rio Treaty)—A regional alliance, signed in Rio de Janeiro in 1947, that established a mutual security system to safeguard the Western Hemisphere from aggression from within or outside the zone. Signatories include the United States and twenty Latin American republics. In 1975 a special conference approved, over United States objections, a Protocol of Amendment to the Rio Treaty that, once ratified, would establish the principle of "ideological pluralism" and would simplify the rescinding of sanctions imposed on an aggressor party.

International Monetary Fund (IMF)—Established on December 27, 1945, the IMF began operating on March 1, 1947. The IMF is a specialized agency affiliated with the United Nations that takes responsibility for stabilizing international exchange rates and payments. The IMF's main business is the provision of loans to its members when they experience balance of payments difficulties. These loans often carry conditions that require substantial internal economic adjustments by the recipients. The IMF's capital resources comprise Special Drawing Rights and currencies that the members pay under quotas calculated for them when they join. These resources are supplemented by borrowing. In 1993 the IMF had 175 members.

International Telecommunications Satellite Organization (Intelsat)—Created in 1964 under a multilateral agreement, Intelsat is a nonprofit cooperative of 116 countries that jointly own and operate a global communications satellite system.

Kennedy Amendment—After evidence of severe repression by the military regime following the overthrow of President Salvador Allende Gossens in September 1973, the United States Congress in 1974 adopted the Kennedy Amendment, prohibiting all security assistance and sales to Chile. This restriction was made much more general in the International Security Assistance and Arms Export Control Act of 1976, prohibiting transfers to any country "which engages in a consistent pattern of gross violations of internationally recognized human rights."

latifundio—A large landed estate held as private property, which may be farmed as a plantation, by tenant sharecroppers, or as a traditional hacienda. The latifundio system (*latifundismo*) is a pattern of landownership based on latifundios owned by local gentry, absentee landlords, and domestic or foreign corporations.

Latin American Free Trade Association (LAFTA)—A regional group founded by the Montevideo Treaty of 1960 to increase trade and foster development. LAFTA's failure to make meaningful progress in liberalizing trade among its members or to move toward more extensive integration prompted the leaders of five Andean states to meet in Bogotá in 1966. This meeting led to the creation in 1969 of the Andean Group (*q.v.*)—consisting of Bolivia, Chile, Colombia, Ecuador, and Peru (Venezuela joined in 1973)—to serve as a subregional structure within LAFTA. LAFTA was replaced in 1980 by the Latin American Integration Association (Asociación Latinoamericana de Integración—ALADI), which advocated a regional tariff preference for goods originating in member states. ALADI has since declined as a major Latin American integration effort in favor of regional efforts, such as the Southern Cone Common Market (*q.v.*).

League of Nations—An international organization whose covenant arose out of the Paris Peace Conference in 1919. It was created for the purpose of preserving international peace and security and promoting disarmament by obligating nations to submit their conflicts to arbitration, judicial settlement, or to the League Council for consideration. The League of Nations contravened traditional principles of neutrality and the right to employ force to resolve disputes. By not signing the Treaty of Versailles, the United States refused to join, but the organization had fifty-three members by 1923. Although the League of Nations considered sixty-six disputes and conflicts between 1920 and 1939, it proved ineffective against German, Italian, Japanese, and Soviet aggression in the 1930s. Formally disbanded in April 1946, its functions were transferred to the United Nations.

liberation theology—An activist movement led by Roman Catholic clergy who trace their inspiration to the Second Vatican Council (1962–65), when some church procedures were liberalized, and the second meeting of the Latin American Bishops' Conference (Conferencia Episcopal Latinoamericana—CELAM) in Medellín (1968), which endorsed greater direct efforts to improve the lot of the poor. Advocates of liberation theology—sometimes referred to as ''liberationists''—work mainly through Christian Base Communities (*q.v.*).

marginality—A concept used to explain the poor political, economic, and social conditions of individuals within a society, social classes within a nation, or nations within the larger world community. Refers often to poverty-stricken groups left behind in the modernization process. They are not integrated into the socioeconomic system, and their relative poverty increases. Marginality is sometimes referred to as dualism or the dual society thesis.

mayorazgo—Colonial system whereby the elder son inherited the titles and properties of the family.

Mercosur—*See* Southern Cone Common Market.

mestizo—Originally, term designated the offspring of a Spaniard and a native American. It now means any obviously nonwhite individual who is fluent in Spanish and observes Hispanic cultural norms.

monetarism—An economic policy based on the control of a country's money supply. Monetarists assume that the quantity of money in an economy determines its economic activity, particularly its rate of inflation. A rapid increase in the money supply creates rising prices, resulting in inflation. To curb inflationary pressures, governments need to reduce the supply of money and raise interest rates. Monetarists believe that conservative monetary policies, by controlling inflation, will increase export earnings and encourage foreign and domestic investments. Monetarists have generally sought support for their policies from the International Monetary Fund (*q.v.*), the World Bank (*q.v.*), and private enterprise, especially multinational corporations. The University of Chicago economist Milton Friedman is considered to be a leading monetarist.

North American Free Trade Agreement (NAFTA)—A free-trade agreement comprising Canada, Mexico, and the United States. Tripartite negotiations to form NAFTA began among these countries in June 1991 and were concluded in August 1992. The United States Congress finally ratified NAFTA in November 1993, and the agreement went into effect on January 1, 1994. NAFTA was expected to create a free-trade area with a combined population of 356 million and a GDP (*q.v.*) of more than US$6 trillion. Chile was expected to be incorporated into NAFTA on January 1, 1995.

Organisation for Economic Co-operation and Development (OECD)—A Paris-based organization of twenty-four European countries, Australia, Canada, and the United States that promotes economic and social welfare throughout the OECD area by assisting its member governments in the formulation of policies designed to this end and by coordinating these policies.

It also helps coordinate its members' efforts in favor of developing countries.

Organization of American States (OAS)—Established by the Ninth International Conference of American States held in Bogotá on April 30, 1948, and effective since December 13, 1951, the OAS has served as a major regional organization composed of thirty-five members, including most Latin American states and the United States and Canada. Determines common political, defense, economic, and social policies and provides for coordination of various inter-American agencies. Responsible for implementing the Inter-American Treaty of Reciprocal Assistance (Rio Treaty—*q.v.*) when any threat to the security of the region arises.

patronato real—The "king's patronage" was the absolute control of clerical patronage in the colonies that the papacy gave to the kings of Spain. The Spanish crown maintained this extensive power over the church throughout the colonial period. It ended with independence, when the church lost the protection of royal support.

Peronism—An eclectic Argentine political movement formed in 1945–46 to support the successful presidential candidacy of Juan Domingo Perón. The movement later splintered, with left-wingers forming the Montoneros urban guerrilla group. Nevertheless, the fractious movement survived Perón's death in 1974 and made a good showing in the congressional elections of 1986. The political, economic, and social ideology of Peronism was formally labeled "social justice" (Justicialismo) in 1949. It combines nationalism, social democracy, loyalty to the memory of Perón, and personalism, which is the dominance of a nation's political life by an individual, often a charismatic personality.

plebiscite—A device of direct democracy whereby the electorate can pronounce, usually for or against, some measure put before it by a government. Also known as a referendum. A Chilean president may convoke a plebiscite, under Article 117 of the constitution, if the president totally rejects an amendment approved by Congress. Articles 118 and 119 further specify the conditions under which a plebiscite may be held.

"popular" sectors—A term similar to popular culture, referring to the masses of working-class, underemployed, and unemployed citizens.

positivism—The theory that genuine knowledge is acquired by science and that metaphysical speculation has no validity. Positivism, based largely on the ideas of the French philosopher

Auguste Comte, was adopted by many Latin American intellectuals in the late nineteenth and early twentieth centuries. Chilean positivists promoted secular education, free inquiry, the scientific method, and social reform.

real exchange rate—The value of foreign exchange corrected for differences between external and domestic inflation.

reformed sector—Under an unprecedentedly strong agrarian reform law proposed by the administration of Eduardo Frei Montalva (1964–70) in late 1965 and adopted in July 1967, the reformed sector, consisting of cooperatives, was created.

Richter scale—A logarithmic scale, invented in 1935 by United States geophysicist Charles Richter, for representing the energy released by an earthquake. A figure of 2 or less indicates the earthquake is barely perceptible; a figure of 5 or more indicates the earthquake may be destructive, and a figure of 8 or more indicates the earthquake is a major earthquake.

Rio Group—A permanent mechanism for consultation and political coordination that succeeded the Contadora Support Group. Founded in December 1986, the Contadora Support Group consisted of Argentina, Brazil, Colombia, Mexico, Panama, Peru, Uruguay, and Venezuela. Its second meeting, attended by the presidents of the seven member countries (Panama's membership was temporarily suspended in February 1988), was held in Punta del Este, Uruguay, in October 1988. In 1990 Chile joined the Rio Group. In 1993 the Rio Group had twelve members: Argentina, Bolivia, Brazil, Chile, Colombia, Ecuador, Mexico, Panama, Paraguay, Peru, Uruguay, and Venezuela. The seventh summit of the Rio Group was held in Santiago, Chile, on October 15–16, 1993.

Rio Treaty—*See* Inter-American Treaty of Reciprocal Assistance.

Southern Cone Common Market (Mercado Común del Cono Sur—Mercosur)—An organization established on March 26, 1991, by Argentina, Brazil, Paraguay, and Uruguay for the purpose of promoting regional economic cooperation. Chile was conspicuously absent because of its insistence that the other four countries first had to lower their tariffs to the Chilean level before Chile could join. Mercosur aimed to form a common market by December 31, 1994.

state of exception—States of assembly, siege, emergency, and catastrophe that may be declared under Article 40 of the constitution by the president of the republic, with the consent of the National Security Council, cover the following exceptional situations, respectively: a foreign war, an internal war or internal commotion, an internal disturbance, and an emergency or public calamity.

structuralism—An economic policy that blames chronic inflation primarily on foreign trade dependency, insufficient local production (especially in agriculture), and political struggles among entrenched vested interests over government contracts. Structuralists advocate encouraging economic development and modernization through Keynesian and neo-Keynesian policies of governmental stimulative actions, accompanied by organizational reforms. Structuralists contend that the policies of monetarism (*q.v.*) retard growth and support the status quo.

terms of trade—The ratio between prices of exports and prices of imports. In international economics, the concept of "terms of trade" plays an important role in evaluating exchange relationships between nations. The terms of trade shift whenever a country's exports will buy more or fewer imports. An improvement in the terms of trade occurs when export prices rise relative to import prices. The terms of trade turn unfavorable in the event of a slump in export prices relative to import prices.

Third International—Created in 1921 by the Russian Bolsheviks, its founding involved the emergence of separate communist parties sharply opposed to socialist or social democratic parties. These new communist parties were organized along Marxist-Leninist lines.

value-added tax (VAT)—An incremental tax applied to the value added at each stage of the processing of a raw material or the production and distribution of a commodity. It is calculated as the difference between the product value at a given state and the cost of all materials and services purchased as inputs. The value-added tax is a form of indirect taxation, and its impact on the ultimate consumer is the same as that of a sales tax.

World Bank—The informal name for the International Bank for Reconstruction and Development (IBRD). The IBRD was conceived at the Bretton Woods Conference on July 22, 1944, and became effective on December 27, 1945. Its primary purpose is to provide technical assistance and loans at market-related rates of interest to developing countries at more advanced stages of development. The World Bank Group consists of the IBRD, the International Development Association (IDA), the International Finance Corporation (IFC), and the Multilateral Investment Guarantee Agency (MIGA). The IDA, a legally separate loan fund administered by the staff of the IBRD, was established in 1960 to furnish credits to the poorest developing countries on much easier terms than those of conventional IBRD loans.

The IFC, founded in 1956, supplements the activities of the IBRD through loans and assistance designed specifically to encourage the growth of productive private enterprises in developing countries. The MIGA, founded in 1988, insures private foreign investment in developing countries against various noncommercial risks. The president and certain senior officers of the IBRD hold the same positions in the IFC. The affiliated international organizations of the World Bank Group are owned by the governments of the countries that subscribe their capital. To participate in the World Bank Group, member states must first belong to the International Monetary Fund (IMF— *q.v.*). In 1993 the World Bank Group included 174 member countries. By the early 1990s, the Latin American and Caribbean region had received more loan aid through the World Bank Group than any other region.

Index

abortion, 129-30, 245, 249, 256-57
Academia de Guerra. *See* War Academy
Academia de Guerra Naval. *See* Naval War Academy
Academia Politécnica Aérea. *See* Air Force Technical College
Academia Politécnica Militar. *See* Military Polytechnical Academy
Acción Chilena Anticomunista. *See* Chilean Anti-Communist Action Group
AChA. *See* Chilean Anti-Communist Action Group
Aconcagua, 64
acquired immune deficiency syndrome (AIDS), 106-7
Adimark, xli, 118, 119, 129
Administradoras de Fondos de Pensiones. *See* Pension Fund Administrators
Aeronautic Constructions, S.A. (Construcciones Aeronáuticas, S.A.—CASA), 307
AFL-CIO. *See* American Federation of Labor-Congress of Industrial Organizations
AFPs. *See* Pension Fund Administrators
Agrarian Labor Party, 41, 42
agrarian reform. *See* land reform
Agrarian Reform Corporation (Corporación de Reforma Agraria—Cora), 145
Agrarian Reform Law (1962), 145
agricultural products (*see also under individual crops*): demand for, 25; export of, 72, 74, 140-41, 191; fruit, 71, 72, 74, 165-66; grapes, 84, 266; import of, 165-66; wheat, 141
agriculture, 163, 165-66; of Araucanians, 6; changes in, 90; employment in, 91; export crops, 20; in far north, 70; in near north, 71; as percentage of gross domestic product, 161-62; potential for, 78; prices, control of, 144; privatization in, ; productivity of, 162; slash-and-burn, 6; unions, 33
Aguirre Cerda, Pedro, 31, 35
AIDS. *See* acquired immune deficiency syndrome
air force, 305-8; aircraft of, 305, 307, 322-23; civic-action role of, 308; class

consciousness in, 29, 310; commander in chief of, 297; commands of, 305; conditions of service in, 310-11; creation of, 288; education requirements for, 311; foreign influences on, 289, 290; insignia, 316; matériel, 290, 307, 309-10, 316, 322-23; number of personnel in, 278, 305; organization of, 305-8; ranks, 316; recruitment for, 310-11; schools, 312; spending on, 309-10; training of, 264, 307; uniforms, 316
Air Force Technical College (Academia Politécnica Aérea), 312
airports, 178
Albania: relations with, 48
Alessandri Besa, Arturo, xli, 254
Alessandri Palma, Arturo, 4; as president, 30-31, 34-36, 123, 200, 217; support for, 30
Alessandri Rodríguez, Jorge, 204, 250, 257; in election of 1958, 43-44; in election of 1970, 46, 47
Alessandri Rodríguez administration (1958-64), 44-45
Allende Gossens, Salvador, xxxv, 31; career of, 35, 41; in election of 1958, 43-44; in election of 1964, 44; in election of 1970, 46, 47, 145, 199, 202, 247; suicide of, xxxvi-xxxvii, 51, 149, 203
Allende Gossens administration (1970-73), xxxv, 47-51; analysis of, xxxvi, 51; businesses under, 258; economy under, 47-48, 139, 145-46; labor under, 259; land reform under, 47, 89; nationalization under, 218; opposition to, xxxv-xxxvi, 50, 249, 250, 265; overthrown, xxxvi, 50-51, 139, 149, 203, 247, 278; public sector under, 219; relations of, with Catholic Church, 256; relations of, with judiciary, 231
Alliance for Progress, 44
Almagro, Diego de, xxxv, 7, 279
Almeyda, Clodomiro, 146
American Federation of Labor-Congress of Industrial Organizations (AFL-CIO), 39

431

221; local, of 1992, 240–41; manipulation of, 17, 33, 201, 294
Electoral Certification Tribunal (Tribunal de Certificación Electoral—TCE), 236
electoral system, 242–45; abuses of, 236; binomial, xlii, 243–44; boundaries for, 243
electric power, 170; generation, 170; nationalized, 142; stations, 170
elite class, 4; criticism of, 30; economic power of, 40; political affiliations in, 5, 43; political power of, 8, 16; support of, for Alessandri, 30
Elizabeth II, 268
El Mercurio, 261, 262
El Mercurio Company, 262
El Salvador: military training for, 289
El Siglo, 261
El Tepual Military Air Base, 307
Embraer. *See* Brazilian Aeronautics Company
EMDN. *See* National Defense Staff
employment, 182–83; under Aylwin, 183; distribution of, 91; in public sector, 217; rate of, 90–91, 183; of women, 90
Employment Program for Heads of Household (Programa de Ocupación para Jefes de Hogar—POJH), 156
employment programs, public, 155–56
Employment Security Law, 154
Empresa de Ferrocarriles del Estado. *See* State Railroad Company
Empresa Nacional de Aeronáutica. *See* National Aeronautical Enterprise
Empresa Nacional de Electricidad. *See* National Electric Company
Empresa Nacional de Petróleo. *See* National Petroleum Enterprise
Empresa Nacional de Telecomunicaciones. *See* National Telecommunications Enterprise
Enaer. *See* National Aeronautical Enterprise
ENAP. *See* National Petroleum Enterprise
encomenderos, 11, 141
encomienda system, 11; outlawed, 11
ENDESA. *See* National Electric Company
energy (*see also* electric power), 170–73; privatized, 170
Engineers' School (Regimiento Escuela de Ingenieros), 311
Enlightenment, 12–13
Enríquez, Miguel, 337

Entel. *See* National Telecommunications Enterprise
environmental pollution, 86, 193
Ercilla, 262
Errázuriz Talavera, Francisco Javier, 215; in elections of 1989, 215
Errázuriz Zañartu, Federico, 22, 251
Escuela de Abastecimientos y Servicios. *See* Supplies and Services School
Escuela de Aeronáutica Militar "Capitán Ávalos Prado." *See* Captain Ávalos Prado Military Aviation School
Escuela de Armamentos. *See* Armaments School
Escuela de Educación Física. *See* Physical Education School
Escuela de Especialidades. *See* Specialists' School
Escuela de Fuerzas Blindadas. *See* Armored Forces School
Escuela de Infantería de Marina. *See* Marine Corps School
Escuela de Ingeniería Naval. *See* School of Naval Engineering
Escuela de Navegación Antártica "Piloto Luis Pardo Villalón." *See* Pilot Luis Pardo Villalón Antarctic Navigation School
Escuela de Operaciones. *See* School of Operations
Escuela de Suboficiales y Clases. *See* Noncommissioned Officers' School
Escuela Militar Femenina. *See* Women's Military School
Escuela Militar "General Bernardo O'Higgins." *See* General Bernardo O'Higgins Military Academy
Escuela Naval. *See* Naval School
Escuela Naval Arturo Prat. *See* Arturo Prat Naval School
Escuela Superior de Guerra. *See* War College
ESG. *See* War College
Estado Mayor de la Defensa Nacional. *See* National Defense Staff
Estado Mayor General. *See* General Staff
ethnic groups: conflict among, 8; diversification of representation by, 78
Europe: immigrants from, 21, 25–26, 79; relations with, 18, 56; support of, for Frei Montalva, 44; trade with, 12
Europeans: relations of, with native Americans, 9–10

Regimiento Escuela de Caballería Blindada. *See* Armored Cavalry School
Regimiento Escuela de Fuerzas Especiales y Paracaidistas. *See* Special Forces School
Regimiento Escuela de Infantería. *See* Infantry School
Regimiento Escuela de Ingenieros. *See* Engineers' School
Regimiento Escuela de Montaña. *See* Mountain Warfare School
Regimiento Escuela de Telecomunicaciones. *See* Signals School
Región Militar Austral. *See* Southern Military Region
religion (*see also under individual denominations*): freedom of, 122–23; historical perspective of, 120–25; popular beliefs in, 125–28; syncretic, 125
religious affiliations, 118–20; of women, 119–20
Renewed Socialists, 247
Renovación Nacional. *See* National Renewal
Republican Militia (Milicia Republicana), 34
Rerum Novarum (1891), 255
research institutes, 117
reservations, native, 25, 79
retirement, 102
Rettig Commission. *See* National Commission on Truth and Reconciliation
Río Bío-Bío, 72
Río Calle Calle, 72, 178
Rio Group, 268
Río Lauca, 70
Río Loa, 70
Ríos Morales, Juan Antonio, 37–39
Rio Treaty. *See* Inter-American Treaty of Reciprocal Assistance
Rivera, Alonso de, 279
rivers: in central Chile, 71; in far north, 70; in near north, 71
roads, 177; rural, 90
Rodríguez, Manuel, 13
Roman Catholic Church. *See* Catholic Church, Roman
rural areas, 88–90; crime in, 331; education in, 80; labor unions in, 37, 38, 39, 95; political orientations in, 43, 256; workers in, 4, 20, 37, 40, 41, 42, 45, 89
rural enterprises, 89

Rural Police Law (1881), 326
rural-urban dichotomy, 5

Samoré, Antonio, 268
San Antonio: port of, 178
San Bernardo Prison, 336
Sandok Austral of South Africa, 321
San Martín, José de, 14, 280
Santa Cruz y Calahumana, Andrés de, 18, 282
Santa María González, Domingo, 22
Santiago: air pollution in, 193; city services in, 86; climate of, 71; distribution of social classes in, 84–86; founded, 7, 83; growth of, 28, 84; housing in, 86–87; migration to, 84, 86; population of, 83, 84, 182; public transportation in, 84, 86; roads in, 177; suburbanization of, 86
Santiago College, 123
Santiago International Airport, 178
Schneider Chereau, René, 47
School of Naval Engineering (Escuela de Ingeniería Naval), 302
School of Operations (Escuela de Operaciones), 302
schools: administration of, 112–14; and associations, 97; attendance in, 62; enrollment in, 108–14; for girls, 110; under Montt, 21; preprimary, 111–12; primary, 112–13; private, 110, 112–14; reforms in, 113–14; rural, 90; secondary, 110, 112–14; state, 113; subsidies for, 112–13, 118; vocational, 110, 114
secularization, 22
Security Assistance Institutions (Mutuales de Seguridad), 105
Selkirk, Alexander, 67
Senate, 225; designated senators, xlii, 161, 207, 216, 226, 227, 294, 296; members of, 226
Sernam. *See* National Women's Service
Sernatur. *See* National Tourism Service
service sector: employment in, 91
Servicio de Aviación Naval. *See* Naval Aviation Service
Servicio de Seguro Social. *See* Social Insurance Service
Servicio Nacional de la Mujer. *See* National Women's Service

Contributors

Paul W. Drake is Professor of Political Science, Department of Political Science; Adjunct Professor, Department of History; and Adjunct Professor, Graduate School of International Relations and Pacific Studies, University of California at San Diego, La Jolla, California. From September through December 1993, he was a Visiting Scholar at the Instituto Juan March, Madrid, Spain.

Alejandra Cox Edwards is Professor of Economics at California State University, Long Beach, and, in 1993–94, an economist with the World Bank, Washington, D.C.

Sebastian Edwards is Henry Ford II Professor of International Business Economics in the John E. Anderson Graduate School of Management at the University of California, Los Angeles, and, in 1993–94, Chief Economist, Latin American Division, the World Bank, Washington, D.C.

Adrian J. English is Defence Consultant and Analyst, Dublin, Ireland.

Rex A. Hudson is Senior Research Specialist in Latin American Affairs with the Federal Research Division of the Library of Congress, Washington, D.C.

Scott D. Tollefson is Assistant Professor of Comparative Politics and Latin American Studies in the Department of National Security Affairs at the Naval Postgraduate School in Monterey, California. From August 1993 through April 1994, he lived in Viña del Mar, Chile, while engaging in research as a Visiting Researcher at the Latin American School of Social Sciences (Facultad Latinoamericana de Ciencias Sociales—FLACSO) in Santiago, Chile.

Arturo Valenzuela is Deputy Assistant to Assistant Secretary for Inter-American Affairs Alexander F. Watson, United States Department of State. Prior to assuming that position on January 3, 1994, he was Director, Center for Latin American Studies, and Professor, Department of Political Science, at Georgetown University, Washington, D.C.

J. Samuel Valenzuela is Senior Fellow at The Helen Kellogg Institute for International Studies, University of Notre Dame, Notre Dame, Indiana, and Professor and Chair of Sociology at the University's Department of Sociology. From September 30, 1992, until August 1993, he was a Visiting Fellow at Oxford University (St. Antony's College), Oxford, England.

Published Country Studies

(Area Handbook Series)

550-65	Afghanistan		550-87	Greece
550-98	Albania		550-78	Guatemala
550-44	Algeria		550-174	Guinea
550-59	Angola		550-82	Guyana and Belize
550-73	Argentina		550-151	Honduras
550-169	Australia		550-165	Hungary
550-176	Austria		550-21	India
550-175	Bangladesh		550-154	Indian Ocean
550-170	Belgium		550-39	Indonesia
550-66	Bolivia		550-68	Iran
550-20	Brazil		550-31	Iraq
550-168	Bulgaria		550-25	Israel
550-61	Burma		550-182	Italy
550-50	Cambodia		550-30	Japan
550-166	Cameroon		550-34	Jordan
550-159	Chad		550-56	Kenya
550-77	Chile		550-81	Korea, North
550-60	China		550-41	Korea, South
550-26	Colombia		550-58	Laos
550-33	Commonwealth Caribbean, Islands of the		550-24	Lebanon
550-91	Congo		550-38	Liberia
550-90	Costa Rica		550-85	Libya
550-69	Côte d'Ivoire (Ivory Coast)		550-172	Malawi
550-152	Cuba		550-45	Malaysia
550-22	Cyprus		550-161	Mauritania
550-158	Czechoslovakia		550-79	Mexico
550-36	Dominican Republic and Haiti		550-76	Mongolia
550-52	Ecuador		550-49	Morocco
550-43	Egypt		550-64	Mozambique
550-150	El Salvador		550-35	Nepal and Bhutan
550-28	Ethiopia		550-88	Nicaragua
550-167	Finland		550-157	Nigeria
550-155	Germany, East		550-94	Oceania
550-173	Germany, Fed. Rep. of		550-48	Pakistan
550-153	Ghana		550-46	Panama

550-156	Paraguay		550-53	Thailand
550-185	Persian Gulf States		550-89	Tunisia
550-42	Peru		550-80	Turkey
550-72	Philippines		550-74	Uganda
550-162	Poland		550-97	Uruguay
550-181	Portugal		550-71	Venezuela
550-160	Romania		550-32	Vietnam
550-37	Rwanda and Burundi		550-183	Yemens, The
550-51	Saudi Arabia		550-99	Yugoslavia
550-70	Senegal		550-67	Zaire
550-180	Sierra Leone		550-75	Zambia
550-184	Singapore		550-171	Zimbabwe
550-86	Somalia			
550-93	South Africa			
550-95	Soviet Union			
550-179	Spain			
550-96	Sri Lanka			
550-27	Sudan			
550-47	Syria			
550-62	Tanzania			